NEWCOMER'S HANDBOOK®

FOR MOVING TO AND LIVING IN

LOS ANGELES

Including Santa Monica, Pasadena,
Orange County, and the San Fernando Valley

4th Edition

6750 SW Franklin
Portland, OR 97223
503-968-6777
www.firstbooks.com

4th Edition

Newcomer's Handbook® is a registered trademark of Firstbooks.com, Inc.

Author: Joan Wai
Series Editor: Bernadette Duperron
Proofreader: Linda Weinerman
Publisher: Jeremy Solomon
Cover and interior design, composition: Erin Johnson Design
Maps: Scott Lockheed and Jim Miller/fennana design
Transit map courtesy of the Los Angeles County Metropolitan Transportation Authority (Metro). Used with permission.

Published by Firstbooks.com, Inc., 6750 SW Franklin Street, Portland, OR 97223-2542, 503-968-6777, www.firstbooks.com.

ISBN 0-912301-60-0
ISSN 1086-8879

Printed in the USA on recycled paper.

What readers are saying about Newcomer's Handbooks:

I recently got a copy of your Newcomer's Handbook for Chicago, and wanted to let you know how invaluable it was for my move. I must have consulted it a dozen times a day preparing for my move. It helped me find my way around town, find a place to live, and so many other things. Thanks.

—Mike L.
Chicago, Illinois

Excellent reading (Newcomer's Handbook for San Francisco and the Bay Area) ... balanced and trustworthy. One of the very best guides if you are considering moving/relocation. Way above the usual tourist crap.

—Gunnar E.
Stockholm, Sweden

I was very impressed with the latest edition of the Newcomer's Handbook for Los Angeles. It is well organized, concise and up-to-date. I would recommend this book to anyone considering a move to Los Angeles.

—Jannette L.
Attorney Recruiting Administrator for a large Los Angeles law firm

I recently moved to Atlanta from San Francisco, and LOVE the Newcomer's Handbook for Atlanta. It has been an invaluable resource – it's helped me find everything from a neighborhood in which to live to the local hardware store. I look something up in it everyday, and know I will continue to use it to find things long after I'm no longer a newcomer. And if I ever decide to move again, your book will be the first thing I buy for my next destination.

—Courtney R.
Atlanta, Georgia

In looking to move to the Boston area, a potential employer in that area gave me a copy of the Newcomer's Handbook for Boston. It's a great book that's very comprehensive, outlining good and bad points about each neighborhood in the Boston area. Very helpful in helping me decide where to move.

—no name given (online submit form)

TABLE OF CONTENTS

CONTENTS

CONTENTS

WELCOME TO EL PUEBLO DE NUESTRA SEÑORA LA REINA DE LOS Angeles (in English, the Town of Our Lady the Queen of the Angels). That's the name the Spanish gave to this city in 1781 when 44 settlers made their home in what is now downtown Los Angeles. Today, LA is a multi-ethnic, multicultural society as diverse as any city in the world. The city is so large you can fit St. Louis, Milwaukee, Cleveland, Minneapolis, San Francisco, Boston, Pittsburgh, and Manhattan all within the municipal boundaries! People from more than 140 countries live in Los Angeles County, including the largest population of Mexican, Armenian, Korean, Filipino, Salvadoran, and Guatemalan communities outside their respective home nations. Los Angeles ranks as the second largest city in the nation behind New York City; the County of Los Angeles alone would rank as the ninth most populated state. It's safe to say that with 9.8 million people living in LA County, there is indeed something for everyone.

For decades, people around the world have been attracted to Los Angeles for its promises of fame and fortune, and excellent year-round weather. While only a sliver of the population is famous and wealthy, the good weather here is no myth. Average temperatures range from 58 degrees Fahrenheit in December to 76 degrees in September, and it's not uncommon to have an 80-degree day at the beach in February, while much of the rest of the country shivers under a layer of snow.

Greater Los Angeles's traffic and other negatives like crime and racial tensions are perhaps as famous now as her pluses. But, as someone once said of LA, "If this is hell, why is it so popular?" For those who choose to call Los Angeles "home," she welcomes you with a wealth of opportunities.

WHAT TO BRING

- **A car**; although LA has a large bus transit system and an underground subway and light rail system that are slowly growing, LA is simply too big to get around effectively without a car. And, public transportation by bus often means an even longer commute time than if you drove yourself. Small, compact model cars are the most economical and ideal for maneuvering LA's tight parking spots. Be prepared to shell out the bucks for insurance coverage; the cost for auto insurance in LA is among the nation's highest.
- **A map**; it'll take newcomers a while to create a mental map of where one community is in relation to another, and to figure out how much time is necessary to get from one place to another. Traffic patterns create situations where the shortest route is not always the fastest. Although many city streets are laid out in a grid, there are plenty of exceptions with streets that cross over, change names, and create not four, but five junctions at an intersection. A *Thomas Guide* street map (loose-leaf books of detailed LA neighborhood road maps) is perfect for finding alternate routes around gridlocked freeways. The *LA County, LA County/Ventura*, and *LA County/Orange Thomas Guides*, veritable LA bibles, can be purchased through First Books at www.firstbooks.com or at most local bookstores.
- **An open mind and positive attitude**; if this is your first time in Los Angeles, be prepared to interact with many different cultures and ethnicities. In general, Californians are famous for their laid-back attitudes, and Angelenos are no exception; however, the pace of life here is faster and more energetic than in smaller cities—but that's what makes it so fun!

While this *Newcomer's Handbook® for Moving to and Living in Los Angeles* will introduce you to the area, nothing compares to discovering Los Angeles's many beautiful facets yourself. Welcome and enjoy.

MOST MAJOR LOS ANGELES STREETS FOLLOW A STANDARD GRID pattern, running east-west and north-south, but there are plenty that snake around, stop at one block, then continue down another with little rhyme or reason. We offer a general guide to LA's thoroughfares and city layout. Nearby cities may have their grids laid out differently. Ultimately, the best way to figure out where you are, or where you want to go, is to pull out your trusty *Thomas Guide*. And, unless you're in a tough part of town, don't be shy about asking for directions. Every Angeleno has gotten lost at one time or another in this sprawling metropolis.

Roads that run east-west are usually boulevards (Pico Boulevard) and if they're numerical, they're streets (Third Street). Those that run north-south are avenues (but there are plenty of exceptions like Westwood Boulevard). The grid pattern extends to downtown, except the grid is tilted about 45 degrees to Hoover Street. Continue south, and downtown returns to an upright grid at Martin Luther King Junior Boulevard. (The east-west street numbers continue through South Central.)

The approximate center of the grid is downtown at Main Street and First Street. All streets that run north-south below First Street increase in number as you travel south. For north-south streets above First Street, the numbers increase in number as you head north. For example, La Brea Avenue is one long north-south street. First Street bisects La Brea Avenue into South La Brea Avenue (south of First) and North La Brea Avenue (north of First) in Hancock Park—but most Angelenos refer to a street without the "south" or "north." So an address like 1400 La Brea Avenue can be in Culver City or Hollywood. (Always ask for a cross street when getting the address of a new location.) The same goes for many of the streets that run east-west. If the east-west street runs west of Main Street, "West" is attached to the street moniker and the numbers increase as you head further west; if the east-west street runs east of Main Street, "East" is the modifier and the street numbers increase as you head further east of Main Street.

Outside of downtown, some numbered streets make up the side streets, while main thoroughfares have names such as Wilshire Boulevard or Beverly Boulevard. Beyond that, there is little logic behind the names of city streets. Until you familiarize yourself with the city, keeping a map in the car is almost as important as your insurance card.

The lack of a formal system in street planning might be blamed on the fact that many of the communities came into being before incorporating with the City of Los Angeles. Fortunately, the city's main thoroughfares are easy to identify—they're heavy with traffic because they're used as alternatives to the freeways. Some of the **main arteries** include:

- **Santa Monica Boulevard**: begins in Silver Lake at Sunset Boulevard and runs west, ending in Santa Monica on Ocean Avenue. This is a heavily traveled street on the Westside.

- **Wilshire Boulevard**: begins at Grand Avenue, downtown, and ends at Ocean Avenue on Santa Monica Boulevard. It is heavily traveled throughout its length.

- **Ventura Boulevard**: this valley-based street begins in Universal City where Cahuenga Boulevard ends and runs west to Woodland Avenue in Woodland Hills.

- **Sepulveda Boulevard**: begins at San Fernando Boulevard in Mission Hills (in the Valley) and runs south, paralleling the 405 Freeway into the 91 Artesia Freeway in Manhattan Beach.

A T FIRST GLANCE, LOS ANGELES APPEARS TO BE A SPRAWLING metropolis, with no clear demarcations from one municipality to the next, let alone distinct neighborhoods. It takes time and patience to understand the subtle qualities that make Santa Monica different from Venice, or Silver Lake from the Fairfax District, but, after a while, you will find neighborhoods in Los Angeles have different characteristics. Exploring LA's communities is easy and fun, and for newcomers especially, it's encouraged.

While cruising through the city you will no doubt encounter the "strip mall" phenomenon; that is, the appearance of one- to three-story mini-malls on every other block. While some consider these modern strip malls eyesores, take a closer look. They may be architecturally uninspiring, but some of these strip centers have become little neighborhood commerce centers in areas that previously had none.

Los Angeles's problems of crime and violence may be notorious, but in reality they reflect the nation's urban woes, and are certainly no better or worse here than in other major US cities. In fact, in a recent survey of FBI crime statistics, which ranked crime levels of the 100 largest metropolitan areas in the country, Los Angeles didn't even make the top 25. As in any city, a good dose of street smarts and common sense will help steer you away from trouble, and, as safety experts are fond of reminding us, always be aware of your surroundings. Certain high-crime neighborhoods such as South-Central and Watts are not recommended for outsiders or newcomers, but there are plenty of safe and affordable areas in which to live, work, and play.

In terms of climate, the warmest temperatures and worst air pollution occur in the summer months and, in general, you can expect the climate and air quality to be hotter and smoggier the further east you go. The Los Angeles metropolitan area reliably ranks at or near the top of ozone pollu-

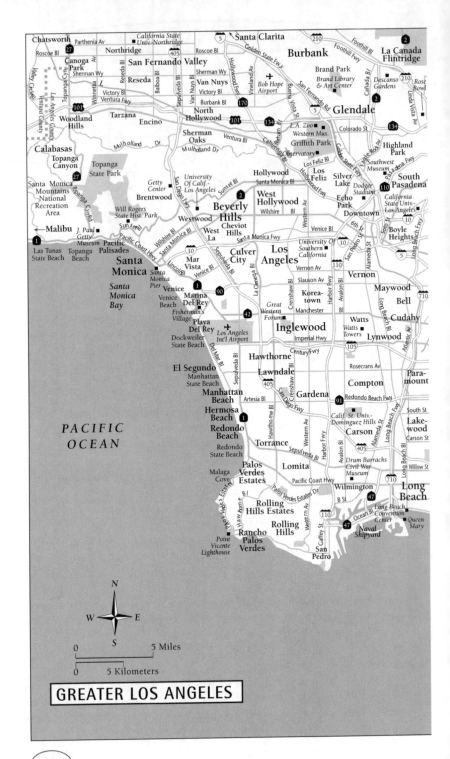

GREATER LOS ANGELES

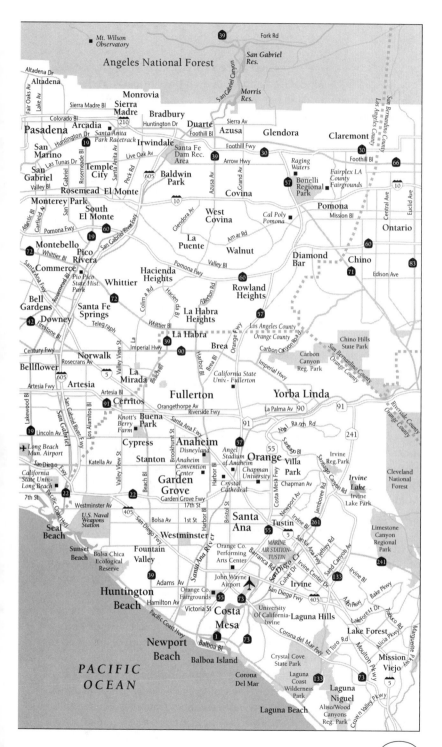

tion lists, so if smog-related illnesses are a particular concern, choose your location carefully. For detailed information on the air quality in the areas you are considering calling home, contact the **South Coast Air Quality Management District** at 909-396-2000, www.aqmd.gov.

The City of Los Angeles is the second most populated city in the USA, with an estimated population of over 3.9 million in 2004; Los Angeles County is comprised of 9.8 million residents. Due to the vastness of LA County, this guide does not attempt to cover every neighborhood, but it does cover many. Some profiled communities, while very much a part of LA, are incorporated cities in their own right; others are distinct neighborhoods within the City of Los Angeles proper. What follows are comprehensive yet concise descriptions of neighborhoods and cities that would be appropriate to those relocating to LA or its environs. We start on the Westside with the beach communities and then move east, more or less, through downtown, and then north, covering the Valley. In this latest edition we have profiled the Orange County communities of Irvine, Newport Beach, Balboa Island, Corona del Mar, and Tustin as well.

Including the City of LA, Los Angeles County consists of 88 cities, such as Glendale, West Hollywood, and Beverly Hills. (There are usually signs posted on major thoroughfares identifying the border of a particular city.) Each city has an independent city council and provides municipal services. Many residents proudly identify with their municipality and its reputation—taking offense when referred to as "Angelenos." Neighborhoods within the City of LA, which measures roughly 470 square miles or 12% of the county, include Fairfax, Westwood, West LA, Hollywood, Downtown, and North Hollywood. The city's patchwork quilt–like composition resulted from battles over a surprisingly simple commodity during its formation: water. Municipalities that were annexed by the City of LA because of their water supplies often retained their community name.

Other useful information such as area codes: 213 (downtown); 323 (areas surrounding downtown, including Hollywood); 310 (Westside and South Bay); 562 (Long Beach); 818 (the Valley, Glendale, and Burbank); 661 (Santa Clarita); 626 (Pasadena); 949 and 714 (Orange County); as well as zip codes, post offices, district police stations, neighborhood hospitals, public libraries, community resources, and public school districts follows each neighborhood description. In some cases, the neighborhood boundaries are approximations, since areas that are not distinct cities tend to blend into one another.

Unless otherwise noted, housing statistics included in the neighborhood profiles are derived from the California Association of Realtors, www.car.org and Dataquick, www.dqnews.com (same resource used by the *LA Times*). In January 2005, the *LA Times* reported that the median sale price for homes in Los Angeles County was $418,000, up more than 21%

from a year earlier, and the median price of an Orange County home surged 18% to $551,00. In itself, this number doesn't tell the full story since homes vary widely in price here, but the double-digit rising percentages are a good indicator of where the LA market is headed. Many local real estate agents predict no end in sight as the demand for housing here continues to exceed the supply.

LA NEIGHBORHOODS AND COMMUNITIES—WEST

MALIBU

Boundaries: **North**: Mulholland Highway; **East**: Tuna Canyon Road, Saddle Creek Road; **South**: Santa Monica Bay; **West**: Mulholland Highway

"Malibu—it's a state of mind." This message seen on license plate holders across Los Angeles may leave you scratching your head and wondering what it all means ... until you get to the City of Malibu. Once you've traveled the twenty miles northwest of Santa Monica on the Pacific Coast Highway (PCH) you'll find Malibu is not so much a place as a peaceful vibe, something often absent in other parts of the region.

In fact, upon arrival Malibu is not so impressive. You'll find the usual fast-food stands, small shopping centers, and surf shops, sprinkled with a few fancy restaurants like Wolfgang Puck's star hangout, Granita. The pretty Malibu Pier offers fishing and food. Most nonresidents come to Malibu for the beaches, which are some of the loveliest and cleanest (both sand and water) in the Los Angeles area. Zuma Beach is the most visited, nearby Point Dume is a bit less crowded, and Leo Carrillo, a 1,600-acre beach situated further northwest, features three campgrounds. Surfrider Beach is still popular with surfers, as it was in the 1950s and '60s when Annette Funicello and Frankie Avalon frolicked here in their Beach Blanket Bingo movies. Even Pepperdine University has an ocean view in Malibu.

As for residents, Malibu is the home, or second home (or third, or fourth), to the rich and famous who enjoy its scenery and privacy. Particularly popular with celebrities is the Malibu Beach Colony, a gated community right on the sand. Note: While the streets and homes in the Colony are not accessible to outsiders, the ocean is. The tidelands in California, defined as the area below the mean high tide, are considered public land. Hence, you can park along the road before or after the Colony property (or, for that matter, almost any other private beach area in the state), and walk along the wet, packed sand for a look at these beachside villas. A few private beach communities have guards that will chase you off

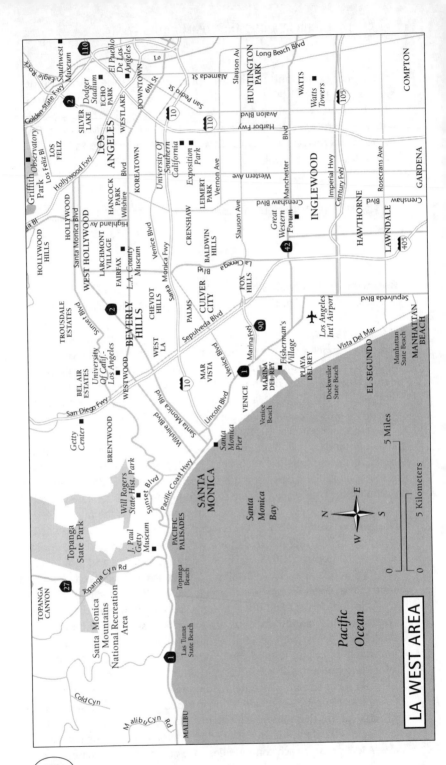

LA WEST AREA

the dry, sandy part of the beach, but stick to the hard, wet sand along the tide and you should be fine.

Aside from the famous folks, Malibu has a fair share of successful professionals, surfer dudes and dudettes, and just plain beach lovers calling it home. As you might imagine, rents and house prices in Malibu are most expensive at the coast, a median of $1.9 million (beachfront property easily sells for more), and then decrease as you move inland, into the canyons. While the area is mostly owner-occupied, a diligent hunter can locate a sprinkling of apartments, condominiums, guesthouses, and town-homes for rent.

Because much of Malibu is hilly, dry canyon country, almost every summer brush fires are a problem. Then in the winter, in places where hillside vegetation has been burned, winter rains can cause landslides, which then cause flooding. During heavy rains, rockslides are responsible for the occasional closures of the Pacific Coast Highway, the main artery in and out of Malibu. Through it all, most residents say the privacy and beauty of Malibu make residing here worthwhile.

Web Sites: www.ci.malibu.ca.us, http://lacounty.info

Area Code: 310

Zip Codes: 90264, 90265

Post Offices: Main Post Office, 23648 Pacific Coast Highway; La Costa Station, 21229 Pacific Coast Highway; Point Dume Station, 29160 Heathercliff Road; 800-275-8777

Police District: Malibu is served by the Los Angeles County Sheriff's Department, 27050 Agoura Road, Agoura, 818-878-1808, www.lasd.org.

Emergency Hospitals: Malibu Urgent Center, 23656 Pacific Coast Highway, 310-456-7551; Santa Monica UCLA Medical Center, 1250 16th Street, Santa Monica, 310-319-4000, www.healthcare.ucla.edu.

Libraries: Malibu Library, 23519 West Civic Center Way, 310-456-6438, www.colapublib.org; Palisades Library, 861 Alma Real Drive, 310-459-2754, www.lapl.org

Public School Education: Santa Monica-Malibu Unified School District: 1651 16th Street, Santa Monica, CA 90405, 310-450-8338, www.smmusd.org

Community Resources: Pepperdine University, 24255 West Pacific Coast Highway, Malibu, 310-456-4000, www.pepperdine.edu; Malibu Bluffs Park, 24250 Pacific Coast Highway, 310-317-1364; Malibu Equestrian Center, 6225 Merritt Drive, 310-317-1364; Charmlee Nature Preserve, 2577 South Encinal Canyon Road, 310-457-7247; Malibu Parks and Recreation Department, 310-317-1364, www.ci.malibu.ca.us

Public Transportation: call 800-COMMUTE or visit www.mta.net, for specific bus route schedule and information.

TOPANGA CANYON

Boundaries: **North**: Mulholland Drive; **East**: Topanga State Park; **South**: Santa Monica Bay; **West**: Los Flores Canyon

Curvy mountain roads, tangled trees and vines, an occasional hippie-type hitchhiking alongside the canyon passageway—are we in LA? Nestled in the Santa Monica Mountains between Santa Monica and Malibu, Topanga Canyon hardly seems like a part of a major metropolis. Its roots are firmly planted in the hippie, artist, and other alternative communities that have populated this unincorporated part of Los Angeles County for decades.

It's easy to see why people choose to live in Topanga Canyon. For starters, there is the beautiful, natural setting, complete with vistas (in some spots) of the Pacific Ocean. Another bonus is the relatively low cost of housing. Residences run the gamut from mountain cabins to newer, high-end houses, and rents and home prices are much lower compared with nearby, chic Malibu. Most area housing was built after 1950, and much is filled by newcomers, many of whom previously were residents of the City of LA. Yes, the word is out, Topanga is more than just a good state park to take a day hike; hence today your next-door neighbor here is as likely to be a downtown lawyer as a stained-glass artist.

However, people accustomed to the convenience of home-delivered Chinese food or 2 a.m. grocery shopping should think twice about living in Topanga Canyon. Although only a few miles up the Pacific Coast Highway from Pacific Palisades, Topanga feels remote. At the crest of Old Topanga Canyon Road, a commercial strip caters to the basics like food and gas, but for the most part, once you've driven up the hill towards home, you've probably left the day's errands behind. And that's just the way locals like it.

Hikers frequent Topanga Canyon, especially along the beautiful, hilly trails at Topanga State Park. Within Topanga Canyon is Topanga Creek, the third largest watershed draining into Santa Monica Bay. (Look out for the three turtle crossing signs in the neighborhood.) Another fun spot in the canyon is the Will Geer Theatricum Botanicum, a rustic outdoor theater now headed by actor Will Geer's daughter Ellen. It is a place where, on a warm summer evening, you can have a romantic, candle-lit picnic and then sit under the stars on comfy throw pillows and view a Shakespearean drama or other play or musical production.

Finally, it's worth noting that if heavy rains hit during the winter, certain sections of Old Topanga Canyon Road and Topanga Canyon Boulevard, the primary arteries serving this community, are prone to closure due to landslides, especially along the creek beds. City crews are quick to bring in bulldozers, so the residents consider this a minor nuisance in exchange for mountain living.

Web Sites: www.topangaonline.com, http://lacounty.info

Zip Code: 90290

Area Codes: 310, 424

Post Office: 101 South Topanga Canyon Blvd., 800-275-8777

Police District: Topanga Canyon is served by the Los Angeles County Sheriff's Department, 27050 Agoura Road, Agoura, 818-878-1808, www.lasd.org.

Emergency Hospitals: Saint John's Hospital and Health Center, 1328 22nd Street, Santa Monica, 310-829-5511; Santa Monica UCLA Medical Center, 1250 16th Street, Santa Monica, 310-319-4000

Libraries: Malibu Library, 23519 West Civic Center Way, Malibu, 310-456-6438, www.colapublib.org; Palisades Library, 861 Alma Real Drive, Malibu, 310-459-2754, www.lapl.org

Public School Education: LA Unified School District, 333 South Beaudry Avenue, LA, CA 90017, 213-241-1000; www.lausd.k12.ca.us

Community Resources: Topanga State Park in the Santa Monica Mountains National Recreation Area, 310-454-8212, www.parks.ca.gov; Topanga Community House, 1440 Topanga Canyon Blvd., 310-455-1980, www.topangacommunityclub.org; Will Geer Theatricum Botanicum, 1419 North Topanga Canyon Blvd., 310-455-3723, www.theatricum.com

Public Transportation: call 800-COMMUTE or www.mta.net for specific Metro bus route and schedule information.

SANTA MONICA

PACIFIC PALISADES, RUSTIC CANYON

Boundaries: **North**: San Vicente Boulevard; **East**: Centinela Avenue; **South**: Dewey Street; **West**: Santa Monica Bay, Pacific Ocean

Nicknamed "Santa Moscow" for its liberal city politics, Santa Monica, which is its own municipality, was once a highly coveted neighborhood for its rent-controlled, seaside apartments. However, rent control has ended and in its place is "vacancy decontrol" (started in 1999—see **Finding a Place to Live**) that allows landlords to set rent at whatever price they deem appropriate, once a formerly rent-controlled apartment has been vacated. Rental prices now reflect the higher price tag expected of seaside living.

To soften the blow for renters, the City of Santa Monica maintains some level of control over the amount rent may be increased. Each year, at the beginning of September, the city's Rent Control Board determines the maximum percentage by which landlords may raise rent. So, while newcomers moving into an apartment will shell out some dollars to live here, annual rental increases are typically held in check. Typically, the general adjustment agreed upon by the board varies between 3% and 4%. In Santa Monica, Rent Control Board determinations apply only to multiple-unit dwellings built before April 10, 1979. The majority of the rental units qualify. With so much potential for confusion, the rent control office provides special coordinators (310-458-8751, www.santa-monica.org/rentcontrol) to help renters determine what their legal rent should be.

Potential home buyers with low to moderate incomes can seek assistance from the **Santa Monica Housing and Redevelopment Division**, 310-458-8702, www.santa-monica.org, an organization designed to provide affordable housing options, including low-cost housing for seniors and the disabled.

Committed to social and environmental sensitivity, Santa Monica has become one the first US cities to make it a matter of city policy to rely on sustainable or renewable resources, overseen by the Environmental Programs Division of the Environmental and Public Works Management Department. Electricity (generated by sustainable sources) and natural gas are the primary sources of energy within the city. There is also a recycling program in place for homeowners and renters, and aggressive campaigns to encourage residents to use water- and energy-efficient devices.

These environment-friendly policies must be having an effect. Area residents like to brag that the air is cleaner and the weather cooler here than anywhere else in LA, and it's true. While summer temperatures in Los Angeles can hover in the eighties and nineties, it's not uncommon for Santa Monica to sport temperatures that are fifteen degrees cooler than downtown or the Valley. Many apartments do not have air conditioners.

Approximately 20% of the housing stock in Santa Monica is composed of single-family homes; the rest consist of multi-unit apartments and condos. Residential streets are lined with either rows of mature magnolia trees or towering palms. The area north of upscale shopping street Montana Avenue features some of LA's most beautiful (and priciest) homes, most built in the early 1960s. For those less financially endowed, the area south of Santa Monica Avenue offers mostly apartments and condominiums, while still boasting easy access to the area's cafes, coffeehouses, and shops. Be aware, street parking is extremely difficult to procure, especially in apartment neighborhoods.

Main Street is probably the hippest and beachiest area in this small city. The art galleries, restaurants and bars with patio seating, shops, and coffeehouses overflow with ever-so-chic singles (the median age here is 39) or young families with strollers in tow. To the west of Main Street are several walking lanes lined with some nice and some run-down beach cottages, but regardless, prices are high due to the proximity to the ocean. The hilly neighborhood just east of Main Street consists of apartments and condominiums with a few funky houses mixed in.

The focus in downtown Santa Monica is the lively outdoor mall, Third Street Promenade, with shops, restaurants, and a multitude of theaters attracting huge crowds (and enterprising street performers) on weekends. The Santa Monica Place Mall is on the southern end of the promenade, and walk just a bit west to the Santa Monica Pier, which is the western end of famed Route 66. Santa Monica Civic Center, Santa Monica College, and Santa Monica Municipal Airport are also located nearby. Well-tended community parks, active neighborhood watch programs, and strongly supported social services for the elderly and disabled round out this seaside neighborhood's offerings, making Santa Monica a favorite for families and singles, both young and old.

A small suburb of Santa Monica is **Pacific Palisades**. This seaside community, part of Los Angeles City, is surrounded by six major canyons and has the look of a posh small town. Upscale stores and restaurants are patronized by well-to-do residents who live nearby in multimillion-dollar homes. Next door is an even more secluded enclave called **Rustic Canyon**. Aptly named, the canyon neighborhood consists of a little over 200 homes in the densely wooded forest.

Web Sites: www.ci.santa-monica.ca.us, http://santa-monica.org, www.cityofla.org, http://lacounty.info

Area Code: 310

Zip Codes: 90401, 90402, 90403, 90404, 90405, 90406, 90272

Post Offices: Main Post Office, 1248 5th Street; Colorado Station, 1025 Colorado Avenue; Will Rogers Station, 1217 Wilshire Blvd.; 800-275-8777

Police District: Santa Monica Police Headquarters, 1685 Main Street, 310-458-8458, www.santamonicapd.org

Emergency Hospitals: Saint John's Hospital and Health Center, 1328 22nd Street, 310-829-5511, www.stjohns.org; Santa Monica UCLA Medical Center, 1250 16th Street, 310-319-4000, www.healthcare.ucla.edu

Libraries: Main Library, 1324 Fifth Street, 310-458-8859; Fairview branch, 2101 Ocean Park Blvd., 310-450-0443; Montana Avenue branch, 1704 Montana Avenue, 310-829-7081; Ocean Park branch, 2601 Main Street, 310-392-3804; www.smpl.org

Public School Education: Santa Monica-Malibu Unified School District, 1651 16th Street, Santa Monica, CA 90404, 310-450-8338; www.smmusd.org

Community Resources: Santa Monica City Information Desk, 310-458-8411; parking permits, 310-458-8291; Santa Monica College, 1900 Pico Blvd., 310-434-4000, www.smc.edu; Lincoln Park, 1150 Lincoln Blvd.; Memorial Park, 1401 Olympic Blvd.; Santa Monica Recreation Division, 310-458-8300, www.santa-monica.org; Santa Monica Pier, 310-458-8900, www.santamonicapier.org

Public Transportation: the affectionately named Big Blue Bus serves Santa Monica residents. Call 310-451-5444 for specific Santa Monica Municipal Bus Line routes and schedule information, or check www.BigBlueBus.com.

VENICE

Boundaries: **North**: Dewey Street; **East**: Walgrove Avenue; **South**: Washington Street; **West**: Santa Monica Bay, Pacific Ocean

The funkiest of Los Angeles's beach communities, Venice is an eclectic mix of artists, surfers, bodybuilders, and sightseers. It was founded in 1900 by Abbot Kinney, whose dream was to foster a cultural renaissance in America by recreating an Italian "Venice" here. Some of the area's original Venetian-style architecture still stands near the boardwalk, as do a few of the canals (located between Washington Boulevard and Venice Boulevard at Dell). Despite these Venetian touches, it is doubtful that Abbot Kinney had any idea just what kind of culture Venice would become known for. Yes, men and women in skimpy bathing suits do rollerblade down the streets here, and yes, burly muscle men and women do perform their workouts and flex for tourists at Muscle Beach, but Venice is also home to a strong and thriving artists' community, composed of first-rate studios, galleries, and artists' residences. The heart of the area is Ocean Front Walk (known as the boardwalk), a beachfront collection of shops, outdoor cafes, street performers, jewelry and sunglasses stands, and the liveliest place in town to get your palm read, hair braided, or back massaged. Housing runs the gamut from beach cottages to reasonably priced apartments to oceanfront villas that, in total, support a residential population of over 40,000. Prices and quality vary greatly, but generally the closer you are to the ocean, the more you pay.

East of the boardwalk is Abbot Kinney Boulevard. While this street hasn't caught on like Santa Monica's Main Street (and some think that's just fine), it features an interesting mix of art galleries, antique stores, restaurants, and shops. The surrounding homes and apartments are somewhat run down as the mode of lifestyle here suggests comfort over polish. More recently, some homebuyers, who have to shell out an average of $765,000 for a home, are opting to tear down the old house and start fresh. Rentals, however, especially bungalows, more readily dot the main thoroughfares like Abbot Kinney Boulevard and Pacific Avenue and its side streets.

Each spring, artists open their studios and homes for the Venice Artwalk, an area fundraiser. The Canal Neighborhood, located between Venice and Washington boulevards east of Pacific Avenue, offers a unique and charming living situation. The houses along the canals vary from ramshackle cottages to newly built mini-mansions. Many residents have their own rowboats for tooling through the area, and visiting romantics can even rent a gondola for a little taste of Italy, LA style.

While Venice's proximity to the beach and boardwalk and general outdoor lifestyle are definite pluses, beware that crime here is higher than average, and east of Sixth Avenue is a rough neighborhood called Oakwood. As Venice is one of the most popular tourist attractions in California, the City of Los Angeles is rectifying the crime situation with increased patrol efforts, especially on weekends.

Web Sites: www.cityofla.org, www.venice.net, www.westland.net, http://lacounty.info

Area Code: 310

Zip Code: 90291

Post Office: Main Post Office, 1601 Main Street; Venice Carrier Annex Station, 313 Grand Blvd.; 800-275-8777

Police District: Pacific Division, 12312 Culver Blvd., 310-202-4501, www.lapd.org

Emergency Hospital: Daniel Freeman Marina Hospital, 4650 Lincoln Blvd., 310-823-8911, www.danielfreemanmarinahospital.com

Library: Venice-Abbot Kinney Memorial branch, 501 South Venice Blvd., 310-821-1769, www.lapl.org

Public School Education: LA Unified School District, 333 South Beaudry Avenue, LA, CA 90017, 213-241-1000; www.lausd.k12.ca.us

Community Resources: Venice Recreation Center, 1531 Ocean Front Walk, 310-399-2775, www.laparks.org; Westminster Park, 1234 Pacific Avenue; Pacific Resident Theatre, 703 Venice Blvd., 310-822-8392, www.pacificresidenttheatre.com; Penmar Recreation Center, 1341 Lake Street, 310-396-8735, www.laparks.org

Public Transportation: call 800-COMMUTE or visit www.mta.net for specific Metro bus route and schedule information.

MARINA DEL REY

Boundaries: **North**: Washington Street; **East:** Centinela Boulevard; **South**: Ballona Creek; **West**: Santa Monica Bay, Pacific Ocean

Situated around the world's largest manmade small-boat harbor, Marina del Rey has a reputation as a singles area, many of whom enjoy the Marina's waterfront locale and proximity to boating, sailing, windsurfing, water-skiing, tennis, and jogging and bicycling paths. And, Marina del Rey boasts the highest density of restaurant seating in a one-square-mile area, outside of New York City, making it popular with locals and visitors alike.

In Marina del Rey, the area known as the Marina Peninsula, a strip of land between the ocean and the boat harbor, is composed of streets and walkways that run perpendicular to the beach. Locals use the alphabetically arranged nautical street names, "Anchorage" down to "Yawl," to refer not only to the streets themselves but also to the beaches they abut. The Marina Peninsula offers both large (50-unit plus) and small condominiums and apartments, as well as upscale mini-mansions. In fact, real estate is at such a premium here that almost 90% of the residential buildings in Marina del Rey are multi-unit housing. Less than 3% are single detached homes, and these are primarily beach cottages. All are priced over a million dollars.

There is an abundance of modern apartments, many built since the 1980s, throughout the rest of Marina del Rey. Gyms, swimming pools, and tennis courts are common features. At the western end of the 90 Freeway, you'll find new million-dollar condos offering sweeping views of the city and ocean, complete with the finest amenities within their slender towers. Overall, housing prices in Marina del Rey lean toward the high end, so many young professionals fresh out of college team up here as housemates.

Web Sites: www.cityofla.org, www.marinadelrey.com, www.visitthe marina.com, http://lacounty.info
Area Code: 310
Zip Code: 90292
Post Office: Marina del Rey branch, 4766 Admiralty Way; 800-275-8777
Police District: Pacific Division, 12312 Culver Blvd., 310-202-4501, www.lapd.org.
Emergency Hospital: Daniel Freeman Marina Hospital, 4650 Lincoln Blvd., 310-823-8911, www.danielfreemanmarinahospital.com
Library: Marina del Rey branch, 4533 Admiralty Way, 310-821-3415, www.colapublib.org
Public School Education: LA Unified School District, 333 South Beaudry Avenue, LA, CA 90017, 213-241-1000, www.lausd.k12.ca.us

Community Resources: Fisherman's Village, 13723 Fiji Way, 310-301-6000; UCLA Marina Aquatic Center, 14001 Fiji Way, 310-823-0048; LA County's Department of Beaches and Harbors, 13837 Fiji Way, 310-305-9504, http://beaches.co.la.ca.us

Public Transportation: call 800-COMMUTE or visit www.mta.net for Metro bus route and schedule information.

PLAYA DEL REY

Boundaries: **North**: Ballona Creek; **East**: Lincoln Boulevard; **South**: Manchester Avenue; **West**: Pacific Ocean

Tucked in between Marina del Rey and LAX, residents say Playa del Rey (Spanish for "King's Beach") is their little private hideaway. Isolated from the rest of Los Angeles by wetlands and featuring a shack-style downtown strip of mom-and-pop restaurants and shops, Playa del Rey has the feel of a small California beach town. Since there are no public parking lots and street parking is limited, the beaches here are relatively uncrowded, even during the hot summer months. For years, there was talk of developing the wetlands, once owned by Howard Hughes, with an office/residential park or movie production facilities such as Dreamworks Studios, but in 2001, the California Wildlife Conservation Board purchased the wetlands to protect it from development, making this nature preserve an effective and now permanent barrier from the rest of the city. The area is, however, adjacent to the controversial and massive Playa Vista development, planned to accommodate around 13,000 residents. The first phase houses about 4,000 people in a mix of condos, town homes, and single-family homes. The second phase, approved by the LA City Council in 2004, is expected to include 2,600 housing units, in addition to office and retail space.

Housing in Playa del Rey is approximately 45% owner-occupied and 55% renter-occupied. **Lower Playa del Rey** consists of the few streets right along the beach, and features mostly modern townhomes, condominiums, and apartments. Heading east on Manchester Avenue is **Upper Playa del Rey**, and with the exception of some housing that offers magnificent views, this residential area is considered a bit less desirable than the spots right down by the water. On the other hand, if you're looking to rent or buy a house, you'll have more opportunities in this upper area. Another plus, homes here tend to be newer than those found in other communities; many were built in the 1980s.

Playa del Rey is located just north of LAX, a fact that can be a plus or minus, depending on your needs. Frequent travelers will appreciate the easy commute to the airport, but the noise, especially in Upper Playa del Rey, can be a nuisance. On the eastern border of this community is the Catholic Loyola Marymount University. Founded in 1865, it is the first college built in Los Angeles, and it offers entertainment and educational opportunities to the public. Golf fans will notice the Westchester Golf Course is also adjacent.

Prospective residents might also like to know that Playa del Rey is the site of the Hyperion Treatment Plant, a sewage treatment facility at 12000 Vista del Mar. The Department of Public Works assures that state-of-the-art technology is used both to monitor the environmental impact of the plant and to maintain safe standards (visit ww.lacity.org/SAN/htp.htm for more information about the plant). If you would like more information on the environmental monitoring of the plant, contact **Heal the Bay**, 310-581-4188, www.healthebay.org, a volunteer organization that monitors the health of the Santa Monica Bay.

Web Sites: www.cityofla.org, http://lacounty.info
Area Code: 310
Zip Code: 90293
Post Office: Playa del Rey branch, 215 Culver Blvd.; 800-275-8777
Police District: Pacific Division, 12312 Culver Blvd., 310-202-4501, www.lapd.org
Emergency Hospital: Daniel Freeman Marina Hospital, 4650 Lincoln Blvd., 310-823-8911, www.danielfreemanmarinahospital.com
Library: Marina del Rey branch, 4533 Admiralty Way, 310-821-3415, www.colapublib.org
Public School Education: LA Unified School District, 333 South Beaudry Avenue, LA, CA 90017, 213-241-1000, www.lausd.k12.ca.us
Community Resources: Loyola Marymount University, Loyola Blvd. at West 80th Street, 310-338-2700, www.lmu.edu; Del Rey Lagoon Park, 6660 Esplanade; Los Angeles City Department of Recreation and Parks, 888-LA-PARKS, www.laparks.org; Westchester Senior Recreation Center, 8740 Lincoln Blvd., 310-649-3317; Westchester Golf Course, 6900 West Manchester Avenue, 310-649-9168
Public Transportation: call 800-COMMUTE or visit www.mta.net for specific Metro bus route and schedule information.

EL SEGUNDO

Boundaries: **North**: Imperial Highway; **East**: Aviation Boulevard; **South**: Rosecrans Boulevard; **West**: Vista del Mar Boulevard

Located directly south of Los Angeles International Airport and fourteen miles southwest of downtown LA, the city of El Segundo, Spanish for "the second," is so named because in 1911, Standard Oil Company selected it as the site of its second oil refinery. In fact, a 1920s newspaper advertisement described the town as "the Standard Oil payroll city." The 1,000-acre refinery, now run by Chevron USA, is still a major part of El Segundo, encompassing the southwestern quadrant of the city. The rest of the city is 80% zoned for commercial/industrial use and 20% is composed of the tranquil residential enclave west of Sepulveda Boulevard.

In addition to the oil refinery, El Segundo is the long-time home to Mattel Toys, Northrop Grumman, Unocal, and Computer Sciences Corporation. Many people commute to this community to work. In fact, its daytime population exceeds approximately 70,000, compared with its resident population of about 15,000. A 1980s hot spot for aviation and defense industry companies, it also makes sense that the Los Angeles Air Force Base and its Space and Missile Systems Center are here.

You can expect most of the housing here to be modern—generally built between 1950 and 1980, but rather nondescript. The need for housing by corporate execs wanting to keep their commutes short has pushed home prices higher, but price tags remain cheaper than the surrounding areas. Apartments are rare, but when available are more affordable than most Westside communities. El Segundo residents love the small-town atmosphere and the fact that it has its own school district. However, due to its proximity to LAX, overhead noise can be distracting. Also, intermittent fumes from the Hyperion sewage treatment plant (see section on Playa del Rey) have given the area the nickname "El Stinko." On the upside, big business has provided the community with the means for recreational amenities including The Lakes at El Segundo Golf Course and a recreational park located at East Pine Avenue and Eucalyptus Drive. Serviced by the 405 San Diego and 105 Century/Glen Anderson freeways and the Metro Green Line, access to the southwestern part of LA and its beaches is second to none.

Web Sites: www.elsegundo.org, http://lacounty.info
Area Codes: 310, 424
Zip Code: 90245
Post Offices: El Segundo branch, 200 Main Street; Airport Station, 9029 Airport Blvd., Los Angeles, 800-275-8777, www.usps.com
Police District: El Segundo Police Headquarters: 348 Main Street, 310-524-2200, www.elsegundo.org/police
Emergency Hospitals: Centinela Hospital Medical Center, 555 East Hardy Street, 310-673-4660, www.centinelahospital.com; Daniel Freeman Memorial Hospital, 4650 Lincoln Blvd., 310-823-8911, www.danielfreeman marinahospital.com
Library: El Segundo Public Library, 111 West Mariposa Avenue, 310-524-2722; www.elsegundo.org

Public School Education: El Segundo Unified School District, 641 Sheldon Street, El Segundo, CA 90245; 310-615-2650, www.elsegundo usd.com

Community Resources: The Lakes at El Segundo Golf Course, 400 South Sepulveda Blvd., 310-322-0202; Recreation Park, East Pine Avenue and Eucalyptus Drive; El Segundo Parks and Recreation Department, 310-524-2300, www.elsegundo.org.

Public Transportation: call 800-COMMUTE or visit www.mta.net for specific Metro Green Line and Metro bus route and schedule information.

MANHATTAN BEACH

Boundaries: North: Rosecrans Avenue; **East**: Aviation Boulevard; **South**: Artesia Boulevard; **West**: Pacific Ocean

Ever wondered what happened to Susie Sorority and Frank Fraternity after graduation? They moved to Manhattan Beach. It may be a bit more of a commute to work, but the youthful residents, generally in their thirties, think the beautiful beaches and lively shops, restaurants, and bars are worth the drive.

Upscale beach life here centers around The Strand, a cement promenade popular with skaters, joggers, and walkers, and the South Bay Bicycle Trail that also runs along the beach. The white sand draws droves of sunbathers and volleyball players, who can choose their game site from among over one hundred courts located just steps away from beachfront homes.

A short walk from the city's sandy beach is the vibrant and charming shopping district, centered around Manhattan Avenue and Manhattan Beach Boulevard. The area is densely packed with cafes, bars, bookstores, and clothing shops. Weekend nights can take on the feel of a college town as scores of young hipsters walk the streets to take in the local bar and restaurant scene.

Housing options near the ocean include quaint beach cottages with porches or balconies that open right onto the sandy strip and multi-unit apartment buildings, most of which were built during the 1950s. Since Manhattan Beach is on a slight hill, many units boast ocean views. Rents for these units are higher than if not comparable to LA's other beach communities. The area east of Ardmore Avenue is more family oriented, with mostly single-family houses.

As with many beach communities, residential streets are narrow and parking is impossible, especially on weekends when beachgoers flock to the area. It is important to note that, although Manhattan Beach is located only about 20 miles southwest of downtown Los Angeles, the weekday commute to downtown can be as long as 45 minutes to over an hour, each way. If your job requires a lot of flying, though, Manhattan Beach is conveniently located near LAX.

Web Sites: www.ci.manhattan-beach.ca.us, http://lacounty.info
Area Code: 310
Zip Code: 90266
Post Offices: Main Post Office, 1007 North Sepulveda Blvd.; Substation, 425 15th Street; 800-275-8777
Police District: Manhattan Beach Police Headquarters, 1501 North Peck Avenue, 310-802-5100, www.ci.manhattan-beach.ca.us/police
Emergency Hospital: (nearest) Little Company of Mary, 4101 Torrance Blvd., Torrance, 310-540-7676, www.lcmweb.org
Library: Main Library, 1320 Highland Avenue, 310-545-8595, www.cola publib.org
Public School Education: Manhattan Beach Unified School District, 325 South Peck Avenue, Manhattan Beach, CA 90266, 310-318-7345, www.manhattan.k12.ca.us
Community Resources: Marine Avenue Park, Marina Avenue and Redondo Avenue; Live Oak Park, North Valley Drive and 21st Street; Polliwog Park, Manhattan Beach Blvd. and North Peck Avenue; Manhattan Beach Recreation Department, 310-802-5408 or 310-802-5409, www.ci.manhattan-beach.ca.us/parksrec; Manhattan Village Mall, 3200 North Sepulveda Blvd., 310-426-6313, http://shopman hattanvillage.com
Public Transportation: call 800-COMMUTE or visit www.mta.net for specific Metro bus route and schedule information.

INGLEWOOD

Boundaries: **North**: 64th Street; **East**: Van Ness Avenue; **South**: Imperial Highway; **West**: 405 Freeway

Sports fans remember the City of Inglewood as the home of The Great Western Forum (at Prairie Avenue and Manchester Boulevard), the original site of the Los Angeles Lakers, Kings, and Clippers before their move to the Staples Center downtown. In late 2000, the Great Western Forum was purchased by the Faithful Central Bible Church of Inglewood to provide Sunday worship services to its 10,000-member, primarily African-American, congregation. The church continues to allow concerts and other entertainment events to book the Forum. Inglewood is also the site of the Hollywood Park Racetrack where bettors play the ponies. Planes departing and approaching nearby LAX are quite apparent, and security bars and gates are a must in this urban neighborhood, though the eastern side is generally thought of as more secure with its gated streets.

Housing in Inglewood consists of two- and three-bedroom homes, the majority built between 1940 and 1960. Some streets seem to be waging an ongoing fight with graffiti and litter; others are neater and tidier. A handful of multi-unit apartment buildings are also located here. It's recommended that potential renters locate vacancies that include secured parking. Downtown Inglewood is centered around the shopping district of Market Street and Manchester Avenue, offering day-to-day amenities such as grocery stores, pharmacies, and hair salons. The largest patch of green in the community is the Inglewood Park Cemetery, located to the north of the racetrack. The 405 San Diego Freeway borders the western edge, and the relatively new 105 Transit Highway, which is elevated above Inglewood, creates an unwelcome forest of concrete pillars along Inglewood's southern border.

Web Site: www.cityofinglewood.org, http://lacounty.info
Area Code: 310
Zip Codes: 90301-5
Post Offices: Main Post Office, 300 East Hillcrest Blvd.; Alla Vista Station, 13031 West Jefferson Blvd.; Lennox Branch, 4443 Lennox Blvd.; Morningside Park Station, 3212 West 85th Street; North Station, 811 North La Brea Avenue; 800-275-8777
Police District: **Inglewood Police** headquarters, 1 Manchester Blvd., 310 412-5210, www.cityofinglewood.org/depts/police/default.asp
Emergency Hospitals: Daniel Freeman Memorial Hospital, 4650 Lincoln Blvd., 310-823-8911, www.danielfreemanmarinahospital.com; Centinela Hospital Medical Center, 555 East Hardy Street, 310-673-4660, www.centinelahospital.com
Libraries: Main Library, 101 West Manchester Blvd., 310-412-5380; Crenshaw-Imperial Branch, 11141 Crenshaw Blvd., 310-412-5403; Morningside Park Branch, 3202 West 85th Street; 310-412-5400, www.cityofinglewood.org
Public School Education: Inglewood Unified School District, 401 South Inglewood Avenue, Inglewood, CA 90301, 310-419-2700, www.inglewood.k12.ca.us
Community Resources: Hollywood Park Racetrack, 1050 South Prairie Avenue, 310-419-1500, www.hollywoodpark.com; Centinela Park, 700 Warren Lane; Rogers Park, North Oak Street and North Eucalyptus Avenue; Inglewood Parks and Recreation Department, 310-412-8750, www.cityofinglewood.org; Centinela Adobe Complex, 7643 Midfield, 310-412-8750; Inglewood Senior Citizens Center, 111 North Locust Street, 310-412-5338

Public Transportation: call 800-COMMUTE or visit www.mta.net for specific Metro Green Line and Metro bus route and schedule information.

MAR VISTA, PALMS, CHEVIOT HILLS

Boundaries: **North**: 10 Santa Monica Freeway; **East**: Motor Avenue; **South**: Venice Boulevard; **West**: 405 Freeway

Located within the City of LA, Mar Vista and Palms, just northwest of Culver City, attract those looking for reasonably priced housing (for the Westside), both for rent and purchase. These more urban neighborhoods with Spanish exteriors may not be as well manicured as nearby pricier communities, but many young, ethnically diverse families appreciate the break on their pocketbook. This easy-to-access Westside location not only offers plenty to choose from in terms of housing, but its small commercial center with a good selection of neighborhood restaurants and easy shopping along Motor Avenue is popular with the locals as well.

Palms is the oldest community on the Westside; the first streets were laid down in 1886. The Palms Depot first served the Southern Pacific Railroad and then the Pacific Electric Railway. In the 1920s, Laurel and Hardy often filmed their comedy flicks in Palms, using its famous Red Cars on the railroad as a backdrop. Over time, this historic depot, a rare example of that period's Victoria "Eastlake" style architecture, fell into disrepair, but in 1975 it was moved to and restored by the Heritage Square Museum. Today, this modest middle-class town offers mostly rental housing.

Between Palms and **Mar Vista**, the latter is more geared toward family living, offering a bigger selection of single-family homes and fewer apartment buildings. Affordable home prices in Mar Vista attract many young families. A few streets running atop the hill in Mar Vista boast ocean and city views. As evidence of the population in this area, the lovely Mar Vista Park at McLaughlin and Palms is usually filled with families (or kids with nannies). The park's recreation department caters to children, offering summer camps, gym classes, and toddler programs.

The Santa Monica Airport, which sits on the northern border of Mar Vista, can be a noise nuisance. (Those viewing Mar Vista should know that many people often confuse this neighborhood with the housing project located west of Culver City called Mar Vista Gardens.)

Venice Boulevard, the southernmost boundary for both Palms and Mar Vista, is a commercial strip seemingly overflowing with businesses where you can find everything from ethnic food to discount futons to auto parts. A short drive or walk north on Motor Avenue just under the 10 Freeway leads to lovely **Cheviot Hills**, a hilly residential enclave of mostly vintage Southern California homes. Continuing north on Motor Avenue will lead to the popular Cheviot Hills Park, offering 14 lit tennis courts, archery, swimming, basketball courts, and baseball diamonds, and to Rancho Park, reputed to be one of the busiest public golf courses in the country. Motor Avenue continues north into the Twentieth Century Fox studio lot, and although it's closed to the public, you may spot the old movie set street from "Hello, Dolly" as you drive by.

Web Sites: www.palms-california.us, www.cityofla.org, http://lacounty.info

Area Code: 310

Zip Code: 90034

Post Offices: Mar Vista Station, 3826 Grand View Blvd.; Palms Station, 3751 Motor Avenue; 800-275-8777

Police District: Pacific Division, 12312 Culver Blvd., 310-202-4501, www.lapd.org

Emergency Hospital: Brotman Medical Center, 3828 Delmas Terrace, Culver City, 310-836-7000, www.brotmanmedicalcenter.com

Libraries: Mar Vista branch, 12006 Venice Blvd., 310-390-3454; Palms-Rancho Park Library, 2920 Overland Avenue, 310-840-2142; www.lapl.org

Public School Education: LA Unified School District, 333 South Beaudry Avenue, LA, CA 90017; 213-241-1000; www.lausd.k12.ca.us

Community Resources: Mar Vista Recreation Center, 11430 Woodbine Street, 310-398-5982; Palms Recreation Center, 2950 Overland Avenue, 310-838-3838; Cheviot Hills Park and Recreation Center, 2551 Motor Avenue, 310-837-5186, www.laparks.org; Rancho Park Golf Course, 10460 West Pico Blvd., 310-838-7373; Hillcrest Country Club, 10000 West Pico Blvd., 310-553-8911

Public Transportation: call 800-COMMUTE or go to www.mta.net for specific Metro bus routes and schedule information. Santa Monica's Municipal Big Blue Bus has lines in the area; call 310-451-5444, www.bigbluebus.com for route and schedule information. For the Culver City Municipal Bus Line, call 310-253-6510, www.culvercity.org.

CULVER CITY

Boundaries: North: Venice Boulevard; **East**: Jefferson Boulevard; **South**: Slauson Avenue; **West**: 405 Freeway

Culver City is the original and current home to several major movie studios, including the landmark site of Metro-Goldwyn-Mayer, now the location of Sony Studios. Such movie classics as "Citizen Kane," "King Kong," "ET," and the scene of Atlanta burning in "Gone with the Wind" were all filmed on the lots of Culver City movie studios. Today Columbia, Tri-Star, and several other major film and televisions producers are located here.

Though only five square miles and bordered on all sides by parts of LA, Culver City is its own municipal entity. It is bisected by Ballona Creek, which empties into the Pacific Ocean. The majority of Culver City is zoned for commercial, industrial, and light industrial business; however, those looking to reside here can find pockets of single-family homes. The majority of homes are simple, two- or three-bedroom homes, generally built between 1950 and 1980. Because Culver City did not begin developing until the 1940s, homes in this community are newer than many other Los Angeles neighborhoods. Apartment rentals are pricey due to its Westside location, but are less than what might be found in Santa Monica.

The lively commercial district of Culver City has over three million square feet of shopping space. Retailers include the 140-store Fox Hills Mall and a handful of auto dealerships. As a workplace hub, the old industrial area known as the Hayden Tract, located between National Boulevard and Higuera Street and north of Ballona Creek, now consists of a collection of recently built art and design studios, high-tech marketing firms, and architecture offices. Two unique buildings designed by award-winning architect Eric Owen Moss, one on National Boulevard and another on Hayden Avenue, have also focused attention on this area for their eye-catching appearance.

On weekends, residents take to the sidewalk cafes and retail stores along Washington Boulevard, while kids wheel over to the Culver City Skateboard Park. Dog owners, with pooches in tow, head to "the bone yard," the city's only off-leash dog park. Both the skateboard and dog parks are located within the 45-acre Culver City Park. During weekdays, the wide thoroughfares of Venice, Washington, and Culver boulevards provide alternatives to the 10 Santa Monica Freeway into Marina del Rey and Santa Monica. After rush hour, when Culver City's daytime workforce population has left, area residents are able to enjoy a less hurried pace.

Web Sites: www.ci.culver-city.ca.us, http://lacounty.info

Area Code: 310

Zip Code: 90230, 90232

Post Offices: Main Post Office, 11111 Jefferson Blvd.; Gateway Station, 9942 Culver Blvd.; 800-275-8777

Police District: Culver City Police headquarters, 4040 Duquesne Avenue, 310-837-1221, www.culvercity.org/police/police.html

Emergency Hospital: Brotman Medical Center, 3828 Delmas Terrace, 310-836-7000, www.brotmanmedicalcenter.com

Library: Culver City Library, 4975 Overland Avenue, 310-559-1676, www.colapublib.org

Public School Education: Culver City Unified School District, 4034 Irving Place, Culver City, CA 90232, 310-842-4220; www.ccusd.k12.ca.us

Community Resources: Veterans Memorial Park, 4417 Overland Avenue; Culver City Park, Duquesne Avenue and Jefferson Blvd., 310-558-8638; Culver City Recreation Department, 310-253-6650, www.culvercity.org; Culver City Dog Park, www.culvercitydogpark.org; Culver City Skateboard Park, 310-558-8638

Public Transportation: for the Culver City Municipal Bus Line, call 310-253-6510 or visit www.culvercity.org. Call 800-COMMUTE, or visit www.mta.net for specific Metro bus route and schedule information. Santa Monica's Big Blue Bus has lines in the area; call 310-451-5444, www.bigbluebus.com for route and schedule information.

WEST LOS ANGELES

Boundaries: **North**: Santa Monica Boulevard; **East**: Beverly Glen Boulevard; **South**: Pico Boulevard; **West**: Centinela Avenue

While still centrally located on the Westside, the area known as West LA tends to be less expensive than nearby Westwood and Brentwood. Here, the streets are more urban, dotted with convenience shops, gas stations, and strip malls, many of which could use a new coat of paint.

Housing stock mainly consists of bunched together, nondescript, three-story apartments dating from the 1960s and '70s. Many do not have air conditioners, though the air is cooler here, with the ocean just a stone's throw away in the beach community of Santa Monica. Street parking generally is available, and some buildings provide back-alley parking spaces, though many are not gated. The positives for this Westside location include convenient access to major freeways, including the 10 Santa Monica and 405 San Diego, and mid- to low-end rental rates. The area certainly makes up for in affordability what it lacks in architectural charm, creating a good choice for people on a budget who want to live in the Westside.

Aficionados of Japanese food and culture should check out Sawtelle Boulevard north of Olympic Boulevard, where a number of Japanese restaurants and Japanese-owned nurseries can be found. Also worth a visit is the funky Art Deco movie house called the Nuart (on Santa Monica Boulevard just west of the 405 Freeway), which features foreign and alternative films, plus a weekly Saturday midnight showing of "The Rocky Horror Picture Show."

Parents will enjoy the green space in Westwood Park, which features two playgrounds, playing fields, and picnic tables. Shoppers from all over come to West LA, the locale of two major malls. The indoor Westside Pavilion mall offers typical shopping amenities. The upscale outdoor Century City Shopping Mall caters to a fashion-conscious crowd and even offers valet parking. The Century City Mall's movie theater complex is especially popular with Westsiders and is frequently sold out on weekends. The weekday lunch crowd—business-suited men and women from the nearby work district (heavy in the entertainment and law fields)—fills the mall's food court.

According to recent demographic statistics by the US Census Bureau, the Westside comprises only 3% of Los Angeles County's total land area, yet 7% of the county's population and 13% of the county's jobs are in this coveted part of town—explaining why the bordering 405 San Diego Freeway is such a heavily used (and frequently clogged) thoroughfare.

Web Sites: www.cityofla.org, http://lacounty.info
Area Code: 310
Zip Code: 90025
Post Offices: West Los Angeles branch, 11420 Santa Monica Blvd.; West Los Angeles branch, 11270 Exposition Blvd. Fl. 2; Veterans Administration, 11301 Wilshire Blvd., Building #306; Village Station, 11000 Wilshire Blvd.; 800-275-8777
Police District: West Los Angeles Division, 1663 Butler Avenue, 310-575-8402, www.lapd.org
Emergency Hospital: UCLA Medical Center, 10833 LeConte Avenue, 310-825-9111, www.healthcare.ucla.edu
Library: West Los Angeles Library, 11360 Santa Monica Blvd., 310-575-8323, www.lapl.org
Public School Education: LA Unified School District, 333 South Beaudry Avenue, LA, CA 90017; 213-241-1000; www.lausd.k12.ca.us
Community Resources: Westwood Park, 1350 South Sepulveda Blvd.; Los Angeles City Department of Recreation and Parks, 888-LA-PARKS, www.laparks.org; Westside Pavilion Shopping Mall, Overland Avenue and Ayres Avenue; Century City Shopping Mall, 10250 Santa Monica Blvd.
Public Transportation: call 800-COMMUTE or visit www.mta.net for specific Metro bus route and schedule information. Santa Monica's Big Blue Bus has lines in the area; call 310-451-5444, www.bigbluebus.com for route and schedule information.

BRENTWOOD

Boundaries: **North**: Sunset Boulevard; **East**: 405 Freeway; **South**: Wilshire Boulevard; **West**: Centinela Avenue

The lushly planted, upscale Brentwood exudes prestige for those with the means to live here. Brentwood's central position on the Westside and numerous apartment buildings make it a natural choice for new and established professionals. What this community may lack in character, it makes up for with a vanilla safe environment. Running through Brentwood's center, the busy San Vicente Boulevard offers brand-name clothiers, upscale restaurants, bookstores, coffee shops, and gourmet groceries. The boulevard also acts as a divider for area residences, with houses located to the north of it, and stylish contemporary apartments and condominiums to the south. The northwestern-most part of Brentwood is an affluent residential area of palatial homes on shady streets. Multiple bedrooms, i.e., more than three, are typical in these custom homes tucked on quiet streets that curve through hills. These hillside residences translate into big price tags (often in the millions). Higher-end prices also apply to Brentwood's apartments.

The area around Brentwood Village, the quaint shopping area where Barrington Avenue meets Sunset Boulevard, includes cafes, bakeries, hair salons, a post office, and park. Many joggers and dog walkers especially love the wide, grassy median that makes up San Vicente Boulevard, which, for the truly motivated, will take exercisers all the way west to the coastline in Santa Monica.

Brentwood is also home to the Getty Center, a billion-dollar "campus" of buildings housing, among other art-related programs and institutions, the late J. Paul Getty's collection of European antiquities and art. Designed by noted architect Richard Meier, the mountain-top museum has been a hit with locals and visitors alike who are treated to a great view of the 405 San Diego Freeway in a meandering electric tram ride up the mountain.

Proximity to the 405, the main north/south artery in and out of Brentwood, can be both a blessing and a curse. Commuters spill over from the frequently sardine-packed 405 into Sepulveda Boulevard and nearby parallel streets in a mad dash to trim minutes from their rush-hour drive.

Web Sites: www.cityofla.org, http://lacounty.info
Area Code: 310
Zip Code: 90049
Post Office: Brentwood Main Office, 18 Oak Street; Barrington Station, 200 South Barrington Avenue, 800-275-8777

Police District: West Los Angeles Division, 1663 Butler Avenue, 310-575-8402, www.lapd.org

Emergency Hospital: UCLA Medical Center, 10833 LeConte Avenue, 310-825-9111, www.healthcare.ucla.edu

Library: Brentwood branch-Donald Bruce Kauffman Library, 11820 San Vicente Blvd., 310-575-8273, www.lapl.org

Public School Education: LA Unified School District, 333 South Beaudry Avenue, LA, CA 90017; 213-241-1000; www.lausd.k12.ca.us

Community Resources: The Getty Center, 1200 Getty Center Drive, 310-440-7300, www.getty.edu; Barrington Recreation Center, 333 South Barrington Avenue, 310-476-3807; Brentwood Country Club, 590 Burlingame Avenue, 310-451-8011; Los Angeles City Department of Recreation and Parks, 888-LA-PARKS, www.laparks.org

Public Transportation: call 800-COMMUTE, or visit www.mta.net for specific Metro bus route and schedule information. Santa Monica's Big Blue Bus has lines in the area; call 310-451-5444, www.bigbluebus.com for route and schedule information.

WESTWOOD

Boundaries: **North**: Sunset Boulevard; **East**: Beverly Glen Boulevard; **South**: Santa Monica Boulevard; **West**: 405 Freeway

South of the tony hills of Bel Air lies Westwood, most famous for being the home of the University of California Los Angeles (UCLA). The area around the campus is filled with fraternities, sororities, and student-inhabited apartment buildings, but non-students also enjoy the proximity to Westwood Village's many shops, restaurants, and movie theaters, as well as the sporting and cultural events held on campus.

Westwood doesn't quite hum with the same amount of enthusiasm as in its heyday in the eighties, but this college town has a healthy nightlife that's supported by plenty of twenty-somethings. That must explain the dense population of big-screen movie theaters here. In fact, many feature films make their star-studded debut here.

Apartment rentals in Westwood are expensive due to the student population's voracious need for housing. Especially during the school year, it is not unusual for students to double up in a one-bedroom, or bunk four to a two-bedroom.

For those newcomers to Westwood with a car and no garage, a word of warning: hunting down street parking in Westwood requires diligence and a lot of patience. And beware of the meter maids—Westwood has some of the quickest ticket writers in the county.

In the northern portion of Westwood are custom-built homes along winding, eucalyptus-lined streets, many on cul-de-sacs. With the exception of the city's meticulously groomed National Cemetery located between Veteran Avenue and the 405 Sepulveda Freeway, Westwood is surrounded by affluence. The Bel Air Country Club lies just to the north, the Los Angeles Country Club to the east, and the posh outdoor shopping mall, Century City Center, to the south. The price of comfort and convenience isn't cheap; housing prices are on par with Santa Monica.

Prices ease up a bit as you move farther away from campus, especially going south toward the 10 Santa Monica Freeway. There's a little less green (both the kind you grow and the kind you earn) found south of Wilshire Boulevard, the trade-offs here being cheaper housing and easier parking. As you head closer to Los Angeles, apartments and houses are still modern and clean, but mingle with commercial zones, making for heavier traffic. Many professionals and singles reside and work in the area. The Federal Office Building, where many of the city's federal offices are housed, is at Wilshire and Sepulveda boulevards, and the high-profile Getty Museum is a stone's throw across the 405 Sepulveda Freeway in neighboring Brentwood.

Web Sites: www.cityofla.org, http://lacounty.info
Area Code: 310
Zip Code: 90024
Post Offices: UCLA-Wilshire branch, 10920 Wilshire Blvd. Ste. 150; UCLA Medical branch, 308 Westwood Plaza Ste. A233a; Village Station, 11000 Wilshire Blvd.; Veterans Administration Building branch, 11301 Wilshire Blvd., Building #306; 800-275-8777
Police District: West Los Angeles Division, 1663 Butler Avenue, 310-575-8402, www.lapd.org
Emergency Hospital: UCLA Medical Center, 10833 LeConte Avenue, 310-825-9111, www.healthcare.ucla.edu
Library: West Los Angeles Branch, 11360 Santa Monica Blvd., 310-575-8323
Public School Education: LA Unified School District, 333 South Beaudry Avenue, LA, CA 90017; 213-241-1000; www.lausd.k12.ca.us
Community Resources: Westwood Park, 1350 South Sepulveda Blvd.; Holmby Park, 601 Club View Drive; Los Angeles City Department of Recreation and Parks, 888-LA-PARKS, www.laparks.org; Los Angeles Country Club, 10101 Wilshire Blvd., 323-272-2134; UCLA-Armand Hammer Museum, 10889 Wilshire Blvd., 310-443-7000, www.hammer.ucla.edu
Public Transportation: call 800-COMMUTE or go to www.mta.net for specific Metro bus route and schedule information. Santa Monica's Big

Blue Bus has lines in the area; call 310-451-5444 or visit www.bigblue bus.com for route and schedule information. LADOT also operates here; call 310-808-2273 or visit www.ladottransit.com for commuter route and schedule information.

BEVERLY HILLS

TROUSDALE ESTATES
BEL AIR ESTATES

Boundaries: **North**: hills above Sunset Boulevard; **East**: Doheny Drive; **South**: Whitworth Drive; **West**: Whittier Drive

The above boundaries are rough outlines of Beverly Hills—residents are very particular about what constitutes a Beverly Hills address. There's even something called "Beverly Hills P.O.," which refers to areas that may not look as meticulously groomed as Beverly Hills, but fall within the coveted Beverly Hills postal code, therefore entitling such residents to the city's civic amenities. One reason that locals are so concerned about who's in and who's out is that, as its own city, and a well-funded one at that, Beverly Hills' municipal services (police, fire, public education, etc.) are considered top notch in Los Angeles County. Even the well-stocked Beverly Hills public library requires its patrons have library cards (that are gold-colored, by the way) separate from the Los Angeles Public Library's system.

With a worldwide reputation as the home of the rich and famous, the many multi-bedroomed residences in the Beverly Hills housing market feature hefty price tags. The tree-rich **Trousdale Estates** is another exclusive community of custom-built homes tucked in the winding hills north of Beverly Hills, and **Bel Air Estates** sports mansions nestled in canyon country to the west. Apartments, though similar in look and style to much of West Los Angeles (i.e., Spanish stucco), are harder to find and understandably pricier too. Tenacious bargain hunters may find more affordable pricing in the area known as "below the tracks." Though long since removed, train tracks once ran through Beverly Hills along Santa Monica Boulevard, and the site serves to demarcate the high rent from the not-so-high rent district of the city.

Downtown Beverly Hills (including the famous Rodeo Drive) starts south of Santa Monica Boulevard and continues south to Wilshire Boulevard. Along Wilshire Boulevard are high-rise office buildings, large upscale department stores (Neiman Marcus, Saks Fifth Avenue), and the stately Regent Beverly Wilshire Hotel. South of Wilshire Boulevard is the area where more affordable apartments and flats are located. The majority of these buildings were constructed before the 1940s, and many offer hardwood floors and molded ceilings. Harder to find, but worth hunting for are the gatehouses and apartments over garages that are part of many of the Beverly Hills homes in "the flats" (the palm tree-lined residential streets between Sunset and Santa Monica boulevards), and to a lesser extent in the hills above Sunset Boulevard.

Beverly Hills streets are kept clean and have strict parking rules that nearly fill the length of the lampposts on which they're posted. No freeways are immediately accessible from Beverly Hills, which means surface streets such as Wilshire Boulevard and Santa Monica Boulevard serve as surrogate freeways in and out of this city—preserving the exclusivity of the neighborhood, just the way residents like it.

For housing leads in Beverly Hills try the classifieds in the local *Beverly Hills Courier* (310-278-1322, www.thebeverlyhillscourier.com).

Web Sites: www.ci.beverly-hills.ca.us, www.beverlyhills.org, http://lacounty.info

Area Codes: 310, 424

Zip Codes: 90210, 90211, 90212

Post Offices: Main Post Office, 325 North Maple Drive; Crescent Postal Store, 323 North Crescent Drive; Beverly Station, 312 South Beverly Drive; 800-275-8777

Police District: Beverly Hills Police headquarters, 464 North Rexford Drive, 310-550-4951, www.beverlyhills.org

Emergency Hospital: Cedars-Sinai Medical Center, 8700 Beverly Blvd., 310-423-3277, www.csmc.edu

Library: Beverly Hills Library, 444 North Rexford Drive, 310-288-2220, www.beverlyhills.org

Public School Education: Beverly Hills Unified School District, 255 South Lasky Drive, Beverly Hills, CA 90212, 310-551-5100, www.beverly hills.k12.ca.us

Community Resources: Beverly Hills parking permits, 310-285-2551; La Cienega Park Community Center, 8400 Gregory Way, 310-550-4625; Roxbury Park Community Center, 471 South Roxbury Drive, 310-550-4761; Beverly Gardens Park, Santa Monica Blvd. and Beverly Drive, 310-285-2537, www.beverlyhills.org

Public Transportation: call 800-COMMUTE or go to www.mta.net for specific Metro bus route and schedule information.

LA NEIGHBORHOODS AND COMMUNITIES—EAST

WEST HOLLYWOOD

Boundaries: **North**: Sunset Boulevard (to the west), Fountain Avenue (to the east); **East**: La Brea Avenue; **South**: Beverly Boulevard (to the west), Willoughby Avenue (to the east); **West**: Doheny Drive

Although only 1.9 square miles in size with 35,000+ residents, West Hollywood, identified by a lush grass- and rainbow flag–lined median down Santa Monica Boulevard, is high profile for its gay and lesbian community, particularly on the western side. As well, the area is home to a large Jewish community and a Russian immigrant population that both cluster on the southern and eastern borders. Jewish immigrants were the first group to come to the area, spilling west from the Fairfax District where they had settled post-World War II. The gay community was next to discover West Hollywood. Some were attracted to the growing design community here and others by the relative security of living in this then-unincorporated area in LA County, which was under the jurisdiction of the county sheriff and not the Los Angeles Police Department (said to frequently raid gay clubs).

On a stroll through Plummer Park on Santa Monica Boulevard, you can see the mosaic of neighbors who make up the area. As an example of how the local government is responsive to its citizenry, West Hollywood was the first US city to declare Yom Kippur (the Jewish Day of Atonement) a legal holiday, and the social and politically minded residents of this community were responsible for paving the way to outlaw discrimination against people with AIDS. One weekend every June the city plays host to one of the largest gay pride festivals in the country.

Residents enjoy the city's numerous amenities, including chic shopping and dining, and the beautiful Spanish-style architecture that graces many West Hollywood streets. Santa Monica Boulevard runs the length of the city and has a business base as diverse as the community itself. On the western end of the street there are many retail stores, cafes, and nightclubs catering to the gay and lesbian community. A burgeoning group of gyms and related fitness and beauty businesses have transformed the area near city hall into Health Row. And further east, the boulevard is home to the entrepreneurial efforts of West Hollywood's thriving immigrant community. Head south to Melrose and you'll find many more posh eateries including Elixir, 8612 Melrose Avenue, which features a lab-coated Asian herbalist concocting restorative tonics.

West Hollywood is also the site of the Pacific Design Center (www.pacific designcenter.com), a huge collection (1.2 million square feet) of interior

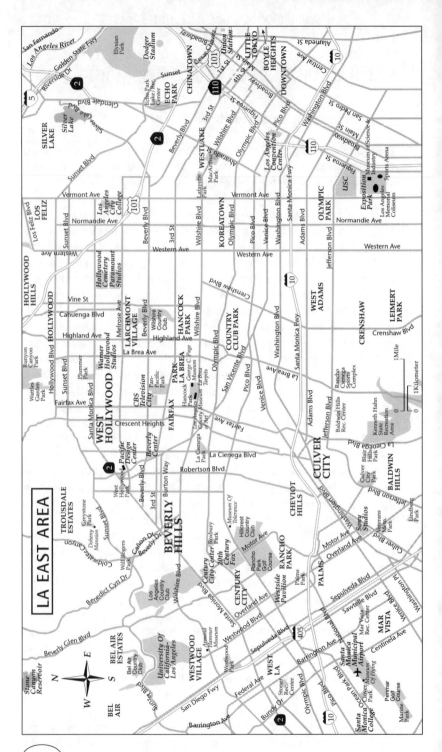

LA EAST AREA

design showrooms that anchors the myriad interior decorating businesses along Melrose, Beverly, and Robertson boulevards. The center itself is affectionately known as "the blue whale," due to the large scale and bright blue hue of the original building. Added later was an equally large and bright green building, Center Green, with even more showrooms. Further south on La Cienega Boulevard is the chic Beverly Center, a multi-level indoor mall, and its humbler sister the Beverly Connection, a smaller outdoor mall.

The northernmost part of West Hollywood features some of the trendiest sites on Sunset Boulevard, including nightclubs like House of Blues, The Viper Room, and The Laugh Factory. The club *du jour*, Standard, is at 8300 Sunset Boulevard in the Sunset Strip Hotel; lit up like a gray-blue mirage it exudes plenty of too-cool-for-you attitude. On weekend nights you'll find this section of the boulevard choked with traffic and exhausted car valets as club-goers cruise the scene, hoping for a peep through the windows of Larry Flynt's Hustler Hollywood. Farther west is Sunset Plaza, a tony strip of sidewalk cafes and designer label retailers, where celebrity sightings are not unusual.

Clean and well-tended apartments and condominiums make up the majority of residences lining the leafy streets radiating out from the night scene section of Santa Monica Boulevard. The buildings are a mix of older Spanish-style homes and the modern but boxy three- to four-story stuccos. A handful of retirement/assisted living apartments are also located in the area.

While the "vacancy decontrol," phased-in in 1996 by the Costa-Hawkins bill (which allows landlords to raise rent in a previously rent-controlled apartment to market value, after a tenant vacates the apartment) is in effect for all of California, including West Hollywood, prospective renters will be interested to know that the City of West Hollywood has a strict and intricate rent control law that regulates the maximum percentage (typically around 1.5% or less) that a landlord may raise rent. This adjustment is based on the consumer price index and is released every July. Rent control does not apply to single-family dwellings, some condominiums, and any apartments that received a certificate of residency after 1979. Apartment vacancies are not difficult to find and the stock of available condominiums is especially healthy. Only 7% of the housing in West Hollywood consists of detached homes. West Hollywood's **Department of Rent Stabilization** publishes a list of residential units available for rent. Call their 24-hour **Rental Referral Service Hotline**, 323-848-6419, for more information. Limited street parking dictates the use of parking permits. Weekend parking is made scarcer by Angelenos of all persuasions looking for a night on the town in West Hollywood.

Web Sites: www.weho.org, http://lacounty.info
Area Code: 310

Zip Code: 90069

Post Office: West Branch, 820 North San Vicente Blvd., 800-275-8777, www.usps.com

Police District: West Hollywood contracts with the County of Los Angeles Sheriff's Department, 720 North San Vicente Blvd., 310-855-8850, www.wehosheriff.com

Emergency Hospital: Cedars-Sinai Medical Center, 8700 Beverly Blvd., 310-423-3277, www.csmc.edu

Library: 715 North San Vicente Blvd., 310-652-5340, www.colapublib.org

Public School Education: LA Unified School District, 333 South Beaudry Avenue, LA, CA 90017; 213-241-1000; www.lausd.k12.ca.us

Community Resources: West Hollywood Permit Parking Division, 323-848-6392, www.weho.org; Department of Rent Stabilization, 323-848-6450; www.weho.org; Convention and Visitor Bureau, 800-368-6020, www.visitwesthollywood.com; West Hollywood Recreation Department, 323-848-6308, www.weho.org

Public Transportation: the West Hollywood City Line offers shuttle services within the city of West Hollywood; call 800-447-2189 for specific route and schedule information. Santa Monica's Big Blue Bus services West Los Angeles and Santa Monica; call 310-451-5444 or visit www.bigbluebus.com for route and schedule information. For all other areas, call 800-COMMUTE, or visit www.mta.net for specific Metro bus route and schedule information.

FAIRFAX DISTRICT (MID-WILSHIRE)

Boundaries: **North**: Willoughby Avenue; **East**: La Brea Avenue; **South**: Pico Boulevard; **West**: La Cienega Boulevard

Long the center of Los Angeles's Orthodox Jewish community, the Fairfax District includes a blend of cultures and lifestyles, including Indian, Ethiopian, African-American, and urban hip mixed in with the daytime office folk. Indeed, Fairfax Avenue itself is a cultural mish-mash where one can find family-run kosher butchers, Ethiopian restaurants, African artifacts, and Indian spice shops. Even Canter's Delicatessen reflects the diversity of the neighborhood, serving up matzo ball soup to elderly Jewish residents by day while featuring jazz and blues in the adjoining "Kibitz (Yiddish for 'chat') Room" at night.

The Farmers' Market at Fairfax Avenue and Third Street is a favorite for tour bus stops and Fairfax District locals who come for fresh, picture-perfect fruits and vegetables and cafes. It's also a busy lunch spot for business people, especially the nearby television and movie industry executives (CBS's Television City is right next door and the Writers Guild of America is across the street). The Grove, an outdoor pedestrian mall that opened in 2003, is right next door to the Farmers' Market. This bustling mall consists of flagship stores from several major retailers and a 14-screen movie theater with an art deco entrance. Intimate and polished, this upscale mall also features an on-site concierge, a small fountain, and a clanging cable car that transfers tourists and locals the short distance between the mall and market at no charge.

A retail district along Third Street between La Cienega Boulevard and Crescent Heights is dotted with new and used clothing and furniture stores, and La Brea Avenue to the east boasts several trendy furniture stores and eateries, as well as some of the area's most well kept Spanish-style apartment buildings along Sycamore Avenue, just east of La Brea. Finally, there is the famous, incense-infused Melrose Avenue. Melrose, on the Hollywood border, is LA's funkiest shopping street and definitely the place to go to find the latest chic fashion and food items. The street's denizens are some of LA's most urban and cutting-edge, with pierces, tattoos, and body scars practically *de rigueur*.

Besides the interesting mix of local residents in the Fairfax District, the architecture of much of the housing here is another plus. You can find reasonably priced rentals in everything from multi-unit apartment buildings to small houses. If it's within your budget and you're lucky enough to locate a vacancy, the real gems are the 1920s and '30s duplexes. Usually two-story stuccos, with one unit on the top and another below, many of these duplexes feature such touches as hardwood floors, built-in cabinetry, leaded or stained glass windows, ceramic tiled bathrooms and kitchens, and spacious rooms. It's typical for the landlord to live in one unit and rent out the other, and often the backyard is available for shared access.

Web Sites: www.fairfaxla.com, http://lacounty.info
Area Codes: 310, 213
Zip Codes: 90035, 90211, 90048, 90036, 90019
Post Office: Bicentennial Station, 7610 Beverly Blvd., 800-275-8777
Police District: (north of Beverly Blvd.) Hollywood Division, 1358 North Wilcox Avenue, 213-485-4302; (south of Beverly Blvd.) Wilshire Division, 4861 Venice Blvd., 213-485-4022, www.lapdonline.org
Emergency Hospital: Cedars-Sinai Medical Center, 8700 Beverly Blvd., 310-423-3277, www.csmc.edu
Libraries: Fairfax Branch, 161 South Gardner Street, 323-936-6191; Wilshire Branch, 149 North Saint Andrews Place, 323-957-4550, www.lapl.org

Public School Education: LA Unified School District, 333 South Beaudry Avenue, Los Angeles, CA 90017, 213-241-1000, www.lausd.k12.ca.us

Community Resources: Parking Permits, 310-843-5936 or 323-913-4600, www.lacity-parking.org; Wiltern Theatre, 3790 Wilshire Blvd., 213-380-5005, www.thewiltern.com; Kodak Theatre, 6801 Hollywood Blvd., 323-308-6363, www.kodaktheatre.com; The Grove, 189 The Grove Drive, 323-900-8080, www.thegrovela.com; Los Angeles City Department of Recreation and Parks, 888-LA-PARKS, www.laparks.org

Public Transportation: call 800-COMMUTE, or visit www.mta.net for specific Metro bus route and schedule information.

HANCOCK PARK

LARCHMONT VILLAGE

Boundaries: **North**: Melrose Avenue; **East**: Western Avenue; **South**: Wilshire Boulevard; **West**: La Brea Avenue

Hancock Park is noted for its rolling, well-groomed front lawns and stately pre-WW II homes, previous residences of Los Angeles's powerful elite. Some of the area's oldest and grandest homes may be viewed here. The Getty House, built in 1921, is the Mayor's official residence, located on Irving Boulevard. Hardwood floors and built-in cabinetry are typical features of homes in this area. The posh Wilshire Country Club begins just north of Third Street, and residents enjoy the proximity to the business district along Wilshire Boulevard. Miracle Mile, as the boulevard is called, was developed during the 1930s when art deco was in its heyday, and many buildings display this architectural influence. Here, the LA County Museum of Art and the Wiltern Theater, preserved in all its art deco glory, offer cultural entertainment year round. Tony Beverly Hills is located to the west, much to the delight of "shopaholics." And for all you bread lovers, the La Brea Bakery, 624 South La Brea Avenue, is known for its artisan breads, including a fresh baked chocolate cherry creation, and scrumptious rectangular toasting bread. Banks, gas stations, and bus stops are conveniently dotted throughout the area. Hancock Park is popular with Jewish families, and a number of orthodox and conservative synagogues are located within walking distance.

Bordered by Koreatown to the east and Mid-City to the south, Hancock Park offers homes that are a little less expensive than what can be found on the Westside. Pricey modern apartments are clustered in Park La

Brea, a gated and grassy community just east of Hancock Park. Parking within Hancock Park is never easy for visitors as many streets are restricted and require permits after business hours.

More affordable apartments and flats—and slightly more relaxed parking regulations—may be found near quaint **Larchmont Village** and along upper Rossmore Avenue. Within Larchmont Village, you'll find a string of mom-and-pop retail businesses and restaurants located along Larchmont Avenue. The small older buildings along the street and general lack of pretension of the stores and cafes are in stark contrast to many of Los Angeles's more trendy neighborhoods, though the boutique shops lend an upscale feel. Business owners can be seen sweeping their sidewalks and addressing their customers by name. No tourist attractions here, just tidy residences with well-kept lawns and small florists, dry cleaners, bookstores, eateries, and the like.

Web Sites: www.cityofla.org, http://lacounty.info, www.larchmont.com
Area Codes: 323, 213
Zip Codes: 90004-5 90019-20, 90010, 90036
Post Offices: Oakwood Station, 265 South Western Avenue; Sanford Station, 3751 West 6th Street, 800-275-8777, www.usps.com
Police District: (north of Beverly Blvd.) Hollywood Division, 1358 North Wilcox Avenue, 323-485-4302; (south of Beverly Blvd.) Wilshire Division, 4861 Venice Blvd., 323-485-4022, www.lapdonline.org
Emergency Hospitals: Queens of Angels-Hollywood Presbyterian Medical Center, 1300 North Vermont Avenue, 213-413-3000, www.qahpmc.com; Children's Hospital of Los Angeles, 4650 Sunset Blvd., 323-660-2450, www.childrenshospitalla.org
Libraries: Memorial Branch, 4625 West Olympic Blvd., 323-938-2732; Wilshire Branch, 149 North Saint Andrews Place; 323-957-4550; Fairfax Branch, 161 South Gardner Street, 323-936-6191, www.lapl.org
Public School Education: LA Unified School District, 333 South Beaudry Avenue, Los Angeles, CA 90017, 213-241-1000; www.lausd.k12.ca.us
Community Resources: Parking Permits, 310-843–5936 or 323-913-4600, www.lacity-parking.org; Pan Pacific Recreation Center, 7600 Beverly Blvd., 323-939-8874, www.laparks.org; Los Angeles County Museum of Art (LACMA), 5905 Wilshire Blvd., 323-857-6000, www.lacma.org; Los Angeles City Department of Recreation and Parks, 888-LA-PARKS, www.laparks.org
Public Transportation: call 800-COMMUTE, or visit www.mta.net for specific Metro bus route and schedule information.

HOLLYWOOD

HOLLYWOOD HILLS

Boundaries: North: Mulholland Drive (in the west), Griffith Park (in the east); **East:** Vermont Avenue; **South:** Melrose Avenue; **West:** Crescent Heights

With images from Hollywood's golden era often in newcomers' minds, many come to Hollywood expecting to rub elbows with the stars and find work in the studios. The reality is that only a handful of studios, Paramount among them, remain in Hollywood, and most working actors try to avoid the tourists. In fact, much of Hollywood has become a budget-rent apartment district and tired tourist destination, dotted with souvenir shops and strip clubs, and is further tarnished by the urban realities of homelessness and crime. The closest most get to a star is at the Walk of Fame where the celebrities' names are engraved in stars lining the sidewalk. The good news, however, is the presence of transients and prostitutes has been reduced and some glamour restored to Hollywood, thanks to an aggressive revitalization effort.

The famous Sunset Boulevard ("the Strip") runs through the heart of Hollywood, providing access to neighboring West Hollywood, a place known for its bustling nightlife. Along Hollywood Boulevard, the recently built Hollywood and Highland (at the intersection of the same name) is a multi-story outdoor mall that, from its third-floor pedestrian bridge, offers the best view anywhere of the Hollywood sign. It is anchored by the hip Hollywood Renaissance Hotel and classy Kodak Theatre (host to the annual Academy Awards). Step out onto the Boulevard and you'll find a cluster of twenties-era theaters: Mann's Chinese, the Egyptian, and the El Capitan, known as the places to go for opening night movies. Many die-hard movie fans will happily stand in line two or more hours for seats and costume themselves according to the movie's theme.

To be content to call Hollywood home, you must love the energy and edginess of the area. Most apartment complexes in central Hollywood were built in the 1950s and '60s, and despite the area's lack of garages and tight street parking, these apartments are filled with many budget-minded singles pursuing their American dream. Amenities much appreciated by the locals include plentiful laundromats, car washes, and cheap eats.

In sharp contrast, the exclusive **Hollywood Hills** is but a few minutes north of Sunset Boulevard. The Hills feature some of Los Angeles's most sought-after residential areas, and many in the entertainment business call the neighborhood home. Here you'll find million-dollar custom-built homes located on windy, twisting hillsides, complete with the prerequisite Lexus or Mercedes-Benz, or both. The Lake Hollywood Reservoir provides beautiful lakeside views and jogging trails for residents within the Hills. Formerly used for chlorinated water storage, the open reservoir was retired from service (due to concerns with water quality from nearby runoff) but will remain full, to be tapped only in case of emergency.

Nestled at the base of the Hills is the Hollywood Bowl, summer home of the Los Angeles Philharmonic and a popular attraction among Angelenos of all ages. The summer series includes orchestral, jazz, and popular tunes, and some nights a fireworks show accompanies the performance. And if these entertainment amenities aren't enough, the Hollywood Hills location also offers quick access to neighboring Beverly Hills and the Westside via Sunset Boulevard.

Outside the Hills and south of the apartments, but just north of hip Melrose Avenue, a pocket of charming, Santa Fe style homes run along tree-lined sidewalks. Rental and housing prices tend to be high, due to the proximity to Melrose Avenue's trendy shopping boutiques and restaurants.

Overall, Hollywood is tiered into a geographic hierarchy of the entertainment business, with those who have "made it" living in the Hills north of Franklin Avenue and those still trying, living south. In-between the hills and the flats, you'll find a few gentrified bohemian enclaves, but overall, Hollywood's population is a mix of working class folk, professionals, artists, and aspiring actors.

Web Sites: www.chamberhollywood.org, www.cityofla.org, http://lacounty.info

Area Code: 323

Zip Codes: 90028, 90068, 90078

Post Office: Hollywood Station, 1615 North Wilcox Avenue, 800-275-8777

Police District: Hollywood Division, 1358 North Wilcox Avenue, 213-485-4302, www.lapdonline.org

Emergency Hospitals: Kaiser Permanente Hospital, 4867 Sunset Blvd., 323-783-4011, www.kaiserpermanente.org; Queens of Angels-Hollywood Presbyterian Medical Center, 1300 North Vermont Avenue, 213-413-3000, www.qahpmc.com

Libraries: Frances Howard Goldwyn Hollywood Library, 1623 North Ivar Avenue, 323-856-8260; John C. Fremont Branch, 6121 Melrose Avenue, 323-962-3521

Public School Education: LA Unified School District, 333 South Beaudry Avenue, LA, CA 90017, 213-241-1000; www.lausd.k12.ca.us

Community Resources: Lake Hollywood Reservoir, northern end of Weidlake Drive, 323-463-0830; Barnsdall Park, 4800 Hollywood Blvd.; Plummer Park, 7377 Santa Monica Blvd., www.laparks.org; Hollywood and Highland, www.hollywoodandhighland.com; Kodak Theatre, 6801 Hollywood Blvd., 323-308-6363, www.kodaktheatre.com; Los Angeles City Department of Recreation and Parks, 888-LA-PARKS, www.laparks.org

Public Transportation: call 800-COMMUTE, or visit www.mta.net for specific Metro bus route and schedule information.

LOS FELIZ, SILVER LAKE, ECHO PARK

Boundaries: **North**: Mulholland Drive (in the west), Griffith Park (in the east); **East**: Vermont Avenue; **South**: Melrose Avenue; **West**: Crescent Heights

More affordable than the Westside, these are the funky communities that hug the Santa Monica Mountains, between Hollywood and Dodger Stadium. Los Feliz, Silver Lake, and Echo Park residents vary greatly, from white-collar entertainment industry executives to the working class. The appearance of residential (a near 50-50 mix of houses and apartments) and commercial zones is likewise varied, ranging from mansion-sized homes with well-tended lawns to modest residences with security bars.

Los Feliz defines the start of East Los Angeles and is the furthest north among these three communities. Residents here are typically well off financially and are sometimes a colorful lot with outrageous hairdos, pierced tongues, and cutting edge urban fashion quite the norm. Los Feliz residents enjoy the closest proximity to Griffith Park, the largest publicly owned park in the United States. The park occupies 4,400 acres in the hills and features the Los Angeles Zoo, the Griffith Park Observatory Planetarium and Laserium, the Greek Theater, Travel Town Train Park, and the Gene Autry Western Heritage Museum. There are also picnic areas, a soccer field, and 50 miles of hiking and horseback riding trails. Along Hillhurst Avenue near Franklin Avenue is Los Feliz Village, the site of bookstores, trendy eateries, and clothing boutiques to the stars. Speaking of trendy, many wing-tipped dancers frequent The Derby, 4500 Los Feliz Boulevard, a bar and restaurant that offers free swing lessons in the evenings.

Located along Franklin Avenue, the two-story, multi-bedroom homes, built in the old-style of Hollywood mansions, attract many a budding star-let. Madonna once resided behind wrought iron gates with the letter "M" sculpted on it. Area architecture varies greatly from stucco to medieval, but the majority of the residences feature 1930s opulence. The houses are of mansion proportions with price tags to match. Homes in Los Feliz cost a good deal more than those in Silver Lake or Echo Park, and street access to residences is occasionally congested by concertgoers heading in and out of the Greek Theater in Griffith Park.

Silver Lake, located further south, offers several shopping districts with the usual cafes, antique stores, and bookstores along Vermont and Hyperion avenues. A number of private residences designed by 1930s architect Richard Neutra line the 2200 block of East Silver Lake Boulevard. Lucky residents even get a view of the tree-lined Silver Lake Reservoir. The well-kept Spanish-style homes seem modest when compared with their neighbors to the north. Silver Lake's gay enclave too is toned down when compared with West Hollywood, but gay and lesbian residents enjoy their own cluster of bars and clubs in the area, and transsexuals, cross-dressers and other alternative lifestylists seem to prefer Silver Lake. The 5 Golden State Freeway borders the northeast section of Silver Lake.

Further southeast is **Echo Park**. Established in the 1920s, this largely blue-collar, Latino community hugs the base of the hills, facing a man-made lake that offers paddle boating on sunny weekends. Well-preserved Victorian and Craftsman-style homes, built when the area was in its heyday, are clustered along Carroll Avenue. Spanish architecture makes up the rest of the selection in the neighborhood's housing stock. There are a variety of mom-and-pop shops and restaurants in Echo Park offering the latest in Latino pop music and the best in Mexican and Spanish food and wares.

Also located in Echo Park is Dodger Stadium (near Elysian Park Avenue and West Sunset Boulevard), which can make navigation into these communities difficult during sporting events, and Elysian Park, second in size only to Griffith. Proximity to downtown LA (just a hop onto the nearby 110 Pasadena Freeway) is a plus for local commuters. Heat and smog become especially noticeable during the summer, but nothing air conditioners can't handle. Housing prices in this urban neighborhood tend to be reasonable, and architecturally interesting older homes abound. Security, however, may be an issue, and many homeowners elect to subscribe to private patrols to supplement the city's.

Web Sites: www.losfelizvillageonline.com, www.cityofla.org, http:// lacounty.info

Area Code: 323

Zip Code: 90026

Post Office: Edendale station, 1525 North Alvarado Street; 800-275-8777, www.usps.com

Police District: Northeast Division, 3353 San Fernando Drive, 213-485-2563, www.lapdonline.org

Emergency Hospitals: Children's Hospital of Los Angeles, 4650 Sunset Blvd., 323-660-2450, www.childrenshospitalla.org; Queens of Angels-Hollywood Presbyterian Medical Center, 1300 North Vermont Avenue, 213-413-3000, www.qahpmc.com

Libraries: Los Feliz Branch, 1874 Hillhurst Avenue, 323-913-4710; Echo Park Branch, 1410 West Temple Street, 213-250-7808; www.lapl.org

Public School Education: LA Unified School District, 333 South Beaudry Avenue, LA, CA 90017, 213-241-1000; www.lausd.k12.ca.us

Community Resources: Barnsdall Park, 4800 Hollywood Blvd.; Echo Park Lake and Recreation Center, Bellevue Avenue and Glendale Blvd., 213-250-3578; Elysian Park, 1880 Academy Drive, 323-226-1402, www.laparks.org; Dodger Stadium, 1000 Elysian Park Avenue, 323-224-1448, www.dodgers.com

Public Transportation: call 800-COMMUTE, or visit www.mta.net for specific Metro bus route and schedule information.

LEIMERT PARK

LEIMERT PARK VILLAGE
BALDWIN HILLS
CRENSHAW

Boundaries: **North**: Martin Luther King Jr. Boulevard; **East**: Leimert Boulevard; **South**: Vernon Avenue; **West**: Crenshaw Boulevard

Located seven miles southwest of downtown LA and nestled in the Crenshaw District, Leimert Park is one of the first planned communities in Los Angeles. Development here began in the early 1930s and grew around the park itself (located at the triangular intersection of Leimert and Crenshaw), created by Olmsted & Olmsted, a later incarnation of the same firm that designed New York's Central Park. The surrounding area of shops, 1940s-style duplexes, and houses on wide, tree-lined streets is known as **Leimert Park Village**.

Leimert Park is characterized by its lovely homes and close-knit African-American community. Most residences in Leimert Park consist of homes and duplexes boasting 1930s and 1940s architecture, which is not found in many other parts of the city. Housing costs are moderate, with a typical home price comparable to that of East Los Angeles communities like Echo Park and Silver Lake.

Stroll down Degnan Boulevard and you will find galleries, art centers, jazz clubs, and bookstores, all highlighting African-American themes. In August, an annual jazz festival here draws music lovers from all over the city. The large Baldwin Hills Crenshaw Plaza mall offers convenient shopping.

In comparison, the nearby **Crenshaw** neighborhood, distinguishable by its gridded city streets, has a more urban feel, with wrought iron security bars on houses and businesses a common sight. This neighborhood gained notoriety as the flashpoint for the infamous 1992 Los Angeles riots.

The LAX airport, located a few miles to the southwest, is a convenience to those who fly frequently, and a noise nuisance to others.

Neighboring to the west is the community of **Baldwin Hills**, an unincorporated patch of oil-rich, but hilly land dotted with more oil pumps than homes.

Web Sites: www.cityofla.org, http://lacounty.info

Area Code: 213

Zip Code: 90008

Post Offices: Crenshaw Station, 3894 Crenshaw Blvd.; Baldwin Hills Branch, 3650 West Martin Luther King Jr. Blvd., 800-275-8777, www.usps.com

Police District: Southwest Division, 1546 West Martin Luther King Jr. Blvd., 213-485-2582, www.lapdonline.org

Emergency Hospitals: LA County - USC Medical Center, 1200 North State Street, 323-226-2622, www.usc.edu/patient_care/hospitals/lac_usc; Daniel Freeman Memorial Hospital, 333 North Prairie Avenue, 310-674-7050, www.danielfreemanmemorialhospital.com

Libraries: Angeles Mesa Branch, 2700 West 52nd Street, 323-292-4328; Exposition Park Branch, 3665 South Vermont Avenue, 323-732-0169; www.lapl.org

Public School Education: LA Unified School District, 333 South Beaudry Avenue, LA, CA 90017, 213-241-1000; www.lausd.k12.ca.us

Community Resources: Leimert Park Village, 43rd Place and Crenshaw Blvd., 213-694-1499; Baldwin Hills Crenshaw Plaza, 3650 West Martin Luther King Jr. Blvd., 323-290-6636, www.crenshawplaza.com; Rancho Cienega Park, 5001 Rodeo Road, 323-290-3141, www.laparks.org

Public Transportation: call 800-COMMUTE, or visit www.mta.net for specific Metro bus route and schedule information.

DOWNTOWN

WESTLAKE
BOYLE HEIGHTS
CHINATOWN
LITTLE TOKYO

Boundaries: **North**: Montana Street (in the west), Washington Boulevard (in the east); **East**: west of Michilinda Avenue; **South**: Columbia Street (in the west), California Boulevard (in the east); **West**: Hills West of Linda Vista Avenue

Generally, Downtown is considered a business district, not a residential neighborhood. During the day, a large number of employees in law, finance, and advertising occupy the tightly packed high-rise office build- ings. At night, after most day-timers have gone home and retailers have pulled down iron gates over storefronts, the streets take on a ghost-town feel. The district's homeless, estimated at 41,000, seek refuge in the city's cluster of homeless shelters and soup kitchens at Fourth and Los Angeles streets. With this in mind, LA's downtown core may not be where you want to take up residence, though many of the city's finest cultural institutions are situated here. The Arata Isozaki-designed Museum of Contemporary Art (MOCA), the Music Center, the Dorothy Chandler Pavilion, LA's newly restored Central Library, the Downtown Convention Center, the largest on the West Coast, and the newly built Staples Center sports arena are all located Downtown. And, the gleaming Frank Gehry-designed Disney Concert Hall draws classical music fans. Also calling these environs home is the University of Southern California, a compact but beautiful private col- lege campus. The 110 Harbor Freeway, 10 Santa Monica Freeway, and 101 Hollywood Freeway all border Downtown, making entry to and exit from this area easy, albeit slow during rush hour.

Downtown is where you'll find the city's flower, jewelry, textile, gar- ment, toy, and produce districts. While primarily a wholesale district, many businesses do retail to the public, which makes for beaucoup savings for savvy bargain hunters unmindful of the no-frills display of wares. The eth- nic hamlets of Chinatown, Little Tokyo, and the Mexican village-style Olvera Street are also situated in Downtown.

In 1993, Los Angeles opened the first phase of the long-awaited sub- way, the Metro Red Line. Starting at the beautiful, historic Union Station on North Alameda Street, riders zip through most of Downtown in seven min- utes. The Red Line extends to Hollywood through Universal City and ends in North Hollywood. The Blue Line transports passengers from Downtown to Long Beach; the Green Line serves LA International Airport; and the Gold Line route goes to Pasadena. Although these established lines have been well received by riders, in 1998, LA County voters, angry with management and funding troubles, banned local tax revenues from funding any future subway tunnel construction, effectively freezing any further development of the subway.

For those looking to set up residence in Downtown, and some do, a smattering of artists-in-residence and loft-type housing dots central LA, including the large Santa Fe Art Colony at 2401 South Santa Fe and The Brewery at 1920 North Main Street. A new "resort style" apartment complex at 725 Bixel Street, which features over 600 units, is part of a recent trend offering Downtown apartments, lofts, and condominiums; until recently, housing in Downtown had been limited mostly to low-rent single-occupancy hotels and apartments.

Those wanting a central locale might consider the business districts in the ethnically diverse neighborhoods of **Westlake** (west of Alvarado Street), Boyle Heights (east of the Los Angeles River), **Chinatown** (slightly north of Cesar E. Chavez Avenue), or Little Tokyo (east of San Pedro Street) to locate housing. Blue- and white-collar families and recent immigrants (mostly Hispanic, Chinese, and Japanese) are the majority of residents in these neighborhoods. The quality of housing is uneven, varying from aging buildings in need of improvement to the well preserved or newly built. Most, if not all, of the stores and restaurants are bilingual and cater to the tastes of area residents. **Little Tokyo** is easily the most polished of these enclaves. Despite its proximity to litter-ridden parts of Downtown LA, tidy apartments and well-tended streets reflect the residents' sense of pride in their neighborhood. Japanese ex-pats seeking the tastes and comforts of home have an array of dining and shopping choices in the Japanese Village Plaza and Little Tokyo Mall. The Japanese American Cultural & Community Center at 244 South San Pedro Street, with its Japan America Theatre, an 880-seat performance space, and the Japanese American National Museum on East First Street round out the cultural offerings in the Little Tokyo cityscape.

Web Sites: www.cityofla.org, http://lacounty.info
Area Code: 213
Zip Codes: 90012-15, 90017, 90057
Post Offices: Alameda Station, 760 North Main Street; Arcade Station, 508 South Spring Street, 800-275-8777
Police District: Hollywood Division, 1358 North Wilcox Avenue, 213-485-4302, www.lapdonline.org
Emergency Hospitals: Good Samaritan Hospital, 1225 Wilshire Blvd., 213-977-2121, www.goodsam.org; White Memorial Medical Center,

1720 East Cesar Chavez Avenue, 323-268-5000, www.white memorial.com; LA County - USC Medical Center, 1200 North State Street; 323-226-2622, www.usc.edu/patient_care/hospitals/lac_usc

Libraries: Central Library, 630 West 5th Street, 213-228-7000; Little Tokyo Branch, 244 South Alameda Street, 213-612-0525; Chinatown Branch, 639 North Hill Street, 213-620-0925

Public Schools: LA Unified School District, 333 South Beaudry Avenue, LA, CA 90017, 213-241-1000; www.lausd.k12.ca.us

Community Resources: Los Angeles Conservancy provides downtown walking tours, 213-623-2489, www.laconservancy.org; Exposition Park at Figueroa Street and Exposition Blvd., www.laparks.org; University of Southern California at Figueroa Street and Jefferson Blvd., 213-740-2311, www.usc.edu; Los Angeles Memorial Coliseum, 3911 South Figueroa Street, www.lacoliseum.com; Dodger Stadium, 1000 Elysian Park Avenue, 323-224-1448, www.dodgers.com; Staples Center, 1111 South Figueroa Street, 213-742-7100, www.staplescenter.com; Japanese American Cultural & Community Center, 244 South San Pedro Street, 213-628-2725, www.jaccc.org; Japanese American National Museum, 369 East First Street, 213-625-0414, www.janm.org; Los Angeles City Department of Recreation and Parks, 888-LA-PARKS, www.laparks.org

Public Transportation: call 800-COMMUTE or 800-371-LINK for specific Metro bus or Metro Rail (respectively) route and schedule information (www.mta.net). The DASH is a $.25 fare mini-bus that runs exclusively in downtown between the area's major tourist stops and office buildings; call 213-808-2273 for route and schedule information.

LA NEIGHBORHOODS AND COMMUNITIES – SOUTH

Fifty years after Columbus came upon the shores of America, Cabrillo and his crew of explorers anchored along the shore of what is present day Long Beach, and by the late 1700s, Spanish settlements and missions began to shape this part of the country. In fact, much of the southern end of Los Angeles County started out as a Spanish ranchero. When the Southern Pacific Railroad's "iron horse" laid railroad tracks through the land in the 1870s, mass transportation brought in hordes of settlers. Shrewd developers like John G. Downey and the brothers Atwood and Gilbert Sproul correctly predicted that the sprouting communities along the railroad lines would become flourishing towns. Downey developed a section of his rancho into a town and gave the community his family name, and the Sproul brothers demanded successfully that passenger trains stop in Norwalk, or "North-walk" as it was called then. Long Beach too saw masses of settlers disembarking at its station. The surrounding undeveloped countryside serv-

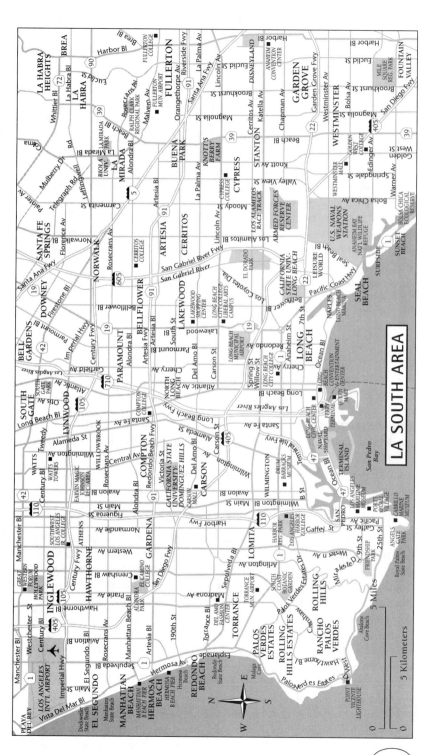

LA SOUTH AREA

iced the cattle and farm industries. Some of the largest sugar beet farms in the state were in Norwalk. The discovery of oil in the southern end of Los Angeles during the 1920s and '30s rocketed the area's growth toward industry and manufacturing. Much of this area—the southwest peninsula of LA County as well as Long Beach—is usually referred to as the South Bay.

The biggest housing boom in southern LA came after WW II when the Lakewood Park Company started developing what would become the nation's first post-war housing tract: 17,500 homes on about 3,500 acres, transforming Lakewood from a sugar beet field into a planned community. In 1954, Lakewood residents rejected annexing to the neighboring City of Long Beach. They voted instead to incorporate as a city, with the novel idea of continuing to contract with Los Angeles County for county services such as road maintenance, utility services, and fire protection. This "Lakewood Plan" was so successful it served as a blueprint for incorporating many future cities in the state and across the country.

DOWNEY

BELLFLOWER
LAKEWOOD

Boundaries: **North**: Telegraph Road; **East**: San Gabriel River; **South**: Forest Road (in the east), Gardendale Street (in the west); **West**: the Rio Hondo River

A southern suburb of Los Angeles, the **City of Downey** is a self-contained community with its own downtown, civic theater, school district, and fire and police departments. A majority of the housing is owner-occupied, with two to three bedrooms, and built between 1950 and 1980.

Despite its tract housing origins, many homes here have since been customized. Remodeling styles vary, and the presence of security bars and doors appears to be the exception rather than the rule. While 40% of the housing stock consists of apartments and condos, the single-family home dominates here at 60%, making this a comfortable south-of-central LA community for first-time homebuyers.

Historically, this traditionally working class community's biggest employer was the Rockwell International Space Division, near Lakewood Boulevard off the 105 Century Freeway. However, cutbacks in the aerospace industry caused the company to scale down its workforce drastically and to eventually close its doors in 1999. Today, Rancho Los Amigos Hospital, a spinal injury treatment center, and the home improvement stores All American Home Center and Home Depot make up the area's biggest employers. Bordered by the 710 Long Beach Freeway to the west and the 5

Santa Monica Freeway to the east, Downey offers quick access to the southern border of Los Angeles County, explaining why more than three-quarters of its residents work outside of Downey in other parts of LA County. The busy international Port of Long Beach/Los Angeles is approximately 12 miles away and equally close is the northern border of Orange County.

The Civic Theater in downtown Downey presents Broadway shows and musicals and is home to the Downey Symphony Orchestra and the Downey Civic Light Opera. Typical of other downtowns, there are a number of restaurants, hotels, and office buildings to be found here. For strolling, the intersection of Florence Avenue and Paramount Boulevard is a busy commercial hub dotted with bookstores, restaurants, gift shops, grocery stores and offices. The Stonewood Center Mall at Firestone and Lakewood boulevards is a large enclosed shopping mall with over 170 stores. The prominent presence of parks (nearly 100 acres), playgrounds, and movie theaters typifies this family-centered community. In fact, children of all ages can boast that Downey is home to the oldest McDonald's still in operation, at Lakewood Boulevard and Florence Avenue. The fast-food icon also operates a museum and gift shop.

Further south, heading toward Long Beach, is the cozy, 6.4-square-mile **City of Bellflower**. In terms of housing, it is similar in composition to Downey; however, the presence of overhead power and telephone lines is noticeable here, especially down the wide thoroughfares that define Bellflower's city blocks. (Many LA cities route their power lines underground.) These imposing steel posts fade away, however, once you turn off onto the side streets. Lots of green yards and trees complement the tidy, single-story homes in this working class community.

A story similar to Bellflower can be told of the **City of Lakewood**, located to the south, 25 miles southeast of LA. Defined by the San Gabriel River to the east and Long Beach to the south, Lakewood is slightly larger, occupying nearly 10 square miles. Having celebrated 50 years in 2004, this city, it can be said, defines suburbia. Now home to 80,000, it was built in the early 1950s for working-class families, many of them returning G.I.'s. Although sidewalks are showing signs of wear and commercial buildings could use some sprucing up, most residents are pleased to call Lakewood home. The city-sponsored Lakewood Beautiful Awards, recognizing well-groomed homes, only hints at the area's civic pride. The neighborhood around Lakewood High School is especially picturesque, and a number of parks dot the primarily residential neighborhood. There's also the Lakewood Center Mall for shopping. According to the 2000 Census, almost 40% of Lakewood households have school-aged youngsters. Several non-Lakewood school districts cover this area, although Lakewood residents have been trying to form their own school district for some time. Just to the east, past the river, runs the 605 San Gabriel River Freeway for easy access into Orange County.

Web Sites: www.downeyca.org, www.bellflower.org, www.lakewood city.org, http://lacounty.info

Area Code: 562

Zip Codes: 90241-2, 90706, 90712-3

Post Offices: Downey branches: 10409 Lakewood Blvd., 13003 Dahlia Street, 7911 Imperial Highway, 8111 Firestone Blvd.; Bellflower branch, 9835 Flower Street; Lakewood branch, 5200 Clark Avenue; 800-275-8777, www.usps.com

Police District: Downey is patrolled by its own police force, Downey City Police, 10911 Brookshire Avenue, 562-861-0771, www.downeypd.org. The cities of Bellflower and Lakewood contract with the Los Angeles County Sheriff's Department for law enforcement services. Lakewood Sheriff's Station, 5130 North Clark Avenue, 562-866-9061; Bellflower substation, 16615 Bellflower Blvd., 562-925-0124; www.lasd.org.

Emergency Hospitals: Downey Community/Rio Hondo Hospital, 11500 Brookshire Avenue, 562-904-5000; Kaiser Foundation Hospital - Bellflower, 9542 East Artesia Avenue, 562-925-8355, www.kaiser permanente.org; Lakewood Regional Medical Center, 3700 East South Street, 562-531-2550, www.lakewoodregional.com

Libraries: Downey, 11121 Brookshire Avenue, 562-904-7360, www.downeylibrary.org; Norwalk: Alondra Library, 11949 East Alondra Blvd., 562-868-7771; Bellflower: Clifton M. Brakensiek, 9945 East Flower Street, 562-925-5543; Lakewood: Angelo M. Iacoboni Library, 4990 Clark Avenue, 562-866-1777; George Nye Jr. Library, 6600 Del Amo Blvd., 562-421-8497; www.colapublib.org

Public School Education: Downey Unified School District, 11627 Brookshire Avenue, Downey, CA 90241, 562-904-6500, www.dusd.net; Bellflower Unified School District, 16703 Clark Avenue, Bellflower, CA 90706, 562-866-9011, www.busd.k12.ca.us. For Lakewood, consult the following districts: Bellflower Unified School District (see above); Long Beach Unified School District, 1515 Hughes Way, Long Beach, CA 90810, 562-997-8000, www.lbusd.k12.ca.us; and LA Unified School District, 333 South Beaudry Avenue, LA, CA 90017, 213-241-1000; www.lausd. k12.ca.us.

Community Resources: Heritage Park, 12100 Mora Drive; Dennis the Menace Park, 9125 Arrington Avenue, 310-904-7127; Furman Park, 10419 South Rives Avenue; Downey Recreation Parks and Department, 562-904-7238, www.downeyca.org; Los Amigos Golf Course, 7295 Quill Drive, 562-869-0302, http://parks.co.la.ca.us/los_amigos.html; Downey Art Museum, 10419 South Rives Avenue, 562-861-0419; Downey Civic Theatre, 8345 Firestone Blvd., 562-904-7230, www.downeytheatre.com; Lakewood City Information Line, 562-925-4357.

Public Transportation: call 800-COMMUTE, or visit www.mta.net for specific Metro bus route and schedule information. This area is also serviced by Downey LINK, 562-529-LINK; the Metro Greenline 800-320-9442; and the Bellflower Bus, 562-865-7433, www.bellflower.org.

LA MIRADA, NORWALK

Boundaries: **North**: Leffingwell Road; **East**: Beach Boulevard; **South**: Alondra Boulevard; **West**: San Gabriel River

A modest southern suburb of Los Angeles, on the northern border of Orange County, is the **City of La Mirada**. This relatively new community (incorporated in 1960) occupies just 7.8 square miles and includes the large La Mirada Park and Golf Course and the private, theologically conservative Biola University. An island of Republicanism in a largely Democratic county, La Mirada is known for its civic beauty, landscaped streets, and lush greenbelts, with pine, palm, and other trees lining its residential streets. While the city's cultural and sporting amenities have yet to fully blossom, the La Mirada Performing Arts Center and its ten parks are nice options for local entertainment.

Two recently built tract housing communities along Visions Drive, Treasures and Visions, feature three- and four-bedroom homes. The median range for existing three-bedroom, single-story homes is slightly higher than the median for the county, but La Mirada is one of the few California cities that does not levy a property tax above the 1% levy by the County of Los Angeles. La Mirada operates its own school district, but receives some city services (such as fire) from Los Angeles County. Typical of many new or yet-to-be-developed communities with land to spare, residences are comfortably spaced apart. The 5 Santa Ana Freeway borders La Mirada's southern edge, making access easy to downtown LA.

Directly west of La Mirada is the **City of Norwalk**, a working-class community dating back to the nationwide housing boom of the 1940s. Correspondingly, the houses tend to be modest single-story, two- and three-bedroom homes, similar in composition to neighboring Downey. Area homes are neat and well-kept, but more tightly packed together compared with La Mirada. Some homes share driveways, but most everybody has a front or back yard. Architecturally speaking, most of these 1950s homes are unremarkable, but their affordability, slightly less than homes in La Mirada, appeals to many first-time, budget-minded homeowners. Security doors and windows are visible. Typically, the breadwinners of Norwalk commute to neighboring commercial districts such as Downey's

Rockwell International Space Division for work. Norwalk civic amenities include Cerritos College, located on the southwest corner of Norwalk, the Norwalk Sports Complex, and Paddison Square Mall. The city also boasts great freeway access; it's served by the 91 Riverside Freeway to the south and the 605 San Gabriel Freeway to the west; interstates 5 Santa Ana Freeway and 105 Century Freeway pass through the community.

Web Sites: www.cityoflamirada.org, www.ci.norwalk.ca.us, http://lacounty.info

Area Code: 562

Zip Codes: 90638, 90650

Post Offices: La Mirada, 14901 Adelfa Drive; Norwalk: 12415 Norwalk Blvd.; 14011 Clarkdale Avenue; 800-275-8777, www.usps.com

Police District: La Mirada and Norwalk contract with the Los Angeles County Sheriff's Department for law enforcement services. Norwalk-La Mirada Sheriff's station, 12335 Civic Center Drive, 562-863-8711, www.lasd.org

Emergency Hospitals: Los Angeles Community Hospital of Norwalk, 13222 Bloomfield Avenue, 562-863-4763; Metropolitan State Hospital, 11400 Norwalk Blvd., Norwalk, 562-863-7011

Libraries: La Mirada Library, 13800 La Mirada Blvd., 562-943-0277; Norwalk Library, 12350 Imperial Highway, 562-868-0775; Alondra Library, 11949 East Alondra Blvd., 562-868-7771; www.colapublib.org

Public School Education: Downey Unified School District, 11627 Brookshire Avenue, Downey, CA 90241, 562-904-6500, www.dusd.net; Norwalk-La Mirada Unified School District, 12820 Pioneer Blvd., Norwalk, CA 90650, 562-868-0431, www.nlmusd.k12.ca.us

Community Resources: La Mirada Park, 13701 South Adelfa Road; Biola University, 13800 Biola Avenue, 562-903-6000, www.biola.edu; La Mirada Theatre for Performing Arts, 14900 La Mirada Blvd., 562-944-9801, www.lamiradatheatre.com; Cerritos College, 11110 Alondra Blvd., 562-860-2451, www.cerritos.edu; Norwalk Sports Complex, 13000 Clarkdale Avenue, 562-929-5566, www.ci.norwalk.ca.us; La Mirada Public Works (Parks Division), 562-902-2385, www.cityoflamirada.org/parks.htm.

Public Transportation: call 800-COMMUTE, or visit www.mta.net for specific Metro bus route and schedule information. This area is also serviced by Downey LINK, 562-529-LINK and the Metro Greenline 800-320-9442.

CITY OF LONG BEACH

CITY OF PARAMOUNT

Boundaries: **North**: Carson Street; **East**: 605 San Gabriel River Freeway; **South**: Pacific Ocean; **West**: 710 Long Beach Freeway

With 35 miles of beach, in a city of 50 square miles, it's easy to see why this city, incorporated in 1888, was called "Long Beach." From a population of 1,500 and an area of just three square miles in those early years, the city has grown to an estimated 480,000, making it the second most populous city in LA County. As host to the busiest port on the west coast, the Port of Los Angeles/Long Beach and the Long Beach Marina (the largest city-run marina in the country with nearly 4,000 slips), many area residents are employed in the shipping industry. Visitors come to tour the dry-docked luxury cruise ship of yesteryear, the Queen Mary, and the popular Aquarium of the Pacific. Opened in 1998, the Aquarium was part of a $650 million renovation of the Long Beach waterfront. Adjacent is downtown Long Beach, a pleasant outdoor shopping village of New England-style buildings, known as Shoreline Village, and the Long Beach Convention & Entertainment Center, which was expanded to triple its original size in the early 1990s. Along the coast, favorable sailing waters with offshore break-waters and a natural bay host the Congressional Cup, Transpac, and Olympic trial races. Further inland are three major golf courses and a country club. Hugging the 405 San Diego Freeway is the Long Beach Municipal Airport (see **Transportation**). The city is a popular and convenient weekend getaway for Angelenos who come to enjoy a sparkling waterfront and all the amenities of a full-fledged city without the urban grit.

Considering the city's proximity to the coast, home prices span a healthy range, from $800,000 down to the lower $400,000 range (as of late 2004). Residents are almost equally divided between renters and owners. Over 40% of the single-family dwellings were constructed between 1940 and 1960. The quality of housing differs from other beachfront communities in that older, lower-income neighborhoods surround the water and downtown, and homes get newer and costlier as you move inland toward Cal State University Long Beach. Just down the street from the university is the newly built Los Altos Market Center (at North Bellflower Boulevard and Stearns Street), which offers local shopping options, including a major grocer and bookstore. The residential streets and main thoroughfares of Long Beach are well tended and tree lined.

Getting in and out of Long Beach can be a bit of a hassle because the 710 Long Beach Freeway, which runs north-south, is narrow and often clogged with trucks taking shipments in and out of the port; running east-west is the perpetually busy 405 San Diego Freeway. In an effort to ease local congestion, the nation's first public bike station was constructed at First Street and The Promenade (for more info, call 562-436-2453 or visit www.bikestation. org). Billed as a bike-transit facility, members (who pay a $20 administrative fee and $96 for a year's membership) can rent cruiser-type bicycles and lockers at a reduced fee. There are more than 30 miles of shoreline and riverside bicycle paths in the city. The public bus and light rail also make stops at this bike facility. While the 30-mile car commute to downtown LA may be an inconvenience, it is often viewed as a relatively minor trade-off by those seeking affordable housing in a bustling seaside community.

The **City of Paramount** is north of Long Beach and is best known as the birthplace of the Zamboni ice resurfacing machine and the Paramount Iceland rink—training ground of skating great Dorothy Hamill. Today, the city has a tarnished reputation for blight and crime, but over the last two decades the city has cracked down on gangs and been able to lower its crime rates. The city has also spent $62 million on city improvements, including upgrading/adding parks, fountains, and landscaping. Housing prices tend toward the low end of the Long Beach price spectrum, making it attractive for many first-time homebuyers. The city's turnaround has been especially noticeable in the commercial districts, with big business chains like Home Depot setting up shop in the area.

Web Sites: www.ci.long-beach.ca.us, www.paramountcity.com, http:// lacounty.info

Area Code: 562

Zip Codes: 90802-46, 90723

Post Offices: 1920 Pacific Avenue; 2727 East Anaheim Street; 300 North Long Beach Blvd.; 800-275-8777, www.usps.com

Police District: Long Beach Police Department, 100 Long Beach Blvd., Long Beach, 562-570-7401, www.longbeachpd.org. Paramount contracts with the Los Angeles County Sheriff's Department for law enforcement services: Paramount Station, 15001 Paramount Blvd., 562-220-2002, www.lasd.org.

Emergency Hospitals: Community Hospital of Long Beach, 1720 Termino Avenue, 562-498-1000, www.chlb.org; Long Beach Memorial Medical Center, 2801 Atlantic Avenue, 562-933-2000; Pacific Hospital of Long Beach, 2776 Pacific Avenue, 562-595-1911; St. Mary Medical Center, 1050 Linden Avenue, Long Beach, 562-491-9074, www.stmary medicalcenter.com

Libraries: Long Beach Public Library, 101 Pacific Avenue, 562-570-7500; Alamitos Neighborhood Library, 1836 East Third Street, 562-570-1037; Bay Shore Neighborhood Library, 195 Bay Shore Avenue, 562-570-1039; Mark Twain Neighborhood Library, 1325 East Anaheim Street, 562-570-1046; North Neighborhood Library, 5571 Orange Avenue, 562-570-1047; www.lbpl.org

Public School Education: Long Beach Unified School District, 1515 Hughes Way, Long Beach, CA 90810, 562-997-8000, www.lbusd.k12.ca.us; Paramount Unified School District, 15110 California Avenue, Paramount, CA 90723, 562-602-6000, www.paramount.k12.ca.us

Community Resources: Shoreline Park, East Shoreline Drive and Pine Avenue; Bixby Park, Cherry Avenue and East Ocean Blvd.; Long Beach Parks and Recreation, 562-570-3232, www.ci.long-beach.ca.us/park; Skylinks Golf Course, 4800 Wardlow Road, 562-421-3388; Virginia Country Club, 4602 Virginia Road, 562-424-5211; Paramount Iceland, 8041 Jackson Street, 562-633-1171, www.paramounticeland.com

Public Transportation: call 800-COMMUTE, or visit www.mta.net for specific Metro bus route and schedule information. The Metro Blue Line runs between Long Beach and downtown LA; call 213-626-4455 for Metro schedule information. For Long Beach Transit, call 562-591-2301 or visit www.lbtransit.com for route and schedule info. The Long Beach Passport Bus Shuttle is a free downtown bus shuttle, 562-591-2301. The Long Beach Bikestation is at 105 The Promenade North; call 562-436-2453 or go to www.bikestation.org for more information. The Paramount Easy Rider Shuttle transports residents along a fixed route; call 562-981-6300 for information.

Additional South Bay communities you might want to consider...

- **Hermosa Beach**, just south of Manhattan Beach: 310-318-0239, www.hermosabch.org
- **Palos Verdes Estates**, south of Torrance, on the Palos Verdes peninsula: 310-378-0383, www.palosverdes.com/pve
- **Rancho Palos Verdes,** also on the Palos Verdes peninsula: 310-377-8111, www.palosverdes.com/rpv
- **Redondo Beach**, south of Hermosa Beach: 310-372-1171, www.redondo.org
- **Torrance**, south of Redondo Beach: 310-328-5310, www.torrnet.com

SAN FERNANDO VALLEY AND OTHER POINTS NORTH

Just north of the Hollywood Hills, via either the 405 San Diego Freeway or 101 Hollywood/Ventura Freeway, is a large, flat basin called the San Fernando Valley, known as "the Valley," and a stronghold of suburban, middle- and upper-middle-class neighborhoods. Its earliest settlers, the Gabrielino Indians, and later the missionaries who founded the San Fernando Rey de Espana Mission in 1797, recognized the Valley's great qualities, grooming its fertile land into prosperous farming and ranching communities, which became world-famous for its orange, lemon, walnut, and persimmon groves. Following WW II, housing tracts sprouted across the Valley and the area became a working model for the American dream. By the 1950s, the Valley was a bastion of suburbia, offering Angelenos affordable homes complete with two-car garages and a patch of lawn to call their own. Today, nearly four million people live in the Valley. (In 1999, some Valley residents started a secession measure to make the Valley its own municipality. Measure F went before voters citywide in 2002, where only 51% of Valley voters cast votes in favor of it, and Los Angeles voters were soundly against it.)

So what, you ask, does the Valley offer that is so different from its southerly neighbor? Generally, the Valley's living options are more suburban in feel, a bit scaled down, but still with close proximity to many businesses, including the entertainment studios and related businesses in the eastern communities of Burbank, Glendale, and Universal City. Homebuyers typically find that they can get more house for their money in the Valley and, while the temperatures are hotter (by 10 to 20 degrees) and the smog worse, the 'burbs lifestyle is what many seek. In addition, this formerly white enclave has taken on a more racially and ethnically mixed flavor, with a steady influx of African-American, Asian, and Latino residents.

Ventura Boulevard runs east-west through the southern portion of the Valley, and is a thriving business and restaurant strip. All forms of housing are represented; single-family homes tend to be located on the side streets that run east and west while apartments and condos line the main streets going north and south. Ventura Boulevard (running parallel to the Ventura Freeway) begins in Studio City, and heads west through Sherman Oaks, Van Nuys, the City of Encino, Woodland Hills, and the City of Calabasas (the latter three are known as the West Valley). Continuing northeast from the western border of the Valley are the communities of West Hills, Reseda, and Northridge (the East Valley).

In the West Valley, the well-established planned communities have been so well tended they still feel new. There are occasional pockets of redevelopment where new homes have been built over old, but they're rare. People looking for newly built homes now search westward in the

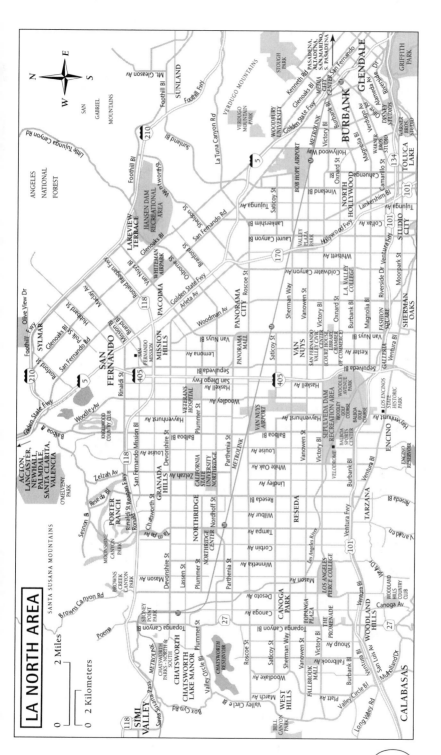

LA NORTH AREA

neighborhoods of Ventura County, which offer the planned and gated communities of Thousand Oaks and Westlake Village. Others search north-ward in the City of Santa Clarita, where the communities of Valencia and Newhall occupy the northernmost border of LA County. The commute from these northern areas can be an hour plus for those who work in Los Angeles proper, but for many, the suburban lifestyle offered by these envi-rons makes the hours spent behind the wheel worthwhile.

The eastern communities of LA County (that is, east of the 5 Golden State Freeway) defy easy categorization as they're not part of the San Fernando Valley nor are they technically part of the City of LA. These com-munities start with the City of Burbank and City of Glendale, and include the City of Pasadena, City of South Pasadena, and unincorporated Altadena. The freeways that service these areas are confusing. The 134 Ventura Freeway runs east-west and eventually becomes the 210 Foothill Freeway in Pasadena. The northern tip of the 110 Harbor Freeway begins in Pasadena, but this wide strip of pavement isn't really a freeway and is also known as South Arroyo Parkway, which is also a leg of the Historic Route 66. This busy road and bustling commercial strip transforms in South Pasadena to a true freeway (the 110), which takes commuters downtown. To add more confusion, the 210 Foothill Freeway also runs north (at the junction that the 134 Ventura Freeway becomes the 210) and yet still has the same name as its twin, the other 210 Foothill Freeway, which runs east. (Just be sure to buy a *Thomas Guide!*)

But enough about freeways, let's look at the communities...

WEST VALLEY

ENCINO
WOODLAND HILLS
SHERMAN OAKS
VAN NUYS

Boundaries: **East**: 405 San Diego Freeway; **South**: Santa Monica Mountains; **North**: 101 Ventura Freeway; **West**: Reseda Boulevard
Pretty and lined with old-growth oaks, Encino (which means "oak tree" in Spanish) is located on the north side of the Santa Monica Mountains, fac-ing the San Fernando Valley. Adjacent and to the west is another well-tended community, Woodland Hills, and to the northeast is Van Nuys, a busy but more middle-class community in comparison. Homey Sherman Oaks is Encino's eastern neighbor and not as modest as Van Nuys, but not as polished as Encino or Woodland Hills either. The bordering 405 San Diego and 101 Ventura freeways provide easy access for commuters.

Encino and **Woodland Hills** are similar in that they're both upper-middle-class, homogeneous communities. Streets are clean and homes well maintained. A number of celebrities reside in these family-oriented neighborhoods that feature modern or Spanish-style architecture. Most of the single-family homes have three or four bedrooms with single-level floor plans; their prices run higher in Encino than in Woodland Hills. The reason for the difference is that Woodland Hills is not as fully developed as Encino, but that gap will certainly close as growth here continues. The business districts of Encino and Woodland Hills, the bulk of which line Ventura Boulevard and Warner Center, boast the greatest number of banks and savings and loans of any Valley community, and retail districts are being developed or expanded, especially in Woodland Hills. Three large malls, Topanga Canyon Plaza, Fall Brook Mall, and The Promenade Mall, are within a few blocks of each other. Residents can enjoy six golf courses, and there are several parks in the area. The Sepulveda Dam Recreation Area offers 2,000 acres of open space and is popular for hiking, picnicking, biking, and paddle boating. The Los Encinos State Historical Park offers five acres dedicated to the preservation of the area's history, including a building that is over 150 years old.

Van Nuys is host to the Anheuser-Busch Brewery and to the Van Nuys Airport, which does not take commercial flights but serves as home base for private and corporate jets and helicopters. Car dealerships cluster along Van Nuys Boulevard, just north of Riverside Drive, and discount retailers located further north on the same street blare Mexican pop music, reflecting the preferences of many area residents. The LA Valley College campus is also here. Most Van Nuys residences are in the form of apartments, with only about 30% of housing in the form of single-family residences. Housing here is much cheaper than in neighboring Encino, and the affordability has made this community attractive to recent immigrants and blue-collar workers, many employed by the manufacturing and industrial assembly plants nearby. Upkeep of residences varies greatly; some streets show a lot of care while others sport security bars and could use sprucing up. To meet the issue of neighborhood neglect, one particular Van Nuys neighborhood formed its own neighborhood association and beautification committee, naming the area **Valley Glen** in 1996. Its borders are Victory Boulevard on the north, Coldwater Canyon on the east, Burbank Boulevard on the south, and Hazeltine Avenue on the west. As a result of this concentrated community effort, Valley Glen property values are slightly higher than the surrounding area.

Sherman Oaks is a mix of flat and hilly land. Residential streets south of Ventura Boulevard wind into the hills, where the neighborhoods and housing styles are less prototypical suburbia and sport higher price tags than much of the Valley. It is north of Ventura Boulevard where you will find more middle-class homes lining the side streets and a respectable choice of apartments along main thoroughfares. Residential architecture varies from ranch homes to boxy stuccos. Many have back and front yards that are tended by hired gardeners who mow and trim their way from one house to the next. Housing prices tend to be up a little here, but still less than what it costs in Encino; apartments are also not too difficult to find. When the Northridge earthquake of 1994 hit (Northridge is northwest of Sherman Oaks), scattered parts of Sherman Oaks were hard hit, especially along Hazeltine Avenue. But with the rebuilding of apartments and homes, the community looks better than ever. Typical of many neighborhoods in the Valley, the majority of area businesses line Ventura Boulevard, including a pleasant mall called the Sherman Oaks Fashion Square, chain grocery stores, banks, restaurants, and a variety of other retailers serving the needs of the local community. Weekend evenings find the locals, their children, and the family dog out on the sidewalks of Ventura Boulevard just west of Van Nuys Boulevard for dinner, ice cream, and window gazing.

Web Sites: www.cityofla.org, www.valleyglen.org, www.encinochamber.org, http://lacounty.info

Area Code: 818

Zip Codes: Encino: 91316, 91436; Woodland Hills: 91364-7; Van Nuys/ Valley Glen: 91401-35; Sherman Oaks: 91401

Post Offices: Encino branch, 5805 White Oak Avenue; Woodland Hills Main Post Office, 22121 Clarendon Street; Van Nuys Main Post Office, 15701 Sherman Way; Sherman Oaks branch, 14900 Magnolia Blvd.; 800-275-8777, www.usps.com

Police District: Encino and Woodland Hills are patrolled by the LAPD's West Valley Division: 19020 Vanowen Street, 818-756-8542; Van Nuys and Sherman Oaks are patrolled by the LAPD's Van Nuys Division: 6240 Sylmar Avenue, 818-756-8343; www.lapdonline.org.

Emergency Hospitals: Encino Tarzana Regional Medical Center - Encino Campus, 16237 Ventura Blvd., 818-995-5000, www.encino-tarzana.com; Kaiser Foundation Hospital - Woodland Hills, 5601 De Soto Avenue, 818-719-2000, www.kaiserpermanente.org; Van Nuys Hospital, 15220 Vanowen Street, 818-787-0123; Valley Presbyterian Hospital, 15107 Vanowen Street, Van Nuys, 818-782-6600, www.valley pres.org; Sherman Oaks Hospital & Health Center, 4929 Van Nuys Blvd., 818-981-7111, www.shermanoakshospital.com

Libraries: Encino-Tarzana Library, 18231 Ventura Blvd., 818-343-1983; Woodland Hills Library, 22200 Ventura Blvd., 818-226-0017; Platt Branch Library, 23600 Victory Blvd., 818-340-9386; Van Nuys Library, 6250 Sylmar Avenue, 818-756-8453; Sherman Oaks Library, 14245

Moorpark Street, 818-205-9716; www.lapl.org

Public School Education: LA Unified School District, 333 South Beaudry Avenue, LA, CA 90017, 213-241-1000; www.lausd.k12.ca.us

Community Resources: Sepulveda Basin Recreation Area, 405 Freeway and Victory Blvd., 818-784-5180, www.laparks.org; Los Encinos State Historic Park, 16756 Moorpark Street, 818-784-4849, www.parks.ca.gov; Encino Community Center, Balboa and Ventura boulevards, 818-995-1690, www.laparks.org; Van Nuys-Sherman Oaks Park, Huston Street near Hazeltine Avenue

Public Transportation: call 800-COMMUTE or visit www.mta.net for specific Metro bus route and schedule information.

NORTH HOLLYWOOD

TOLUCA LAKE
STUDIO CITY

Boundaries: **East**: Cahuenga Boulevard; **South**: Ventura Boulevard; **North**: Saticoy Street; **West**: Van Nuys Boulevard

North Hollywood, located within the Valley, is great for inexpensive apartments and easy access to almost any place in LA without actually being in Los Angeles proper—as long as you have a car. Serviced by the 101 Hollywood Freeway/Ventura Freeway (driver beware, this tricky freeway goes both north-south and east-west), the largely Hispanic North Hollywood neighborhood is a working-class enclave. You'll find rents are more affordable as you go north, though proximity to industrial and commercial zones makes for noisier and grittier living. If you stick close to main thoroughfares like Riverside Drive or Moorpark Street (the southern end of North Hollywood) you will find residences that combine North Hollywood's affordability with the neighboring security of the Toluca Lake (to the east) and Studio City (to the west) communities.

Available street parking runs the gamut and depends on whether the street you live on is crowded with apartments or homes. The good news is permits are not required, street parking is usually unrestricted, and most apartments provide gated parking spaces.

Vacancies in apartments or homes are not hard to find. Among other things, rents here depend on proximity to the more prestigious Toluca Lake and Studio City zip codes. Affordable housing and easy access to the studios make North Hollywood a good bet for transplants interested in the entertainment business.

Judging by the large selection of individual serving-sized portions of food in neighborhood grocery stores, this town is home to a significant singles population. Grocery shopping abounds, with every major supermarket chain represented in the area. For those on the move, dry cleaners and gas stations can be found on virtually every street corner. Used bookstores (Dutton's Books at 5146 Laurel Canyon Boulevard is considered the best in LA) and thrift shops dot the area, convincing many bargain hunters they've died and gone to heaven.

Eateries to satisfy every stomach and wallet size, from the cell phone-armed executive with a fat expense account to the would-be starlet, abound. Actors, writers, and producers, with their irregular work schedules, keep stores and restaurants hopping throughout the week and weekend.

The renovation of NoHo, North Hollywood's ambitious attempt to create a folksy arts district, has yielded a collection of small actors theaters, coffee shops, used bookstores and bargain furniture stores along Lankershim Boulevard. Occasional weekend crafts fairs add to the pickings. The Academy of Television Arts and Sciences also calls this area home.

A pleasant place for a stroll is City Walk at nearby Universal Studios. It's a self-contained outdoor "entertainment complex" (read: theme restaurants, stores, and movie theaters) drawing tourists and locals alike, especially on weekends. (Residents who live within qualifying zip codes may request a booklet of free parking passes from Universal's corporate communications office at 818-777-3591.) Natives who like to keep up with the latest movie releases will appreciate the selection at Odyssey Video or Eddie Brant's Saturday Matinee on Vineland Avenue.

The neighboring communities of **Toluca Lake** and **Studio City** are higher income neighborhoods with plush apartments, recently built condos, and single-family homes hidden among leafy trees. The fact that Toluca Lake and Studio City are just minutes from the media districts of Burbank and Universal City means that a lot of entertainment industry people live in the area. Comedian Jay Leno, an avid car collector, can sometimes be seen hanging with fellow grease monkeys at the oldest remaining Big Boy Restaurant, Bob's Big Boy, 4211 Riverside Drive, which hosts antique car shows and car hop service on weekends.

Within Studio City, you'll find a mix of owners and renters. Single-family residences that cluster behind magnolia trees, south of Ventura Boulevard (the main thoroughfare), are slightly more expensive than the homes lining streets that run east-west, just north of Ventura Boulevard. Apartments and condos are grouped to the north of Ventura along north-south running streets. Ventura Boulevard is a long, bustling street with a wide variety of restaurants and retail merchants; a great place to meander and browse or just people watch.

Web Sites: www.noho.org, http://lacounty.info
Area Code: 818
Zip Codes: 91601-6
Post Offices: North Hollywood Station, 7035 Laurel Canyon Blvd.;
Chandler Station, 11304 Chandler Blvd.; Toluca Lake Station, 10063
Riverside Drive; Studio City Station, 3950 Laurel Canyon Blvd.; 800-275-
8777, www.usps.com
Police District: North Hollywood Division: 11640 Burbank Blvd., 818-
623-4016, www.lapdonline.org
Emergency Hospitals: hospitals serving this area are located within
neighboring communities: Providence Saint Joseph Medical Center,
501 South Buena Vista Avenue, Burbank, 818-843-5111, www.providence.
org; Sherman Oaks Hospital & Health Center, 4929 Van Nuys Blvd.,
Sherman Oaks, 818-981-7111, www.shermanoakshospital.com.
Libraries: North Hollywood Regional Branch, 5211 Tujunga Avenue, 818-
766-7185; Valley Plaza Branch, 12311 Vanowen Street, 818-765-9251;
Studio City Branch, 12511 Moorpark Street, 818-755-7873; www.lapl.org
Public School Education: LA Unified School District, 333 South Beaudry
Avenue, LA, CA 90017, 213-241-1000; www.lausd.k12.ca.us
Community Resources: North Hollywood Recreation Center, Chandler
Blvd. and Tujunga Avenue, 818-763-7651; Studio City Recreation Center,
Rye Street and Beeman Avenue, 818-769-4415; www.laparks.org
Public Transportation: call 800-COMMUTE or visit www.mta.net for
specific Metro bus routes and schedule information.

BURBANK, GLENDALE

Boundaries: **East**: 5 Golden State Freeway; **South**: 134 Ventura Freeway;
North: Verdugo Mountains; **West**: Clybourn Avenue

One of the oldest Los Angeles suburbs, the **City of Burbank** began life as
a humble sheep pasture. Named after Dr. David Burbank, a sheep ranching
dentist, it wasn't until 1928, with the development of a small airplane manufacturing site owned by Alan Loughead (who changed the spelling to
Lockheed), that modern Burbank began to form. Around the same time, a
motion picture studio laid roots here and was eventually acquired by
Warner Brothers. Today, Burbank's big industry is entertainment, home to
NBC's West Coast headquarters, Disney Studios, Nickelodeon Animation
Studios, and a host of other entertainment-related businesses. City leaders,
in a campaign to establish Burbank as the "Media Capital of the World,"
have nicknamed the town Media City.

With an older town, you might expect worn architecture and fully filled out lands. By those standards, Burbank hardly reveals its true age. Most of its existing homes were built in the 1960s and have been well cared for. The residences here are well tended and often display the unique characteristics of their owners. While this community may not be as leafy as others, many of the stucco homes, built to maximize the land allotted to them, sport lush lawns. The housing stock is nicely balanced between renters and homeowners; about 45% are single-family homes and the remaining 55% are townhomes, condos, and apartments. Many condos have been recently built; apartments, however, range from the recently built to the well preserved. Rents vary; you'll find bargain rates for a one-bedroom in an older building but you can expect to pay one quarter to one third more to live in the same in a new building. Prospective homebuyers might want to check nearby **Verdugo Hills** (dubbed the Burbank Hills) for newly built three- to eight- bedroom Spanish architecture homes, complete with panoramic views.

The cost of living in Burbank is slightly lower than in many of Los Angeles County's upper-middle class communities; and business taxes and licenses cost less, as do water and electricity. The Bob Hope Airport (formerly Burbank Airport) offers travelers the choice of some major airlines (see **Transportation**), without the congestion of LAX. The airport was trying to establish a new passenger terminal, but area residents who did not want the additional noise pollution opposed it. To date, airport authorities have agreed to put off building a new passenger terminal until after 2014.

Starting in the mid 1990s, community leaders revamped the city's 22 parks (including three senior centers), built a brand new police and fire headquarters, and opened a three-story, indoor mall, the Media City Shopping Center at 201 East Magnolia Boulevard. Nearby, Brand Avenue in downtown Burbank is a popular evening hangout for residents who patronize the mall's large theater complex. The huge Swedish discount furniture store, Ikea, is located here, providing put-it-together-yourself furniture at reasonable prices. Horse lovers should note that the lovely Los Angeles Equestrian Center is in Burbank. Neighborhood restaurants lean toward comfort food rather than gourmet type fare. The decades-old Barrons Family Restaurant, 4130 West Burbank Boulevard, serves one of the best breakfasts in the nation, this according to *Gourmet Magazine* and morning crowds.

With a small-town feel, clean streets, and one of the most responsive police departments around, Burbank also feels contemporary and metropolitan. It is this city's charm, affordability, and total lack of attitude common to other LA towns that makes Burbank a stand-out for young families and senior citizens.

Adjacent to Burbank, just east of the 5 Golden State Freeway, is the **City of Glendale**. It too has undergone a great deal of change in the past two decades, becoming an ethnically diverse population of nearly 200,000 people in its 30 square miles. Glendale, the third largest city in Los Angeles County, has a more urban feel and pace in comparison to Burbank, though housing prices are a close match.

Multi-family units, many of which were built in the 1980s, today comprise 60% of the city's housing stock. In fact, Glendale has one of the highest percentages of multi-family dwelling units of any city in California. Most apartment buildings are clustered around downtown—a bright and cheery business district located just south of the 134 Ventura Freeway. Some of the newest two-story, stucco, red-tiled homes are poised above Chevy Chase Drive, east of Highway 2. Most existing homes were built between 1950 and 1980 and can be found north of Foothill Boulevard.

Glendale has attracted a large Asian, Middle Eastern, and Mediterranean population. In fact, Colorado Street, Glendale's main thoroughfare, is lined with the charming restaurants and sumptuous bakeries of many ethnic persuasions. Overall, streets are clean, business districts well tended, and social amenities abundant, including the large indoor mall, Glendale Galleria, and 32 city parks. Recently, the city's growth has slowed somewhat, and available land has been built out, giving city leaders a chance to catch up with civic beautification, including the renovation of Colorado Street and tree plantings along its neighborhood streets.

Web Sites: www.ci.burbank.ca.us; www.ci.glendale.ca.us, http://la county.info

Area Code: 818

Zip Codes: 91501-91523, 91201-91213

Post Offices: Burbank Main Post Office, 2140 North Hollywood Way; Glendale Main Post Office, 313 East Broadway Street; many more locations, call 800-275-8777, www.usps.com.

Police District: Burbank and Glendale operate their own municipal police forces: Burbank Police Headquarters: 200 North Third Street, 818-840-8830, www.ci.burbank.ca.us/police; Glendale Police Department: 140 North Isabel, 818-548-4840, http://police.ci.glendale.ca.us.

Emergency Hospitals: Providence Saint Joseph Medical Center, 501 South Buena Vista Avenue, Burbank, 818-843-5111, www.providence. org; Glendale Memorial Hospital and Health Center, 1420 South Central Avenue, Glendale, 818-502-1900, www.glendalememorial.com

Libraries: Main Burbank Library, 110 North Glenoaks Blvd., 818-238-5600; Buena Vista Branch, 300 North Buena Vista, 818-238-5620; Northwest Branch, 3323 West Victory Blvd., 818-238-5640; www. burbank.lib.ca.us; Main Glendale Library, 222 East Harvard Street, 818-548-2030; Brand Art & Music Center, 1601 West Mountain Street, 818-548-2051; Casa Verdugo Branch Library, 1151 North Brand Blvd.,

818-548-2047; Chevy Chase Branch, 3301 East Chevy Chase Drive, 818-548-2046; Grandview Branch Library, 1535 Fifth Street, 818-548-2049; Pacific Park Branch Library, 501 South Pacific Avenue, 818-548-3760; http://library.ci.glendale.ca.us

Public School Education: Burbank Unified School District, 1900 West Olive Avenue, Burbank, 91506, 818-729-4400; www.burbank.k12.ca.us; Glendale Unified School District, 223 North Jackson Street, Glendale, 91206-4380, 818-241-3111, www.www.glendale.k12.ca.us

Community Resources: Olive Recreation Center and George Izay Park, 1111 West Olive Avenue, 818-238-5385; Verdugo Recreation Center, 3201 West Verdugo Avenue, 818-238-5390; Burbank Tennis Center, 1515 North Glenoaks Blvd., 818-843-4105, www.burbanktenniscenter.com; Johnny Carson Park, 400 South Bob Hope Drive; Starlight Amphitheatre, 1249 Lockheed View Drive, 818-238-5300; De Bell Municipal Golf Course, 1500 East Walnut Avenue, 818-845-5052/0022; Burbank Family YMCA, 321 East Magnolia Blvd., 818-845-8551, www.burbankymca.org; Burbank Parks and Recreation Department, 818-238-5300, www.ci.burbank.ca.us; Los Angeles Equestrian Center, 480 Riverside Drive, 818-840-9063, www.la-equestriancenter.com; Glendale Central Park, East Colorado Street and South Louise Street, 818-548-2000, http://parks.ci.glendale.ca.us/parks.htm

Public Transportation: call 800-COMMUTE, or visit www.mta.net for specific Metro bus routes and schedule information. Downtown Glendale has a shuttle known as the "Beeline"; call 818-548-3960, or visit www.glendalebeeline.com for route and schedule information.

PASADENA

ALTADENA
SAN MARINO
SOUTH PASADENA

Boundaries: **North**: Montana Street (in the west), Washington Boulevard (in the east); **East**: West of Michilinda Avenue; **South**: Columbia Street (in the west), California Boulevard (in the east); **West**: Hills west of Linda Vista Mountain Way

Pasadena's claim to fame is the always-sunny New Year's Day Tournament of Roses Parade and Rose Bowl, but this city's roots, like much of the Valley, are in agriculture. Pioneers who came to this area in the late 1800s found success growing oranges and olives, and named their community Pasadena (derived from an Ojibwa word and translated into "Crown of the Valley").

By the turn of the 20th century, the town had become a winter retreat for wealthy Midwesterners such as David B. Gamble of Procter & Gamble and chewing gum magnate William Wrigley Jr. Through the next several decades it was known as a quiet, pretty, and conservative place in which to raise a family.

Over the past few years, a revitalized "old town" has sparked new interest in the area. Colorado Boulevard is Pasadena's main artery, and the heart of Old Pasadena. The city's original business district, Old Pasadena is bounded by Pasadena Avenue, Walnut Street, Arroyo Parkway, and Green Street; newly renovated historic buildings offer a unique array of retailers, art galleries, movie theaters, antique shops, restaurants, and offices. On weekend nights, the sidewalks are brimming with people. The outdoor pedestrian mall, Paseo Colorado, opened in 2002, adds to the area's shopping possibilities. Those arriving in Pasadena via the 134 Ventura Freeway are greeted by a magnificent view of the intricate and recently restored Colorado Street Bridge (Colorado Boulevard at Arroyo Seco). Carefully preserved, turn-of-the-century homes grace the streets, and Pasadena residents take pride in the city's small town atmosphere. At first glance, single-family homes appear to make up the majority of the residential offerings; however, about half of the city's residents are renters. Most homes were built in the 1950s, with about 30% constructed before 1939. Housing prices in Pasadena start at about the county median and go up from there. The neighborhood is clean, palm tree-lined, with plenty of grassy front yards. "Pah-sad-na," as some intentionally but affectionately mispronounce the name, is a lovely place to own a home. Twenty-three square miles in size, it has an average of nine residents per acre.

Would-be homebuyers who fall in love with Pasadena may elect to buy in the neighboring, yet to be incorporated, **Altadena**, just north of Pasadena. Residents of this leafy suburb find they can still enjoy the benefits of Pasadena without the higher price tag; homes here hover at about the county median. Suburban to its core, Altadena has plenty of room yet for development. Some homeowners keep horses on their land and many backyards open right onto mountain trails. Paved sidewalks and apartment buildings are scarce.

If money is not a concern, try the **City of San Marino**, Pasadena's southern neighbor, which also offers a cozy community with beautiful, rolling tree-lined streets. The posh Ritz-Carlton Huntington Hotel & Spa offers pampering to the ladies who lunch—they number more than a handful here. The picture-perfect, multiple-bedroom homes are in the million-dollar to millions of dollars range, more expensive than Pasadena. This storybook neighborhood was featured in the Steve Martin film, "Father of the Bride."

To the south of Pasadena is—surprise—the **City of South Pasadena**. It features Craftsman-style and Mission Revival architecture. Located between Pasadena and Los Angeles, it acts as a buffer between these two environs, and consequently some streets aren't as well tended in comparison to its northerly sister. Despite its more urban feel, homes here consistently fetch prices that rival those in Pasadena.

In the commercial districts of these residential neighborhoods, boutique shops and gourmet grocery stores mingle with general retailers, providing plentiful shopping options. South Lake Avenue is where you'll find designer label boutiques. Preservation of area historic sites adds to the village-like feel of these communities. Pasadena's public library is housed in a Renaissance-style building. One of the country's oldest soda fountains, the Fair Oaks Pharmacy and Soda Fountain, 1526 Mission Street, South Pasadena, still dishes out malts and egg creams much like it did back in the 1920s.

The Jet Propulsion Laboratory, Cal Tech, Pasadena Center (the city's convention center), Pasadena Playhouse (built in 1917), the lavish Huntington Gardens and Library, and the privately owned and recently renovated Norton Simon Museum, featuring Western European painting and Asian sculpture, round out the first-rate cultural and educational offerings in the area.

Depending on where you work, Pasadena, serviced by the 210 Foothill and 134 Ventura Freeways, can be a half-hour commute to downtown Los Angeles or parts of the Valley—or a long haul if you need to head to the western and southern communities of Los Angeles. A car is definitely needed here, unless you plan to work in an area easily accessed by bus. The Metro also runs the Gold Line from downtown Los Angeles to Pasadena.

On the downside, Pasadena, nestled as it is in the foothills of the San Gabriel Mountains, can get hot and smoggy. Still, Pasadena and its neighboring cities remain a wonderful place to call home...just be on the lookout for central air conditioning when house hunting here.

Web Sites: www.ci.pasadena.ca.us, www.pasadenacal.com, www.ci. south-pasadena.ca.us, www.cityofsanmarino.org, www.aaaim. com/Altadena, http://lacounty.info

Area Code: 626

Zip Codes: Pasadena: 91101-91126; South Pasadena: 91030; San Marino: 91108; Altadena: 91001

Post Offices: Pasadena Main Post Office, 600 North Lincoln Avenue; South Pasadena Main Post Office, 1001 Fremont Avenue; Altadena Main Post Office: 2271 Lake Avenue; many more locations, call 800-275-8777, www.usps.com

Police District: Pasadena Police Headquarters, 207 North Garfield Avenue, 626-744-4501, www.ci.pasadena.ca.us/police; South Pasadena Police Headquarters, 1422 Mission Street, 626-403-7270, www.ci.south-pasadena.ca.us; San Marino Police Department Headquarters, 2200 Huntington Drive, 626-300-0720, www.ci.san-marino.ca.us

Emergency Hospitals: Huntington Memorial Hospital, 100 West California Blvd., 626-397-5000, www.huntingtonhospital.com; Las Encinas Hospital, 2900 East Del Mar Blvd., 626-795-9901, www.lasencinas hospital.com

Libraries: Main Library, 285 East Walnut Street, 626-744-4066, www.ci.pasadena.ca.us/library; South Pasadena Public Library, 1100 Oxley Street, 626-403-7330, www.ci.south-pasadena.ca.us; San Marino Public Library, 1890 Huntington Drive, 626-300-0777, http://sanmarinopl.org; Altadena Main Library, 600 East Mariposa Street, 626-798-0833, http://library.altadena.ca.us

Public School Education: Pasadena Unified School District, 351 South Hudson Avenue, Pasadena, 91109, 626-795-6981, www.pasadena. k12.ca.us; South Pasadena Unified School District, 1020 El Centro Street, South Pasadena, 626-441-5700, www.spusd.k12.ca.us; San Marino Unified School District, 1665 West Drive, San Marino, 91108, 626-299-7000, www.san-marino.k12.ca.us; Altadena is part of the La Canada Unified School District, 5039 Palm Drive, La Canada, 91011, 818-952-8300, www.lcusd.net

Community Resources: Norton Simon Museum, 411 West Colorado Blvd., Pasadena, 626-449-6840, www.nortonsimon.org; Huntington Library, Art Collections & Botanical Gardens, 1151 Oxford Road, San Marino, 626-405-2100, www.huntington.org; Pacific Asia Museum, 46 North Los Robles Avenue, Pasadena, 626-449-2742, www.pacificasia museum.org; Tournament House & Wrigley Gardens, 391 South Orange Grove Blvd., 626-449-4100, www.tournamentofroses.com; Rose Bowl, 991 Rosemont Blvd., Pasadena, 626-577-3100, www.rose bowlstadium.com; Brookside Park, 360 North Arroyo Blvd., Pasadena; Pasadena Human Services & Recreation Department, 626-744-4000, www.ci.pasadena.ca.us; California Institute of Technology, 1201 East California Blvd., Pasadena, 626-395-6811, www.caltech.edu

Public Transportation: call 800-COMMUTE, or visit www.mta.net for route and schedule information for Metro bus and the Metro Gold Line. Foothill Transit contributes regular and express bus service here, 626-967-3147, www.foothilltransit.org. LADOT also operates commuter express lines here, 800-363-1317, www.ladottransit.com. Free Pasadena ARTS Buses shuttle the shopping and entertainment districts; inquire with Transit Operations at 626-398-8973, www.ci.pasadena.ca.us/trans/transit/trans_arts.asp for routes and hours.

SANTA CLARITA

NEWHALL
VALENCIA
LANCASTER
PALMDALE
ACTON

Boundaries: **East**: Angeles National Forest; **South**: Junction of the 5 Golden State and 14 Antelope Valley freeways; **North**: Angeles National Forest; **West**: 5 Golden State Freeway

Santa Clarita only became a city in 1987 and by 1999 was selected as one of 30 finalists in the All-American City Award competition. That same year, the city was also named the fifth most kid-friendly suburban city in the nation by Zero Population Growth. The group cited the community's schools, low crime, and low high school drop-out rates as factors. In fact, the city claims its schools consistently rank in the top 10% in California.

Forty-six square miles in size and with a population of over 160,000, according to the 2000 Census, Santa Clarita is the fourth largest in LA County (after Los Angeles, Long Beach, and Glendale). It is located 35 miles north of downtown Los Angeles, in between the 5 Golden State and the 14 Antelope Valley freeways, near the Six Flags Magic Mountain Theme Park (incidentally, the city's largest employer). The established community of Newhall and the new tract-housing community of Valencia are both within Santa Clarita.

Much of Santa Clarita's existing housing was built in the 1960s; however, during the late 1990s the city experienced another housing boom. Prices here are reasonable, primarily due to Santa Clarita's far-flung location, making it one of the fastest growing cities in the county. While 35 miles may not sound far, with traffic, an hour-plus commute into central LA would not be unusual. (You could opt for the Metrolink, which takes residents to Burbank, Glendale, or downtown LA.) Despite the longer than average commute to LA, many newcomers are drawn to Santa Clarita's affordable housing and newness. And, according to FBI statistics, Santa Clarita is the safest city of its size in the state and the nation.

Typical housing in Santa Clarita consists of newer four-bedroom/two-story homes. Newly built condominiums run about two-thirds the price of a new home. Rentals, with a slightly lower vacancy rate than the rest of the county, are moderately priced. Young families make up a large segment of the population—the median age here is about 34. Santa Clarita sponsors Pride Week every April, an organized effort to keep the community clean. Call organizers at 661-255-4918 for more details. A word of warning to newcomers from cold climates, Santa Clarita is in desert country and gets quite hot during the summer.

"New" seems to be the best adjective to describe the communities of Santa Clarita. Three parks were recently constructed: 17-acre Canyon Country Park and five-acre Begonias Lane Neighborhood Park (both in the Canyon Country community); and, most recently, the eight-acre Creekview Park in Newhall. The city's commitment to creating a family-friendly environment is obvious. Those who can't easily get to a park can ask the city to bring its "mobile park," a sort of playground on wheels, to their community (call 661-255-4910).

Revitalization efforts and civic dollars are also being invested in downtown **Newhall**. The typical chain restaurants, houseware stores, and grocery stores can be found in the myriad of recently built strip malls. School buildings here are also new. (Note that separate districts represent elementary schools and high schools here.) The California Institute of the Arts (Cal Arts), the Disney-sponsored arts college where many top animators graduate, is located in Newhall, and a new theater complex, major recreation area, and skateboard park in adjacent Canyon Country are some of the more recently available community offerings.

In **Valencia**, community amenities are similar to neighboring Newhall's but the buildings appear even newer. Valencia residents are especially keen on preserving the neighborhood's spacious environs. Oak trees and generous greenbelts are plentiful here, supported by residents who pay an annual assessment for public landscape upkeep. (Not so in other nearby communities where *au naturel* tends to be the rule.) This tract-housing community is also noted for excellent traffic flow within its well-planned streets.

Further north of Santa Clarita are the **City of Acton**, the **City of Lancaster**, and the **City of Palmdale**. All three are located in Antelope Valley, with Lancaster and Palmdale bordering Edwards Air Force Base. This is truly desert country, hot dry air, no smog, and bargain-priced homes garnished with freshly planted trees. The commute to LA is even longer than what it would be from Santa Clarita. Acton is the most southern of the trio and nearly 50 miles from LA. Homes in this intimate equestrian community are the most expensive of the three. About 40% of the two-story, two-bedroom homes in this area were built in the mid 1980s. The older residences date from between 1950 and 1970. Rentals make up a modest 27% of the housing stock here. Three- to four-bedroom homes are sprouting up all over with commercial districts blossoming alongside. New homebuyers might be interested in the Legends Way development in Palmdale. The prices of these homes run well below the county median. These towns make lovely selections for first-time homebuyers who enjoy desert suburban life.

Web Sites: www.santa-clarita.com, www.cityoflancasterca.org, www.city ofpalmdale.org, www.cityofacton.org, http://lacounty.info

Area Code: 661

Zip Codes: Santa Clarita: 91381-2, Acton: 93510, Lancaster: 93534, Palmdale: 93550

Post Offices: Santa Clarita Main Post Office, 24355 Creekside Road; Acton Main Post Office, 3632 Smith Avenue; Lancaster Main Post Office: 1008 West Avenue J2, Cedar Station, 567 West Lancaster Blvd.; Palmdale Main Post Office, 38917 20th Street East; Palmdale branches: 2220 East Palmdale Blvd., 38560 9th Street East, 829 West Palmdale Blvd.; 800-275-8777, www.usps.com

Police District: all communities are patrolled by the LA County Sheriffs. The Santa Clarita Valley station is at 23740 Magic Mountain Parkway, 661-255-1121; Lancaster station: 501 West Lancaster Blvd., 661-948-8466; Palmdale Station: 1020 East Palmdale Blvd., 661-267-4300, www.lasd.org

Emergency Hospitals: in Valencia and Newhall, Henry Mayo Newhall Memorial Hospital, 23845 West McBean Parkway, 661-253-8000, www.henrymayo.com; for Lancaster and Acton: Antelope Valley Hospital Medical Center, 1600 West Avenue J, 661-949-5000, www.avhospital.org; LAC-High Desert Hospital, 44900 North 60th Street West, 661-948-8581; Lancaster Community Hospital, 43830 North 10th Street West, 661-948-4781, www.lancastercommunity hospital.net; in Palmdale: South Antelope Valley Health Center, 38350 40th Street East, 661-272-5000

Libraries: Valencia Library, 23743 West Valencia Blvd., 661-259-8942; Newhall Library, 22704 West Ninth Street, 661-259-0750; Santa Clarita Valley Bookmobile for Acton, 661-260-1792; Lancaster Library, 601 West Lancaster Blvd., 661-948-5029; www.colapublib.org; Palmdale City Library, 700 East Palmdale Blvd., 661-267-5600, www.palmdalelibrary.org

Public School Education: Saugus Union School District, 24930 Avenue Stanford, Santa Clarita, 91355, 661-294-5300, www.saugus.k12.ca.us; William S. Hart Union High School District, 21515 Centre Pointe Parkway, Santa Clarita, 91350, 661-259-0033, www.hart.k12.ca.us; Newhall School District, 25375 Orchard Village Road, Valencia, 91355, 661-286-2200, www.newhall.k12.ca.us; Acton-Agua Dulce Unified School District, 32248 North Crown Valley Road, Acton, 93510, 661-269-5999, www.aadusd.k12.ca.us; Antelope Valley Union High School District, 44811 Sierra Highway, Lancaster, 93534, 661-948-7655, www.avdistrict.org; Lancaster School District, 44711 North Cedar Avenue, Lancaster 93534, 661-948-4661, www.lancaster.k12.ca.us; Palmdale School District, 39139 North 10th Street East, Palmdale, 93550, 661-947-7191, www.psd.k12.ca.us

Community Resources: Santa Clarita Community Center, 24406 San Fernando Road, 661-284-1476, www.santa-clarita.com; Newhall Park, 24923 Newhall Avenue, 661-286-4000; Valencia Meadows Park, 25671 Fedala Road, 661-286-4000; Canyon Country Park, 17815 West Soledad Canyon Road, Santa Clarita; Santa Clarita Park, 27285 Seco Canyon Road, 661-799-1198 (outdoor) or 661-250-3706 (indoor), www.santa-clarita.com; Santa Clarita City recreation programs, 661-250-3700; Cal Arts, 24700 McBean Parkway, Valencia, 661-225-1050, www.calarts.edu; Acton County Park, Syracuse Avenue and Crown Valley Road, 661-269-0133, www.cityofacton.org/park.htm

Public Transportation: Antelope Valley Transit Authority route and schedule information: 661-945-9445, www.avta.com; Santa Clarita Transit/Bus route and schedule information: 661-294-1287, www.santa-clarita.com/cityhall/field/transit; for Metrolink information, 800-371-LINK, www.metrolinktrains.com

ORANGE COUNTY COMMUNITIES

Disneyland is what many people think of when Orange County (the "OC") is mentioned, that and orange groves, many of which can still be seen from Interstate 5. This sleepy agricultural community between Los Angeles and San Diego, long ignored through the years, has been discovered and then rediscovered, transformed by farmers, entrepreneurs, and families, many of whom in more recent years have been squeezed out by the ravenous housing demands in Los Angeles and San Diego.

The year was 1889 when Orange County was established, formally breaking off from the County of Los Angeles. Orange County, known for its crops of Valencia oranges, lemons, avocados, and walnuts, was named after its bountiful orange groves. In the early 1900s, Buena Park farmer Walter Knott founded a farm stand and restaurant, which eventually evolved into the Knott's Berry Farm Theme Park. And in 1955, Walt Disney opened the Magic Kingdom in nearby Anaheim. It was in the 1960s when some of Los Angeles County's population began spilling over into Santa Ana Valley that Orange County really began to boom.

Today, Orange County consists of 798 square miles, 42 miles of coastline, 34 cities, and a population of 2.9 million. Oranges are still grown here, but it's mainly nursery stock and cut flowers that are the agricultural breadwinners now. In the last decade or so, the OC has developed into a desirable, affluent, and ethnically diverse suburban community. According to

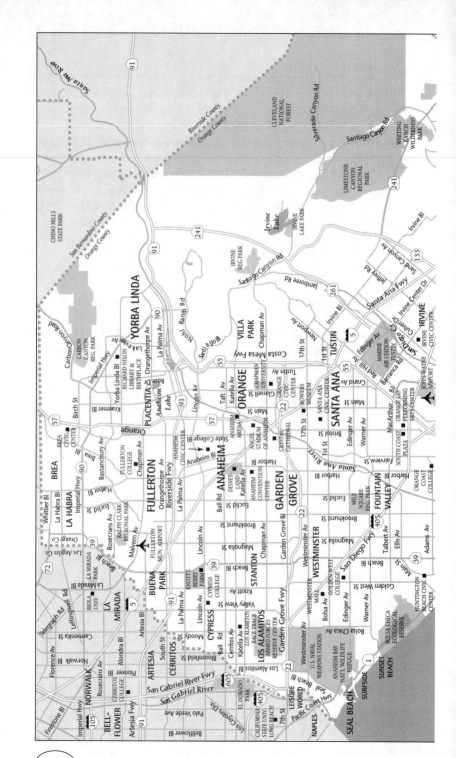

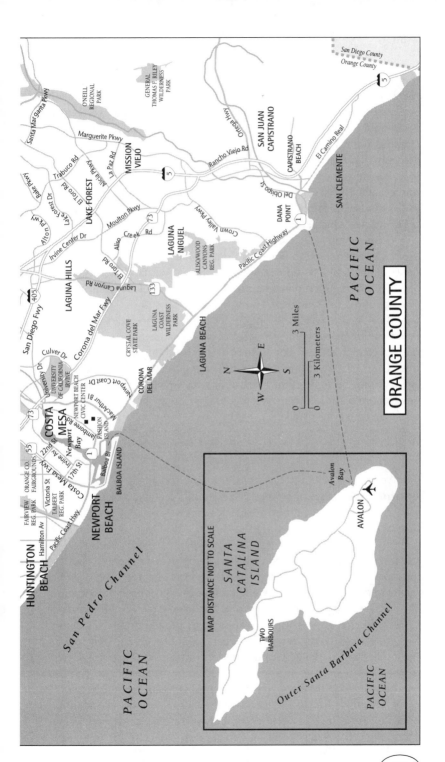

ORANGE COUNTY

the National Association of Realtors, in the second quarter of 2004, the median price of homes in Orange County ran well over the half million mark, more than $200,000 over LA County's median, and more even than San Francisco's median price of $647,000. Area amenities abound: The Orange County Performing Arts Center in Costa Mesa, the Orange County Museum of Art in Newport Beach, and the Verizon Wireless Amphitheatre in Irvine are some of the cultural venues here. Also calling this county home is the Crystal Cathedral, a twelve-story nondenominational church in Garden Grove, famous for its Christmas and Easter services inside the glass and steel sanctuary.

There are many OC cities worth investigating for newcomers. Along the shore, where median prices for homes trend toward the millions, are the communities of Newport Beach, Corona del Mar, and Laguna Beach. The beach lifestyle is prominent, drawing people who love residing just a few steps from the sand, surf, and sun. Some of the priciest real estate in California and the nation is along this coastline. Further inland, the more urban communities of Anaheim, Santa Ana, and Irvine offer much more in the way of affordable to middle-range housing. Although most residents of the OC work locally, some do drive the hour-plus commute to LA. Below we have profiled some of the more developed Orange County communities that are particularly noteworthy for their variety of housing, cultural resources, and city amenities.

IRVINE

Boundaries: **East**: Interstate 5 San Diego Freeway; **South**: 73 San Joaquin Hills Freeway; **North**: Barranca Parkway and Portola Parkway; **West**: MacArthur Boulevard

James Irvine, one of four sheep ranchers in this sleepy backlands south of Los Angeles, acquired hundreds of thousands of acres of land for his ranching operations. It was his son, James Irvine Jr., who in 1894 created The Irvine Company, changing from ranching to growing orchards of olives and citrus. When the company was passed down to his son, Myford, in 1947, urban development became the focus. The University of California purchased a thousand acres from The Irvine Company in 1959 to build UC Irvine, and an additional 500 acres surrounding its campus was purchased to develop a master community plan for 50,000 people called The Irvine Ranch. The Irvine Business Complex and the neighborhoods of Turtle Rock/University Park, Culverdale, The Ranch, and Walnut soon followed. Architect William Pereira, best known for designing the

Transamerica Building, was the head of this master plan, which was so large in scope that today it remains one of the nation's largest planned communities. In 1971, residents voted to incorporate their community and an even larger radius of land, for a total of 55 square miles, to create the City of Irvine. The Irvine Company continues to develop Irvine from its headquarters in Newport Beach.

The relative newness of this city is apparent in the clean lines of its modern architecture and the tidiness of both its business and residential sections. Open land continues to give way to new business parks and residential developments, making it possible to buy a brand new home in the city's many "villages"—as the neighborhoods here are called. In particular, those looking for a new home should look to the villages of **Turtle Ridge**, **Shady Canyon**, and **Northwood**. Housing demand in Irvine has been growing due to its relative affordability and convenient location in the Center of Orange County. Many folks, drawn to the coastal communities of Costa Mesa and Newport Beach that sit just west of Irvine, find living a little further inland slightly easier on their pocketbooks. Homes in Irvine, which sell at slightly above the county's median price, span the spectrum of apartments, town-homes, larger family homes (the average home has five bedrooms), and custom estates. The City of Irvine has an affordable housing office that provides assistance to lower-income households, with a number of master planned communities having a portion of housing set aside for lower incomes. Visit www.cityofirvine.org for more information.

The villages here are family-friendly with parks and recreation centers scattered throughout. The Disc Golf Course at Deerfield Community Park has been popular with disc golfers since 1980, and the Harvard Sk8 Park on Harvard Avenue features bowls, rails, and spines where skateboarders show off their stuff day and night. Adults too have their share of recreational offerings. The Irvine Museum at 18881 Von Karman Avenue specializes in California art from the Impressionist period, and the Irvine Spectrum Center and The Market Place are shopping-entertainment complexes with movie theaters, restaurants, and retail stores (see listings below). And if you can't find what you need at either of these places, head to neighboring Costa Mesa for the South Coast Plaza at 3333 Bristol Street, Costa Mesa (800-782-8888, www.southcoastplaza.com). With over 300 shops, many exclusive to California, a shopper's day is easily filled. The California Scenario Sculpture Garden by Isamu Noguchi, next to the mall, is wonderful.

As for the college that started it all, UCI has blossomed into a well-respected four-year college and the county's third largest employer. It was the first public university to have faculty win two Nobel Prizes in chemistry and physics. In 2004, UCI was listed among the top 50 colleges in "U.S. News and World Report." The student population of over 23,000 drives some of the demand for housing in the University's surrounding villages of **Turtle Rock/University Park** to the south, and **West Park** and **Woodbridge** to the east. Housing that is most coveted by the student population is University Town Center, a collection of apartments and condos (with its own shopping area and cinema) connected to campus by a pedestrian bridge. Rents for apartments in these areas tend to increase every year, causing some forward-thinking parents to buy a home or condo for their child to reside in during his or her school years and then sell it (usually at a profit) after graduation.

Web Sites: www.ci.irvine.ca.us, www.irvineranch.com
Area Code: 949
Zip Codes: 92602-20
Post Offices: Main Office, 15642 Sand Canyon Avenue; East Irvine, 14982 Sand Canyon Avenue; Harvest Station, 17192 Murphy Avenue; University Station, 4255 Campus Drive, Ste A100; 800-275-8777, www.usps.com
Police District: Irvine Police Department, 1 Civic Center Plaza, Irvine, 949-724-7000, www.cityofirvine.org/ipd
Emergency Hospitals: Irvine Regional Hospital and Medical Center, 16200 Sand Canyon Avenue, 949-753-2000, www.irvineregional hospital.com; UCI Medical Center, 101 The City Drive South, 877-UCI-DOC, www.ucihealth.com
Libraries: Heritage Park Regional Library, 14361 Yale Avenue, 949-551-7151; University Park Library, 4512 Sandburg Way, 949-786-4001; www.ocpl.org
Public School Education: Irvine Unified School District, 5050 Barranca Parkway, Irvine, CA 92604; 949-936-5000, www.iusd.org; Tustin Unified School District, 300 South C Street, Tustin, CA 92780, 714-730-7301, www.tustin.k12.ca.us
Community Resources: Heritage Park Community Center, 14301 Yale Avenue, 949-724-6750; University Community Park, 1 Beech Tree Lane, 949-724-6815; Deerfield Community Park Disc Golf Course, 949-551-8638, www.ci.irvine.ca.us; Laguna Niguel Regional Park, 28241 La Paz Road, Laguna Niguel, www.destinationirvine.com; South Coast Plaza, 3333 Bristol Street, Costa Mesa, 800-782-8888, www.southcoast plaza.com; Harvard Sk8 Park, 14701 Harvard Avenue, 949-337-6577, www.ci.irvine.ca.us; Irvine Museum, 18881 Von Karman Avenue, 949-476-2565, www.irvinemuseum.org; Irvine Spectrum Center, Irvine Center Drive and I-405, 949-753-5180, www.irvinespectrumcenter.com;

The Market Place, 2777 El Camino Real, 714-731-5701, www.shopthe
marketplace.com
Transportation: Orange County Transportation Authority (OCTA), 714-
636-7433, www.octa.net

NEWPORT BEACH

**BALBOA ISLAND
CORONA DEL MAR**

Boundaries: East: 73 San Joaquin Hills Freeway; **South**: Crystal Cove State
Park; **North**: Irvine Avenue and Upper Newport Bay; **West**: Pacific Ocean

Newport Beach is a homogeneous, upper-class community and the
largest coastal city in Orange County. Known for its yacht clubs and beachfront property, it's also the setting for the popular TV series "The O.C.,"
which has elevated the Newport Beach lifestyle to the stuff of legend. Leafy
coral trees and purple bougainvilleas, the city's official tree and flower, decorate the picturesque residential streets. Temperatures are impressively
moderate year-round, with high temperatures averaging 75 degrees in the
summer and 65 degrees in the winter. With an average annual rainfall of
only 12 inches, the sunny weather makes this city an ideal resort town. The
exclusive Balboa Bay Club & Resort and Four Seasons are just two of many
resorts in the area. Newport Beach's average population of 76,000 swells to
100,000+ in the summer due to an influx of visitors. Many Angelenos trek
the 50 miles south from LA for weekend getaways here.

This beachside city consists of 55% owner-occupied residences; the rest
are renters. Most single-family homes were built between the 1960s and
1970s. Condos, town-homes, and villas round out the offerings. Home sales
have been running between one and three million dollars; anything under is
a "steal." Rental rates are consistent with rates found at any upper-class
beachside community. Newport Coast is a newer luxury residential development with breathtaking views of the Pacific Ocean. The Pelican Hill Golf
Club is next door for those who want to be close to the putting greens.

A number of private estates and beach houses line Newport Harbor.
This huge sparkling marina is home to more than 9,000 boats and yachts,
making it one of the world's busiest small boat harbors. More than a handful of yacht clubs call it home. Boating is the main draw, but there is also
fishing, swimming, and volleyball.

The primary shopping district for Newport Beach is Fashion Island, an
upscale open-air mall that occupies a small man-man island. The annual

Taste of Newport is a popular September event; 70,000 locals and visitors sample the best of local dining over three days. The Orange County Museum of Art is also in Newport Beach. Exhibits emphasize modern works of art, and curators frequently showcase emerging artists from the state.

The man-made **Balboa Island**, located just a five-minute ferry ride from the Balboa Peninsula or a short drive over a bridge at the end of Jamboree Boulevard, is an intimate, exclusive, and picturesque neighborhood. The ferry ride is especially popular during the summer season, and waits to board the ferry (which transports people and cars) can run as long as an hour. Marine Avenue and accompanying side streets are popular for shopping and dining. The island itself, including the bridge, is a mere 2.6 miles. Since land is at a premium here, many of the houses, most with extraordinary bay views, are packed close together—reminiscent of San Francisco. When the island was developed during World War I, land parcels were doled out for $250. Today, if you can find a cottage for sale, you're easily looking at a million dollars and more. That said, the island is widely popular among UCI students for its fully furnished rentals and, sitting only six miles from campus, its convenient location. The close-knit population of 2,200 maintains the island's storybook character with streets named after gems like Sapphire and Ruby and an annual Christmas boat parade (running since 1908). The peninsula side has a "Fun Zone" as well as a Pavilion where you can board ships to Catalina Island.

On the southern end of Newport, about four miles southwest of UCI, is **Corona del Mar** (Spanish for "Crown of the Sea"). This Orange County jewel starts at the base of the San Joaquin Hills and runs east of Avocado Street to the city limits. The seaside village's small town allure comes with a big city price tag. House hunters can expect to pay a million dollars plus for estates of varying architectural styles. Rentals are limited and run slightly higher than rentals on Balboa Island. The main commercial drag is California State Route 1, dotted by galleries, restaurants, and boutiques. The community even has its own beach, the Corona del Mar State Beach, which is well groomed and popular with swimmers and sunbathers.

Web Sites: www.city.newport-beach.ca.us, www.balboa-island.com, www.cdmchamber.com

Area Code: 949

Zip Codes: Newport Beach: 92660-3, Corona del Mar: 92625, Balboa Island: 92662

Post Offices: Main Office, 1133 Camelback Street; Bay Station, 191 Riverside Avenue; Balboa Station, 204 Main Street; Balboa Island Station, 206 Marine Avenue; Corona del Mar Main Office, 406 Orchid Avenue; 800-275-8777, www.usps.com

Police District: Newport Beach Police Department, 870 Santa Barbara Drive, Newport Beach, 949-633-3681, www.nbpd.org

Emergency Hospitals: Hoag Memorial Hospital Presbyterian, One Hoag Drive, 949-645-8600, www.hoag.org; Newport Bay Hospital, 1501 East 16th Street, 949-650-9750

Libraries: Central Library, 1000 Avocado Avenue, 949-717-3800; Crean Mariners Branch, 2005 Dover Drive, 949-644-3078; Corona del Mar Branch, 420 Marigold Avenue, Corona del Mar, 949-644-3075; Balboa Branch, 100 East Balboa Boulevard, Balboa, 949-644-3076; www.newport beachlibrary.org

Public School Education: Newport-Mesa Unified School District, 2985-A Bear Street, Costa Mesa, CA 92626, 714-424-5000, www.nmusd.k12.ca.us

Community Resources: Newport Beach Park and Marine Department, 949-644-3151, www.city.newport-beach.ca.us; Newport Harbor, 18712 University Drive, Irvine, 949-923-2250, www.ocparks.com; Sherman Library & Gardens, 2647 East Pacific Coast Highway, Corona del Mar, 949-673-2261, www.slgardens.org; Orange County Museum of Art, 850 San Clemente Drive, 949-759-1122, www.ocma.net; Upper Newport Bay, 2301 University Drive, 949-923-2290, www.ocparks.com; Corona del Mar State Beach, Ocean Boulevard and Iris Avenue, 949-673-3047, www.parks.ca.gov; Pelican Hill Golf Club, 22651 Pelican Hill Road South, 949-760-0707, www.pelicanhill.com; Fashion Island, Pacific Coast Highway and Newport Center Drive, 949-721-2000, www.fashionisland-nb.com

Public Transportation: Orange County Transportation Authority (OCTA), 714-636-7433, www.octa.net

TUSTIN

Boundaries: **East**: Jamboree Road; South: Barranca Parkway; **North**: Irvine Boulevard; **West**: 55 Costa Mesa Freeway

The City of Tustin, about ten miles north of UCI, has been slowly but steadily growing. Its allure: outright affordability in comparison to the coastal cities. Easy access to I-5 and I-15, plus the 55 and 91 freeways, is another perk. Residents of this conservative city, which occupies just 11 square miles, make up a little over 2% of the county's population. Sycamore, eucalyptus, pepper, palm, pine and oak trees were once so plentiful in Tustin, it dubbed itself the City of Trees. Some of these trees gave way to the El Toro Marine Corps Air Station in WW II, the establishment of which helped fuel Tustin's early growth.

The newer and more popular residential area is east of downtown at **Tustin Ranch**, which consists of single-family homes and condos. A lavish golf club and shopping centers have added to its popularity. Home prices hover at just above the county's median price, and condos run significantly less than that, making them a hot commodity. Further north, million dollar estates dot the hillsides next to Peters Canyon Regional Park and Reservoir, which come with panoramic views of the Saddleback Mountains and Pacific Coast. Outside of Tustin Ranch, homes run below the county median. In the south central part of town, **Laurelwood** is a 50-50 mix of condominiums and detached homes. The majority of Tustin's existing housing stock, generally consisting of two- to four-bedroom homes, was built in the 1960s or later. Single-family homes are slightly edged out in number by multi-family dwellings, but that's likely to change as land developers ramp up construction of new homes. Rentals, usually in the one- or two-bedroom range, are favored by UCI students and by workers from local industry—Ricoh Electronics, Inc. and Steelcase, Inc., are the two biggest manufacturers in the area. Many business parks are situated on and around Red Hill Avenue between Edinger Avenue and Barranca Parkway. Sycamores and other trees grace many of the city streets.

With the closure of the 1,500-acre El Toro Marine Corps Air Station in 1999, the land was renamed Tustin Legacy, and city planners established an ambitious community plan regarding its use. Urban parks, schools, residential villages, and commercial zones are part of the plan, with the first 376 homes being finished at Tustin Field, a 29-acre parcel between Harvard Avenue and Jamboree Road and adjacent Edinger Avenue. Construction on Phase II is expected soon. The fledgling neighborhood will feature a mix of traditional detached houses, urban-style row houses, and cluster townhouses meant to resemble a village square. **North Tustin** is still unincorporated and has plenty of room for expansion and development.

Possibly the county's oldest "old town" is in Tustin on Main Street and El Camino Real. Well-preserved commercial buildings, some dating back to the 1880s, and a Victorian mansion are still standing. The Tustin Museum documents the street's evolution from a blacksmith store and Wells Fargo Express stop to present day. More modern commercial districts are in the Marketplace on El Camino Real, which it shares with Irvine.

Web Site: www.tustinca.org
Area Code: 714
Zip Codes: 92780-2
Post Offices: Main Office, 340 East 1st Street, 800-275-8777, www.usps.com
Police District: Tustin Police Department, 300 Centennial Way, 714-573-3200, www.tustinpd.org

Emergency Hospital: Tustin Hospital and Medical Center, 14662 Newport Avenue, 714-669-5880

Library: Tustin branch, 345 East Main Street, 714-544-7725, www.ocpl.org

Public School Education: Tustin Unified School District, 300 South C Street, Tustin, CA 92780, 714-730-7301, www.tustin.k12.ca.us

Community Resources: Peppertree Park, 230 West 1st Street, 714-573-3326; Tustin Parks and Recreation, 714-573-3326, www.tustinca.org; Tustin Museum, 714-731-5701, www.tustinhistory.org; Peters Canyon Regional Park and Reservoir, 714-973-6611, www.ocparks.com; Tustin Ranch Golf Club, 12442 Tustin Ranch Road, 714-734-2104, www.tustinranchgolf.com; Tustin Chamber of Commerce, 714-544-5341, www.tustinchamber.com; Tustin Legacy Planning, 714-573-3000, www.tustinlegacy.com; The Marketplace, 2777 El Camino Real, 714-731-5701, www.shopthemarketplace.com

Transportation: Orange County Transportation Authority (OCTA), 714-636-7433, www.octa.net

Additional OC cities you might want to consider...
- **Anaheim**, 714-765- 5100, www.anaheim.net
- **Costa Mesa**, 714-754-5223, www.ci.costa-mesa.ca.us
- **Fountain Valley**, 714-593-4400, www.fountainvalley.org
- **Laguna Beach**, 949-497-3311, www.laguna-beach.ca.us, www.lagunabeachinfo.org
- **City of Orange**, 714-744-5511, www.cityoforange.org
- **San Juan Capistrano**, 949-493-1171, www.sanjuancapistrano.org
- **Seal Beach**, 562-431-2527, www.ci.seal-beach.ca.us
- **Westminster**, 714-898-3311, www.ci.westminster.ca.us
- **Yorba Linda**, 714-961-7100, www.ci.yorba-linda.ca.us

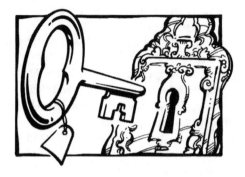

A S IN ALL MAJOR METROPOLITAN AREAS, YOU CAN FIND APART-
ments, condos, single-family homes, mansions, and everything in
between in Los Angeles. Your choice will depend on your needs and
your financial resources.

Unless you're moving here from New York, San Francisco, or San
Diego, brace yourself for sticker shock. In the second quarter of 2004, the
National Association of Realtors' ranking of the top 20 US metropolitan
areas with the highest median sale price for existing single-family homes
placed Los Angeles fifth, at $438,400; Orange County topped the list.
What's more, in terms of cost of living, in 2004, Los Angeles was rated by
Money Magazine to be the second most expensive city in the USA in which
to live, following New York, more even than San Francisco, and the 27th
most expensive city in the world. Between 1998 and 2002, rental vacancies
in the city declined from 7% to 3.5%, and current trends show the median
cost of a house in LA continues to rise each year by double-digit percentages (up 21.2% between December 2003 and December 2004).

As far as rentals, it's impossible to state what the "average" rents are
for one-bedroom apartments in Los Angeles since the locale, area
resources, and building amenities greatly affect the going rates. Keep in
mind, location can mean the difference between a cramped single with
ancient appliances in Santa Monica and a cheery one-bedroom with central air and a fireplace in Van Nuys—and the Santa Monica place would cost
more! Speaking in very general terms, beachside community rentals tend
to consist of two- or three-level apartment buildings (sometimes cramped
and usually pricier due to their proximity to the Pacific Ocean); inland
architecture fluctuates from duplexes in Beverly Hills to modern, major
complexes like those downtown and in the Fairfax District, to quirky art-
deco units and apartments in the modern clean lines of the 1960s and 70s,
which are scattered throughout the county. Prices are generally tied into a

neighborhood's prestige and general upkeep. Housing around the major universities, particularly UCLA and USC, is tight because of the student population. The recent trend toward revitalization has seen a sprinkling of new buildings throughout the city, as landowners raze old deteriorating units to build new complexes.

If you're looking to own, condominiums are typically less expensive than a townhouse or detached house. Condos and townhouses are popular choices here for would-be homeowners who find the down payment for a single-family detached home out of their means. Another option is the high-end condo, which costs more than a house and feels like a mansion...once you step inside.

New or old home? If you're looking for a new home within greater LA, you'll have better luck finding a recently built condo rather than a new house. Residential land in Los Angeles is fully built out and buyers will have to look at the suburbs, often outside of LA County, if they want a newly built home. Some homebuyers who want to stay in the city opt to purchase an existing home with the intent of remodeling it or tearing it down to build anew.

To get the most current information on what homes are going for in various southern California communities, check out the **LA Times** web site: www.latimes.com/dataquick or visit **DataQuick's** site directly at www.dqnews.com. The **US Department of Housing and Urban Development's (HUD)** web site is a good clearinghouse of information for prospective homeowners and renters in California: www.hud.gov. The Los Angeles HUD branch can be reached at 213-894-8000. To compare quality-of-life and cost-of-living data for about 3,000 US cities and towns, including 300 metropolitan areas, go to **BestPlaces**, www.bestplaces.net.

RENTING

Finding an apartment in the Los Angeles area can be simple or difficult, depending on where you are looking and your budget. Rental market conditions within the greater Los Angeles area vary. More units are available in luxury, high-end complexes; in the more economical units, vacancies are harder to come by. The best bet for a new and relatively affordable apartment may lie in downtown LA. The Downtown Center Business Improvement District predicts almost 5,000 units of housing will become available in the near future as many newly built apartment complexes are nearing completion.

Before hitting the internet, the newsstands, or the pavement to look for an apartment, first determine how much money you are willing to spend on your monthly rent and what size apartment you want. If you need a two-bedroom place but can only afford $1,000 per month, you can cross Beverly Hills off your list. Since competition for the lower rent one-bedroom units is high, the next best thing is to opt for a two-bedroom, two-bath, and split the rent with a roommate; you may even spend less in this scenario.

APARTMENT HUNTING

Once you have determined your housing budget and desired apartment size, walk or drive through the neighborhoods in which you would like to live. Not only will this give you a feel for the areas, but often you can find "For Rent" signs posted on available apartments. Finally, ask around. Co-workers and friends may know of vacancies in their buildings, and land-lords are often quite willing to take a referral from a trustworthy tenant. Below are the resources available to you as you search for the perfect place to call home.

NEWSPAPER CLASSIFIED ADVERTISEMENTS

A key resource for those hunting for an apartment is the classifieds. The *Los Angeles Times* lists pages of rentals, with the largest selection in its Sunday edition; web-goers: www.latimes.com. (Tip: most grocery and conven-ience stores and newsstands get an early Sunday edition of the *Los Angeles Times*, including the classified ads, on Saturday morning.) Smaller regional and weekly alternative newspapers like the *LA Weekly*, the *Santa Monica Outlook*, *Beverly Hills Courier*, and *The Tolucan Times* also have rental ads (see **Newspapers and Magazines** in **Getting Settled** for contact infor-mation for these publications). For those looking at mid- to higher-end apartments, you can pick up free, monthly apartment listing directories from Von's and Ralph's grocery stores, 7-Eleven stores, AM-PM Mini Markets, and other convenience stores, motels and hotels, real estate agents, banks, moving companies, and airports. Look for the **Apartment Guide**, www.apartmentguide.com (trial period, then annual fee), or the **Original Apartment Magazine**, www.aptmag.com (no fee).

RENTAL AGENTS

Using a real estate agency for apartment rentals is not the norm here, as area agents generally are used for those trying to locate townhouses, con-dos, or houses for sale. However, apartment-listing services, which let you browse for free, but require a fee before they'll release the contact informa-tion for the rental, are common. These services have become so successful that their ads have largely replaced the rental ads that landlords/managers place in the local papers.

- **Westside Rentals**, 800-RENT-005, www.westsiderentals.com; for a $60 fee, you can view their 14,000+ listings for 60 days.
- **Rent Times**, 323-653-RENT, www.rentimes.com; $49 fee, offers online listings that include vacancies and sublets, including houses and guest homes for three months.
- **Metro Rent**, 323-848-3490, www.metrorent.com; $34.95 fee, offers 45 days of listings.
- **Crown Relocation**, 714-898-0955, www.crownrelo.com; specializes in corporate employee relocations. But for a fee, individuals can hire a moving consultant to do all the legwork of locating a home based on preferences and lifestyle.

SHARING

Sharing a two-bedroom with a roommate is often more economical than getting a one-bedroom by yourself. The same classified ads sources mentioned above also have a "Rentals to Share" section. A roommate service may also be an option. Similar to rental agencies, a fee is charged to conduct a search for a compatible roomie. Consider one of the following:

- **Roommate Matchers**, 323-653-ROOM, www.roommatematchers.com; for a $49 membership fee, they will match you up with compatible roommates for 12 weeks. You can also browse pictures of potential roomies and descriptions of their housing.
- **Roommate Express**, 800-487-8050, www.e-roommate.com; $29 membership fee, will match you with a roommate looking to rent or one who already has a place to share.
- **Roommate Access**, 866-823-2200, www.roommateaccess.com; fee-based matching service.

SHORT-TERM/SUBLETS

If you prefer to take your time finding just the right place, consider a **sublet**. Some UCLA and USC students who are departing for the summer months as well as landlords desiring to fill student apartments during the summer may offer sublets. If you are interested in finding a temporary housing arrangement, go the same route as apartment seekers (above). In particular, local papers like the *Los Angeles Times*, the *LA Weekly*, http://losangeles.sublet.com, and roommate-matching services (listed above) are great resources for sublet listings. In addition, sublet seekers will do well to check for notices posted on college kiosks (or via college housing services directly) and neighborhood notice boards (at laundries, cafes, metro stops, etc.) Short-term rental opportunities might include a weekly or monthly rental situation. See the **Temporary Lodgings** chapter near the end of this guide for additional ideas.

OTHER PLACES TO LOOK

Keep your eyes peeled. Many neighborhood coffee shops, grocery stores, pet stores, and laundries have bulletin boards or wall space devoted to posting neighborhood announcements. Tucked between flyers for yoga classes and dog walkers, you may find notices of apartment or house rentals. More often, you'll find flyers for apartment shares. Some of the best rental bargains are advertised only with a sign on the window or front yard of an apartment building. The web sites of the city or neighborhood you're interested in will likely have leads as well. (Refer to the neighborhood profiles at the beginning of the book.)

ONLINE RESOURCES—RENTING

Los Angeles is well covered in terms of online sites for those seeking rentals. Many sites post apartment listings only; others help match roommates, and/or supply moving-related information or links to other moving-related sites. Here are a few:

- **Apartment Access**, www.apartmentaccess.com; listings for large metropolitan areas in the USA, including Los Angeles. Skim their listings of apartments; then, if it looks promising, pay a flat rate of $40 to use the service. Since landlords can list their units at no cost, your subscription buys you access to updated listings of apartments that you can lease without an agent fee.
- **Apartment Ratings**, www.aptratings.com; not an apartment listing service but rather a nationwide rating service. Residents of the Los Angeles area post assessments of where they live for the benefit of those in search of an apartment.
- **Craig's List**, http://losangeles.craigslist.org; the Los Angeles component of this popular web site posts listings for fee and no-fee apartment rentals, roommates, and sublets.
- **Easy Rent**, www.easyrent.com, for a flat rate of either $39 for seven days, $79 for one month, or $99 for two months, you can search apartments in the Los Angeles area. This web site is also connected to a roommate-matching service: www.easyroommate.com.

- **Homebuilder.com**, www.homebuilder.com; comprehensive web site where you can find apartments, homes (both sales and rentals), and roommates in Los Angeles. Free to renters.
- **Homestore**, www.homestore.com, a comprehensive portal that's very similar to www.homebuilder.com.
- **Roommates**, www.roommates.com, pay $5.99 for a three-day trial, $19.99 for 30 days, and $29.99 for 60 days for listings from this room-mate-matching company.

CHECKING IT OUT

It's two months into your lease and suddenly, that cozy budget bachelor pad you found is feeling claustrophobic and the police choppers buzzing overhead are keeping you awake at night. To avoid this scenario we suggest you bring a checklist of your musts and must-nots. In addition, you should make a quick inspection to make sure the apartment's beauty is not just skin deep. A little time and a few questions asked now can save you a lot of time, money, and headaches later. Specifically, you may want to look for the following:

- Are the kitchen appliances clean and in working order? Do the stove's burners work? How about the oven? Is there enough counter and shelf space? Be aware, apartments in Los Angeles do not usually come with refrigerators, and you may need to buy or rent your own. Some land-lords offer rentals on refrigerators they have in the building.
- Do the windows open, close, and lock? Do the bedroom windows open onto a noisy or potentially dangerous area? Is there an air-conditioning unit or central air?
- Are there enough closets and is there enough storage space?
- Are there enough electrical outlets for your needs? Do the outlets work?
- Are there any signs of insects?
- What about laundry facilities? Are they in the building or nearby?
- How did the building fare in the last earthquake? Superficial cracks along the walls or ceiling don't necessarily indicate a serious structural problem. The city's building inspector office (213-977-6941 or 888-LA4BUILD) can provide you with information if you are unsure.
- Outside, do you feel comfortable? Will you feel safe here at night? Is there secured parking? How many spaces? If two, are they tandem (so that one car blocks the other) or side by side? Is there an extra fee for parking? What about public transportation and shopping?
- Are you responsible for paying gas, water, and/or electricity? This policy varies from place to place, and paying any combination or none at all is possible.

- How quick to respond is the landlord or manager to work orders for repairs in the apartment? If possible, ask current tenants about this. Does the manager live on the premises?

Ed Sacks' *Savvy Renter's Kit* contains a thorough renter's checklist for those interested in augmenting theirs.

If all passes muster, be prepared to stake your claim without delay!

STAKING A CLAIM

While it is not necessary to wear your Sunday best, coming on time and appearing neat and well-kept, no matter how superficial, is certain to give a good impression to a prospective landlord. Also come with checkbook in hand. Often the person who is willing to put down a deposit first will get the apartment. Have ready access to your references, both credit and personal, and bring your rental history with you: previous residence addresses, manager contact information, and length of tenancy for the past five years or more to fill out a rental application.

LEASES, SECURITY DEPOSITS, AND RENT CONTROL

The lease is a legally binding contract that outlines both your obligations to your landlord, and your landlord's obligations to you. Of course, you should read your lease carefully, and get a full written explanation for anything that does not make sense to you, *before* signing. If you have any questions regarding your lease, security deposit, or rent control, contact your rent stabilization board (see below).

Here are some things to consider in your lease:
- Is this a month-to-month rental, or a one- or two-year lease?
- Are pets allowed?
- Are water beds allowed?
- Are you allowed to barbecue on the property?
- Can you sublet your unit?

Under California law, in most instances the security deposit cannot exceed two months' rent for an unfurnished unit or three months' rent for a furnished unit. The deposit can be collected in addition to the first month's rent. In some cities, for instance in West Hollywood, landlords are required to pay interest on your security deposit. Check with your rent board for specifics in your city. In addition, your landlord cannot raise your rent during a lease period unless it is so stated in your lease—read carefully before signing. If you have a month-to-month agreement, your landlord can increase rent after giving you 30-days' notice.

LANDLORD PROBLEMS

You should try to resolve any problems with your landlord first. However, if your efforts are fruitless, there are a number of city and state housing advocates available:

- **California Department of Fair Employment and Housing**, 800-233-3212, www.dfeh.ca.gov; handles discrimination claims
- **City of LA Tenant & Landlord Information Line**, 800-994-4444, www.ci.la.ca.us/lahd/ten_land.htm; provides information and helps handle landlord-tenant disputes including information on eviction procedures. If you reside in another city, contact the housing department or general information line of your city for a referral.
- **Coalition for Economic Survival**, 323-656-4410, www.cesin action.org; specializes in legal problems with regards to tenants' rights.
- **Fair Housing Council of San Fernando Valley**, 818-373-1185; investigates housing discrimination in the Valley.
- **Legal Aid Foundation of Los Angeles**, 213-640-3881, www.lafla. org; can refer a lawyer for handling disputes.
- **San Fernando Valley Neighborhood Legal Services**, 800-433-6251; provides information and assistance to low-income renters regarding evictions and landlord problems.
- **US Department of Housing and Urban Development**, 800-669-9777, www.hud.gov; handles discrimination and other housing problems.

RENT STABILIZATION

In an effort to offer affordable rental housing, several cities in the Los Angeles area have enacted rent stabilization. Rent control laws and their effects vary according to city. In Los Angeles City, for example, rent stabilization is applicable only to buildings built before 1979. If you're renting in a building built after this date, the landlord can issue annual increases at whatever amount he/she pleases with 30-days' notice.

The most recent development in rent control, and one that is more beneficial to the landlord than to the tenant, is the Costa-Hawkins Bill (also known as "vacancy decontrol"), which went into effect in 1999. This bill allows landlords to raise the rents of vacated rent-controlled units to current market value, which has resulted in a significant loss of bargain-priced rentals. It is worth noting that rental units affected by the Costa-Hawkins Bill are still covered by rent control in terms of how much rent may be raised from year to year during a tenancy. However, this type of rent control does nothing to prevent the rent of recently vacated apartments from being immediately raised to current market value. Cities with rent control have counselors who can help a renter sort it all out. Contact the following rent stabilization boards to learn how rent control works in your area.

- **Beverly Hills Rent Office**, 455 North Rexford Drive, 310-285-1031, www.ci.beverly-hills.ca.us
- **City of LA Department of Housing**, 3550 Wilshire Blvd., 866-557-7368, www.lacity.org/lahd
- **Santa Monica Rent Control Board**, 1685 Main Street, Room 202, 310-458-8751, www.santa-monica.org/rentcontrol
- **West Hollywood Department of Rent Stabilization**, 8611 Santa Monica Blvd., 323-848-6450, www.weho.org

RENTER'S/HOMEOWNER'S INSURANCE

Renter's insurance provides a relatively inexpensive policy against theft, water damage, fire, and in many cases personal liability. Earthquake insurance usually has to be purchased separately. Renter's insurance does not cover structural damage to the building, only personal belongings. Go for the replacement value over cash-value policy. As with all insurance, be sure you understand your policy completely and ask questions. While most insurance companies offer renter's insurance, call to be sure. (Check with your auto insurance agency to see if they offer renter's insurance—many agencies offer discounts for multiple policy holders.) Allstate, Farmers, Metlife, Prudential, and State Farm are some of the larger insurance agencies in the area. Homeowners in need of financing will be required to obtain a homeowner's insurance policy as part of the home buying process. Insurance customer satisfaction ratings and comparisons are possible at www.insure.com; also the **State of California Department of Insurance** does an annual survey of homeowner insurance providers in Los Angeles: Go to www.insurance.ca.gov/docs/FS-Surveys, 800-927-4357. After the 1994 Northridge earthquake, some companies stopped selling earthquake insurance altogether. In response, in 1996, the California Legislature established the **California Earthquake Authority**, 916-325-3800, www.earthquakeauthority.com, which is a privately funded, publicly operated organization to provide earthquake coverage to Californians. This coverage is not required, but certainly recommended. Due to the variances in local geography, additional natural disasters that may pose some risk to your home include wildfires, landslides, flooding, and environmental hazards—all should be disclosed in your title inspection report to help you determine which additional protections you might need. A thorough home inspection will address the home's structural integrity as well. When you obtain insurance, many insurance companies will require that you provide a detailed inventory of your possessions. Photograph or videotape your furniture, jewelry, electronics, and anything else of value to supplement your documentation. Store this inventory separate from your home, in a safe-deposit box or with a family member or trusted friend. To order your CLUE (Comprehensive Loss Underwriting Exchange) report, write to **Choice Point Asset**, P.O. Box 105108, Atlanta, GA 30348-5108, or go to www.choicetrust.com. This national database of consumers' automobile and homeowner's insurance claims is used by insurers when determining rates or denying coverage. Contact Choice Point if you find any errors in your report.

BUYING

In Southern California's tight housing market, becoming a homeowner can be a good financial investment. Over the long term, the cost of renting can exceed that of owning, especially in high-rent districts. If you expect to spend at least seven years in one place and if you can afford it, purchasing a home is worth investigating. That said, a newcomer to Los Angeles would be well advised to rent or sublet for at least one year before buying, giving time to learn about various neighborhoods, commuting issues, and local schools. Realtors recommend that buyers get pre-qualified for a loan before house hunting (see **The Buying Process** below), so that when you spot the home of your dreams, you can act quickly—a necessity in this sellers' market. Sellers who entertain multiple bids are common in today's marketplace. Making a good impression on the seller when viewing a house will be to your advantage in a multiple-bid situation. The search for a condo, town-home, or house requires resourceful and aggressive search tactics. Your best bet is to work with an attentive broker who has access to homes waiting to be listed with the Multiple Listing Service. Assisting your broker's efforts by browsing the "Housing" section of the Sunday *Los Angeles Times* as well as the numerous home-for-sale listings on the web is a good idea. Free real estate guides—**Homes & Land**, 800-277-7800, www.homes.com, **The New Home Buyers Guide**, 800-273-HOUSE, www.hbg.com, and **Coldwell Banker Homes**, 800-733-1380 or 800-589-9866, www.californiamoves.com—can be found on racks at grocery stores, pharmacies, and newspaper stands. City web sites (see **Neighborhoods**) will often offer links to real estate options.

REAL ESTATE BROKERS

Most people selling a home in Los Angeles use a real estate broker/agent, which is helpful for buyers. An agent is knowledgeable about the maze of legal paperwork required in California and will have access to brand-new listings. The real estate broker takes a percentage of the sale, usually 5% to 6% of the price of the home (paid by the seller) to cover services, which include writing and making an offer, guiding the buyer through escrow and settlement, and answering questions.

RECOMMENDATIONS FOR FINDING A REAL ESTATE BROKER

Seek the referrals of friends, family, and co-workers, and/or browse the classifieds and/or internet for a broker who handles listings in neighborhoods that appeal to you. Any search should include a visit to the www.realtor.com site, since working with a licensed broker ensures a certain level of professionalism. (Do not rely on the Realtor symbol on the real estate brokers' business cards as sole proof that they're Realtor licensed.) Investigate the vicinity in which you're interested and look for smaller offices that operate only in the area—that broker will likely have intimate knowledge of the neighborhood. Call a realty agency or check their web site for a field office in the community in which you're interested.

The following large **realty firms** have offices throughout Los Angeles and can direct you to their branch offices:

- **Coldwell Banker–Jon Douglas Company**, 800-733-1380, www.coldwellbanker.com
- **Century 21**, 800-346-9118, www.c21allproperties.com
- **Dilbeck**, 626-584-0101, www.dilbeck.com; in Pasadena call Jeff Huang, 626-665-8860, www.jeffhuanghomes.com
- **Prudential California Realty**, 818-889-1431, www.prucalhomes.com
- **Ramsey-Shilling Associates**, 818-763-5162, www.ramseyshilling.com
- **Re/Max**, 800-603-7828, www.remax.com

Of a concern to some, many real estate brokers alternate between representing a buyer or seller at different times. For those looking for an agent that specializes in representing only buyers, seek out an accredited Buyer's Representative via the **Real Estate Buyer's Agent Council** of the National Association of Realtors, 800-648-6224, www.rebac.net, or contact **Buyers Broker**, 888-302-0001, www.homesoflosangelescounty.com and www.homesoforangecounty.com.

Some of the larger real estate agencies offer **concierge** or **relocation services**. Expect an organized network of prescreened local vendors to provide every service a homebuyer could need, from locksmiths to maid service to upholstery cleaning, often offered at a discount. Inquire with your realtor to see if they offer this service.

THE BUYING PROCESS

PRE-QUALIFICATION/PRE-APPROVAL

The first thing you need to consider when buying a house is how much you can spend. Start with your gross monthly income, then tally up your monthly debt load: credit cards, car loans, personal debt, child support, alimony, etc. For revolving debt (like credit card debt), use your minimum monthly payment for the calculation. For the purposes of this calculation, ignore any debts you expect to have paid off entirely within six months' time. As a rule, your monthly housing costs shouldn't exceed 28% of your total monthly income, and your debt load shouldn't exceed 36% of it. That said, these days lenders might tailor the 28/36 ratio depending on your situation (assets, liability, job, credit history). When calculating your budget, don't forget to factor in closing costs, which include insurance, appraisals, attorney's fees, transfer taxes, and loan fees. Fees normally range from 3% to 7% of the purchase price. Likewise, when figuring out your budget, be sure to factor in the additional monthly outgoes of homeowner's insurance, property taxes (tax deductible), utilities, condo fees, improvements, and maintenance.

Lenders suggest that you "pre-qualify" or, better still, get "pre-approved" for a loan. **Pre-qualification** is, in essence, an educated guess as to what you'll be able to afford for a loan. To be **pre-approved**, your loan officer will review your financial situation (by running a credit check, going over your proof of employment, savings, etc.) and then you will be given a letter documenting that the bank is willing to lend you a particular amount based on your proven financial situation. Pre-approval is a bit more labor-intensive for you and the lender, but sellers and real estate agents will take you more seriously if you show up with a pre-approval letter in hand.

For either pre-qualification or pre-approval of a loan, go to your lender with documentation of your financial history and a list of your debt load, and contact the three major credit bureaus (listed below) beforehand to make sure your credit history is accurate. You will need to provide your name, address, previous address, and social security number with your request. Contact each company for specific instructions, or visit **www.annualcreditreport.com** for online access to all three. A credit report will list your credit activity for the past seven years, including your highest balance, current balance, and promptness or tardiness of payments. After seven years, the slate is wiped clean for any credit transgressions, except in the case of bankruptcy and foreclosure, which will appear on your record for 10 years. If you find your credit score is not as good as it could be, keep in mind that lenders are more concerned with your most recent track record than how you behaved seven years ago. It's best to try to pay all your bills in full and on time for at least a year before you apply for a loan, and be aware that even if you pay your bills on time, having too much credit can be a problem. Even if your credit report isn't stellar, you most likely can still get a loan, though your rates (interest and fees) may be higher. A substantial down payment can counteract credit flaws as well.

The major **credit bureaus** are:

- **Experian**, P.O. Box 2104, Allen, TX 75002-2104, 888-397-3742
- **TransUnion**, P.O. Box 390, Springfield, PA 19064-0390, 800-916-8800
- **Equifax**, P.O. Box 105873, Atlanta, GA 30348, 800-685-1111

It's best to get a copy of your credit report from each bureau, as each report may be different. Your credit report will have a FICO (Fair Isaac and Company). Typically, lenders will give a standard loan for scores of 650+; if your score is lower, you'll probably get a sub-prime loan (from a non-major lender and with a higher interest rate). If you discover any inaccuracies on your credit report, you should contact the service immediately and request that it be corrected. By law, credit bureaus must respond to your request within 30 days. If you have questions about your credit record, call Fannie Mae's non-profit credit counseling service at 800-732-6643 before you apply for a mortgage. Be aware that too many credit record inquiries can lower your credit status.

FINANCING

Most buyers need a **mortgage** to pay for a house. A typical house mortgage is for either 15 or 30 years and consists of four parts, commonly referred to as "PITI" (principal, interest, taxes, and insurance). The **principal** is the flat sum of money that you borrowed from the lender to pay for the property. The larger the down payment, the less you will need to borrow to meet the total purchase price of your home. The lender charges **interest**, a percentage of the principal, as repayment for the use of the money that you've borrowed. (Points, each one equal to 1% of the amount you borrow for your mortgage, might also contribute to the interest.) Your community charges you **taxes** based on a percentage of your property value, which you'll continue paying even after your mortgage is paid off. The final component of PITI is house **insurance** against calamities such as fire, theft, and natural disasters. In many cases, people deposit funds into an escrow or trust account to cover insurance and taxes. Within three business days of applying for your loan, your lender must give you a "good faith estimate" of how much your closing costs will be.

There are many loan programs around. Search the internet, newspapers, and books, and speak with financial planners, real estate agents, and mortgage brokers to find out what's available. Direct lenders (banks) and mortgage brokers are the most common places to go for a loan. A **direct lender** is an institution with a finite number of in-house loans, whose terms and conditions are controlled by the lender. A **mortgage broker**, on the other hand, is a middleman who shops around to various lenders and loan programs to find what's best for your needs. Because brokers shop around for the best interest rates, it's often worth paying their fee. Most major lenders and brokers have their own web sites. For a list of local banks, look in the **Money Matters** chapter.

When educating yourself about mortgages, be sure to take the time to research institutions' loan costs and restrictions: interest rates, broker fees, points, prepayment penalties, loan term, application fees, credit report fees, and cost of appraisals. The Bank Rate Monitor, www.bankrate. com, offers pages of information on mortgages and interest rates at over 2,000 banks. It may pay to shop around.

DOWN PAYMENT

Down payments vary. Some lenders offer programs that require as little as 5% down or even zero down. An example of these programs is Fannie Mae's three/two loan program, which gives a first-time buyer 95% of the price of a home. The buyer is required to supply 3% of the down payment; the other 2% can be a gift from family, a government program, or a nonprofit agency. Programs requiring no down payment may sound like a dream come true, but the interest will be about 2% higher than what you'd pay at 20% down. The best interest rate can be obtained with at least 20% down. (A down payment of less than 20% will require private mortgage insurance.) If you are a first-time buyer, which is defined as someone who hasn't owned property within the past three years, you may qualify for state-backed programs that feature lower down payment requirements and below-market interest rates.

MAKING AN OFFER

The longer a home has been on the market, the more likely you can negotiate a discount on the purchase price. The most anxious sellers are those who have already purchased another home. Given LA's current housing market, it is the rare house that lingers on the market. Typically, houses in LA County are sold within a few days of being listed. Buyers need to be prepared to make an offer and a deposit (typically 3% of the home's asking price) immediately upon viewing a house—or risk missing out. When making the offer, minimally, you should protect yourself by making your purchase offer contingent on financing (if applicable) and on the approval of a professional inspector, keeping in mind that sellers and their agents dislike contingencies and in a competitive market, a contingency-free offer is the most attractive bid to the seller. Offers, which should be submitted in writing to the seller, may mention the following:

- Address and legal description of the property
- Price you will pay for the home
- Terms (how you will pay)
- Seller's promise to provide clear title
- Target date for closing (when the property is actually transferred to you, and the funds are transferred to the seller)
- Down payment accompanying the offer—how much and in what form
- Plan for prorating utilities, taxes, etc., between buyer and seller
- Provisions: who will pay what extra costs (e.g., insurance, survey)
- Type of deed
- Contingencies

If you want your offer to be seriously considered, particularly in a tight market, be sure to offer a fair market price, include a statement of the source of your down payment, your pre-approval letter, and even a note to the seller about why/how much you want the house. Buyers offering cash, or with a pre-approval in hand, will be more attractive to the seller, and conversely, an offer made contingent upon the sale of the buyer's home will not be appealing.

CONTINGENCIES, PURCHASE AND SALE (P&S) AGREEMENT

Common **contingencies** include an appraisal of the house that is satisfactory to the bank, financing (in cases where the buyer has not been pre-approved), a free and clear title, selling a current residence, and receiving a satisfactory inspection report of the property. Some buyers put into their offer "on terms to be approved by the buyer's attorney." In the competitive Los Angeles housing market, making the offer is the most important part of the buying process, not the closing. The closing is just signing the paperwork that finalizes what you agreed to in your offer. If the seller agrees to your written offer, it becomes a binding sales contract, called a **purchase and sale (P&S) agreement**. If you default on this contract, you can lose your deposit money. If the seller defaults, you can sue him to force the sale to which he agreed in writing.

That said, after you make an offer, the buyer will accept it, reject it, or make a counter offer; at which point you may accept, reject, or change the counter offer, and so on. When both parties agree, it becomes a binding purchase agreement.

INSPECTION

As mentioned above, **inspections** are crucial, particularly for older homes. Because many Los Angeles residences were built decades ago, hiring an inspector to perform a thorough check of the property you are considering is recommended. You can ask your realtor for a reference or try one of the following:

- **California Real Estate Inspection Association** certified inspector, 800-848-7342, www.creia.org
- **American Society of Home Inspectors**, 800-743-2744, www. ashi.com
- **National Association of Certified Home Inspectors**, www.nachi.org

All of the above should be able to make referrals for more specialized testing of home environmental toxins such as mold, lead, asbestos, radon and the like, which are *not* covered in a standard home inspection.

CLOSING

Assuming the inspection goes well and/or all issues are resolved to your satisfaction, it is time for closing. At the closing, also known as "settlement" or "escrow," costs, such as transfer taxes, closing costs, legal fees, and adjustments are paid. (Closing costs for a $400,000 home will run about $10,000.) This is a brief process in which the title to the property is transferred from seller to buyer; the seller gets his payment and you get the keys, and the closing agent officially records your loan.

FIRST-TIME HOMEBUYERS

Buying a home for the first time can be a financially overwhelming experience. **First-time** buyers can turn to home buying assistance programs through local **Neighborhood Housing Services**:

- **Inglewood**, 310-674-3756, http://homeownershipcenter.com
- **LA County**, 888-895-2647, www.lanhs.org
- **Pasadena**, 626-744-8316, www.ci.pasadena.ca.us/housing

- **San Fernando Valley Homeownership Center**, 818-834-7858, www. lanhs.org
- **South Bay Homeownership Center**, 310-514-9444, http://home ownershipcenter.com

Services include down payment and closing-cost assistance, arranging home-rehabilitation loans, and home-maintenance classes.

Another source of assistance is the **LA County Housing Department's Home Ownership Assistance Program**, designed specifically to help low- to moderate-income households and first-time homebuyers purchase a home. Call 323-890-7281 or visit the county's web site, www. lacdc.org/programs/homebuyer/index.shtm for more information. The **California Association of Realtors'** web site, www.car.org, also lists homebuyer assistance programs.

ONLINE RESOURCES—HOUSE HUNTING

Web sites for would-be homeowners include the following:
- **FISBO Registry for Homebuyers**, www.fisbos.com
- **Homebuilder.com**, www.homebuilder.com; comprehensive site where you can find apartments, homes, and roommates; sales and rentals.
- **HomeGain**, www.homegain.com
- **Homes.com**, www.homes.com
- **Homestore**, www.homestore.com
- **MSN House and Home**, http://houseandhome.msn.com
- **The National Association of Realtors**, www.realtor.com
- **Real Estate Book**, http://realestate.citysearch.com
- **ZipRealty**, www.ziprealty.com, a national real estate site.

If you want to investigate homes **for sale by owner**, try:
- **For Sale By Owner**: www.4salebyowner.com
- **IsoldMyHouse.com**: www.isoldmyhouse.com
- **For Sale By Owner Network**: www.fsbonetwork.com
- **HomesByOwner.com**: www.homesbyowner.com

ONLINE RESOURCES—MORTGAGES

In addition to the information included in the text of this chapter, the following sites might help you on your quest to finance a home:

- **Bankrate.com**, www.bankrate.com; everything about mortgages and lending.

- **Countrywide Financial**, www.countrywide.com; nationwide mortgage rates, credit evaluations, etc.
- **Dirs.com**, www.dirs.com; links and information on mortgages and home equity loans.
- **Fannie Mae**, www.fanniemae.com; loans for real estate purchases; dedicated to helping Americans achieve the dream of homeownership.
- **Freddie Mac**, www.freddiemac.com; provides information on low-cost loans, a home inspection kit, and tips to help avoid unfair lending practices.
- **Interest.com**, www.interest.com; shop for mortgages and rates.
- *Los Angeles Times*, http://latimes.interest.com/calculators.asp; link to research daily mortgage rates. Also offers a mortgage calculator.
- **The Mortgage Professor**, www.mtgprofessor.com; demystifies and clarifies the confusing and often expensive world of mortgage brokers, helpfully written by an emeritus Wharton professor who answers questions(!), useful calculators.
- **Owners.com**, www.owners.com; all things mortgage and home sale related.
- **Quicken Home**, www.quickenloans.com

ADDITIONAL RESOURCES—BUYING A HOME

Finally, aside from the selection of books you can pick up at your local bookstore or at an online bookseller, consider the following resources and publications:

- *100 Questions Every First Time Homebuyer Should Ask: With Answers from Top Brokers from Around the Country*, 2nd edition (Times Books) by Ilyce R.Glink
- *The 106 Common Mistakes Homebuyers Make (and How to Avoid Them)*, 3rd edition (Wiley) by Gary W. Eldred
- *The Co-Op Bible: Everything You Need to Know About Co-Ops and Condos: Getting In, Staying In, Surviving, Thriving* (Griffin Trade Paperback) by Sylvia Shapiro
- ***Opening the Door to a Home of Your Own***: a pamphlet by Fannie Mae for first time homebuyers. Call 800-834-3377 for a copy.
- **Score Card**; if you're particularly concerned about environmental toxins at your new property, check out www.scorecard.org, a site sponsored by the Environmental Defense Fund.
- *Your New House: the Alert Consumer's Guide to Buying and Building a Quality New Home* (Windsor Peak Press) by Alan and Denise Fields

HAVING FOUND AND SECURED A PLACE TO LIVE, YOU HAVE NOW the task of getting your stuff here and perhaps finding storage. The how-tos follow, as well as a section detailing which agency to contact regarding consumer complaints against moving companies, information about moving with children, and specifics regarding tax-deductible moving expenses.

TRUCK RENTALS

First determine if you are going to move it yourself or hire someone else to do it for you. If you prefer doing it all yourself, you can rent a vehicle, load it up, and hit the road. Look in the Yellow Pages under "Truck Rental" and call around and compare; also ask about any specials. Below is a list of four national truck rental companies and their toll-free numbers and web sites. For the best information, you should call a local office. Note: most truck rental companies now offer "one-way" rentals as well as packing accessories and storage facilities. Of course, these extras are not free. If you're cost conscious you may want to scavenge boxes in advance of your move or buy some directly from a box company. (Those moving locally should check Smart and Final stores, which frequently offer empty boxes in a bin by the entrance of the store.)

If you're planning to move during the peak moving months (May through September), call well in advance, at least a month ahead of when you think you'll need the vehicle. Remember that Saturday is a popular moving day; you may be able to get cheaper rates if you book a different day.

Once you're on the road, keep in mind that your rental truck may be a tempting target for thieves. If you must park it overnight or for an extended period (more than a couple of hours), try to find a safe place, preferably somewhere well-lit and easily observable by you, and do your best not to leave anything of particular value in the cab. Make sure you lock the back door and, if possible, use a steering wheel lock or other easy-to-purchase safety device.

Four national self-moving companies to consider:

- **Budget**, 800-428-7825, www.budget.com
- **Penske**, 800-222-0277, www.penske.com
- **Ryder**, 800-297-9337, www.ryder.com (now a Budget company, still operating under the Ryder name)
- **U-haul**, 800-468-4285, www.uhaul.com

A little wary of driving the truck yourself? Commercial freight carriers, such as **ABF U–Pack**, 800-355-1696, www.upack.com, offer an in-between service; they deliver a 28-foot trailer to your home, you pack and load as much of it as you need, and they drive the vehicle to your destination (often with some other freight filling the remaining space). However, if you have to share truck space with another customer you may arrive far ahead of your boxes—and bed. Try to estimate your needs beforehand and ask for your load's expected arrival date. You can get an online estimate from some shippers, so you can compare rates.

If you aren't moving an entire house and can't estimate how much truck space you will need, keep in mind this general guideline: two to three furnished rooms equal a 15-foot truck; four to five rooms, a 20-foot truck.

MOVERS

INTERSTATE

First, the good news: Moving can be affordable and problem-free. The bad news: If you're hiring a mover, the chances of it being so are much less.

Probably the best way to find a mover is by **personal recommendation**. Absent a friend or relative who can recommend a trusted moving company, you can turn to what surveys show is the most popular method of finding a mover: the **Yellow Pages**. Then there's the **internet**: just type in "movers" on a search engine and you'll be directed to hundreds of more or less helpful moving-related sites.

In the past, *Consumer Reports*, www.consumerreports.org, has published useful information on moving. You might ask a local realtor, who may be able to steer you towards a good mover, or at least tell you which ones to avoid. Members of the American Automobile Association have a valuable resource at hand in **AAA's Consumer Relocation Services**, which will assign the member a personal consultant to handle every detail of the move free of charge and which offers discounts arranged with premier moving companies. Call 800-839-MOVE, www.aaa.com.

But beware! Since 1995, when the federal government eliminated the Interstate Commerce Commission, the interstate moving business has degenerated into a wild and mostly unregulated industry with thousands of unhappy, ripped-off customers annually. (There are so many reports of unscrupulous carriers that we no longer list movers in this book.) Since states do not have the authority to regulate interstate movers and the federal government has been slow to respond, you are pretty much on your own when it comes to finding an honest, hassle-free mover. That's why we can't emphasize enough the importance of carefully researching and choosing who will move you.

To aid your search for an **interstate mover**, we offer a few general recommendations.

First get the names of a half-dozen movers and check to make sure they are licensed by the US **Department of Transportation's Federal Motor Carrier Safety Administration (FMCSA)**. With the movers' Motor Carrier (MC) numbers in hand, call 888-368-7238 or 202-358-7000 (offers the option of speaking to an agent) or go online to www.fmcsa. dot.gov, to see if the carriers are licensed and insured. If the companies you're considering are federally licensed, your next step should be to check with the **Better Business Bureau**, www.bbb.org, in the state where the moving companies are licensed as well as with the states' consumer protection boards (in Los Angeles call 800-952-5210 or go to www.dca.ca.gov), or attorney generals. Also check FMCSA's **Household Goods Consumer Complaint** web site, www.1-888-dot-saft.com, where they maintain complaints that have been filed on interstate movers. Assuming there is no negative information, you can move on to the next step: asking for references. Particularly important are references from customers who did moves similar to yours. If a moving company is unable or unwilling to provide references, eliminate it from your list. Unscrupulous movers have even been known to give phony references who will falsely sing the mover's praises—so talk to more than one reference and ask questions. If something feels fishy, it probably is. One way to learn more about a prospective mover: Ask them if they have a local office (they should) and then walk in and check it out.

Once you have at least three movers you feel reasonably comfortable with, it's time to ask for price quotes (always free). Best is a binding "not-to-exceed" quote, of course in writing. This will require an on-site visual inspection of what you are shipping. If you have *any* doubts about a prospective moving company, drop it from your list before you invite a stranger into your home to catalog your belongings.

Recent regulations by FMCSA require movers to supply five documents to consumers before executing a contract. These include two booklets: *Important Information for Persons Moving Household Goods (within California)*, which must be provided at the first-person contact between the consumer and the mover, and *Your Rights and Responsibilities When You Move*, is a concise and accurate written estimate of charges; a summary of the mover's arbitration program; the mover's customer complaint and inquiry handling procedure; and the mover's tariff containing rates, rules, regulations, classifications, etc. For more about FMCSA's role in handling household goods, you can go to its consumer page at www.fmcsa.dot.gov/factsfigs/moving.htm.

ADDITIONAL MOVING RECOMMENDATIONS

- If someone recommends a mover to you, get names (the salesperson or estimator, the drivers, the loaders). To paraphrase the NRA, moving companies don't move people, people do. Likewise, if someone tells you they had a bad moving experience, note the name of the company and try to avoid it.
- Remember that price, while important, isn't everything, especially when you're entrusting all of your worldly possessions to strangers.
- Legitimate movers charge by the hour (local moves, under 100 miles), and by weight/mileage (for long-distance moves). Be wary if the mover wants to charge by cubic foot.
- Ask about the other end—subcontracting increases the chances that something could go wrong.
- In general, ask questions, and if you're concerned about something, ask for an explanation in writing. If you change your mind about a moving company after you've signed on the dotted line, write a letter explaining that you've changed your mind and that you won't be using its services. Better safe than sorry.
- Ask about insurance; the "basic" 60 cents per pound industry standard coverage is not enough. If you have homeowner's or renter's insurance, check to see if it will cover your belongings during transit. If not, ask your insurer if you can add that coverage for your move. Otherwise, consider purchasing "full replacement" or "full value" coverage from the carrier for the estimated value of your shipment. Though it's the most expensive type of coverage offered, it's probably worth it. Trucks get into accidents, they catch fire, they get stolen—if such insurance seems pricey to you, ask about a $250 or $500 deductible. This can reduce your cost substantially while still giving you much better protection in case of a catastrophic loss.
- Whatever you do, do not mislead a salesperson/estimator about how much and what you are moving. And make sure you tell prospective movers about how far they'll have to transport your stuff to and from the truck as well as any stairs, driveways, obstacles or difficult vegeta-

tion, long paths or sidewalks, etc. The clearer you are with your mover, the better he or she will be able to serve you.

- Think about packing. If you plan to pack yourself, you can save some money, but if something is damaged because of your packing, you may not be able to file a claim for it. On the other hand, if you hire the mover to do the packing, they may not treat your belongings as well as you will. They will certainly do it faster, that's for sure. Depending on the size of your move and whether or not you are packing yourself, you may need a lot of boxes, tape, and packing material. Mover boxes, while not cheap, are usually sturdy and the right size. Sometimes a mover will give a customer free used boxes. It doesn't hurt to ask. Also, *don't* wait to pack until the last minute. If you're doing the packing, give yourself at least a week to do the job; two or more is better. Be sure to ask the mover about any weight or size restrictions on boxes.

- You should transport all irreplaceable items such as jewelry, photographs, or key work documents personally. Do not put them in the moving van! For less precious items that you do not want to put in the moving truck, consider sending them via the US Postal Service or by UPS.

- Ask your mover what is not permitted in the truck: usually anything flammable or combustible, as well as certain types of valuables.

- Although movers will put numbered labels on your possessions, you should make a numbered list of every box and item that is going in the truck. Detail box contents and photograph anything of particular value. Once the truck arrives on the other end, you can check off every piece and know for sure what did (or did not) make it. In case of claims, this list can be invaluable. Even after the move, keep the list; it can be surprisingly useful.

- Movers are required to issue you a "bill of lading"; do not hire a mover who does not use them.

- Consider keeping a log of every expense you incur for your move, i.e., phone calls, trips to LA, etc. In many instances, the IRS allows you to claim these types of expenses on your income taxes. (See **Taxes** below.)

- Be aware that during the busy season (May through September), demand can exceed supply and moving may be more difficult and more expensive than during the rest of the year. If you must relocate during the peak moving months, call and book service well in advance of when you plan on moving. A month at least. If you can reserve service way in advance, say four to six months early, you may be able to lock in a lower winter rate for your summer move.

- Listen to what the movers say; they are professionals and can give you expert advice about packing and preparing. Also, be ready for the truck on both ends—don't make them wait. Not only will it irritate your movers, but it may cost you. Understand, too, that things can happen on the road that are beyond a carrier's control (weather, accidents, etc.) and your belongings may not get to you at the time or on the day promised.

- Treat your movers well, especially the ones loading your stuff on and off the truck. Offer to buy them lunch, and tip them if they do a good job.
- Before moving pets, attach a tag to your pet's collar with your new address and phone number in case your furry friend accidentally wanders off in the confusion of moving. Your pet should travel with you and you should never plan on moving a pet inside a moving van.
- Be prepared to pay the full moving bill upon delivery. Cash or bank/cashier's check may be required. Some carriers will take VISA and MasterCard but it is a good idea to get it in writing that you will be permitted to pay with a credit card since the delivering driver may not be aware of this and may demand cash. Unless you routinely keep thousands in greenbacks on you, you could have a problem getting your stuff off the truck.

INTRASTATE AND LOCAL MOVERS

The **California Public Utilities Commission (CPUC)**, www.cpuc. ca.gov, regulates the licensing, rates, and rules of the Household Goods moving industry in California. All companies involved in the moving business must be insured and hold a license that permits them to provide moving services within or from/to California. To verify certification of your chosen mover, call the CPUC at 800-877-8867 or the **California Moving and Storage Association (CMSA)** at 800-672-1415 and have the mover's CAL T number (listed on the mover's literature) ready. The CMSA, www.thecmsa.org, is a non-profit trade organization that offers references to legitimate movers and provides information to help consumers avoid "bandit movers" (movers that engage in unlawful practices and/or bully the customer into paying outrageous prices once the move has started). According to the CMSA, 80% of the calls to them involve complaints about bandit movers. They recommend against booking online or over the phone without investigating the company's physical address first and confirming it's licensed (with a CAL T number) with the CPUC. For moves within California, the CPUC regulations require all movers to provide each client with a written "not to exceed price" before the move commences. This price should be clearly disclosed on your Agreement for Service form. The mover will have you sign this form before the move begins.

CONSUMER COMPLAINTS—MOVERS

If a **move goes badly** and you blame the moving company, you should first file a written claim with the mover for loss or damage. If this doesn't work and it's an **intrastate move**, call 800-366-4782 to file a complaint with the CPUC. If the mover is a CMSA member, the CMSA will intervene on the consumer's behalf if there is a problem.

If your grievance is with an **interstate carrier**, your choices are limited. Interstate moves are regulated by the Federal Motor Carriers Safety Administration (FMCSA), 888-368-7238, www.fmcsa.dot.gov, an agency under the Department of Transportation, with whom you can file a complaint against a carrier. While its role in the regulation of interstate carriers historically has been concerned with safety issues rather than consumer issues, in response to the upsurge in unscrupulous movers and unhappy consumers, it has issued a recent set of rules "specifying how interstate household goods (HHG) carriers (movers) and brokers must assist their individual customers shipping household goods." According to its consumer page, carriers in violation of said rules can be fined, and repeat offenders may be barred from doing business. In terms of loss however, "FMCSA does not have statutory authority to resolve loss and damage of consumer complaints, settle disputes against a mover, or obtain reimbursement for consumers seeking payment for specific charges. Consumers are responsible for resolving disputes involving these household goods matters." It is not able to represent you in an arbitration dispute to recover damages for lost or destroyed property, nor enforce a court judgment. If you have a grievance, your best bet is to file a complaint against a mover with FMCSA and with the Better Business Bureau, www.bbb.org, in the state where the moving company is licensed, as well as with that state's attorney general or consumer protection office. To seek redress, hire an attorney.

STORAGE WAREHOUSES

Storage facilities may be required when you have to ship your furniture without an apartment to receive it or if your apartment is too small for all your belongings. The CPUC regulates short-term storage (under 90 days), but not long-term or self-storage. If your mover maintains storage warehouse facilities in the city, as many do, you'll probably want to store with them. Some even offer one month's free storage. Look in the Yellow Pages under "Storage," and shop around for the best and most convenient deal. Below, a couple major moving/storage companies. Listing here does *not* imply endorsement by First Books.

- **Door to Door Storage**, 888-366-7222, www.doortodoor.com, has warehousing for cargo containers, which it delivers to you for packing, and then its trucks transport the container back to its facilities (several throughout Los Angeles).
- **Public Storage**, 800-447-8673, www.publicstorage.com, offers locations throughout the county for self-service storage, pick-up service and storage, full-service moving, and/or truck rentals.

SELF-STORAGE

The ability to rent anything from 5' x 5' rooms to storage rooms large enough to accommodate a car is a great boon to urban dwellers. Collectors, people with old clothes they can't bear to give away, and those with possessions that won't fit in a sublet or shared apartment all find mini-warehouses a solution to too-small living spaces.

Rates for space in Los Angeles self-storage facilities are competitive: Expect to pay at least $80 a month for a 5' x 5' (25 sq ft), $110 a month for a 5' x 10' space (50 sq ft), and so on. Some offer free pick-up, otherwise you or your mover delivers the goods. If you're looking for lower rates, inquire with the storage facility for move-in specials or other locations.

As you shop around, you may want to check the facility for cleanliness and security. Does the building have sprinklers in case of fire? Does it have carts and hand trucks for moving in and out? Does it bill monthly, or will it automatically charge the bill to your credit card? Access should be 24-hour or nearly so, and some are air conditioned, an asset if you plan to visit your locker in the summer. Is the rental month to month or is there a minimum lease?

Finally, a word of warning: Unless you no longer want your stored belongings, pay your storage bill and pay it on time. Storage companies may auction the contents of delinquent customers' lockers.

Here are a few area self-storage companies. For more options, check the Yellow Pages under "Storage."

- **Price Self Storage**, www.priceselfstorage.com, two locations in West LA: 3430 South La Brea Avenue, 323-299-2699 or 10151 National Blvd., 310-837-7700; with individually alarmed units that range in size from 5' x 5' to 12' x 30'. It also offers truck and driver services.
- **Extra Space Storage**, 323-464-4780, www.extraspace.com, has facilities in Hollywood, Silverlake, and Culver City.
- **EZ Storage**, 877-769-9720; a variety of locations in Los Angeles including Santa Monica, Marina del Rey, Burbank, Van Nuys, Encino, Sherman Oaks, Northridge, also offers truck rentals at some locations.

- **Mobile Mini, Inc.**, 800-234-5669, www.mobileminiinc.com; delivers storage containers from 5' x 8' to 40' x 10' that you fill and it will transport to a location you specify or to its own secured facilities.
- **Public Storage**, 800-447-8673, www.publicstorage.com; also offers pick-up and delivery services at certain locations: 877-777-4258, www.pspickup.com.
- **Los Angeles Security Storage**, 323-469-1402, 6372 Santa Monica Blvd., LA; has been in business at this location since 1923.
- **U-Haul Self-Storage** has seven warehouses in Los Angeles, Glendale, and Pasadena, 800-GO-U-HAUL, www.uhaul.com. Prices for rooms vary by their location and availability; a 5' x 5' goes for approximately $80 and 8' x 10' for $110.

CHILDREN AND MOVING

Studies show that moving, especially frequent moving, can be hard on children. According to an American Medical Association study, children who move often are more likely to suffer from such problems as depression, low self-esteem, and aggression. Often their academic performance suffers as well. Aside from not moving more than is necessary, there are a few things you can do to help your children through this stressful time:

- Talk about the move with your kids. Be honest but positive. Listen to their concerns. To the extent possible, involve them in the process.
- Make sure children have their favorite possessions with them on the trip; don't pack "blankey" in the moving van.
- Make sure you have some social life planned on the other end. Your children may feel lonely in your new home, and such activities can ease the transition. If you move during the summer you might find a local camp (check with the YWCA or YMCA) at which they can sign up for a couple of weeks in August to make new friends.
- Keep in touch with family and loved ones as much as possible. Photos and phone calls are important ways of maintaining links to the important people you have left behind.
- If your children are school age, take the time to involve yourself in their new school and in their academic life. Don't let them fall through the cracks.
- Try to schedule a move during the summer so they can start the new school year at the beginning of the term.
- If possible, spend some time in the area prior to the move doing fun things in the area to which you are moving, such visiting a local playground or playing ball in a local park or checking out the neighborhood stores with teenagers. With any luck they will meet some other kids their own age.

For children ages 6-11, ***The Moving Book: A Kids' Survival Guide*** by Gabriel Davis is a wonderful gift. For general guidance, read ***Smart Moves: Your Guide Through the Emotional Maze of Relocation*** by Nadia Jensen, Audrey McCollum, and Stuart Copans.

TAXES AND MOVING

If your move is work-related, some or all of your moving expenses may be tax-deductible—so you may want to keep those receipts. Though eligibility varies, depending, for example, on whether you have a job or are self-employed, generally, the cost of moving yourself, your family, and your belongings is tax deductible, even if you don't itemize. The criteria: In order to take the deduction your move must be employment-related, your new job must be more than 50 miles away from your current residence, and you must be here for at least 39 weeks during the first 12 months after your arrival. If you take the deduction and then fail to meet the requirements, you will have to pay the IRS back, unless you were laid off through no fault of your own or transferred again by your employer. It's probably a good idea to consult a tax expert regarding IRS rules related to moving. However, if you're a confident soul, get a copy of IRS Form 3903 (www.irs.gov) and do it yourself!

ADDITIONAL RELOCATION AND MOVING INFORMATION

- **www.firstbooks.com**, relocation resources and information on moving to Atlanta, Boston, Chicago, Minneapolis-St. Paul, New York, San Francisco, Seattle, Washington, D.C., as well as London, England. Also publisher of the *Newcomer's Handbook® for Moving to and Living in the USA*, *The Moving Book: A Kids' Survival Guide*, and *The Pet-Moving Handbook*.
- **BestPlaces**, www.bestplaces.net; compares quality-of-life and cost-of-living data of US cities.
- **DataMasters**, www.datamasters.com; for basic community statistics by zip code
- ***How to Move Handbook*** by Clyde and Shari Steiner, an excellent general guidebook
- **http://houseandhome.msn.com**; online quotes
- **The Riley Guide**, www.rileyguide.com/relocate.html; online moving and relocation clearinghouse. Lists moving and relocation guides and web sites, offers links to sites that cover cost of living/demographics as well as real estate links and school and health care directories.
- **www.allamericanmovers.com**, 800-989-6683; online quotes

- **www.american-car-transport.com**; if you need help moving your car
- **www.erc.org**; the Employee Relocation Council, a professional organization, offers members specialized reports on the relocation and moving industries
- **www.homestore.com**; relocation resources, including a handy salary calculator that will compare the cost of living in US cities
- **www.usps.com**; relocation information from the United States Postal Service

AFTER FINDING YOUR NEW PLACE OF RESIDENCE, THE NEWCOMER'S first order of business probably will be opening a bank account. The following information about personal savings, checking accounts, and credit unions should make the task less daunting. Most major national and some international financial institutions have branches in Los Angeles, so shop around for what suits your needs. A section on credit cards and credit reports follows, and, for your edification come April 15, we've included information about federal and state income tax procedures, as well as details for those wanting to start or move a business.

BANKING

Bank of America, 800-792-0808, www.bankamerica.com, **California National Bank**, 800-434-3354, www.calnationalbank.com, and **Wells Fargo**, 800-869-3557, www.wellsfargo.com, are the three largest banks on the West Coast, and the numerous branches each bank offers can be convenient. In addition to direct deposit, ATM service, and computerized telephone systems for checking your balance and tracking transactions, most banks offer online banking.

Additional banks serving LA and its environs include (check the Yellow Pages for a complete listing):
- **Santa Monica Bank**, 310-394-9611
- **First Bank of Beverly Hills**, 888-359-4605, www.fbbh.com
- **East West Bank**, 888-895-5650, www.eastwestbank.com
- **Union Bank of California**, 800-238-4486, www.uboc.com
- **Washington Mutual**, 800-756-8000, www.washingtonmutual.com
- **CitiBank**, 800-374-9700, www.citibank.com
- **Ing Direct**, 877-469-0232, www.ingdirect.com
- **Bank of the West**, 800-488-2265, www.bankofthewest.com

To compete with the giants some of the smaller banks offer no or fewer fees, free checking, and other customer perks. The primary trade-offs: fewer branches, a limited number of ATMs, and your chosen bank may end up merging with the very bank you were trying to avoid.

CREDIT UNIONS

According to the **National Credit Union Administration (NCUA)**, "A federal credit union is a nonprofit, cooperative financial institution owned and run by its members." Organized to serve and democratically controlled, credit unions provide their members with a safe place to save and borrow at reasonable rates. Most who qualify for membership to a credit union elect to join. Credit unions offer nearly the same services as regular banks, but they typically offer lower fees and higher interest rates. Perks, such as discount coupons for movies, theme parks, and other entertainment options, are sometimes part of the package as well. Membership generally is limited to a specific group or employee association; the **LA Federal Credit Union**, 818-242-8640, for example, is limited to Los Angeles city employees and their families.

For a complete list of local credit unions or for more information about them, you can visit the **National Association of Credit Union Service Organizations**, www.nacuso.org, or the **NCUA**, http://ncua.gov.

CHECKING AND SAVINGS ACCOUNTS

Many establishments will not take your check unless it is local and imprinted with your name, address, and telephone number. Needless to say, it helps to get your checking (and savings) accounts set up as soon as possible. If you have moved to Los Angeles from another US city and previously banked with a large national institution with offices in LA, chances are you can simply transfer your account. Otherwise, a minimum deposit (amounts vary by bank) is required to open an account, and you'll need to bring a photo ID and your new address. For fee-free checking, you may need to maintain a certain monthly balance (fee-free accounts typically are not interest-bearing accounts). Some opt to connect checking with savings for overdraft protection. Other products and services to inquire about: online or telephone banking, certificates of deposit, safe deposit boxes, hours, and fees. You can expect a debit card to be issued with your checking account.

ONLINE BANKING

Today, it is rare when a bank does not offer online banking. Generally this includes balance and other account information inquiries, making transfers, paying bills, and even applying for loans. Security should be a chief concern when accessing your private financial information over the internet. While banks should encrypt your personal information and password, the user should also take standard precautions as well. Don't share your password with anyone, and change it often; don't send confidential information through e-mail or over unsecured web space; and restrict your banking interactions to private computers—not a work computer with a shared network or at an internet café.

Online access services and fees vary from bank to bank, so check with individual institutions for information. Sometimes access is directly through the bank's web site; sometimes you'll first need to download a program or use specialized banking software.

CONSUMER COMPLAINTS—BANKING

Federal and state government regulates bank policies on discrimination, credit, anti-redlining, truth-in-lending, etc. If you have a problem with your financial institution, you should first attempt to resolve the issue directly with the bank. Should you need to **file a formal complaint**, you can do so through the Board of Governors of the **Federal Reserve System, Division of Consumer and Community Affairs**. For specifics, call 202-452-3693 or go to www.federalreserve.gov/pubs/complaints. You can also pursue the issue with the following agencies:

- Nationally chartered commercial banks go through the **US Comptroller of the Currency**, Customer Assistance Group, 1301 McKinney Street, Suite 3710, Houston, TX 77010; 800-613-6743; www.occ.treas.gov.
- **US Office of Thrift Supervision**, 1700 G Street NW, Washington, D.C. 20552, 202-906-6000, www.ots.treas.gov; for thrift institutions insured by the Savings Association Insurance Fund and/or federally chartered (i.e., members of the Federal Home Loan Bank System).
- Federally chartered credit unions; state chartered credit unions with federal insurance: **National Credit Union Administration**, 9 Washington Square, Washington Avenue Extension, Albany, NY 12205, 518-862-7400, www.ncua.gov.

CREDIT CARDS

A list of low-rate card issuers can be found on the internet at **CardWeb**, www.cardweb.com, 301-631-9100; **Consumer Action**, www.consumer-action.org; and **BankRate.com**, www.bankrate.com, 561-630-2400. For consumer information regarding credit cards, check with CardWeb or the Consumer Action Organization. In addition, you might want to investigate reward cards; some cards are offering rebates on certain types of purchases (groceries, gasoline, restaurant meals, etc.) for an indefinite period; such cards could be worth your while.

To request a credit card application you can contact one of the following:

- **American Express**, 800-THE-CARD, www.americanexpress.com
- **Diners Club**, 800-2-DINERS, www.dinersclubnorthamerica.com
- **Discover Card**, 800-347-2683 (or apply at a Sears store), www.discover card.com
- **VISA** and **MasterCard** can be obtained through banks and other financial service associations. Check first with your bank, and shop around for the lowest interest rate, annual fees, and frequent flyer miles deals.
- **Department stores in Los Angeles** also offer their own store credit cards, although most department stores will take local personal checks with proper identification or major credit cards. The advantages of having a store credit card include advance notice of sales and often no annual fee.

CREDIT REPORTS

Those interested in seeing a personal credit report can go to www.annual creditreport.com, where you can obtain a copy of your credit report from the three main credit bureaus (Equifax, Experian, and TransUnion). It's best to get a copy from each service because each company's report may be different. If you discover any inaccuracies, you should contact the service immediately and request that it be corrected. By law they must respond to your request within 30 days. Under a new federal law, these reports can be ordered without charge by consumers. **Credit scores**, however, still cost between $4 and $8. Note: Checking your credit report frequently can adversely affect your credit rating.

You can also visit or call each bureau individually:

- **Equifax**, P.O. Box 105873, Atlanta, GA 30348, 800-685-1111, www.equifax.com
- **Experian**, P.O. Box 2104, Allen, TX 75002-2104, 888-397-3742
- **TransUnion**, P.O. Box 390, Springfield, PA 19064-0390, 800-916-8800

TAXES

There is no city income tax for residents of the City of Los Angeles, Beverly Hills, Burbank, Culver City, Glendale, West Hollywood, Malibu, or Santa Monica.

STATE INCOME TAX

State income tax forms can be obtained from the **State Franchise Tax Board Office**, 300 South Spring Street, downtown LA, or by calling 800-852-5711, www.ftb.ca.gov. The Franchise Tax Board office is open from 8 a.m. to 5 p.m., Monday-Friday. As with federal forms, your local post office or library may have state forms, as well.

The **Franchise Tax Board** is the department that administers personal income taxes and corporation taxes for the State of California. The board's web site has a taxpayer advocate link that provides information on taxpayers' rights and how to request the assistance of an advocate: www.ftb.ca.gov.

STATE SALES TAX

In California, a sales tax is imposed on retail sales or consumption of personal property (fast-food, snacks, etc.). Statewide, the sales tax is 7.25%, but LA County tacks on an additional 1% for the Metropolitan Transit Authority. The breakdown of the tax follows:

State General Fund:	5.5%
Public Safety Augmentation:	0.5%
County:	0.25%
City:	1.00%
Metro:	1.00%
Total:	8.25%

FEDERAL INCOME TAX

Resources for federal income tax information and forms:
- **Federal income tax forms** can be obtained by calling 800-829-FORM or going to the lobby of the Federal Building, 11000 Wilshire Boulevard, Westwood, 310-235-7110. In Orange County, go to the Ronald Reagan Federal Building & United States Courthouse, 411 West Fourth Street, Santa Ana, 714-338-5300. Or visit your local post office or library (the Beverly Hills Library frequently has the most complete selection of forms).

- **IRS Tax Help Line,** 800-829-1040, www.irs.gov; for consumers with questions and/or in need of forms.
- **Federal Teletax Information Line**, 800-829-4477

MOVING OR STARTING A BUSINESS

In order to do business in Los Angeles, you'll need to file your Fictitious Business Name (FBN) statement with the County Recorder's office (fee $10). Within 30 days of filing, you must publish the FBN statement for four weeks in a newspaper of general circulation in the county in which the principal place of business is located. You can download the FBN form and view said newspapers at http://regrec.co.la.ca.us/main.htm, or write the **Registrar**, **Recorder/County Clerk**, **Business Filing and Registration**, P.O. Box 53115, Los Angeles, CA 90053-0115 to request the form. You may also call 562-462-2028 with any questions.

To obtain a business license, contact the **city hall** of the municipality where your business will be conducted. For a business to be conducted in an unincorporated area of the county, contact the **LA County Business License** office at 213-974-0093. Anyone conducting business within the City of LA must pay business tax. The amount varies depending on your industry, and small businesses may qualify for exemptions. See www.la city.org/finance for a tax registration application, or contact the **City of LA Office of Finance Tax and Permit Office** at 213-473-5901. If your business operates outside the City of LA but you do business within the city, this tax liability may be lower. The city's web site, www.ci.la.ca.us, offers a wealth of information including business incentives and necessary permits for doing business in Los Angeles.

If your business involves sales of tangible personal property, you'll have to apply for a seller's permit from the **State of California Board of Equalization**, 800-400-7115, www.boe.ca.gov. The board's web site provides information about doing business in California, including employer tax forms and the *California Employer's Guide*. The Board of Equalization's information center can also answer your tax questions.

Additional resources for those wanting to start or move a business to LA include:

- **LA County Bar Association**, 213-627-2727, www.lacba.org, 261 South Figueroa, Suite 300, LA, CA 90012
- **Internal Revenue Service**, 800-829-1040, for a tax ID number
- **US Small Business Administration Home Page**, 800-827-5722, www.sba.gov
- **California State's** web site, www.ca.gov, has all sorts of information about starting a business in the state. Tax, license, and permit forms are available online.

O KAY. YOU'VE FOUND A PLACE TO LIVE, ESTABLISHED A CHECKING account, and now you are ready to unpack and truly get settled in. The following covers most of the services you will need: electric, water, gas, and telephone, and those modern almost-necessities of cable television and internet service providers. There is also automobile-related information, including registering your car with the DMV and parking details, as well as specifics on getting a library card, registering to vote, finding a physician, subscribing to local newspapers and magazines, information about owning a pet, and finally some hints about personal safety.

UTILITIES

Upon moving into your Los Angeles apartment or home, your landlord/ building manager or real estate agent will be able to provide you with a list of numbers for setting up utilities. For those establishing service from afar, you'll need to have your new address handy when calling to set up your new accounts. Note: For those of you needing to dig in your yard—say for a garden—call **Under Ground Service Alert**, 800-227-2600, at least two days before. This non-profit organization will notify the water, phone, cable, and electric companies, which will then send representatives to your place to mark their lines.

GAS

Gas service in greater LA and Orange County is provided by **So Cal Gas**, 800-427-2200, www.socalgas.com. A service establishment fee of $25 is required to set up an account. A credit check will be run when setting up service to determine what the amount of your deposit will be (which can range from $20 to $200). The deposit will be refunded after one year of timely payments. If you have only a gas cooking range, you can expect your monthly bill to be minimal. If you have gas heat, your bills will be slightly higher during the winter, but remember, temperatures seldom drop below 45 degrees here, so your heating bills will not be a major part of your budget.

ELECTRICITY AND WATER

Commonly called the DWP, the **Los Angeles Department of Water and Power** is the municipal service that provides electricity and water to the majority of Los Angeles. There is a one-time set-up fee of $13 for an apartment and $15.50 for a home. Those with credit issues (and they'll be able to tell you who you are) or with no identification will have to put down a $205 deposit, which will be refunded after a year of timely payments. (For most apartment rentals, water is covered by the landlord.) Questions regarding LA's water quality (see below) should be directed to the **DWP Water Quality Customer Service** line, 213-367-3182. (Tap water is fluoridated.)

- **Los Angeles Department of Water and Power**, www.ladwp.com
  Metropolitan LA: 213-481-5411
  San Fernando Valley: 818-342-5397
  Other areas: 800-342-5397

The DWP's conservation efforts benefit homeowners and include a shade tree program (attend a free workshop and get up to eight free trees to plant around your home) and a free ultra-low flush toilet in exchange for your non–water-saving toilet.

(For an interesting fictionalized account of the history of this powerful government office, view the movie "Chinatown," with Jack Nicholson. It tells the story of how early Los Angeles officials secured water rights for the city during its boom years. The main character, "Hollis Mulwray," is a thinly veiled reference to William Mulholland, a turn-of-the-century water engineer who is now immortalized by the 22-mile skyline Mulholland Highway on the crest of the Santa Monica Mountains.)

Additional utility providers include (if yours is not listed, check with your municipality):

- **Southern California Edison**, 800-655-4555, www.sce.com, provides electricity to areas not covered by the DWP, including Orange County, and within LA County, the communities of Santa Clarita, Culver City, Santa Monica, South Pasadena, Inglewood, and portions of Marina del Rey and Manhattan Beach.

- **The Municipal Water District of Orange County**, 714-963-3058, www.mwdoc.com, provides water to most of the OC, leaving Anaheim, Fullerton, and Santa Ana to the **Metropolitan Water District**, 213-217-6000, www.mwd.dst.ca.us.
- **Southern California Water Company**, 310-838-2143, services other parts of Los Angeles not covered by the DWP, including Culver City, El Segundo, Hawthorne, Redondo Beach, and Inglewood.
- **Burbank** has its own water and power company, **Public Service, City of Burbank**, 818-238-3700. A $40 deposit is required to set up service, which is refunded after one year of timely payments.
- **Glendale** residents should call **Public Service, City of Glendale**, 818-548-3300.
- **Long Beach** has its own water and power companies, the **Long Beach Water Department**, 562-570-2300, and the **Long Beach Gas & Electric Department**, 562-570-2000.
- **Malibu** is served by the **Las Virgenes Municipal Water Company**, 818-880-4110, and the **Los Angeles County Water District** #29, 310-456-6621.
- **Pasadena** has its own water and power company, **Pasadena Water and Power**; call 626-744-4409 for general information, or 626-744-4005 to set up service.
- **South Pasadena** residents should contact the **City of South Pasadena Water**, 626-403-7200.
- **Santa Clarita** has a number of water companies, by county: **Santa Clarita Water Company**, 661-259-2737; **Valencia Water Company**, 661-294-0828; **Newhall County Water District**, 661-259-3610; **Castiac Lake Water Agency**, 661-257-6024.
- **Santa Monica** has its own water department, the **City of Santa Monica Water Department**, 310-458-8224.

WATER QUALITY

In California, chemical additives are mixed in with gasoline to make it burn cleaner for better air quality. However, scientists have discovered that one of these additives, MTBE, a carcinogen, can contaminate groundwater, and is not as readily removable as other contaminates. The City of Santa Monica, West Los Angeles, and Culver City had their water fields shut down as a result of the contamination. After extensive clean-up, two of these wells returned to service in 2003. The California Department of Health Services requires all water systems in the state to monitor for MTBE and has established a limit for MTBE within tap water at 13 micrograms per liter. In 2000, Governor Gray Davis requested a ban of MTBE, and the planned total phase-out of MTBE was scheduled for the end of 2002, but has been delayed pending a decision at the national level. Visit the **California Department of Health Services** web site at www.dhs.cahwnet.gov to read its report "MTBE in Drinking Water." For additional information about LA area water quality, there are a number of departments to contact: **City of Santa Monica Water Department**, 310-458-8235; **Los Angeles County Department of Health Services**, **Environmental Health Department**, 626-430-5200, www.lapublichealth.org; or the **LA Regional Water Quality Control Board**, 213-576-6600, www.swrcb.ca.gov/rwqcb4.

TELEPHONE

SBC (Southwest Bell Company), 800-310-2355, www.sbc.com, is the primary telephone service provider in Los Angeles, except for the Westside. In Orange County, service is provided by SBC or **Verizon**, 800-483-4000, www.verizon.com. The western portions of Los Angeles—Malibu, Mar Vista, Marina del Rey, Pacific Palisades, Playa del Rey, Santa Monica, Venice, portions of Brentwood, Culver City, and Topanga—are also covered by Verizon. Both SBC and Verizon offer local and long-distance service. Assuming you have an established credit history with a telephone company, and if you have not had your service temporarily or completely disconnected in the last year for non-payment, and you have paid all previous "final" bills older than 45 days, you will not be required to put down a deposit for service. There is a one-time charge of $34.75 to activate your service. Both companies offer additional services, including voice mail, call waiting, call blocking, repeat dialing, and number referral services. For a complete list of the services available, check the front white pages of their respective phone books or call for details.

If you find yourself doing a lot of business with companies outside your immediate calling territory it's a good idea to collect phone books from the different sections of Los Angeles: Beverly Hills & Santa Monica make up one directory, as does Greater Los Angeles, the San Fernando Valley East, the San Fernando Valley West, and Burbank and Glendale. You may order from SBC by calling 800-248-2800—the price varies depending upon which directory you need—or simply ask friends and/or co-workers if they have any extras.

LONG-DISTANCE SERVICE PROVIDERS

At the time you install your telephone service, you will be asked to name a long-distance carrier. Unless you bundle your long-distance service with your local carrier, you will receive separate telephone bills. Currently some of the lowest per-minute rates can be found through calling cards offered at gas stations and grocery stores. If you want to compare long-distance pricing, go to **SmartPrice** at www.smartprice.com or call 877-550-5317. You will be asked questions regarding your phone usage, your area code, and the first three digits of your phone number. They will then provide a free instant analysis of the carriers available in your area. You can also contact **Telecommunications Research and Action Center (TRAC)**, a consumer organization that publishes charts comparing plans and prices at 202-263-2950, www.trac.org.

Major **long-distance service providers** in LA include:

- **AT&T**, 800-222-0300, www.att.com
- **GTC Telecom**, 800-486-4030, www.gtctelecom.com
- **IDT**, 800-889-9126, www.idt.net
- **MCI WorldCom**, 800-444-3333, www.mci.com
- **Sprint**, 800-877-4646, www.sprint.com
- **Verizon**, 800-870-9999, www.verizon.com
- **Working Assets**, 800-362-7127, www.workingforchange.com

CELL PHONES

For many Angelenos, especially actors waiting for a call back, a cellular phone is an absolute must. Many cell phone providers operate out of strip mall storefronts, kiosks in local malls, or outside on campus squares. When you buy a cellular phone, you will need to set up service, typically a minimum one-year contract. Depending on the service contract you select, the cost of your cell phone may be refunded to you, making the cell phone itself free. The largest cellular service operators in the area are **Cingular Wireless**, 866-246-4852, www.cingular.com; **AT&T Wireless**, 800-888-7600, www.attwireless.com; **NexTel**, 800-639-8359, www.nextel.com; **Sprint PCS**, 888-253-1315, www.sprintpcs.com; **T-Mobile**, 800-866-2453, www.t-mobile.com; and **Verizon**, 800-256-4646, www.verizonwireless.com.

Note: In 2003, the California Public Utilities Commission granted local number portability to cell phone users. This means that you can keep your same phone number if you change telephone providers within the same local area and, in limited cases, move a phone number from a land line to a wireless phone. And in another victory for consumers, California adopted the Telecommunications Bill of Rights in 2004, which provides some protections, such as requiring companies to bill customers only for services they request and allowing customers 30 days to drop a service without penalty.

DIRECTORY ASSISTANCE

For local directory assistance calls, the first three of which are free each month (after that they cost 46 cents), dial 411 (for national listings, the charge is $1.50 per request); repair service is 611. For the correct time, dial 853 and any four digits—there is no charge.

INTERNET SERVICE PROVIDERS (ISPs)

Many are cruising the virtual highway (when not sitting on a freeway). Popular standard dial-up service and the faster DSL (Digital Subscriber Line) plans are from **America Online**, 800-827-6364, www.aol.com; **Earthlink**, 800-511-2041, www.earthlink.net; and **SBC**, 800-310-2355, www.swbell.net. Request internet access software by phoning the provider. Availability of DSL service is determined by your proximity to a central switching office; contact the provider you're considering for availability. A cable modem, which you can order through your cable provider (see the **cable** section below), is also an option for high-speed internet access.

Internet services that are advertiser supported cost less, though you must be willing to provide some demographic information about yourself upon signing up (this is for directed advertising) and give up a small portion of your computer screen space for ad banners while online. **Net Zero**, www.netzero.com, is one such advertiser-supported internet service provider.

CONSUMER PROTECTION—UTILITY COMPLAINTS

There are a number of agencies available to contact with problems with your utilities. The **State of California Public Utilities Commission** at 320 West 4th Street, 213-676-7000, www.cpuc.ca.gov, is the place to go with inquiries and complaints about electric, gas, water, and telephone services. The **Consumer Affairs Department of California**, 800-952-5210, www.dca.ca.gov, is another resource, as is the **LA County Department of Consumer Affairs**, 213-974-1452, or 800-593-8222, http://consumer-affairs.co.la.ca.us.

Additionally, if you look at your phone bill and think you've been **slammed** (your long-distance provider or established services were changed without your approval) or **crammed** (calls you didn't make were added to your bill), and you can't get help from your local service provider or from the State of California's **Attorney General's Office**, 916-322-

3360, http://caag.state.ca.us, you can file a complaint with the **Federal Communication Commission's Consumer Center**, 888-225-5322, www.fcc.gov; or the Federal Trade Commission, 202-382-4357, www.ftc.gov.

GARBAGE AND RECYCLING

Apartment dwellers should ask their landlord or building manager about trash pickup and recycling. Homeowners will need to make arrangements for refuse collection by contacting the **Sanitation District of Los Angeles County** at 323-685-5217, www.lacsd.org. In Santa Clarita, contact the **Waste Management** division at 661-286-4098, www.santa-clarita.com/cityhall/field. In Orange County, talk to **Integrated Waste Management** at 714-834-4000, www.oclandfills.com.

Recycling is a way of life in Southern California. Some neighborhoods have curbside pickup along with regular refuse collection, others have drop-off points. For recycling, contact the **LA County Department of Public Works, Recycling and Household Hazardous Waste Program** at 888-253-2652, www.ladpw.org or www.888cleanla.com; in Orange County, call the **County of Orange Integrated Waste Management Department** (see above) to locate the recycling center nearest you. Since old computers and their peripherals require special handling, the City of Los Angeles created an E-waste disposal program. Contact them via the **Bureau of Sanitation**, 213-473-8228, www.la city.org/SAN/ewaste.htm.

PRINT AND BROADCAST MEDIA

TELEVISION

Heaven forbid you should miss an episode of your favorite TV show! The large local station is KCAL - 9. The major television network affiliates in Los Angeles and Orange County are as follows:

- **ABC** - 7
- **CBS** - 2
- **FOX** - 11
- **NBC** - 4
- **PBS** - 28
- **UPN** - 13
- **WB** – 5

CABLE TELEVISION

Aside from offering nearly 100 stations, cable also provides better reception in some areas. Since there are several cable companies in Los Angeles, the City of Los Angeles has an **Information Technology Agency**, 213-485-2751, www.lacity.org, that will help direct you to your cable company. The monthly fee for basic cable ranges from $30 to $45.

Many cable companies now offer digital telephone and high-speed internet service too, all of which can be bundled together with your cable service. It's easy and you get the benefit of a single bill and discounts for subscribing to multiple services from one provider. Obviously, plans and pricing vary widely; contact the cable provider for the most up-to-date information:

- **Adelphia Communications**, 888-683-1000, www.adelphia.net; covers a large section of LA County, from West Los Angeles to East Los Angeles, in addition to portions of Orange County
- **Cox Communications**, 949-240-1212, www.cox.com: Orange County
- **Comcast**, 888-255-5789, www.comcast.com: Hollywood-Wilshire, Southern LA, Sunland-Tujunga, Harbor, parts of Orange County
- **Charter Communications**, 626-300-8228, www.charter.com: Burbank, Glendale, Norwalk, West Covina, Alhambra, Pasadena, Altadena, Monterey Park, Artesia, Cerritos, LA County of Covina, Arcadia, Long Beach, Thousand Oaks, Calabasas, Topanga Canyon, and Malibu
- **Time Warner Communications**, 818-700-6500, 714-903-4000, www.accesstimewarner.com: covers Northridge, Encino, Woodland Hills, and Van Nuys, South Pasadena, parts of Santa Clarita, and areas within Orange County

RADIO

Maddening daily commutes have many tuning in for up-to-the-minute traffic reports. AM stations 980 and 1070 give frequent and regular traffic reports (every 6 minutes for 1070 and "on the one's," 9:01, 9:11, etc., for 980).

Most of the following stations can be received in both Los Angeles and Orange counties.

AM
- **KABC** 790 Talk Radio
- **KFI** 640 Talk/Sports
- **KSPN** 710 Sports

- **KFWB** 980 News
- **KLAC** 570 Standards
- **KNX** 1070 News
- **KDIS** 1110 Radio Disney
- **KTLK** 1150 Progressive Talk Radio
- **KMPC** 1540 Sports

FM
- **KBIG** 104.3 Adult Contemporary
- **KCBS** 93.1 Oldies
- **KHHT** 92.3 Rhythm & Blues Oldies
- **KIIS** 102.7 Top 40
- **KLOS** 95.5 Album Oriented Rock
- **KMZT** 105.1 Classical
- **KOST** 103.5 Adult Contemporary
- **KROQ** 106.7 Rock
- **KRTH** 101.1 Oldies
- **KTWV** 94.7 Smooth Jazz
- **KYSR** 98.7 Modern Adult Contemporary
- **KZLA** 93.9 Country

NEWSPAPERS AND MAGAZINES

Neighborhood publications that focus on community issues include:
- *Arcadia Weekly*, 626-294-1090
- *Argonaut*, 310-822-1629, www.argonautnewspaper.com
- *Beverly Hills Courier*, 310-278-1322
- *Brentwood News*, 310-873-0226, www.brentwoodnews.com
- *Burbank Leader*, 818-843-8700
- *Culver City News*, 310-313-6727, www.culvercityonline.com
- *Daily Breeze*, 310-540-5511, www.dailybreeze.com (Torrance)
- *Downtown Gazette*, 562-433-2000, www.gazettes.com (Long Beach)
- *Downtown News*, 213-481-1448, www.losangelesdowntown.com
- *Glendale News Press*, 818-241-4141
- *Hollywood Independent*, 323-556-5720, www.laindependent.com
- *Malibu Times*, 310-456-5507, www.malibutimes.com
- *Pasadena Weekly*, 626-795-0149, www.pasadenaweekly.com
- *Santa Monica Outlook*, 310-829-0411
- *Signal*, 661-259-1234, www.the-signal.com (Santa Clarita)
- *Tolucan Times*, 818-762-2171, www.tolucantimes.com (Toluca Lake)
- *Vanguard News*, 805-269-2030, www.vanguardnews.com (Acton)
- *Westside Weekly*, 310-314-1297

Citywide publications include:

- *Los Angeles Times*, 888-565-2323, www.latimes.com; primary newspaper in LA, it publishes a separate but similar edition for the Valley. Its Sunday edition (available as early as Saturday morning at convenience stores and newsstands) makes for hefty weekend reading.
- *Daily News*, 818-713-3000, www.dailynews.com; based in the Valley and competitor to the *Times*
- *LA Weekly*, 323-465-9909, www.laweekly.com; this alternative paper is what many Angelenos turn to for information on movies, clubs, and fun (wholesome and not-so-wholesome) in LA. Their provocative personal ads are a hoot. The paper is free for the taking at newsstands, supermarkets, coffeehouses, convenience stores, etc. If you want a home-delivered subscription, you'll have to pay.
- *Los Angeles Magazine*, 800-876-5222; nice glossy spread covering the hip and happening in the LA scene, some fashion and food as well
- *Orange County Register*, 877-469-7344, www.ocregister.com; the major daily in Orange County
- *OC Weekly*, 714-550-5900, www.ocweekly.com; the Orange County counterpart to the *LA Weekly*

AUTOMOBILES

DRIVER'S LICENSES

California drivers must have a valid California driver's license; upon arrival, you have 10 days to get the task done. A California driver's license is valid for up to five years and expires on the birthday of the license holder. You will be sent a renewal notice approximately two months before the expiration date. The renewal fee for a standard Class C and/or M1/M2 license is $24. Bring the notice and your license with you when you renew. You may be eligible to renew your license by mail without taking a test, if you have a good driving record.

If you have an out-of-state or out-of-country license, you must be at least 18 years of age, complete all the steps required for a permit (see below), and surrender your valid out-of-state driver's license. A driving test for license renewals or holders of out-of-state or US territory licenses is normally waived. However, driving tests are required for out-of-country license holders.

To get a permit, you must:

- Be at least 18 years of age (those under 18 who are licensed to drive outside of California should check with the DMV for specifics on how to acquire a California driver's license).

- Fill out the DMV application form (DL 44).
- Provide your full legal name.
- Present an acceptable birth date/legal presence document.
- Provide your social security number.
- Pay the required $24 application fee.
- Pass an eye exam (by law, any person with a corrected-vision score of 20/200 will not be issued a driver's license).
- Have your picture taken.
- Give a thumbprint.
- Pass a traffic laws and road signs test.

The DMV may cancel your license or refuse to issue you a license if you:
- Have a history of alcohol or drug abuse.
- Have used the license illegally.
- Have lied on your application.
- Do not understand traffic laws or signs.
- Do not have the skill to drive.
- Have a health problem that makes your driving unsafe.
- Have an outstanding traffic citation because you failed to appear or failed to pay.
- Have not complied with a judgment or order for family support payments.
- Cheated on any license examination.
- Impersonated an applicant or allowed someone else to impersonate you to fraudulently qualify for a license.
- Refuse to give a thumbprint.
- Refuse to sign the certification on the application (form DL 44).
- Submit a fraudulent birth date/legal presence document or social security document.

STATE IDS

If you don't drive, California IDs are available at the Department of Motor Vehicles. Contact the department at 800-777-0133, or go to www.dmv. ca.gov for locations. There is a $20 application fee for a state ID and it is valid for six years.

AUTOMOBILE REGISTRATION

In California, cars need to be registered and insured, and they must pass emissions inspection (smog check). As with licenses, the **Department of**

Motor Vehicles (DMV) web site is a good resource for those with questions about automobile registration.

Residents who come from out of state need to register their vehicles in California within 20 days. Take your most recently issued auto registration, smog certificate, and purchase information to your nearest DMV office. (A smog certificate is required by the state; the certificate itself is $8.25, but a smog test must be performed to get the certificate, and that price will vary from shop to shop. See your Yellow Pages under "Automobile Repairing & Service" for ones that conduct smog checks or look for repair garages in your neighborhood that hang a sign with a red check mark, indicating smog check service.) Various fees are due upon registering your vehicle—amounts vary by vehicle—they include a registration fee of $31 and CHP (California Highway Patrol) fee of $9; a $1 plate fee; and a vehicle license fee or VLF. The formula for VLF assessment is based upon the purchase price of the vehicle or the value of the vehicle when acquired. The VLF decreases with each renewal for the first 11 years and is tax deductible.

Unfortunately, DMVs are notorious for their long lines. If you are applying for a license or identification card or registering your vehicle, you can reduce your wait time by making an appointment via the phone or their web site. (Or, if you have AAA membership, you can walk into your AAA office to renew your registration once you have a California registration and driver's license.) Following are the **DMV offices** in the Los Angeles area; every office now uses the central number 800-777-0133:

- **Culver City**, 11400 Washington Blvd.
- **Glendale**, 1335 West Glenoaks Blvd.
- **Hollywood**, 803 North Cole Avenue; 1600 Vine Street
- **Inglewood**, 621 North La Brea Avenue
- **Long Beach**, 3700 East Willow Street
- **North Hollywood**, 14920 Vanowen
- **Northridge**, 14920 Vanowen
- **Santa Monica**, 2235 Colorado Avenue
- **Van Nuys**, 14920 Vanowen

Following are some **DMV offices** in the Orange County area:
- **Costa Mesa**, 650 West 19th Street
- **Laguna Hills**, 23535 Moulton Parkway
- **Santa Ana**, 1330 East 1st Street
- **Westminster**, 13700 Hoover Street

AUTOMOBILE INSURANCE

California's Compulsory Financial Responsibility Law requires every driver and every owner of a motor vehicle to have liability coverage.

The minimum amount your insurance must cover per accident is: $15,000 for a single death or injury, $30,000 for death or injury to more than one person, and $5,000 for property damage.

If you recently moved here from out of state, you should know that many out-of-state insurance companies are not authorized to do business in California. Before you drive here you should ask your insurance company if you are covered in case of an accident. Should you become involved in an accident in California before switching to an in-state provider, the DMV requires all three of the following conditions be met to avoid suspension of your license: You must have insured the vehicle before you came to California (you cannot renew the out-of-state policy once the vehicle is registered in California); your insurance company must file a power of attorney, allowing the DMV to act as its agent for legal service in California; and your liability policy must provide bodily injury and property damage coverage that equals or exceeds the limits stated above.

Be aware, Los Angeles has some of the highest automobile insurance rates in the country. In fact, according to a survey conducted in 2004 by a cost-of-living analysis service (Runzheimer International, www.runz heimer.com), LA ranked as the second most expensive metropolitan area in the USA in which to own and operate a car, with LA's insurance rates being the largest contributing factor. To make bare-bones coverage affordable to low-income households, in 2000, the state started a pilot program for Los Angeles residents called the **California Automobile Assigned Risk Plan**; call 800-622-0954 or go to www.aipso.com/lc for more information. The **State of California Department of Insurance** annually surveys auto and homeowner insurance providers in Los Angeles; go to www.insurance.ca.gov/docs/FS-Surveys.htm to see a general side-by-side premium comparison or call 213-897-8921.

For most auto-related information, including insurance, emergency road service, DMV registration renewal, and travel services (including great free maps), you may find it worth the $45 annual membership fee (plus a one-time $20 initiation fee) to join the **Automobile Club of Southern California**, the regional branch of AAA, 800-222-8794, www.aaa-calif.com.

AUTOMOBILE SAFETY

Driving under the influence of drugs or alcohol is illegal in California. The legal blood alcohol limit is .08. If you are pulled over for driving under the influence, you will likely be arrested, have your car towed, and be given a Breathalyzer test. (A first-time refusal of a breath or blood test in California will result in an automatic license suspension for one year; if this is your second refusal, your license will be revoked for two years.) If you fail the chemical test, a first offense will result in a four-month driving suspension. A second or subsequent offense within seven years will result in a one-year suspension. For more information, go to www.dmv.ca.gov/dl/driversafety/dsalcohol.htm.

California has a mandatory **seatbelt law**. All occupants of a vehicle—be it a car, truck, or van—must be properly buckled in, including children in safety seats. The law is very specific with regard to children. Infants under one or who weigh less than 20 pounds are required to ride in rear-facing, reclined (45 degrees) car seats. Toddlers ride in upright forward-facing seats, with a harness, until 40 pounds. Children who are over 40 pounds must use a lap and shoulder belt-positioning booster seat until they are at least six years old or weigh 60 pounds. Visit the California Highway Patrol's web site for further information: www.chp.ca.gov/html/safetyseats.html.

PURCHASING AN AUTOMOBILE

The experience of purchasing a car is both exciting and a hassle, and always a big expense. It pays to conduct research beforehand to determine the worth of the car you're thinking of purchasing. For used cars, check out the Kelley Blue Book site at www.kbb.com. To research dealer invoice prices for new cars, check www.autovantage.com. AAA offers a walk-in vehicle pricing report service to members and non-members for a nominal fee. Also, *Consumer Reports* offers a low-cost auto pricing information service, available via their web site: www.consumerreports.org.

Many local automobile dealers publish advertised specials of new and used vehicles in the automotive classifieds of the *Los Angeles Times* and run internet specials on their web pages. Used cars also can be purchased through the classified advertisements in local newspapers. Or visit your local newsstand for a free copy of the *Auto Trader*, 800-395-SELL, or *Recycler Auto Buys*, 323-660-5116 or 818-988-3647. It's a good idea to pay to have an auto mechanic inspect and evaluate any used vehicle you are considering buying.

CONSUMER PROTECTION—AUTOMOBILES

When you buy a new car in California, it's good to know about the state's Motor Vehicle Warranty and Lemon Law for new and leased vehicles. The Lemon Law is applicable during the first 18 months or within the first 18,000 miles, whichever occurs first. A new or leased car is a "lemon" if it has a defect that "substantially impairs the use, value, or safety of the vehicle" and cannot be fixed after a "reasonable" number of repair attempts, i.e., four or more times for the same problem or 30 days out of service for any combination of problems.

If it is determined in court or arbitration that your car is indeed a lemon, you are entitled to either a refund or a replacement vehicle. Keep in mind, a car manufacturer can argue that it has not had "reasonable" opportunity to repair your car, or that the defect is the result of abuse or does not substantially affect the vehicle's use, value or safety to you, to negate its Lemon Law obligations, so be sure to keep a record of all repair attempts, number of days in the shop, and any comments from the mechanics who worked on your vehicle to build your case.

The **California Department of Consumer Affairs** offers a free booklet on this law at www.dca.ca.gov or 800-952-5210. You may apply for the state-certified arbitration program via the Better Business Bureau's Auto Line: 800-952-5100, www.bbb.org.

PARKING

Parking regulations vary from neighborhood to neighborhood. Some areas require residents to display a permit to park on the street in front of their apartment building, others, particularly ones that are close to shopping and business districts, allow only two-hour parking, unless you have a residential parking permit. Parts of Beverly Hills and Burbank allow no overnight parking on the street. Certain parts of the Westside, particularly Santa Monica and Westwood, have some of the fastest meter maids in the county.

Once each week most residential streets are cleaned by sweepers; during this time there is usually a two-hour block of time when cars may not park; look for signs posting the day and hours. If you forget about your car on street sweeping day, you're likely to find a ticket on it afterwards. Be especially aware of restricted parking on high-traffic streets, effective during certain parts of the day, usually at rush hour. Tow truck operators are known to lie in wait for the minute they can begin towing offending cars.

Do not be lax about paying parking tickets. After five unpaid tickets, a meter maid will boot your car. This immobilizes the vehicle and if your booted car is parked in restricted parking, your car will be ticketed for continued parking violations where it sits. A large sticker on your vehicle will give you the parking violation division's phone number as well as the place you'll need to contact to pay off all unpaid tickets plus an additional $100 for the boot removal.

The best advice is to read carefully the signs in your neighborhood. If permits are required for on-street parking, contact the permit department in your local city hall. The following are direct numbers for obtaining **residential parking permits** where they are required:

- **Beverly Hills**, 310-285-2551, www.beverlyhills.org
- **Los Angeles**, 310-843–5936 or 323-913-4600, www.lacity-parking.org
- **Santa Monica**, 310-458-8291, http://santa-monica.ca.us/planning/transportation
- **West Hollywood**, 323-848-6392, www.weho.org

TOWED OR STOLEN AUTOMOBILES

When an automobile is impounded, the lot will release the car only after collecting storage and tow fees. If you find yourself chasing after a tow truck that's taking your car off into the sunset, don't panic. First call the traffic division of the police department for the area where your car was originally parked (see the neighborhood profiles for contact information). They will then direct you to the impound lot where your car is being held. An impounded car will be released only to the car's registered owner or to the person bearing a notarized letter of authorization from the car's registered owner. Expect to pay approximately $120 in tow fees and $15 to $70 per day for storage fees. Many impound lots are in unsavory parts of town, best to bring a friend along. The process is not a fun one.

If your car has been stolen, contact the police department as soon as possible. The police will need your driver's license, the car's year, make, model, and color as well as the vehicle identification number. Once you file a report, the police department will notify you as soon as your car has been located. If you have engraved a unique identification number on your car stereo or other accessories, the police can better identify those items should they be recovered.

ANTI-THEFT DEVICES

The Automobile Club of Southern California recommends anti-theft devices on cars. The general feeling is that, although few mechanisms will stop a professional car thief determined to take your car, devices do thwart amateurs. If you decide to buy an anti-theft device, be sure to tell your automobile insurer, as they often offer discounts for car owners who have them on their vehicles.

Steering wheel locks, like the Club, are one of the cheapest ways to go. While a pro can break through them with ease (in about 15 seconds), they may still be enough of a deterrent for the thief to move on to the next target. Ditto for audible **car alarms**. Be aware, however, the California Vehicle Code allows police to tow and impound an unattended vehicle after its alarm has blared for 45 minutes, so be careful not to set it too sensitively, and park it where you will be able to hear it. **Kill switches** can be installed to shut down your car's starter, fuel pump, or ignition, unless the switch is first disengaged by the motorist. Those truly serious about anti-theft devices should consider having a tracking transmitter installed, offered by **Lojack** (www.lojack.com) and **Teletrac** (www.tele trac.net). Lojack systems are tracked by police cars with homing devices, while Teletrac does the tracking itself and then tells police where to look for your vehicle. Both systems have excellent recovery rates (about 90%).

VOTER REGISTRATION

Before you can vote, or sign a petition for that matter, you must be registered to vote. For those wanting to take part in an upcoming election, registration must occur 29 days prior to Election Day. Voter registration forms can be obtained at post offices and through the **LA County Registrar of Voters**, 562-466-1323, http://regrec.co.la.ca.us, or the **Orange County Registrar of Voters**, 714-567-7600, www.oc.ca.gov/election. As an election approaches, you will see volunteers from Democratic and Republican parties registering voters at public places like shopping malls and grocery stores.

After the registrar processes your registration, you will be mailed a voting guide, which lists the candidates and propositions on the ballot. Every guide also contains an application to request an absentee ballot by mail. A request for an absentee ballot must be filed with the Registrar at least seven days prior to the election.

If you elect to vote in person, look in the back of your voting guide for the address of the polling location assigned to your mailing address—the location may change from election to election or may even fall outside your precinct, depending on the number of volunteers. Or call the Registrar for assistance with locating your polling location. It is important to vote at the poll set up for your precinct because ballots usually carry candidates for local elections specific to your area. The county is in constant need of volunteer precinct officers (bilingual, especially) and locations for polling. If you want to help or volunteer your place of residence or business for polling to make voting more convenient for your neighbors, call your respective registrar.

The **State of California Voter's Assistance Hotline**, 800-345-8683, is a good resource; call it to report voter fraud, receive an absentee ballot, find out who your elected representatives are, and to locate your polling center.

Area parties and voter information groups include:

- **LA County Democratic Party**, 213-382-0063, www.lacdp.org
- **Republican Party of Los Angeles County**, 323-215-4471, www.cagop.org
- **League of Women Voters**, 213-368-1616 (LA, San Fernando Valley), 818-247-2407 (Glendale, Burbank); www.lwv.org
- **Project Vote Smart**, 888-VOTE-SMART, www.vote-smart.org, provides information on state and national candidates and voting issues
- **State Secretary's Voting Site**: www.ss.ca.gov/elections.htm

PASSPORTS

Many passport renewals can be handled by mail or at one of the city's Passport Application Acceptance Facility locations (usually a post office). For detailed information and to download the proper mail-in forms, you can visit the **US Department of State Bureau of Consular Affairs National Passport Information Service**: http://travel.state.gov/get_forms.html, or call them at 877-487-2778, TDD 888-874-7793, Monday-Friday 8 a.m. to 8 p.m. EST. (General travel information and advisories are available at the Bureau of Consular Affairs' home page, www.travel.state.gov.)

If you are applying for a passport for the first time, you must have (1) proof of citizenship: an original or copy of your birth certificate with a raised seal, or naturalization papers, and (2) proof of your identity: a driver's license or other ID with a photograph and signature. (If you don't have these papers, call the number above for alternatives.) You will need two passport photos (which can be made while you wait in most neighborhood photo shops) and $85 if you are age 16 or older; $70 for those under age 16; renewals are $55. Allow six weeks for your completed passport to be processed. For expedited service, add $60; you can expect to receive your passport in two weeks. New applications for passports use form DS-11, and for minors under age 14 an additional consent form, DS-3053, is required. You will find the necessary forms at many post offices and libraries, at county court offices, or online at the State Bureau of Consular Affairs. You must appear in person to get your first passport; this includes minors.

The **Los Angeles Passport Agency** serves only customers who are traveling within 14 days or are submitting their passports for foreign visas. Their office is at the Federal Building, 11000 Wilshire Boulevard, Ste. 1000, Westwood, CA. For information, call 310-575-5700 or visit http://travel. state.gov/ppt_la.html. Office hours are from 8 a.m. to 3 p.m. Since Los Angeles is a port of immigration, lines for the passport room typically start forming hours beforehand.

Those in need of emergency passports should contact the Bureau of Consular Affairs for assistance. You can also try **Travisa Passport and Visa Services** at 800-222-2589, www.travisa.com, a private service that promises to process an emergency passport application with a one- to two-day turnaround.

LIBRARY CARDS

You can apply for a library card at any local library (check the neighborhood profiles for the one nearest you). Los Angeles County's Central Library is located downtown at 630 West Fifth Street, 213-228-7000, www.lapl.org. Hours are 10 a.m. to 8 p.m., Monday-Saturday, and 1 p.m. to 5 p.m. on Sunday. To renew a book by phone, call 888-577-5275. In Orange County, check with the Orange County Public Library at www.ocpl.org for a list of branches. (See **Literary Life** in the **Cultural Life** chapter for more information about area public libraries and for a list of specialty libraries.)

FINDING A PHYSICIAN

Choosing a personal physician is more like choosing a mate than buying a car. You're looking for a doctor who has graduated from an excellent medical school, done residency in a good teaching hospital, is board certified, has practiced long enough to know what he or she is doing but not so long as to be out of touch with the latest research and technology, and has just the right professional manner—concerned, straightforward, a listener with, perhaps, a good sense of humor. In short, you want a doctor you can rely on. If you put it off until you need one, you're apt to wind up sitting miserably in the nearest emergency room, followed by a big bill.

If you are enrolled in an HMO or PPO through your employer or independently, you are probably limited in your choice of physicians to those listed by that HMO or PPO. This makes choosing somewhat easier, but the criteria for choosing remain the same.

You may choose a physician as many do, on the basis of the recommendation of friends, which can be a good start. Question your friends closely on what exactly they do and do not like about a doctor. Or, if you had physicians you liked before moving here, they may be able to recommend a colleague here who will suit you. The Yellow Pages contains a list of docs in its "Physicians & Surgeons, MD" section, or try a **physician referral line**:

- **Cedars-Sinai Physician Referral Line**, 800-CEDARS-1, www. csmc.edu
- **Columbia Physician Referral**, 800-265-8624
- **Doctor Finder - Glendale Memorial Hospital**, 818-502-2378
- **UCLA Medical Group**, 800-UCLA-MD1

For those wanting to know if their doctor is board certified in a specialty area, check with the **American Board of Medical Specialists**, 866-275-2267, www.abms.org.

PET LAWS AND SERVICES

As a renter, can you bring your Portuguese water dog and your Burmese cat to Los Angeles? Will that pose a problem? Yes and maybe. The biggest hurdle to clear will be the first: finding an apartment that will accept pets (fish don't count). As a general rule, you can expect landlords to prohibit pets, particularly dogs, which means you may have to choose between the perfect apartment and the perfect pet. Be sure to inquire as you search for a pet-friendly home, and don't plan to sneak one in where they are prohibited. As well, California law prohibits ownership of certain animals (although there are groups working to change some of these laws). Currently, prohibited pets include gerbils, ferrets, skunks, and sugar gliders. If you have an unusual animal as a pet, you might want to check on the legality of owning it in California. Dogs and cats being the most common city pets, we'll address their needs here.

Resident dogs (not cats) of the City of Los Angeles are required to be licensed; licenses are available from shelters, through veterinarians, or by mail: write to the **Department of Animal Regulation**, 419 South Spring Street, Room 1400, Los Angeles, CA 90013, or call 888-452-7381. Allow six to eight weeks for processing. If the application is submitted in person to any departmental office (see below), processing takes only minutes. The annual fee for dogs (four months or older) is $10 if spayed or neutered and $30 otherwise. Free licenses for spayed or neutered dogs are available to seniors (62 years or older) who meet financial requirements and to disabled persons who own a guide dog or service dog. As well, the **City of LA Sterilization Fund** provides free spaying and neutering for dogs and cats owned by qualified persons living within the City of Los Angeles—basically, the same persons meeting the criteria for free dog licenses may have their pets altered at no cost. The centers listed below offer spaying and neutering services. All dogs over the age of four months must be vaccinated against rabies. A dog license is issued only when the required rabies vaccination certificate, from a licensed veterinarian, is provided and only as long as the rabies vaccination is current.

Here is a list of **LA County Animal Care and Control Centers**:

- **Burbank Animal Control**, 818-238-3340, 1150 North Victory Place, Burbank
- **East Valley Animal Care and Control Center**, 13131 Sherman Way, North Hollywood, 888-452-7381
- **Harbor Animal Care and Control Center**, 735 Battery Street, San Pedro, 888-452-7381
- **Long Beach Animal Control**, 3001 East Willow, Long Beach, 562-570-7387
- **North Central Animal Care and Control Center**, 3201 Lacy Street, Los Angeles, 888-452-7381
- **Orange County Animal Care Services**, 561 The City Drive, Orange, 714-935-6943, www.ocpetinfo.com
- **Santa Monica Animal Shelter**, 1640 9th Street, Santa Monica, 310-458-8594
- **South Central Animal Care and Control Center**, 3320 West 36th Street, Los Angeles, 888-452-7381
- **Southeast Area Animal Control Center**, 9777 Seaca Street, Downey, 562-803-3301
- **West LA Animal Care and Control Center**, 11950 Missouri Avenue, Los Angeles, 888-452-7381
- **West Valley Animal Care and Control Center**, 20655 Plummer Street, Chatsworth, 888-452-7381

OFF-LEASH PARKS

Off-leash canine parks are popular in this dog-loving city, which otherwise has a zero tolerance policy for off-leash dogs. Some of the dog parks listed below are outfitted with doggie drinking fountains and free scoop-the-poop baggies. While obviously popular with Fido, dog parks have become a hot spot for meeting friends or even a significant other.

- **Calabasas**: Calabasas Bark Park, 4232 Las Virgienes Road, across from A.E. Wright Middle School
- **Encino**: Sepulveda Basin Off-Leash Dog Park, White Oak and Victory Blvd.
- **Hollywood**: Laurel Canyon Park, Mulholland Drive just off Laurel Canyon; open after 3 p.m.; Runyon Canyon Park, top of Fuller Avenue (the north end of Fuller, west of La Brea, north of Franklin Avenue)
- **Long Beach**: Long Beach Dog Park, 7th Street and Park
- **Los Angeles**: Silverlake Dog Park, Silverlake Blvd. at Easterly Terrace
- **Pasadena**: Brookside Park, 360 North Arroyo Blvd.
- **West Los Angeles**: Westminster Park, 1234 Pacific Avenue on east side of Westminster Park

   In Orange County try:
- **Costa Mesa**: Costa Mesa Bark Park, Arlington Drive and Newport Blvd., www.cmbarkpark.org
- **Huntington Beach**: Best Friend Dog Park, on Edwards Street between Slater and Pacific Coast Highway

SAFETY AND CRIME

Every city has its high- and low-crime areas, and Los Angeles is certainly no exception. Check out prospective communities when trying to determine how comfortable and secure you might feel living there. Observe. Is there a lot of graffiti? Litter? Loiterers? Security bars? All these are indicators that should not be ignored.

   Big city rules apply here in LA. Use common sense and be cautious when it comes to your safety:

- Keep your doors and windows locked. If you like fresh air and want to keep your windows open a crack, take extra precautions and buy a window lock (available at hardware stores) that prevents the window from being slid further open or wedge it with a stick. Upper level apartments are not as easy targets for thieves.
- Walk with a purpose, trust your instincts, and keep clear of abandoned areas, especially at night. Be particularly cautious in South Central.
- When taking public transportation, ride toward the front of the bus, next to the driver. On the Metro, sit in a populated car.
- Be extra aware of your surroundings in unfamiliar areas. Once you get a feel for your personal comfort level in your neighborhood, you'll fall right in with the pace of the city and, like most Angelenos, go about your days without incident.

To investigate the safety of a neighborhood, you'll want to inquire with the LAPD, LA Sheriff, or whichever police department patrols your neighborhood of interest. The California Department of Justice maintains a map of registered sex offenders residing in Los Angeles County (available on the internet at http://gismap.co.la.ca.us/sols/default.htm). Megan's Law, which passed in 1996, gives residents the right to know the general whereabouts of registered sex offenders who are classified as either "Serious" or "High Risk." You may view areas of the map by zip code, city/community, or specific address.

You can also be proactive in keeping your new community safe by starting a **Neighborhood Watch Program** if one doesn't exist already. The LAPD (323-526-5541, www.lapdonline.org) or your Sheriff substation (323-267-3435, www.lasd.org) can provide information.

AUTO SAFETY

Safety experts say that with the advent of car alarms and other anti-theft devices, autos are getting more difficult to steal. Unfortunately, thieves who formerly would steal unattended parked cars have learned that violent confrontation, i.e., car-jacking, may be the only way to get the cars they want. Here are some guidelines for auto safety:

- Know how to get to where you are going. Study your route ahead of time to eliminate the need to look at a map while driving.
- Keep your car doors locked while driving, and keep windows up in unfamiliar areas. If it is hot and you have no air conditioning, roll down the window enough to get air in the car, but not enough for an arm to get in.
- Keep your wallet or purse hidden, either under the seat or in the trunk.
- Park in well-lit areas. If you are in a questionable area and need to use a pay phone or purchase gasoline, stop where the attendants can see you. While more costly, having someone pump gas for you is safer than getting out of your car and paying yourself. Avoid parking in alleys; their low visibility makes them a favorite for thieves.
- Do not be tricked into getting out of your car. If you are rear-ended in a remote or dark area and feel uneasy about getting out of your car to exchange insurance information, motion to the other driver to follow you to a police or fire station, or a 24-hour store.
- Do not stop for flashing white lights. Law enforcement vehicles use red flashers or blue and white ones.
- Drive in the middle lane if you feel insecure in a certain area. Try not to get into a lane where you can easily be cut off. If a car blocks you intentionally, honk repeatedly for help, but do not get out of your car.

- Most importantly, if you are confronted, give up your car, your jewelry, your wallet or purse. Often violence occurs when citizens resist a car-jacking or mugging. No possession is more valuable than your life.

POLICE COMPLAINTS

The police have a separate unit to handle complaints about their officers. If an incident occurs between you and an officer, file a complaint with the appropriate officer/sheriff's department. The LAPD has a special number; call 800-339-6868 or file online at www.lapdonline.org.

S ETTING UP YOUR HOME MAY REQUIRE HIRING OUT FOR ASSISTANCE. Some of the services you'll find in this chapter are those designed to make your life easier, like house cleaning and pest control; other sections, such as **Services for People with Disabilities**, **Immigrant Newcomers**, and **Gay and Lesbian Life**, detail services relevant to specific communities.

RENTAL SERVICES

From tables, chairs, dinnerware, and fine linens for an elegant dinner party, to mammoth plasma screen TVs for Oscar night or Super Bowl Sunday, just about anything you need can be rented in Los Angeles. Check the Yellow Pages for the range of services available.

APPLIANCE RENTAL

In LA, it is common to find apartments that are not equipped with major appliances, particularly refrigerators. While most apartment dwellers opt to buy what they need, rental outfits abound. Consider the following or look in the Yellow Pages under "Appliances – Major – Renting" for more listings:

- **Aim Rental**, 3562 Rodeo Drive, 323-293-2000
- **Anthony Rents**, 11012 Ventura Blvd., Studio City, 818-980-1001 or 323-650-7060
- **Rent-A-Center**, 6300 Laurel Canyon Blvd., 818-505-1903; 12735 Van Nuys Blvd., Van Nuys, 818-890-3000
- **J&R Appliances**, 7137 Owensmouth Avenue, Canoga Park, 818-716-5737
- **WebRents**, 800-645-2023, www.webrents.com

DOMESTIC SERVICES

For those who could use some help around the house, the following services may be of interest.

DRY CLEANING DELIVERY

There seems to be a dry cleaner on every other street corner in LA, with many offering a drive-thru window for pick-up and drop-off—this must explain why so few offer delivery service. Nonetheless, here are some that will pick-up and deliver:

- **Burton Way Cleaners**, 9038 Burton Way, West LA, 310-276-8902
- **Effrey's**, 8917 Melrose Avenue, Beverly Hills, 310-858-7400; 8302 Wilshire Blvd., Beverly Hills, 323-653-0525
- **Encino Dry Cleaners**, 16946 Ventura Blvd., Encino, 818-986-8464
- **Merry Go Round**, 8550 West Third Street, 310-275-1782
- **Regal Cleaners**, 12154 Ventura Place, Studio City, 818-762-4350; 17471 Ventura Blvd., Encino, 818-986-9105; 11335 Camarillo, North Hollywood, 818-762-2456
- **The Shirt Shuttle**, 2515 South Barrington Avenue, West LA, 310-822-8771
- **Sterling Cleaners**, 1600 Westwood Blvd., Westwood, 310-474-8525; 3405 Overland Avenue, West LA, www.sterlingcleaners.com

HOUSE CLEANING SERVICES

For those needing maid service there are plenty of options. Check the telephone directory under "House Cleaning" for a complete listing of agencies near you. If you choose a service, make sure it's bonded and insured.

- **AMAIDzing! Inc.**, 310-278-7812, www.amaidzing.com
- **Betty's Maid Service**, 800-877-6243
- **Dana's Housekeeping Personnel Service**, 818-342-3930, 661-255-1988, www.danashousekeeping.com
- **Golden Maid Agency**, 818-783-7777
- **M&M Maid & Janitorial Services**, 818-704-0779
- **Maid with Joy**, 310-823-2990, www.maidwithjoy.com
- **Merry Maids**, 818-508-7411, www.merrymaids.com
- **Oriental Lady Cleaning**, 800-358-4258
- **Queen of Clean**, 800-805-8395

MAIL AND SHIPPING SERVICES

Renting a post box at a mail receiving center is a good option for those still on the hunt for a house, for those who are frequently out of town, or for those who work from home but don't want to use their residence address for business. Aside from mailbox companies, boxes can also be rented at your local post office—however, these typically have a waiting list of three months or more. Check with your local post office or try one of the following:

- **Beverly Hills Mailbox**, Beverly Hills, 310-286-0500
- **Mail Boxes & Accessories**, has two locations in Burbank, 818-843-5803, 818-558-5600
- **The Mail Shoppe** in LA, 323-466-9050
- **The UPS Store** (formerly Mail Boxes Etc.) has multiple locations in Los Angeles; hours and days of operation vary. Call 888-346-3623 or visit www.mbe.com for a complete list of locations.
- **United Mail Boxes**, Beverly Hills, 310-652-7522, www.bhumb.com

JUNK MAIL

Junk mail will surely follow you to your new locale. In order to curtail this kind of unwanted mail we suggest you send a written note, including name and address, asking to be purged from the **Direct Marketing Association's** list (Direct Marketing Association's Mail Preference Service, Box 643, Carmel, NY 15012-0643). Some catalogue companies will need to be contacted directly with a purge request. You can also check the *JunkBusters Guide to Reducing Junk Mail* at www.junkbusters.com. For **junk e-mail**, you may also go to the Direct Marketing web site, www.dmaconsumers.org, and request an opt-out service for your e-mail address. The service will accept three non-business e-mail addresses at a time. This should reduce the amount of e-mail you receive from national e-mail lists. Another option is to call the "opt-out" line at 888-567-8688, and request that the main credit bureaus not release your name and address to interested marketing companies. (**Curb phone solicitations** by going to the government's "do not call registry," www.donotcall.gov, and registering your phone number.)

US POSTAL SERVICE

Mail delivery within the city is fast and efficient. Generally, the only time you have to worry about your mail is once it hits your mailbox, where theft may be a problem. If you are experiencing stolen or missing mail, speak to someone at your local post office or contact the US Post Office's Consumer Affairs at 800-275-8777, www.usps.com.

Most post offices in the county close by 5 p.m., although a few close a little later (there are no 24-hour post offices in LA):

- **LAX Airport Station**, 9029 Airport Blvd., 310-649-7490, open until 11 p.m., it will accept mail until 6 p.m.
- **Los Angeles Main Office**, 7101 South Central Avenue, 323-586-4414, accepts mail until 7 p.m.
- **Alameda Station**, 760 North Main Street, 213-617-4405; accepts mail until 7 p.m.
- **Van Nuys Main Office,** 15701 Sherman Way, Van Nuys, 818-374-5650, accepts mail until 8 p.m.

SHIPPING SERVICES

Couldn't get everything to fit in the moving truck? You can always ship it via one of these services:

- **DHL Worldwide Express**, 800-225-5345, www.dhl.com
- **FedEx**, 800-463-3339, www.fedex.com
- **Roadway Express**, 800-313-4089, www.roadway.com
- **UPS**, 800-742-5877, www.ups.com
- **US Postal Service Express Mail**, 800-222-1811, www.usps.com

CONSUMER PROTECTION

"Buyer beware" may be a cliché, but it is the best line of defense against fraud and consumer victimization. Sometimes, an unscrupulous business operator can hoodwink even the most cautious of us. Here are some agencies that, depending on your concern, may be able to help you on your quest for justice:

- **Automotive Repair Bureau, Department of Consumer Affairs**, 310-410-0024, www.dca.ca.gov
- **California Attorney General's Office**, 800-952-5225, http://caag.state.ca.us
- **California Department of Consumer Affairs**, 800-952-5210, www.dca.ca.gov
- **California Department of Insurance**, 800-927-HELP, www.insurance.ca.gov
- **LA County Bar Association**, 213-243-1525, www.lacba.org; operates an attorney referral line and the Smart Law information line, 213-

243-1500, which has several prerecorded messages providing basic information about many areas of law.

- **LA County Department of Consumer Affairs**, 213-974-1452, http://consumer-affairs.co.la.ca.us
- **Los Angeles Better Business Bureau**, 818-386-5510, www.bbb.org
- **US Consumer Product Safety Commission**, 800-638-2772, www.cpsc.gov

SERVICES FOR PEOPLE WITH DISABILITIES

Los Angeles has a variety of resources for people with special needs. Many public, private, and commercial facilities provide for sight, hearing, and/or mobility impaired people. Public transit provides various types of assistance to the elderly and disabled. Major crosswalks equipped with audio signals and ramps are most common in neighborhoods where colleges and universities are located. Here is a list of some available services and agencies that can offer referrals and assistance:

- **Assistive Technology Network**, 800-390-2699, TTY 800-900-0706, www.atnet.org; provides information on obtaining assistive devices and services.
- **Braille Institute**, 800-272-4553; serves anyone with reading difficulties due to visual impairment or physical disability. Their Books on Tape program, 800-808-2555, is popular.
- **California Telephone Access Program**, 800-806-1191, TTY 800-806-4474; provides information on obtaining assistive devices and services.
- **California Department of Rehabilitation**, 310-348-0965, TDD 310-641-3214
- **Center for the Partially Sighted**, 310-458-3501, www.lowvision.org; counseling, equipment and rehabilitative programs for independent living.
- **Computer Access Center**, 310-338-1597, www.cac.org; information on assistive technology for people with disabilities.
- **Crisis Line for the Handicapped**, 800-426-4363; a 24-hour support and information line.
- **Driving Systems, Inc.**, 818-782-6793, www.drivingsystems.com; develops customized adaptive driving devices.
- **Easter Seal Society**, 818-996-9902, www.easterseals.com; gives infant-care education, adult day programs, and referrals to rehabilitation services.

- **Greater Los Angeles Council on Deafness (GLAD)**, 323-478-8000, TTY 323-478-8000, www.gladinc.org; counseling, job development, translation, and information for the hearing-impaired.
- **Goodwill Industries of Southern California**, 323-223-1211; counseling, job placement, and educational services
- **Independent Living Center of Southern California**, 818-988-9525, TTY 818-988-3533
- **Jay Nolan Community Services**, 818-361-6400; serves people with developmental disabilities, including autism.
- **Los Angeles Caregiver Resource Center**, 800-540-4442; resource for caregivers of brain-impaired adults.
- **Los Angeles County Adult Protective Services**, 213-351-5401, 800-992-1660; report abuse of dependent adults to this number
- **Los Angeles County Commission on Disabilities**, 213-974-1053, TTY 213-974-1707
- **Los Angeles County Deaf Information**, 800-660-4026
- **Los Angeles City Department on Disability**, 213-485-6334, TTY 213-485-6655, www.lacity.org/dod
- **LA Unified School District Parent Resource Network Hotline**, 800-933-8133, www.lausd.k12.ca.us; information and referrals to special education programs.
- **North Los Angeles County Regional Center**, 818-778-1900, www.nlacrc.com; services for people with developmental disabilities
- **Recording for the Blind and Dyslexic**, 800-499-5525, www.lafn.org/community/rfbd; records over 3,000 new books each year on audio cassettes for loan to students and adults who cannot read standard print because of a visual, perceptual, or physical disability: Los Angeles, 323-664-5525.
- **Social Security and Medicare Eligibility Information**, 800-772-1213, TTY 800-288-7185, www.socialsecurity.gov
- **Spinal Cord Injury Network International**, 800-548-2673; information network and video library for people with spinal cord injuries
- **Venice Skills Center**, 310-392-4153, offers free rehabilitation services for people with disabilities, such as sign language interpreters for the hearing impaired, readers for the blind, and job placement assistance and counseling.
- **Westside Regional Center for Independent Living**, 310-258-4000; offers a variety of services, from counseling to living skills, for seniors and people with developmental disabilities.

COMMUNICATION

Telephone relay service for the hearing/speech impaired is available free of charge via the **California Relay Service** (**CRS**). They will relay phone calls between TTY and voice callers. There is no charge for the service itself; however, regular toll and long-distance fees apply. For TTY to voice, call 800-735-2929; voice to TTY, 800-735-2922. You can also dial 711 anywhere in the US to reach the relay service.

Special adaptive telecommunications equipment can be obtained free of charge by qualified California residents via the **California Telephone Access Program**, 800-806-1191, TTY 800-806-4474.

GETTING AROUND

Contact your local **DMV** for handicapped licenses: In LA, call 800-777-0133, TTY 800-368-4327, or visit www.dmv.ca.gov. If you need a blue curb painted at your residence, contact the **Department of Transportation Bureau of Parking Management and Regulations Analysis Section** at 323-913-4620. Expect about two weeks for completion. For those who need other forms of special transportation, these are some options:

- **Access Services** provides curb-to-curb transportation for disabled residents of LA County, 800-827-0829, TTY 800-827-1359, www.asila.org.
- **Cityride** provides curb-to-curb transportation for seniors and mobility-impaired residents of the San Fernando Valley and Los Angeles, 818-908-1901.
- **Culver City Bus**, 310-253-6500, TTY 310-253-6548, www.culvercity.org
- **Lift Van Program**, 323-761-8810, provides inexpensive lift van transportation for wheelchair-bound residents to any destination within an eight-mile radius of the user's departure point (within West Hollywood and Beverly Hills only).
- **Health Link Medi-van**, 888-633-4743, provides non-emergency medical transportation service for Valley and Los Angeles residents.
- **Metrolink**, 800-371-5465, TTY 800-698-4833, www.metrolink trains.com
- **Metro**, 800-266-6883, TTY 800-252-9040, www.mta.net; **Disabled Riders Emergency Hotline**, 800-621-7828
- **Paratransit Information Referral Service**, 800-431-7882, TTY 800-431-9731; clearinghouse of transportation services for seniors and mobility-impaired residents of LA County

- **Santa Monica Municipal Bus Lines**, 310-451-5444, TTY 310-395-6024, www.bigbluebus.com
- **Taxi Coupons**, 323-761-8810; program allows persons age 65 and older, and residents of any age who are wheelchair-users or blind, to purchase one book of discounted taxi coupons per month.

ADDITIONAL RESOURCES—PEOPLE WITH DISABILITIES

- The Los Angeles Housing Department sponsors a **Handyworker** program, providing minor repairs to low- and moderate-income home-owners who are physically disabled, or to senior citizens 62 years and older, free of charge. Repairs can take place anywhere from two weeks to nine months after a request, depending upon the required repair and the demand for services in your area. There is currently a waiting list for service in some communities. Call 213-808-8803, 866-557-7368, or go to www.cityofla.org/lahd for more information.
- The Los Angeles City Fire Department offers a **Fire Safety**, and a **Safety and Earthquake Program for the Disabled**. Contact the Disaster Preparedness Section at 818-756-9672. Their web site also features a detailed "Earthquake Preparedness Handbook": www.lafd.org/eqhbtext.htm.
- **Bet Tzedek Legal Services**, 323-939-0506, www.bettzedek.org, provides free legal services to low- and moderate-income residents, the disabled, and the frail elderly in the areas of nursing home law, power of attorney, and other health issues.
- The **Western Law Center for the Handicapped** at Loyola Law School, 213-736-1031, offers legal advocacy on disability rights issues.
- The **Partners Adult Day Healthcare Center**, 323-883-0330, sponsored by the city of West Hollywood, is for the frail elderly, younger disabled adults, and persons with AIDS.

IMMIGRANT NEWCOMERS

Those new to the USA may find the following information useful.

CONSULATES

There are over 30 consulates in Los Angeles. Here are a few:
- **Consulate General of Australia**, Century Plaza Towers, 19th Floor, 2049 Century Park East, LA, CA 90067, 310-229-4800, www.austemb.org

- **Consulate General of Austria**, 11859 Wilshire Blvd., Ste. 501, LA, CA 90025, 310-444-9310, www.austria.org/tel_la.shtml
- **Consulate General of Brazil**, 8484 Wilshire Blvd., Ste. 730, LA, CA 90211, 323-651-2664, www.brasilemb.org
- **Consulate General of Canada**, 550 South Hope Street, 9th Floor, LA, CA 90071, 213-346-2700, www.canadianembassy.org
- **Consulate General of China**, 443 Shatto Place, LA, CA 90020, 213-807-8088, www.chinaconsulatela.org
- **Consulate General of Columbia**, 8383 Wilshire Blvd., Ste. 420, LA, CA 90211, 323-653-4299, www.colombiaemb.org
- **Consulate General of Costa Rica**, 1605 West Olympic Blvd., Ste. 400, LA, CA 90015, 213-380-7915, http://costarica-embassy.org
- **Consulate General of Finland**, 1801 Century Park East, Ste. 2100, LA, CA 90067, 310-203-9903, www.finlandla.org
- **Consulate General of France**, 10990 Wilshire Blvd., Ste. 300, LA, CA 90024, 310-235-3200, www.consulfrance-losangeles.org
- **Consulate General of the Federal Republic of Germany**, 6222 Wilshire Blvd., Ste. 500, LA, CA 90048, 323-930-2703, www.germany-info.org
- **Consulate General of Greece**, 12424 Wilshire Blvd., Ste. 800, LA, CA 90025, 310-826-5555, www.greekembassy.org
- **Consulate General of Honduras**, 3450 Wilshire Blvd., Ste. 230, LA, CA 90010, 213-383-9244
- **Consulate General of Indonesia**, 3457 Wilshire Blvd., LA, CA 90010, 800-615-8648, www.kjri-la.net
- **Consulate General of Israel**, 6380 Wilshire Blvd., Ste. 1700, LA, CA 90048, 323-852-5500, http://israelemb.org/la
- **Consulate General of Italy**, 12400 Wilshire Blvd., Ste. 300, LA, CA 90025, 310-820-0622, http://sedi.esteri.it/losangeles
- **Consulate General of Japan**, 2350 South Grand Avenue, Ste. 1700, LA, CA 90071, 213-617-6700, www.la.us.emb-japan.go.jp
- **Consulate General of Malaysia**, 550 South Hope Street, Ste. 400, LA, CA 90071-1203, 213-892-1238
- **Consulate General of Mexico**, 2401 West 6th Street, LA, CA 90057, 213-351-6800, www.sre.gob.mx/losangeles
- **Consulate General of The Netherlands**, 11766 Wilshire Blvd., Ste. 1150, LA, CA 90025, 310-268-1598
- **Consulate General of Nicaragua**, 3550 Wilshire Blvd., Ste. 200, LA, CA 90010, 213-252-1178
- **Consulate General of New Zealand**, 12400 Wilshire Blvd., Ste. 1150, LA, CA 90025, 310-207-1605
- **Consulate General of Peru**, 3460 Wilshire Blvd, Ste. 1005, LA, CA 90036, 213-252-8599

- **Consulate General of Philippines**, 3600 Wilshire Blvd. Ste. 500, LA, CA 90010, 213-639-0980
- **Consulate General of Poland**, 12400 Wilshire Blvd. Ste. 555, LA, CA 90025, 310-442-8500, www.polishconsulatela.com
- **Consulate General of Portugal**, 1801 Avenue of the Stars, Ste. 400, LA, CA 90067, 310-277-1491
- **Consulate General of Romania**, 11766 Wilshire Blvd., Ste. 560, LA, CA 90025, 310-444-0043
- **Consulate General of Saudi Arabia**, 2045 Sawtelle Blvd., LA, CA 90025, 310-479-6000
- **Consulate General of South Korea**, 3243 Wilshire Blvd., LA, CA 90010, 213-385-9300
- **Consulate General of Spain**, 5055 Wilshire Blvd., Ste. 960, LA, CA 90036, 323-938-0158
- **Consulate General of Sweden**, 10940 Wilshire Blvd., Ste. 700, LA, CA 90024, 310-445-4008
- **Consulate General of Taipei (Taiwan)**, 3731 Wilshire Blvd., Ste. 700 LA, CA 90010, 213-389-1215, www.taipei.org
- **Consulate General of Thailand**, 611 North Larchmont Blvd., 2nd Floor, LA, CA 90004, 323-962-9574, www.thai-la.net
- **Consulate General of the United Kingdom of Great Britain and Northern Ireland**, 11766 Wilshire Blvd., Ste. 1200, LA, CA 90025-6540, 310-481-0031

CITIZENSHIP AND IMMIGRATION SERVICES

The Los Angeles District Office for the **US Citizenship and Immigration Services (CIS)** is at 300 North Los Angeles Street, Room 1001, Los Angeles, CA 90012, 213-830-5122, http://uscis.gov.

IMMIGRATION RESOURCES

- **Bureau of Immigration and Customs Enforcement**, www.bice. immigration.gov
- **Customs & Border Protection**, www.cbp.gov
- **Department of Homeland Security**, www.dhs.gov, www.white house.gov/deptofhomeland
- **General Government Questions**, 800-688-9889, www.firstgov.gov
- **Social Security Administration**, 800-772-1213, www.ssa.gov
- **US Bureau of Consular Affairs**, www.travel.state.gov

- **US Department of State, Visa Services**, http://travel.state.gov/visa_services
- **US Immigration Online—Green Cards, Visas, Government Specific Forms—USA Immigration Services**, www.usaimmigration service.org

IMMIGRATION PUBLICATIONS

- ***The Immigration Handbook***, 3rd edition, by Henry Liebman (First Books)
- ***Newcomer's Handbook for Moving to and Living in the USA***, by Mike Livingston (First Books)

MOVING PETS TO THE USA

- ***The Pet-Moving Handbook*** (First Books) covers domestic and international moves, via car, airplane, ferry, etc. Primary focus is on cats and dogs.
- **Cosmopolitan Canine Carriers** out of Connecticut, 800-243-9105, has been shipping dogs and cats all over the world for over 25 years. Contact them with questions or concerns regarding air transportation arrangements, vaccinations, and quarantine times.

GAY AND LESBIAN LIFE

When you're in Los Angeles, especially around West Hollywood and Los Feliz, the joke about that cute single man probably being gay is often true. In fact, the City of West Hollywood is *the* openly gay and lesbian enclave, offering a Domestic Partnership Ordinance to its residents. This ordinance officially recognizes domestic partnerships between two adults (regardless of sexual orientation) if they are each other's sole partner and are responsible for each other's welfare. Contact the **Domestic Partnerships Department** at 323-848-6332 or 323-848-6400, www.weho.org for information on how to apply for a Certificate of Domestic Partnership (a $25 fee applies).

Much of the night scene is focused on a long stretch of Santa Monica Boulevard in West Hollywood, from La Brea Avenue to La Cienega Boulevard, where bars, restaurants, and clubs are packed shoulder to shoulder on weekend nights. Every June the Gay Pride Parade is held on this same street. On Halloween night, those of every persuasion converge on the Boulevard in costume. The main event at this free, wild street party is the show by the drag queens, who pull out all the stops. In the summer, head to Silverlake for the annual Sunset Junction Street Festival (323-661-

7771, www.sunsetjunction.org). Originally held in 1980 to ease tensions between the established working class Latino families and the then newer gay residents, today this block party is a well-established and well-received annual event. A donation is requested for entry.

Following is a list of some **local organizations** that specialize in gay and lesbian issues:

- **AIDS Project Los Angeles**, 213-201-1600, www.apla.org; provides comprehensive assistance to persons living with HIV/AIDS, and an AIDS information hotline
- **American Civil Liberties Union (ACLU)**, 213-977-9500, www.aclu-sc.org; provides civil liberties litigation and legal referrals
- **Anti-Gay-Bashing** resources, 323-848-6414
- **GLAAD**, Los Angeles chapter, 323-933-2240, www.glaad.org
- **Gay & Lesbian Association of Santa Clarita**, 661-288-2814, www.glasc.com
- **Gay & Lesbian Adolescent Social Services**, 310-358-8727, www.glassla.org
- **Gay and Lesbian Sports Alliance of Greater Los Angeles**, 310-515-3337, www.lasportsalliance.org; promotes recreational and competitive sports within the community
- **Los Angeles Gay & Lesbian Center**, 323-993-7400, www.laglc.org; provides a variety of social and health services
- **West Hollywood Cares**, 310-659-4840

LOCAL GAY PUBLICATIONS

- *The Advocate*, 800-827-0561, www.advocate.com
- *Frontiers Magazines*, 323-848-2222, www.frontiersnewsmagazine.com
- *The Lesbian News*, 800-458-9888, www.lesbiannews.com

A S IN MOST MAJOR US CITIES, FINDING GOOD DAYCARE CAN BE difficult and waiting lists abound for highly recommended daycare centers. Los Angeles has over 3,000 licensed childcare centers and over 3,800 licensed family childcare providers, the quality of which varies, so screen carefully. California requires a license for any childcare provider who cares for the children of more than one family. To check if your childcare provider's license is up to date, or to investigate any filed complaints against the provider, call the **Department of Social Services Community Care Licensing Offices**, 310-337-4333 or 323-981-3350, or go to www.ccld.ca.gov to conduct a search. If a provider is exempt from licensing, you can contact the **Trust Line**, 800-822-8490, www.trust line.org, to see if she is registered. All providers registered on Trust Line's site have passed a background check. The provider pays a listing fee that subsidizes the cost of the check so there's no charge for the inquiry.

Other resources for parents include the **National Resource Center for Health and Safety and Child Care**, 800-598-KIDS, http:// nrc.uchsc.edu. Los Angeles parents might want to visit www. LAparent.com for its community discussion boards on topics from the going rate for a babysitter to determining when your youngster is ready for kindergarten.

Please note: *Listing in this book is merely informational and is **not** an endorsement. When entrusting your child to strangers, always err on the side of safety and caution.*

CHILDCARE

DAYCARE

When looking for the right daycare, begin with referrals from friends, family, and co-workers or try the **California Child Care Resource & Referral**

Network, 415-882-0234, www.rrnetwork.org, a state resource and referral agency. Additional organizations that offer resources and referrals for day-care providers and in some cases parenting advice or other services include:

- **Center for Community and Family Services**, 888-421-4247, www.chsca.org; provides referrals for the county.
- **Pathways**, 213-427-2700; provides referrals for Central Los Angeles, Hollywood, Silverlake, and Beverly Hills
- **Child Care Resource Center**, Van Nuys, 818-756-3360; refers parents to child daycare and family daycare centers
- **Connections for Children**: Santa Monica, 310-452-3202; West LA, 310-322-1877
- **Early Childhood Parenting Center**, 310-281-9770; information line offering advice on rearing children
- **LA County Child Care Information and Resources Directory**, http://childcare.co.la.ca.us, has an exhaustive directory of licensed childcare centers. Their web site also provides links to local childcare referrals, a childcare provider checklist, and after-school enrichment programs
- **The Help Company**, Santa Monica, 310-828-4111; a childcare referral service.
- **YWCA** of Los Angeles, 213-365-2991, www.ywcagla.org; provides childcare and support services for parents

List of prospective childcare providers in hand, your next step should be to make sure a facility is licensed by visiting http://childcare.co.la.ca.us, and then investigate the centers, visiting each at least a couple times, preferably unannounced. Consider the following:

- Is the center conscientious about how it handles check-ins and check-outs?
- Examine the kitchen, play area, bathroom, and grounds for safety and cleanliness: Is disinfectant used in the kitchen and bathroom; are toys age appropriate and in good condition; are there any potential hazards lying around?
- Check for indoor and outdoor play areas.
- Watch the children at the center: Do they seem happy, well-behaved, and well-supervised? Do they respond well to the attendants? Observe the caregivers with the children.
- Review the daily schedule to make sure the kids have what you think is an appropriate balance of active time and quiet time, and age-appropriate activities.
- You should also determine qualifications of the employees and ask about the staff turnover rate. Also, ask for references—names and

phone numbers of other parents whose children are enrolled whom you can contact.

BABYSITTERS

The best source for babysitting is to ask around—friends, neighbors, co-workers; if you're lucky they may give up a name from their list. Membership in a church or synagogue can be a good source for referrals. In the Yellow Pages, check out the "Baby-Sitters" and "Nurses & Nurses Registries" sections. The **LA Baby Sitters Guild**, 310-837-1800 and the **Glendale, Burbank, Pasadena Baby Sitters Guild**, 818-552-2229, offer referrals. These on-call services (with a four-hour minimum) may be able to point you to someone who will provide regular service.

NANNIES

Need a sitter on a more permanent basis? Tired of toting the kids off to day-care? A nanny may be the right choice for you. If the cost is prohibitive and you aren't in need of a full-time nanny, consider doing a nanny-share with another family and thereby splitting the cost. To find a good match, nanny referral agencies are available and offer the benefit of prescreening applicants for you, but they will cost more than if you locate one yourself. If you are hiring a nanny without the help of an agency (see below), you'll want to do a background check, which can be done online. Go to any search engine and type in "employment screening." A host of companies is available to research criminal records, driving records, and credit information for you. Check local parent magazines or the "Help Wanted" section in the *Los Angeles Times*, or see the resources above under **Babysitters** for more ideas. The following companies offer a range of domestic care providers. For a full listing check the Yellow Pages under "Nannies" (inclusion here does not imply endorsement by First Books):

- **Buckingham Nannies**, 310-247-1877, 818-784-6504, www.buckinghamnannies.com
- **Domestic Solutions**, 323-845-1433, www.domesticsolution.com
- **Family Care Agency**, 818-345-2950, www.familycareagency.com
- **Golden Maid Agency**, 818-981-4444
- **Huntington Nannies**, 888-796-2669, www.huntingtonnannies.com
- **Nannies Etc.**, 310-470-776, 818-342-5454, www.nanniesetc.com
- **Nannies on the Net**, 888-346-2669, www.nannyonthenet.com
- **The Nanny Exchange**, 310-440-1088
- **TeacherCare**, 888-TEACH-07, www.teachercare.com
- **Tender Care Agency**, 818-366-6718

NANNY TAXES

For those hiring a nanny directly (not using a nanny agency) there are certain taxes you will be responsible for calculating, specifically social security and Medicare, and possibly unemployment. For help with such issues, check the **Nanitax** web site, www.4nannytaxes.com, or call 800-626-4829. Nanitax provides household payroll and employment tax preparation services. You can also check with The **Nanny Tax Company**, 800-747-9826, **www.nannytaxprep.com**, or the **IRS's** household employer page, www.irs.gov/taxtopics/tc756.html, which discusses taxes for household employees.

AU PAIRS

If you land the right applicant, an au pair (typically, a young woman—18 to 25—from abroad who will take care of your child and do light housekeeping in exchange for room, board, and a weekly stipend) may be a better alternative than a nanny. However, an au pair will likely not have the extended experience of a professional nanny, usually works for only one year, and is required to enroll in an accredited post-secondary institution for not less than six semester hours of academic credit. The **US Department of State's Bureau of Educational and Cultural Affairs**, 202-647-4000, http://exchanges.state.gov, oversees and approves the organizations that offer this service in the US. The national agencies below can match your family with an au pair:

- **Au Pair in America**, 800-928-7247, www.aupairinamerica.com
- **Go Au Pair**, 888-AUPAIR1, www.goaupair.com
- **Au Pair USA/Interchange**, 212-924-0446 www.interexchange.org
- **Au PairCare Inc.**, 800-4AUPAIR, www.aupaircare.com
- **Cultural Care Au Pair**, 800-333-6056, www.culturalcare.com
- **EurAupair Intercultural Child Care Programs**, 949-494-5500, www.euraupair.com
- **TrekAmerica**, 973-983-1144, www.trekamerica.com

SCHOOLS

The following covers elementary and secondary schools; colleges and universities are discussed in the **Cultural Life** chapter.

PARENT RESOURCES

Newcomers with school-aged children may find it helpful to obtain a listing of schools in LA County when beginning their search for a school. The **LA County Office of Education's (LACOE)** web site, www.lacoe.edu, offers a listing of its school districts. For more information, call or write: 562-922-6111, 9300 East Imperial Highway, Downey, CA 90242. For a listing of all the public and private schools in Los Angeles County, visit the **California Department of Education's** school directory at www.cde.ca.gov/re/sd. You may purchase a hard copy of its "Public Schools Directory" or "Private Schools Directory" by calling 800-995-4099.

Parents researching an appropriate school for their children have a number of resources at their disposal. Comprehensive web sites to investigate public and private school scores and standings include the **California Department of Education's** web site, www.cde.ca.gov, and the **Ed-Data Education Partnership**, www.ed-data.k12.ca.us, which posts the latest fiscal, demographic, and performance data on public schools. Some opt to use **Instant SchoolMatch**, www.schoolmatch. com, 800-992-5323, to research public school districts based on selected criteria for free. There is a fee for their detailed "report card." The **School Report** provides information consisting mainly of statistics (total enrollment, student to teacher ratio, etc.) for any school district of your choice at www.theschoolreport.com. (The web site is advertiser supported, so the service is free, provided you fill out a brief survey.) Another site widely used by real estate agents, which "helps parents get smart about schools" is **School Wise Press**, www.schoolwisepress.com. The site offers school rankings and profiles, as well as school-related news articles. In-depth reports are available for a fee.

Often, parents' involvement in their children's education does not end once the kids are enrolled. Parent groups include the **California State Parent Teacher Association** (PTA), 213-620-1100, www.capta.org, a united forum of parents, teachers, and school administrators that meet to address education issues; **Parents for Unity** (PFU), 323-734-9353, which provides assistance with grievance resolution within LA Unified School District; and the **California Association for the Gifted**, 562-789-9933, www.cagifted.org, which provides support for the academically advanced child.

PUBLIC SCHOOLS

The **Los Angeles Unified School District** (**LAUSD**), www.lausd. k12.ca.us, has the second largest student population in the nation, serving over 740,000 students. And, as with most metropolitan areas in the USA, student test scores tend to be higher in the wealthier communities. Within LA Unified, the Westside and the San Fernando Valley are home to some of the more highly regarded schools, and Beverly Hills Unified School District is lauded as one of the best school districts in LA County. Keep in mind, however, that student achievement scores don't tell the whole story. A school's overall test scores may be affected by immigrant students who have yet to achieve English proficiency, and parental involvement and dedicated teachers have more to do with student performance than income levels.

Individual neighborhood districts within LA Unified are broken into "clusters." When considering a prospective neighborhood, call LA Unified to find out which cluster/district your child would be attending, and whether students are bused in (done to ease overcrowding in certain schools). LA Unified's school locator information line is 213-241-KIDS, or go online to www.lausd.net. To register your child in LA Unified, you must show proof of the child's age, residency, and immunization for polio, diphtheria, tetanus, hepatitis B, whooping cough, rubeola (measles), rubella, and mumps. Call 800-933-8133 for enrollment information. About one-third of the schools within LA Unified are "multi-track" (also called year-around), which is where a student enrolls in one of three to four possible schedules or "tracks"), but most follow traditional "single track" September to June schedules.

LA Unified offers a straightforward open enrollment program: A student who resides in one cluster can petition to attend a school outside of his or her cluster—on a space-available basis; the number of seats available to students who want to take advantage of this program is limited. State law requires that a school accommodate students from its neighborhoods first before offering open enrollments. Factors involved in the scarcity of seats at some schools include the rise in immigration to Los Angeles and the ambitious class-size reduction program (mandating a maximum of 20 students to one teacher in kindergarten through third grades and in some ninth grade classes). Priority is given to current open enrollment students who wish to continue attending schools in the same feeder school pattern, which follows the district's general student transfer policies. Parents may apply for open enrollment transfers to as many schools as they wish. If parents are applying to send several children to the same school, a separate application must be filled out for each child. Applications are typically accepted during May for the following school year. The list of schools with open enrollment seats is usually available in the main office of every school beginning in late April or early May. Once the application period ends in late May, schools with more applicants than seats available will hold random drawings to determine who will be invited to enroll.

Within Los Angeles there are over 100 **magnet schools** and **magnet centers** that emphasize specialty areas, such as mathematics and science, and performing arts. Contact your prospective district for specific information on its magnet programs and to request an application form. Applicants do not have to meet any criteria (grades, test scores, auditions, etc.) to be admitted to a magnet school, the only exception being the highly gifted magnets (applicants must meet intellectual assessment criteria set by the LAUSD). The application deadline is typically late January for enrollment for the following fall. Parents are notified in April or May as to whether their children are accepted or wait listed. Most children accepted for a magnet are provided with transportation.

Some of LA Unified's magnet schools are:

- The **Brentwood Science Magnet School**, 740 Gretna Green Way, West LA, 310-826-5631, www.lausd.k12.ca.us, is the largest magnet elementary school in the LA Unified School District. Over 1,000 students make up the kindergarten through fifth grades. Studies emphasize one of four areas: Biological Science, Physical Science, Earth Science, and Computer Literacy.

- The **32nd Street/USC Magnet School**, 822 West 32nd Street, LA, 213-748-0126; its inner city campus comprises two distinct schools, a visual and performing arts magnet school of K-8th grades and a math/science magnet for high school. It is one of only five campuses in the Los Angeles Unified School District to have all grade school ages. The magnet is a member of the University of Southern California's "Family of Five Schools" program (www.usc.edu/ext-relations/unipark/family_of_five.html) where USC students perform outreach work and share university resources with young students.

- **Portola Middle School**, 18720 Linnet Street, Tarzana, 818-342-6173, www.lausd.net/Portola_Gifted_MS; offers "enriched and accelerated academic opportunities" among a multi-cultural student body. Students must meet the LA Unified's intellectual assessment criteria to apply for enrollment in a highly gifted magnet.

- The **North Hollywood High School**, 5231 Colfax Avenue, North Hollywood, 818-769-8510, www.lausd.k12.ca.us, is a year round school that is the base for two magnet programs, the Biological Sciences Zoo Magnet and the Highly Gifted Magnet. Of special note is that the biological sciences magnet classes are held at the Los Angeles Zoo.

- **Los Angeles High School**, 4650 West Olympic Blvd., 323-937-3210, www.lausd.k12.ca.us/Los_Angeles_HS; math and science magnet.

Their highly touted Academic Decathlon teams frequently advance to the state and national level competitions.

LOS ANGELES COUNTY SCHOOL DISTRICTS

- **Acton-Agua Dulce Unified School District**, 32248 North Crown Valley Road, Acton, CA 93510, 661-269-5999, www.aadusd.k12.ca.us
- **Antelope Valley Union High School District**, 44811 Sierra Highway, Lancaster, CA 93534, 661-948-7655, www.avdistrict.org
- **Bellflower Unified School District**, 16703 Clark Avenue, Bellflower, CA 90706, 562-866-9011, www.busd.k12.ca.us
- **Beverly Hills Unified School District**, 255 South Lasky Drive, Beverly Hills, CA 90212, 310-551-5100, www.beverlyhills.k12.ca.us
- **Burbank Unified School District**, 1900 West Olive Avenue, Burbank, CA 91506, 818-729-4400, www.burbank.k12.ca.us
- **Culver City Unified School District**, 4034 Irving Place, Culver City, CA 90232, 310-842-4220, www.ccusd.k12.ca.us
- **Downey Unified School District**, 11627 Brookshire Avenue, Downey, CA 90241, 562-904-6500, www.dusd.net
- **El Segundo Unified School District**, 641 Sheldon Street, El Segundo, CA 90245, 310-615-2650, www.elsegundousd.com
- **Glendale Unified School District**, 223 North Jackson Street, Glendale, CA 91206, 818-241-3111, www.glendale.k12.ca.us
- **Inglewood Unified School District**, 401 South Inglewood Avenue, Inglewood, CA 90301, 310-419-2700, www.inglewood.k12.ca.us
- **La Canada Unified School District**, 5039 Palm Drive, La Canada, CA 91011, 818-952-8300, www.lcusd.net
- **Lancaster School District**, 44711 North Cedar Avenue, Lancaster, CA 93534, 661-948-4661, www.lancaster.k12.ca.us
- **LA County Office of Education**, 9300 Imperial Hwy., Ste. 109, Downey, CA 90242, 562-922-6111, www.lacoe.edu
- **LA Unified School District**, 333 South Beaudry Avenue, LA, CA 90017, 213-241-1000; www.lausd.k12.ca.us
- **Long Beach Unified School District**, 1515 Hughes Way, Long Beach, CA 90810, 562-997-8000, www.lbusd.k12.ca.us
- **Manhattan Beach Unified School District**, 325 South Peck Avenue, Manhattan Beach, CA 90266, 310-318-7345, www.manhattan.k12.ca.us
- **Newhall School District**, 25375 Orchard Village Road, Valencia, CA 91355, 661-286-2200, www.newhall.k12.ca.us
- **Norwalk-La Mirada Unified School District**, 12820 Pioneer Blvd., Norwalk, CA 90650, 562-868-0431, www.nlmusd.k12.ca.us

- **Palmdale School District**, 39139 North 10th Street East, Palmdale, CA 93550, 661-947-7191, www.psd.k12.ca.us
- **Paramount Unified School District**, 15110 California Avenue, Paramount, CA 90723, 562-602-6000, www.paramount.k12.ca.us
- **Pasadena Unified School District**, 351 South Hudson Avenue, Pasadena, CA 91109, 626-795-6981, www.pasadena.k12.ca.us, www.pusd.us
- **Redondo Beach Unified School District**, 1401 Inglewood Avenue, Redondo Beach, CA 90278, 310-379-5449, www.rbusd.org
- **San Marino Unified School District**, 1665 West Drive, San Marino, CA 91108, 626-299-7000, www.san-marino.k-12.ca.us
- **Santa Monica-Malibu Unified School District**, 1651 16th Street, Santa Monica, CA 90405, 310-450-8338, www.smmusd.org
- **Saugus Union School District**, 24930 Avenue Stanford, Santa Clarita, CA 91355, 661-294-5300, www.saugus.k12.ca.us
- **South Pasadena Unified School District**, 1020 El Centro Street, South Pasadena, CA, 626-441-5700, www.spusd.k12.ca.us
- **Torrance Unified School District**, 2335 Plaza Del Amo, Torrance, CA 90501, 310-972-6500, www.tusd.k12.ca.us
- **William S. Hart Union High School District**, 21515 Centre Point Pkwy., Santa Clarita, CA, 91350, 661-259-0033, www.hart.k12.ca.us

SURROUNDING COUNTY SCHOOL DISTRICTS

- **Irvine Unified School District**, 5050 Barranca Parkway, Irvine, CA 92604; 949-936-5000, www.iusd.org
- **Newport-Mesa Unified School District**, 2985-A Bear Street, Costa Mesa, CA 92626, 714-424-5000, www.nmusd.k12.ca.us
- **Orange County Department of Education**, 200 Kalmus Drive, Costa Mesa, CA 92626, 714-966-4000, www.ocde.k12.ca.us
- **Riverside County Office of Education**, 3939 Thirteenth Street (P.O. Box 868), Riverside, CA 92502-0868, 909-826-6530, www.rcoe.k12.ca.us
- **San Diego County Office of Education**, 6401 Linda Vista Road, San Diego, CA 91111-7399, 858-292-3500, www.sdcoe.k12.ca.us
- **Tustin Unified School District**, 300 South C Street, Tustin, CA 92780, 714-730-7301, www.tustin.k12.ca.us
- **Ventura County Superintendent of Schools Office**, 5189 Verdugo Way, Camarillo, CA 93012, 805-383-1900, www.vcss.k12.ca.us

PRIVATE SCHOOLS

If you are considering private schooling for your child, there are a lot of options. Many parents choose private schooling because of the lower student to teacher ratio and its reputation for higher quality education. However, it doesn't come cheap. Entrance requirements vary from school to school, so get details when you contact them. For a list of all the private schools within LA, check the **California Department of Education's School Directory** at www.cde.ca.gov/re/sd, or call 916-319-0800. As well, the city's **Human Relations Commission**, 213-978-1660, may also be able to provide information. The following list is a sample of private schools. Check **Parent Resources** (see above) for tips on researching schools:

- **Academy of Princeton College Preparatory** (6-12), 14615 Sherman Way, Van Nuys, 818-766-9346
- **Bethel Lutheran Elementary** (K-6), 17500 Burbank Blvd., Encino, 818-788-2663
- **Beverly Hills Prep** (7-12), 9250 Olympic Blvd., Beverly Hills, 310-276-0151
- **Beverly Hills Montessori School** (pre-school-K), 1105 North Laurel Avenue, West Hollywood, 323-650-2922, www.bhms.org
- **Burbank Montessori Academy** (pre-school-3), 217 North Hollywood Way, Burbank, 818-848-8226
- **Fairfield School** (K-8), 16945 Sherman Way, Lake Balboa, 818-996-4560
- **Harvard-Westlake School** (7-12), 3700 Coldwater Canyon, Studio City, 818-980-6692
- **Hillel Hebrew Academy** (K-8), 9120 West Olympic Blvd., Beverly Hills, 310-276-6135
- **Laurel Hall** (K-8), 11919 Oxnard Street, North Hollywood, 818-763-5434, http://laurelhall.angelcities.com
- **Los Angeles Lutheran Junior-Senior High School** (7-12), 13570 Eldridge Avenue, Sylmar, 818-362-5861
- **Montessori Learning Center** (K-6), 11363 Washington Blvd., Culver City, 310-391-7004
- **Montessori School Santa Monica** (K-9), 1909 Colorado Avenue, Santa Monica, 310-829-3551
- **New World Montessori School** (K-6), 10520 Regent Street, West LA, 310-838-4044
- **Saint Monica's Catholic High School** (9-12), 1030 Lincoln Blvd., Santa Monica, 310-394-3701, www.stmonicahs.org
- **Summit View School** (K-12), 6455 Coldwater Canyon Avenue, Valley Glen, 818-779-5262, www.summitview.org

- **Venture School** (9-12), 5333 South Sepulveda Blvd., Culver City, 310-559-2678
- **West LA Baptist School** (7-12), 1609 South Barrington Avenue, West LA, 310-826-2050

HOME SCHOOLING RESOURCES

Those who educate their children at home can turn to the **Home School Association of California**, 805-462-0726, www.hsc.org, for assistance with starting a school at home. The **Alternative Schools of California**, 818-846-8990, is another resource.

I T WOULD BE AN UNDERSTATEMENT TO SAY THAT SHOPPING IS A popular pastime in Los Angeles. From chi-chi boutiques on Rodeo Drive in Beverly Hills to Pasadena's flea market-type Rose Bowl Swap Meet, LA is a slice of heaven for shopping mavens, many of whom liken it to an indoor sport.

Below is a list of full-service department stores where you can do a good portion of your shopping, followed by specialty stores, a list of second-hand shopping districts, and finally food...shopping requires so much energy. (Bookstores are discussed separately in the **Cultural Life** chapter.)

Unless otherwise noted, listings are in Los Angeles.

SHOPPING MALLS AND DISTRICTS

MALLS

The Grove and Hollywood & Highland are the two newest malls within the city and have been wildly successful at revitalizing their neighborhood environs. Most of the full-service department stores like Robinsons-May and Macy's can be found in the larger malls. Here are the major malls, and the big department stores that anchor them

- **The Beverly Center**, 8500 Beverly Blvd., 310-854-0070, www.beverly center.com; this mall includes Macy's and Bed, Bath & Beyond
- **Glendale Galleria**, 2148 Glendale Galleria, Glendale, 818-246-6737, www.glendalegalleria.com; anchored by Nordstrom and Macy's
- **The Grove**, 189 The Grove Drive, 323-900-8080, www.thegrovela. com; European-inspired open-air mall with a trolley that runs through the middle of its cobblestoned street, next door to the year-round Farmers' Market

- **Hollywood & Highland**, 6201 Hollywood Blvd., Hollywood, 323-467-6412, www.hollywoodandhighland.com; home of the Kodak Theater, upscale restaurants, retail stores, a night club, and Renaissance Hollywood Hotel
- **Media City Center**, East Magnolia and North San Fernando boulevards, Burbank, 818-566-8617, www.mediacitymall.com; anchored by Macy's, Sears, and AMC Theaters
- **Northridge Fashion Center**, 9301 Tampa Avenue, Northridge, 818-885-9700, www.northridgefashioncenter.com; features Macy's and Robinsons-May
- **Paseo Colorado**, Colorado Blvd. and Los Robles Avenue, Pasadena, 626-795-8891, www.paseocoloradopasadena.com
- **The Promenade at Howard Hughes Center**, 6081 Center Drive, 310-641-8073, www.hhpromenade.com
- **Santa Monica Place**, 395 Santa Monica Place, Santa Monica, 310-394-1049, www.santamonicaplace.com; anchored by Robinsons-May and Macy's
- **Sunset Plaza**, 8623 West Sunset Blvd., West Hollywood, 310-652-2622; chic outdoor strip lined with designer clothiers and trendy sidewalk cafes
- **Two Rodeo**, 9480 Dayton Way, Beverly Hills, 310-247-7040, www.2rodeo.com; beautiful cobblestone street lined with upscale stores, anchored by Tiffany's
- **Valencia Town Center**, McBean Parkway and Magic Mountain Parkway, Santa Clarita, 661-287-9050, www.valenciatowncenter.com; anchored by Robinsons-May and Sears
- **Westfield Shoppingtown Century City**, 10250 Santa Monica Blvd., Century City, 310-277-3898, www.westfield.com; anchored by Macy's and Bloomingdale's
- **Westfield Shoppingtown Fashion Square**, 14006 Riverside Drive, Sherman Oaks, 818-783-0550, www.westfield.com; anchored by Macy's
- **Westfield Shoppingtown Fox Hills**, 924 Foxhills Mall, Culver City, 310-390-7833, www.westfield.com; major department stores include Robinsons-May and JC Penney
- **Westfield Shoppingtown Promenade**, 6100 Topanga Canyon Blvd., Woodland Hills, 818-594-8732, www.westfield.com
- **Westfield Shoppingtown Topanga**, 6600 Topanga Canyon Blvd., Canoga Park, 818-594-8732, www.westfield.com; featuring Nordstrom and Robinsons-May
- **Westside Pavilion Shopping Center**, 10800 West Pico Blvd., West LA, 310-474-6255, www.westsidepavilion.com; anchored by Nordstrom and Robinsons-May

SHOPPING DISTRICTS

- For the area's choicest department stores head to, where else, **Beverly Hills**, 800-345-2210, www.beverlyhillsbehere.com. Along Wilshire Boulevard, west of Rodeo Drive are Tiffany's, Neiman-Marcus, Saks Fifth Avenue, Barney's, and Bloomingdale's. Go north on Rodeo Drive and you can check out the likes of Cartier, Salvador Ferragamo, and Prada.
- **Downtown** is *the* place to go when you want to buy directly from the wholesaler, often at a significant discount. The flower, produce, toy, textiles and fabrics, and jewelry districts are clustered here. These are wholesalers, some of whom will sell to the public, so don't expect much in the way of presentation: Fresh **flowers** are available at Wall and 7th streets; the **fashion district**, 213-488-1153, www.fashion district.org, is centered at East Olympic Boulevard and Los Angeles Street (Santee Alley, between Santee and Maple, is crammed with stalls that hawk cheap trendy clothing and knock-offs); **produce** dominates along Central Avenue between 8th and 9th streets; **textiles and fabrics** are at Wall and 8th streets; **toys** can be found along 3rd Street between South San Pedro and Los Angeles streets; and finally, **jewelry** is located on Hill Street between 6th and 7th streets. Expect a lot of walking and bring quarters to feed the meter.
- **Melrose Avenue**, between La Brea Avenue and Doheny Drive in Los Angeles, is the old standby for funky fashions and food
- **Old Pasadena**, 626-365-9725, www.oldpasadena.org, is a lovely shopping district where contemporary favorites like Sur La Table, Gap, and Restoration Hardware are housed in well-preserved, historical buildings. It is a 20-block area stretching along Colorado Boulevard, between Pasadena Avenue on the west, and Arroyo Parkway on the east, Walnut Street on the north, and Del Mar on the south. Upscale shopping district **South Lake Avenue**, 626-792-1259, www.south lakeavenue.com, offers 10 blocks of shopping between Colorado and California boulevards, just outside of Old Town Pasadena.
- Santa Monica's **Third Street Promenade**, 310-393-8355, www.third streetpromenade.com; permanently closed to cars between Broadway and Wilshire Boulevard, offers three city blocks of shops, cafes, and the interspersed visual delights of street performers. The Promenade also hosts a farmers' market twice a week.

DEPARTMENT STORES

Check the malls (above) for locations of your favorite department store. The most popular department stores in Los Angeles include the following:

- **Bloomingdale's**, www.bloomingdales.com; high-end, good selection of clothing, jewelry, and make-up.
- **JC Penney**, www.jcpenney.com; affordable chain with your standard department store selections, good variety of children's clothing.
- **Macy's**, www.macys.com; a solid, all-around department store that won't break the bank; very respectable household goods and bedding department.
- **Nordstrom**, www.nordstrom.com, upscale store with a reputation for outstanding, you-gotta-hear-what-they-did-for-me customer service; clothing, shoes, jewelry, make-up, and home decorations too.
- **Robinsons-May**, www.robinsonsmay.com; a popular chain that carries just about anything you'd need for your home, clothing, furniture, household goods, and electronics.

DISCOUNT DEPARTMENT STORES

- **Kmart or Big K**, www.kmart.com; budget chain with numerous locations throughout LA.
- **Ross Dress for Less**; www.rossstores.com, offers discontinued or slightly blemished designer clothing at discount prices.
- **Target**, 800-800-8800, www.target.com; all-around chain for reasonably priced clothing, household goods, food, and furniture. Numerous locations throughout LA.
- **T.J. Maxx**, www.tjmaxx.com; similar to Ross Dress for Less. Limited number of locations.
- **Wal-Mart**, www.walmart.com; limited locations, more expected in the suburbs.

HOUSEHOLD SHOPPING

COMPUTERS, ELECTRONICS, AND APPLIANCES

In addition to the following chains, many department, office supply, and wholesale stores also sell computers and household electronics and appliances.

- **Best Buy**, 11301 West Pico Blvd., West LA, 310-268-9190; 21601 Victory Blvd., Woodland Hills, 818-713-1007; www.bestbuy.com
- **Circuit City**, 401 North First Street, Burbank, 818-558-1172; 5660 Sepulveda Blvd., Culver City, 310-313-6002; 200 East Broadway Street, Glendale, 818-247-0410; 4400 Sunset Blvd., Hollywood, 213-663-6033; 1839 La Cienega Blvd., 310-280-0700; 3115 Sepulveda Blvd.,

West LA, 310-391-3144; 1145 Gayle Avenue, Westwood, 310-208-6885; 25610 North The Old Road, Valencia, 661-260-3751; 13630 Victory Blvd., Van Nuys, 818-782-3355; 6401 Canoga Avenue, Woodland Hills, 818-888-3233; www.circuitcity.com

- **CompUSA**, 761 North San Fernando Blvd., Burbank, 818-848-8588; 11441 Jefferson Blvd., Culver City, 310-390-9993; 2150 North Bellflower Blvd., Long Beach, 562-598-1992; www.compusa.com
- **Fry's Electronics**, 2311 North Hollywood Way, Burbank, 818-526-8100; 3600 Sepulveda Blvd., Manhattan Beach, 310-364-FRYS; 6100 Canoga Avenue, Woodland Hills, 818-227-1000; www.outpost.com
- **The Good Guys**, 142 South Brand Blvd., Glendale, 818-409-1400; 100 North La Cienega, 310-659-6500, open 24 hours; 13450 Maxella Avenue, Marina del Rey, 310-574-1810; 310 South Lake, Pasadena, 626-577-5300; 24840 Pico Canyon Road, Santa Clarita, 661-222-3100; 12050 Ventura Blvd., Studio City, 818-754-6250; 10831 West Pico Blvd., West LA, 310-441-4600; www.goodguys.com

BEDS, BEDDING, AND BATH

MATTRESSES

A good selection of mattresses and bedding can be found at most major department stores or you can try one of the following:

- **Simmons-Beautyrest Mattress**, call 877-399-9397, www.simmons. com; numerous locations
- **Beds Plus**, 7052 Van Nuys Blvd., Van Nuys, 818-994-9461, www. beds-plus.net
- **Discount Mattress Depot**, 8974 Tampa Avenue, Northridge, 818-700-5320; 20829 Ventura Blvd., Woodland Hills, 818-716-5516
- **The Mattress Store**, 10545 West Pico Blvd., West LA, 310-441-1997
- **Leeds Mattress Stores**, 877-905-3337, www.leedsmattress.com
- **Mattress Discounters**, call 800-BUY-A-BED or visit www.mattress discounters.com for a location near you.
- **Ortho Mattress**, 800-734-6784, www.orthomattress.com; 6205 Wilshire Blvd., 323-933-9503; 2570 South Lincoln Blvd., Marina Del Rey, 310-823-0268; 6321 Laurel Canyon Blvd., North Hollywood, 818-760-4163; 10672 West Pico Blvd., West LA, 310-839-0274
- **Sit'n Sleep**, 800-319-3192, www.sitnsleep.com; 3824 Culver Center, Culver City; 18833 Hawthorne Blvd., Torrance

BEDDING

For one-stop shopping for bedding, towels and other linens, try one of these chains:

- **Anna's Linens**, 6340 West 3rd Street, 323-939-7201; 12201 Victory Blvd., North Hollywood, 818-763-3006; 6735 Van Nuys Blvd., Van Nuys, 818-785-6234; 928 North San Fernando Road, Burbank, 818-729-0790; 866-ANNAS-2-U, www.annaslinens.com
- **Bed, Bath & Beyond**, 11801 West Olympic Blvd., 310-478-5767; 142 South San Vicente Blvd., 310-652-1380; 1255 Ventura Blvd., Studio City, 818-980-0260; 19836 Ventura Blvd., Woodland Hills, 818-702-9301; 800-GO BEYOND, www.bedbathandbeyond.com
- **Linens 'N Things**, 11250 Olympic Blvd., 310-479-6655; 19500 Plummer, Northridge, 818-882-3377; 13730 Riverside Drive, Sherman Oaks, 818-461-0770; 1601 North Victory Place, Burbank, 818-260-9110; 866-568-7378, www.lnt.com

CARPETS AND RUGS

In addition to the listings below, don't forget to look into the flooring departments of home improvement chains like Lowe's and Home Depot.
- **Carpet Depot**, 13451 Sherman Way, North Hollywood, 818-765-3622 or 800-640-6595
- **Carpet Market Outlet**, 5900 Kester Avenue, Van Nuys, 818-989-0940
- **Carpet One Carpet Factory**, 5836 Sepulveda Blvd., Sherman Oaks, 818-780-4044
- **The Carpet Showcase**, 1430 Lincoln Blvd., Santa Monica, 310-395-4575
- **Close Out Carpets**, 1446 South Robertson Blvd., West LA, 310-273-1464
- **Culver Carpet Center**, 4026 South Sepulveda Blvd., Culver City, 310-391-5286, 323-870-5797
- **Ikea**, 600 North San Fernando Blvd., Burbank, 818-842-4532; 20700 South Avalon Blvd., Carson, 310-527-4532, www.ikea.com
- **Pier 1 Imports**, locations throughout the city, go to www.pier1.com or call 800-245-4595 for a store locator

FURNITURE/HOUSEWARES

Upscale houseware and furniture stores are scattered throughout LA. Serious shoppers head to Robertson Boulevard and surrounding areas in West Hollywood, the interior design mecca of greater Los Angeles. Here are some of the more popular furniture and housewares establishments:

Find site on internet.
Location here?

- **Cost Plus World Market**, www.costplus.com; locations throughout the city
- **Crate & Barrel**, www.crateandbarrel.com; locations throughout the city
- **Ethan Allen Home Interiors**, www.ethanallen.com; locations throughout the city
- **Home Depot Expo Design Center**, www.expo.com; 10861 Weyburn Avenue, 310-824-8400; 407 West Huntington Drive, Monrovia, 626-599-3400; 1519 Hawthorne Blvd., Redondo Beach, 310-921-1400
- **Horizon Showroom of Contemporary Furniture**, 8600 West Pico Blvd., 310-652-7400, www.horizonfurniture.com
- **Ikea**, 600 North San Fernando Blvd., Burbank, 818-842-4532; 20700 South Avalon Blvd., Carson, 310-527-4532, www.ikea.com
- **Just Like the Model**, 18429 Pacific Street, Fountain Valley, 714-968-9888, www.justlikethemodel.com; this 24,000-square-foot Orange County warehouse sells the furniture used to decorate model homes from housing tracts at 30% to 70% below retail prices.
- **Pier 1 Imports**, www.pier1.com; locations throughout the city
- **Pottery Barn**, www.potterybarn.com; locations throughout the city
- **Plummers Home and Office Interiors**, 12240 Sherman Way, North Hollywood, 818-765-0401; 8876 Venice Blvd., West Los Angeles, 310-837-0138; 21725 Erwin Street, Woodland Hills, 818-888-9474
- **Rapport International Furniture**, 435 North La Brea Avenue, 323-933-4242, www.rapportusa.com
- **Restoration Hardware**, www.restorationhardware.com; locations throughout the city
- **The Sofa Company**, 9500 Jefferson Blvd., Culver City, 310-559-9901, www.thesofaco.com
- **Target**, 800-800-8800, www.target.com; locations throughout the city.
- **Wickes Furniture**, 888-942-5372, www.wickesfurniture.com; locations throughout the city
- **Williams Sonoma**, 877-812-6235, www.williams-sonoma.com; locations throughout the city
- **Z Gallerie**, 800-358-8288, www.zgallerie.com; locations throughout the city

LAMPS AND LIGHTING

In addition to the listings below, also check the Yellow Pages under "Lamps":
- **Ikea**, 600 North San Fernando Blvd., Burbank, 818-842-4532; 20700 South Avalon Blvd., Carson, 310-527-4532, www.ikea.com

- **Lamps Plus**, 200 South Brand Blvd., Glendale, 818-247-3005; 200 South La Brea Avenue, 323-931-1438; 12206 Sherman Way, North Hollywood, 818-764-2666; 2012 Bundy Drive, West LA, 310-820-7567, www.lampsplus.com
- **Light Bulbs Unlimited**, 8383 Beverly Blvd., 323-651-0330; 2309 Wilshire Blvd., Santa Monica, 310-829-7400; 14446 Ventura Blvd., Sherman Oaks, 818-501-3492
- **Lightwave Lighting**, 8211 Melrose Avenue, 323-658-6888; 21732 Ventura Blvd., Woodland Hills, 818-610-0600

HARDWARE, PAINTS, WALLPAPER, AND GARDEN CENTERS

Most homeowners, do-it-yourselfers especially, come to know their local hardware stores quickly. At the mom-and-pops in particular, seasoned associates can be extremely helpful when you're trying to decide exactly which widget you need. In addition to the many Ace Hardware (www.ace hardware.com) and True Value Hardware (www.truevalue.com) stores, you can look for the following:

- **Armstrong Garden Centers**, 800-55-PLANT, www.armstrong garden.com; 5816 San Fernando Road, Glendale, 818-243-4227; 3232 Wilshire Blvd., Santa Monica, 310-829-6766; 12920 Magnolia Blvd., Sherman Oaks, 818-761-1522; 352 East Glenarm Street, Pasadena, 626-799-7139
- **B&B Hardware**, 12450 Washington Blvd., 310-390-9413
- **Burkard Nurseries**, 690 North Orange Grove Blvd., Pasadena, 626-796-4355, www.burkardnurseries.com
- **Do-It Cente**r, www.doitcenter.com; 3221 West Magnolia Blvd., Burbank, 818-845-8301; 23314 West Valencia Blvd., Valencia, 661-255-7355
- **Home Depot**, 800-553-3199, www.homedepot.com; 12975 West Jefferson Blvd., one of several locations
- **Koontz Hardware**, 8914 Santa Monica Blvd., West Hollywood, 310-652-0123, www.koontzhardware.com
- **Lowe's Home Improvement**, 800-445-6937, www.lowes.com; 2000 Empire Avenue, Burbank, 818-557-2300, one of several locations
- **Marina del Rey Garden Center**, 13198 Mindanao Way, Marina del Rey, 310-823-5956, www.marinagardencenter.com
- **Orchard Supply Hardware**, 888-746-7674, www.osh.com

SECOND-HAND SHOPPING

A popular and inexpensive way to shop for furniture, clothing, and vintage housewares is in second-hand stores. Merchandise runs the gamut from trendy to tacky to vintage to designer cast-offs from the costume departments of the local film and TV industries. Check the Yellow Pages under "Clothing-Used" for listings in your area or try one of the following:

- **Aardvark's Odd Ark**, 7579 Melrose Avenue, 323-655-6769; 1253 East Colorado Blvd., Pasadena, 626-583-9109; 85 Market Street, Venice, 310-392-2996; 21434 Sherman Way, Canoga Park, 818-999-3211
- **All American Hero**, 314 Santa Monica Blvd., Santa Monica, 310-395-4452
- **Couture Exchange**, 12402 Ventura Blvd., Studio City, 818-752-6040
- **It's a Wrap**, 3315 West Magnolia Blvd., Burbank, 818-567-7366; selection includes clothing used for film or television tapings, brought in by studio costuming departments. Most of the clothing sizes run small, but stock rotates frequently.
- **Junk for Joy Vintage Clothing**, 3314 West Magnolia Blvd., Burbank, 818-569-4903
- **Out of the Closet Thrift Store**, all donations made to this thrift store are tax deductible at their fair market value; the money benefits the AIDS Healthcare Foundation: 800-558-8220, www.aidshealth.org/otc: 360 North Fairfax Avenue, Fairfax District, 323-934-1956; 1408 North Vine Street, Hollywood, 323-466-0747; 4136 Beverly Blvd., 213-380-8955; 6241 Laurel Canyon Blvd., North Hollywood, 818-769-0503; 1908 Lincoln Blvd., Santa Monica, 310-664-9036; 8224 Santa Monica Blvd., West Hollywood, 310-473-7787; 1608 Sawtelle Blvd., West LA, 310-473-7787; 21703 Sherman Way, Woodland Hills, 818-676-0105
- **The Paperbag Princess**, 883 Westbourne Drive, West Hollywood, 310-360-1343
- **Polkadots & Moonbeams**, 8367 West Third Street, Fairfax District, 323-651-1746
- **Reel Clothes and Props**, 5525 Cahuenga Blvd., North Hollywood, 818-508-7762, www.reelclothes.com; similar to It's a Wrap
- **Scavengers Paradise**, 5453 Satsuma Avenue, North Hollywood, 323-877-7945; 3747 Cahuenga Blvd., Studio City, 818-769-1313
- **Supply Sergeant**, 6664 Hollywood Blvd., 323-463-4730; 1431 Lincoln Blvd., Santa Monica, 310-458-4166; 503 North Victory Blvd., Burbank, 818-845-9433

One of the largest flea markets in the Los Angeles area, the **Rose Bowl Swap Meet**, 323-560-7469, www.rgcshows.com/rosebowl.asp, brings in 2,000 vendors to the Rose Bowl Stadium parking lot. It is held on the second Sunday of every month from 9 a.m. to 3 p.m. Admission charged. Some of the hip Los Angeles furniture retailers shop here, and after some touch-up work on their swap meet purchases, resell them in their stores. The **Valley Indoor Swap Meet**, 6701 Variel Avenue, Woodland Hills, 818-340-9120, www.indoorswap.com, runs every Friday, Saturday, and Sunday 10 a.m. to 6 p.m. Another smart source for used goods is *The Recycler*, www.recycler.com; published each Thursday and available at most convenience stores.

FOOD

GROCERIES

The major supermarket chains that operate here: **Ralphs**, www.ralphs.com, the biggest and most successful chain in Southern California, **Vons**, www.vons.com, the oldest chain in Southern California, and the relative newcomer, **Albertsons**, www.albertsons.com, are your everyday neighborhood grocery stores that also offer member discounts. Many Ralphs and Vons stores have remodeled, making the shopping experience markedly more pleasant. **Pavilions**, www.pavilions.com, is an upscale version of Vons, and **Fresh Faire** is an upscale version of Ralphs. **Gelson's**, www.gelsons.com, and **Bristol Farms**, www.bristolfarms.com, are gourmet market chains with premium prices, but first-rate service. **Trader Joe's**, www.traderjoes.com, is known for its specialty foods and wine sections at bargain prices. **Whole Foods**, www.wholefoods.com, is an upscale health food grocery chain with a large selection of fresh and prepared foods.

WAREHOUSE STORES

Food 4 Less, www.food4less1.com, is a bulk-item grocery store with no-frills presentation, no membership required.
* Hollywood, 5420 West Sunset Blvd., 323-871-8011
* Los Angeles, 1717 South Western Avenue, 323-731-0164
* South Pasadena, 4910 Huntington Drive, 626-222-2659
* Woodland Hills, 20155 Saticoy, 818-998-8074
* Van Nuys, 16530 Sherman Way, 818-997-0170

Costco, www.costco.com, is a members-only warehouse sized store that sells bulk food, as well as cleaning supplies, health and beauty aids, clothing, appliances, and furniture.

- Burbank, 1051 Burbank Blvd., 818-557-3780
- Inglewood, 3560 West Century Blvd., 310-672-1296
- Northridge, 8810 Tampa Avenue, 818-775-1322
- Norwalk, 12324 Hoxie Avenue, 562-029-0826
- Woodland Hills, 21300 Roscoe Blvd., 818-884-8982
- Van Nuys, 6100 North Sepulveda Blvd., 818-989-5256

Smart and Final, www.smartandfinal.com, is a warehouse-sized store that sells groceries and office products in bulk, no membership required.

- Burbank, 1320 West Magnolia Blvd., 818-845-4544
- Encino, 16847 Ventura Blvd., 818-789-0242
- Glendale, 210 North Verdugo Road, 818-243-4239
- Hollywood, 939 North Western Avenue, 323-466-9289
- Los Angeles, 12210 Santa Monica Blvd., 310-207-8688; 7720 Melrose Avenue, 323-655-2211
- North Hollywood, 6601 Laurel Canyon Blvd., 818-769-2292
- Pasadena, 1382 Locust Street, 626-793-2195
- West Hollywood, 1041 Fuller Avenue, 323-876-0421
- West LA, 12210 Santa Monica Blvd., 310-207-8688
- Woodland Hills, 19718 Sherman Way, 818-996-1331
- Van Nuys, 7817 Van Nuys Blvd., 818-780-7222
- Venice, 604 Lincoln Blvd., 310-392-4954

HEALTH FOOD STORES

Local health food outlets (and there are a lot in LA) include the following:

- **Erewhon Natural Foods**, 7660 Beverly Blvd., 323-937-0777; well stocked and has a busy juice bar/deli
- **VP Discount**, 8001 Beverly Blvd., 323-658-6506; an organic grocery that features a great selection of vitamins
- **Whole Foods**, top quality, selection and presentation. Multiple locations: call 888-746-7936 or go to www.wholefoods.com for a location near you.
- **Wild Oats Natural Marketplace**, www.wildoats.com; well-stocked, picture-perfect presentation. In: Pasadena, 603 South Lake Avenue, 626-792-1778; Santa Monica, 1425 Montana Avenue, 310-576-4707; and Santa Monica, 500 Wilshire Blvd., 310-395-4510.

- **Windward Farms**, 105 Windward Avenue, Venice, 310-392-3566; organic market

COMMUNITY GARDENS

In some parts of Los Angeles, neighborhoods are provided with plots of land where neighbors come together to grow fruits, vegetables, and herbs. In addition to providing food, the process develops a sense of community pride, helping to revitalize urban centers. Contact the **City of LA Department of Recreation and Parks**, 888-LA-PARKS, www.laparks. org (go to "horticultural centers") to find out about obtaining gardening space at one of the following community gardens (visit www.lacity.org/san/cgarden.htm for updates):

- **Orcutt Ranch Horticultural,** 23600 Roscoe Blvd., West Hills
- **Sepulveda Garden Center**, 16633 Magnolia Blvd., Encino

The **LA County Common Ground**, an urban gardening program that operates with the assistance of UC Davis, has a help line for would-be green thumbers wanting to grow their own food garden. Contact them at 323-260-3238, or go to http://celosangeles.ucdavis.edu/garden.

FARMERS' MARKETS

There are numerous farmers' markets throughout the city, including the famous, year-round Farmers Market at Third and Fairfax, which offers the adventurous shopper gorgeous seasonal produce stalls, butchers, and tourist-oriented shops. Below are some of the many neighborhood out-door farmers' markets that sell fruits, eggs, fish, vegetables, honey, nuts, cut flowers, plants, and more—usually for less than you would find at supermarkets. (Go to www.cafarmersmarkets.org/marketlist.shtml for a complete listing.) Many stalls feature organically grown produce, but be sure to ask, or look for the certified organic sign, if that's important to you.

- **Beverly Hills**, North Canon Drive between Clifton and Dayton ways, Sundays, 9 a.m. to 1 p.m., 310-285-1048
- **Brentwood**, 11600 block of Chayote Street, between Barrington Place and Sunset Blvd., Wednesdays, 3:30 to 7 p.m. during daylight saving time, 3:30 to 6 p.m. standard time.
- **Burbank**, Orange Grove Avenue and 3rd Street, Saturdays, 8 a.m. to 12:30 p.m.
- **Calabasas**, 23504 Calabasas Road at El Canon Avenue, Saturdays, 8 a.m. to 1 p.m.

- **Culver City**, Media Park, Culver Blvd. and Canfield Avenue, Tuesdays, 3 p.m. to 7 p.m., 310-253-5775
- **El Segundo**, Main Street between Grand and Holly avenues, Thursdays, 3 p.m. to 7 p.m.
- **Encino**, 17400 Victory Blvd. between Balboa Blvd. and White Oak Avenue, Sundays, 8 a.m. to 1 p.m.
- **Glendale**, Brand Blvd. between Broadway and Wilson Avenue, Thursdays, 9:30 a.m. to 1 p.m.
- **Hollywood**, Ivar Avenue between Sunset and Hollywood boulevards, Sundays, 8:30 a.m. to 1 p.m., 323-463-3171
- **Los Angeles**, St. Agnes Church, 1432 West Adams Blvd., Wednesdays, June-August, 1 p.m. to 6 p.m.; September-May, 2 p.m. to 6 p.m.; Seventh Market Place, 735 South Figueroa Street, Thursdays, noon to 4 p.m.
- **Norwalk**, Alondra Blvd., west of Pioneer Blvd., Tuesdays, 9 a.m. to 1 p.m.
- **Pasadena**, Villa Park, 363 East Villa Street, at Garfield Avenue, Tuesdays, 9 a.m. to 1 p.m.; Victory Park, 2800 block of North Sierra Madre Blvd., between Paloma and Washington avenues, Saturdays, 8:30 a.m. to 1 p.m.
- **Santa Clarita**, College of the Canyons lot 8, Valencia Blvd. and Rockwell Canyon Road, Sundays, 8:30 a.m. to noon.
- **Santa Monica**, Arizona Avenue between 2nd and 3rd streets, Wednesdays, 9 a.m. to 2 p.m., Saturdays, 8:30 a.m. to 1 p.m.; Pico Blvd. at Cloverfield Avenue, Saturdays, 8 a.m. to 1 p.m.; 2640 Main Street at Ocean Park Blvd., Sundays, 9:30 a.m. to 1 p.m.; California Heritage Museum Farmers Market, 2612 Main Street, Sundays, 10 a.m. to 4 p.m., 310-392-8537
- **Studio City**, Ventura Place between Ventura and Laurel Canyon boulevards, Sundays, 8 a.m. to 1 p.m.
- **South Pasadena**, Meridian Avenue at Mission Street, Thursdays, 4 p.m. to 8 p.m.
- **Venice**, Venice Blvd. at Venice Way, Fridays, 7 a.m. to 11 a.m.
- **West Hollywood**, Plummer Park, 7377 Santa Monica Blvd., Mondays, 9 a.m. to 2 p.m.
- **Westwood**, Weyburn Avenue at Westwood Blvd., Thursdays, 2 p.m. to 7 p.m.

ETHNIC FOOD

As one of the biggest melting pots in the nation, LA's substantial Middle Eastern, Hispanic, Jewish, and Asian populations mean plenty of stores to go to if you need to stock up on ghee, kreplach, or kimchi. Many of the markets listed below are located within their respective ethnic communities.

Los Angeles' lively Chinatown has experienced a decline lately, at least perhaps in its sense of authenticity. Much of its thunder has been stolen by the community of Monterey Park, nicknamed "Little Hong Kong" because of its burgeoning **Chinese** population, many of whom are recent arrivals. Chinese groceries, restaurants, and goods can be found in this bustling neighborhood. One of the largest Chinese grocery chains is **99 Ranch Market**, 800-600-TAWA, www.99ranch.com, in Monterey Park at 771 West Garvey Avenue, 626-458-3399, and in Van Nuys at 6450 North Sepulveda Boulevard, 818-988-7899.

To stock up on English pantry items, try **Tudor House**, 1403-1409 Second Street, Santa Monica, 310-451-4101. For sturdy German fare, visit **Van Nuys German Deli** at 16155 Roscoe Boulevard, 818-892-2212.

Those in need of a knish should head down to the Fairfax District on North Fairfax Avenue between Melrose Avenue and Beverly Boulevard for mom-and-pop stores that carry kosher food and other supplies. **Jewish** delis like **Jerry's Deli** are dotted throughout LA, so you'll never be far from some good matzo ball soup.

Many know about Koreatown in Los Angeles (Western Avenue between Olympic and Beverly boulevards), the **Hannam Chain** is a popular grocery store at 2740 West Olympic Boulevard (213-382-2922, www.hannamchain.com), but there is also a large **Korean** population in Northridge, just look for the Korean script on signage. **HK Korean Supermarket** in Los Angeles at 124 North Western Avenue, 213-469-8934 and in Van Nuys at 17634 Sherman Way, 818-708-7396, is a favorite. **Koreatown Plaza Market** is another grocer closer to Koreatown: 928 South Western Avenue, 213-385-1100.

Meticulously clean Little Tokyo (between First, 4th, San Pedro and Alameda streets) in LA is popular for a sushi fix. **Mitsuwa Marketplace**, 333 South Alameda Street, 213-613-0573 (go to www.mitsuwa.com for additional locations), can supply all of your ingredients for the perfect California roll.

Need some spice in your life—say a bite of vindaloo? Try the **Indian Bharat Bazaar**, 11510 West Washington Boulevard in Culver City, 310-398-6766, or **India Sweets and Spices** in Los Angeles at 3126 Los Feliz Boulevard, 323-345-0860 (those in the Valley should head to its sister store at 18110 Parthenia Street in Northridge, 818-407-1498).

Pasta aficionados looking for the perfect **Italian** ingredients will want to go to **Bay Cities Importing Co.**, 1517 Lincoln Boulevard, Santa Monica, 310-395-8279 or **Claro's Italian Markets**, 800-507-0450, www.claros.com, 1003 East Valley Boulevard, San Gabriel.

With strong ties to its neighbor to the south, LA is renowned for its fine selection of authentic **Mexican** cuisine and food markets. In particular, Boyle Heights (along First Street and Cesar E. Chavez Avenue), Los Feliz, and East LA are largely Mexican. The best place for a taste of Mexico City is said to be **El Gallo Giro**, a combination bakery, meat market, and cake shop: in East Los Angeles at 5686 East Whittier Boulevard, 213-726-1246; in El Monte at 11912 Valley Boulevard, 626-575-1244; and in Huntington Park at 7148 Pacific Avenue, 213-585-4433. Another popular place for Mexican foodstuffs is at the **Grand Central Market**, 317 South Broadway, downtown, 213-624-2378. For shelves of Mexican foodstuffs, try the growing **Vallarta Supermarkets** chains. Go to www.vallartasuper market.com for a list of locations.

A mix of Armenian, Persian, Israeli, and Greek populations resides along the western border of Los Angeles. In addition, the city of Glendale has a large **Middle Eastern** population; drive through the neighborhood to browse the restaurants, bakeries, and grocers. If you're in Pasadena, check out Allen and Washington boulevards for Middle Eastern goods. Or try these Middle Eastern favorites: **Elat Market**, 8730 West Pico Boulevard, Los Angeles, 310-659-7070; **Good Food**, 1864 East Washington Boulevard, Pasadena, 626-79-5367.

Borscht anyone? Russian groceries can be found at **Royal Gourmet**, 8151 Santa Monica Boulevard, West Hollywood, 213-650-5001, and **Tatiana**, 8205 Santa Monica Boulevard, West Hollywood, 213-656-7500.

To satisfy your injera craving (or at least to find out what this savory crepe/bread tastes like), head to **Little Ethiopia** along a small segment of Fairfax Avenue, south of Olympic Boulevard. There's an excellent selection of buffet restaurants and tiny immigrant-owned shops featuring East African culture.

EATING OUT

In Philly, it's cheesesteaks, Chicago, deep-dish pizza—ask an Angeleno about Los Angeles's equivalent fast food fame and they'll rave to you about LA chili-cheeseburgers. Perhaps it is the exquisite meeting of the Southwest flavors of the chili with the red, white and blue standard hamburger; whatever the reason, the chili-cheeseburgers here are justifiably famous, and everyone swears by their favorite burger joint. Dine around for your favorite; just don't forget the antacid!

- **The Apple Pan**, 10801 Pico Blvd., Westwood, 310-475-3585; a Westwood institution, known for its burgers and for its pies.
- **Carney's**, 12601 Ventura Blvd., Studio City, 818-761-8300; housed in an old train car, Carney's aficionados swear by the chili-burgers and chili-fries.
- **Fatburger**, various locations citywide. These spots stay open late, perfect for those midnight cravings.

- **In-N-Out Burger**, various locations citywide. For the one nearest you, call 800-786-1000.
- **Marty's Hamburger Stand**, 10558 West Pico Blvd., West LA, 310-836-6944; this is the original Marty's. Also at 1255 La Cienega Blvd., 310-652-8047; the brave here go for "the combo," a chili-cheeseburger with a sliced hot-dog on top.
- **Pink's**, 709 North La Brea Blvd., 213-931-4223; a favorite late night chili-dog stop with constant lines, open till 2 a.m. during the week and 3 a.m. on weekends.
- **Tail o' the Pup**, 329 North San Vicente, West Hollywood, 310-652-4517; architecturally famous—the stand is in the shape of a hot-dog.
- **Tito's Tacos**, 11222 Washington Place, Culver City, 310-391-5780; don't be daunted by the line out front, it moves fast.
- **Tommy's**, various locations citywide. A popular chili-burger joint with imitators all over the city.
- **Philippe, The Original**, 1001 North Alameda Street, www.philippes.com; one of LA's oldest restaurants, it claims to be the birth-place of the famous French Dip sandwich.
- **Clifton's Cafeteria**, 648 South Broadway, 213-627-1673, www.cliftonscafeteria.com; this downtown cafeteria has been serving comfort food cafeteria-style at very affordable prices since the thirties. The 20-foot waterfall in their dining room is a refreshing surprise while dining in "old Los Angeles" style.

A S HOME TO THE ENTERTAINMENT INDUSTRY, AS WELL AS TO thousands of artists, musicians, and writers, LA seems to offer an infinite number of things to do to occupy your leisure time. Whatever your interests, from music to theater to the visual arts, Los Angeles has not only a wide variety of cultural offerings, but some of the finest in the world as well.

If you want to find out what's going on this week or this month, check out the following publications:

- **LA Weekly**, www.laweekly.com; most read free weekly newspaper in Los Angeles. Editorial coverage includes social and political issues as well as extensive film, art, music, and restaurant critiques. Each week, the "Calendar" section lists some 50 pages of events—everything from coffeehouse folk performances to Latin dance clubs to political symposiums. (And don't forget the personal ads, they offer entertainment unto themselves!) Distributed on Thursdays.

- **Entertainment Today**, www.ent-today.com; free weekly offering entertainment listings. Distributed on Fridays.

- **Los Angeles Times** publishes a daily "Calendar" section, www.calendar live.com, that covers a variety of cultural and entertainment options throughout LA; check on Thursdays for a list of upcoming weekend events, and on Sundays for a detailed pull-out version.

- **Los Angeles**, www.lamag.com, is a monthly city magazine; check the back section for entertainment listings.

- The **LA Cultural Affairs Department**, 213-473-7700, www.culture la.org, is a great resource for events. For round-the-clock access to the latest information about music, art, dance, theater, special events, festivals, and community events going on throughout Los Angeles, go to www.artscenecal.com or www.lacountyarts.org.

- **LA Convention and Visitors Bureau**, 213-624-7300, www.see myla.org; geared toward visitors, but still a useful resource for local entertainment suggestions and cultural guides.

Tickets to many events can be purchased through each venue's web site or box office, or through **Ticketmaster**, 213-365-3500, www.ticket master.com, or **Telecharge**, 800-233-3123, www.telecharge.com.

Unless otherwise noted, addresses listed are in Los Angeles.

PERFORMING ARTS

MUSIC

For a complete listing of the week's musical offerings, refer to *LA Weekly*, which offers the most comprehensive guide to the vast Los Angeles music scene. Here is a glimpse of classical musical offerings in and around LA.

CLASSICAL

- **Beverly Hills Symphony**, 310-276-8385, www.beverlyhills.org, has been in existence since 1993, and is led by conductor Bogidar Avramov. Its summer series is held outdoors at Greystone Park on the grounds of the historic Doheny Mansion, which was built in 1928. The winter series is held at various civic sites in Beverly Hills.
- **Los Angeles Philharmonic Orchestra**, 213-972-7300, www.la phil.com, presents a variety of concerts, recitals, and special programs. In October 2003, it made its new home at the Walt Disney Concert Hall, a steely architectural marvel designed by Frank Gehry. In the summer, it continues to hold performances at the Hollywood Bowl (renovated in 2004). For more information, call **The Music Center**, 135 North Grand Avenue, downtown, 213-202-2200 or 213-972-7211, or go to www.musiccenter.org.
- **Santa Monica Symphony Orchestra**, 310-996-3260, www.sm symphony.org, has performed for over half a century, and is now led by conductor Allen Robert Gross. Four times a season, it presents free performances of classical and contemporary music to an audience of 5,000. Most of its musicians are nonprofessionals drawn from the community and area colleges and universities.

    Other Los Angeles area orchestral groups include:
- **Glendale Symphony**, 818-500-8720, www.glendalesymphony.org

- **Hollywood Bowl Orchestra**, 323-850-2000, www.hollywoodbowl. com (summer only)
- **Long Beach Symphony Orchestra**, 310-436-3203, www.lbso.org
- **Pasadena Symphony**, 626-793-7172, www.pasadenasymphony.org
- **Santa Clarita Symphony**, 626-284-6044, www.scsymphony.com
- **San Fernando Valley Symphony**, 818-347-4807, www.sfvsymphony. com
- **Symphony in the Glen**, 800-440-4536, www.symphonyinglen.org (summer only)
- **West Hollywood Orchestra**, 866-WHO-CALL, www.wehoorchestra. org

CHORUSES

- **Angeles Chorale**, 818-591-1735, www.angeleschorale.org; as large as the LA Master Chorale, but entirely composed of volunteer community members, the chorus primarily performs at Royce Hall on UCLA campus. Its conductor, Donald Neuen, is also chair of Choral Music at UCLA.
- **Gay Men's Chorus of Los Angeles**, 800-MEN-SING, www.gmcla. org; directed by Jon Bailey, tickets for this popular and talented group may be purchased through Telecharge at 800-233-3123. It performs primarily in the Alex Theatre in Glendale.
- **Los Angeles Master Chorale**, 213-972-0777, www.lamc.org; this 120-voice professional symphonic chorus, conducted by Paul Salamunovich, performs its subscription series at the Walt Disney Concert Hall.
- **Los Angeles Children's Chorus**, 626-793-4231, www.lachildrens chorus.org; made up of 180 children from throughout LA County. Its mission is to provide advanced musical training for children regardless of financial constraints. It presents two major concerts a year, one each in the spring and winter; consult its calendar for additional smaller concerts.

OPERA

The world-class **Los Angeles Opera** performs September through June at The Music Center in the Dorothy Chandler Pavilion, 135 North Grand Avenue, 213-972-7211, www.losangelesopera.com. Tickets may be purchased in person at The Music Center box office, via its web site, or by calling Ticketmaster, 213-365-3500 (fine arts line). Also check out the **Santa**

Monica Civic Light Opera, 310-458-5939, www.smclo.org. Recent performances include "Who's Afraid of Virginia Woolf" and "The Music Man." Performances are in the restored 1938 art deco Barnum Hall Theater.

DANCE

One area of the arts that's a tad underrepresented in Los Angeles is the world of dance. Visiting companies like the Joffrey Ballet have largely overshadowed the smaller productions here. As young dancers make their way through local schools, the artistic directors are ever hopeful that a new rising star will help Los Angeles carve its own niche in the national dance scene.

Local **dance companies** include:

- **Ballet Pacifica**, 1824 Kaiser Avenue, Irvine, 949-851-9930, www.ballet pacifica.org; Southern California's oldest and only resident professional ballet company. Performs a mix of classical and contemporary programs.
- **California Dance Theatre**, 5863 Kanan Road, Agoura Hills, 818-707-3267, www.californiadancetheatre.com; home to three regional performing companies: Pacific Festival Ballet Company; Dazzle, a professional tap/jazz group; and The Dance Connection, a competition team.
- **City Ballet of Los Angeles & School**, 1532 West 11th Street, 323-292-1932, www.cityballetofla.org; just opened in 2000, this newcomer is still searching for a permanent performance space. Check the arts and entertainments guides listed above for upcoming performance information.
- **Joffrey Ballet**, 213-487-8677, www.joffrey.com; founded by Robert Joffrey and Gerald Arpino, the famous Chicago-based touring company makes annual, well-received stops in Los Angeles.
- **Long Beach Ballet Arts Center**, 1122 East Wardlow Road, Long Beach, 562-426-4112, www.longbeachballet.com; established in 1956, this institution has remained grounded in classical productions. Graduating students produce and perform a commencement program each summer; tickets are available to the public.
- **Lula Washington Dance Theater**, 3773 South Crenshaw Blvd., 323-292-5852, www.lulawashington.com; when the company moved to its new home in 2004 it became one of the few non-profit modern dance companies to own and operate its own facility—just in time to celebrate its 25th anniversary in 2005. Founded by the internationally known choreographer Lula Washington and still run by her, the group has toured around the country. Performances include a variety of contemporary works.

- **Pasadena Civic Ballet (PCB)**, 626-792-0873, www.pcballet.com; formed in 1980, the PCB is an organization of pre-professional dancers from ages 10 and up (its members start training as young as 3 1/2 years of age). Every two years, the students put on a large-scale production; "Alice in Wonderland" was a recent show.
- **Pasadena Dance Theatre Conservatory of Performing Arts**, 1985 East Locust Street, Pasadena, 626-683-3459, www.pasadena dance.org; organizes modern and classic performances.
- **West Coast Classical Ballet**, Westwood Dance Center, 1365 Westwood Blvd., Westwood, 310-477-6414, www.balletdesartistes.com; the Westwood Dance Center is the base of the Vaganova Ballet Academy in Los Angeles, the only officially endorsed ballet school in North America authorized to instruct the Vaganova ballet curriculum. It produces "The Nutcracker" annually.

THEATER

Each week there are dozens of fine theatrical productions going on in Los Angeles. Check one of the weekly newspapers for a full listing.

PROFESSIONAL THEATER

Below are some of the larger and/or better-known theaters in the area.
- **Beverly Hills Playhouse**, 254 South Robertson, Beverly Hills, 310-855-1556
- **Canon Theatre**, 205 North Canon Drive, Beverly Hills, 310-859-2830
- **Doolittle Theatre**, 1615 North Vine Street, Hollywood, 323-972-7372
- **East West Players David Henry Hwang Theater**, 120 North Judge John Aiso Street, 213-625-7000, www.eastwestplayers.org
- **Geffen Playhouse**, 10886 Le Conte Avenue, Westwood, 310-208-5454, www.geffenplayhouse.com; formerly the Westwood Playhouse, it was renamed after receiving a generous donation from entertainment mogul David Geffen.
- **Glendale Central Theatre**, 324 North Orange Street, Glendale, 818-244-8481, www.glendalecentraltheatre.com
- **The Music Center** (Dorothy Chandler Pavilion, Mark Taper Forum, and Ahmanson Theatre, Walt Disney Concert Hall), 135 North Grand Avenue, 213-972-7211 or 213-628-2772, www.musiccenter.org
- **Odyssey Theatre Ensemble**, 2055 South Sepulveda Blvd., West LA, 310-477-2055, www.odysseytheatre.com
- **Pantages Theatre**, 6233 Hollywood Blvd., Hollywood, 323-468-1700

- **The Pasadena Playhouse**, 39 South El Molino Avenue, Pasadena, 800-233-3123 (Telecharge), www.pasadenaplayhouse.org
- **Santa Monica Playhouse**, 1211 4th Street, 310-394-9779, www.santa monicaplayhouse.com
- **Theatre/Theater**, 6425 Hollywood Blvd., 323-871-0210
- **Tiffany Theatres**, 8532 Sunset Blvd., West Hollywood, 310-289-2999
- **Will Geer Theatricum Botanicum**, 1419 North Topanga Canyon Blvd., Topanga Canyon, 310-455-3723, www.theatricum.com; features Shakespeare and more, in a rustic, outdoor amphitheater.

COMMUNITY THEATER

In this city of actors, community theaters are everywhere, and often are quite good. Many theaters are clustered in Hollywood. Check out the LA Stage Alliance's web site, www.theatrela.org, or browse through one of the weekly newspapers for a complete list.

- **68 Cent Crew Theatre Company**, 5419 Sunset Blvd., Hollywood, 323-467-6688, http://68centcrew.com
- **Actors' Gang Theater**, 6209 Santa Monica Blvd., Hollywood, 323-465-0566, www.theactorsgang.com
- **Celebration Theater**, 7051 Santa Monica Blvd., Hollywood, 310-289-2999
- **Downtown Playhouse**, 929 East 2nd Street, Ste. 105, 213-626-6906
- **Eclectic Theatre Company**, 5312 Laurel Canyon Blvd., North Hollywood, 818-508-3003, www.eclecticcompanytheatre.org
- **Hollywood Court Theater** in the Hollywood Methodist Church, 6817 Franklin Avenue, Hollywood, 323-550-1000, www.hollywood courttheater.com
- **Open Fist Theater Company,** 1625 North La Brea Avenue, Hollywood, 323-882-6912, www.openfist.org
- **Theater of Hope**, 11050 Magnolia Blvd., North Hollywood, 818-779-2101
- **Theatre of NOTE**, 1517 Cahuenga Blvd., Hollywood, 323-856-8611, www.theatreofnote.com

COMEDY

Famous comedians often "drop by" various clubs around LA to try out new material, so you never know when you might be in for a special treat. There are several popular comedy clubs in and around Los Angeles, including:

- **Acme Comedy Theater**, 135 North La Brea Blvd., 323-525-0202, www.acmecomedy.com
- **Comedy Store**, 8433 Sunset Blvd., West Hollywood, 323-656-6225, www.thecomedystore.com
- **Conga Room**, 5364 Wilshire Blvd., 323-938-1696, www.congaroom.com
- **Groundlings Theatre**, 7307 Melrose Avenue, 323-934-9700, www.groundlings.com; this improvisational comedy troupe was the training ground for several "Saturday Night Live" veterans, such as Phil Hartman and Julia Sweeney.
- **Ice House**, 24 North Mentor Avenue, Pasadena, 626-577-1894, www.icehousecomedy.com
- **The Improv**, 8162 Melrose Avenue, 323-651-2583, www.improv.com
- **Improv Olympic**, 6468 Santa Monica Blvd., Hollywood, 323-694-2935, www.improv.com
- **LA Connection Comedy Theatre**, 13442 Ventura Blvd., Sherman Oaks, 818-710-1320, www.laconnectioncomedy.com
- **Laugh Factory**, 8001 Sunset Blvd., Hollywood, 323-656-1336, www.laughfactory.com

MOVIE THEATERS

As one might expect, movies are a big deal in Los Angeles. Most feature flicks open here and in New York ahead of the rest of the country. You may be approached in front of theaters to attend market survey screenings, where you can watch a free movie in exchange for filling out a questionnaire at the end of the show. While the large multi-screen theaters are everywhere (the biggies are AMC, Mann, Loews, and Edwards/Regal/UA)—check the telephone directory or newspaper for the one nearest you—here are a few alternative theaters that feature foreign, classic, budget and/or art films.

- **American Cinematheque**, 6712 Hollywood Blvd., Hollywood, 323-466-3456, www.egyptiantheatre.com; screens alternative, classic, foreign, and art house movies at the Egyptian Theatre; $15 million was spent on renovating the Egyptian-themed 1920s landmark.
- **ArcLight Cinema**, 6360 West Sunset Blvd., 323-464-1478, www.arclightcinemas.com; features 14 auditoriums and the Cinerama Dome (a unique, geodesic-shaped theater that's the ultimate in giant movie screens), and all-reserved seating for a premium movie-going experience.
- **The Bridge Cinema De Luxe**, 6081 Center Drive, 310-568-3375, www.thebridgecinema.com; located inside the Promenade at Howard Hughes Center, this 16-screen complex houses a full-service restaurant,

plus an IMAX screen, concierge services, and reserved seating (for an additional charge). Its Silver Screen Classics program allows patrons to revisit classic films from the 1930s through the '80s once a month on the big screen for just $1 (includes popcorn and a soda).

- **Laemmle Theatres**: www.laemmle.com; Figueroa at Third Street, 213-617-0268; Music Hall, 9036 Wilshire Blvd., Beverly Hills, 310-274-6869; Town Center 5, 17200 Ventura Blvd., Encino, 818-981-9811; Playhouse, 673 East Colorado Blvd., Pasadena, 626-844-6500; One Colorado Cinemas, 42 Miller Alley, Pasadena, 626-744-1224; Monica 4, 1332 2nd Street, Santa Monica, 310-394-9741; Sunset 5, 8000 Sunset Blvd., West Hollywood, 323-848-3500; Royal, 11523 Santa Monica Blvd., West LA, 310-477-5581
- **Landmark Theaters**: www.landmarktheaters.com; Cecchi Gori Fine Arts, 8556 Wilshire Blvd., Beverly Hills, 310-652-1330; NuWilshire, 1314 Wilshire Blvd., Santa Monica, 310-394-8099; Rialto, 1023 South Fair Oaks, South Pasadena, 626-799-9567; Nuart, 11272 Santa Monica Blvd., West LA, 310-478-6379; Royal, 11523 Santa Monica Blvd., West LA, 310-477-5581; Westside Pavilion, 10800 Pico Blvd., West LA, 310-475-0202
- **Levitt Pavilion at Memorial Park,** at Walnut and Raymond Avenues in Old Pasadena, 626-666-4156, www.oldpasadena.org; the Old Pasadena Management District presents "Cinema in the Park," a free movie series that screens a classic every Saturday in May under the stars beginning at sunset (pick up your free ticket one week prior).
- **Silent Movie**, 611 North Fairfax, Fairfax District, 323-655-2520, www.silentmovietheatre.com; the only movie house in the nation that features only "pre-talkies," accompanied by a live band.

TELEVISION TAPINGS

Live-audience TV shows are mostly filmed during the week. Watching a sit-com taping is a guaranteed way to see a celebrity. Mementos from shows, such as T-shirts and autographed scripts, are sometimes given away to audience members. Be prepared to devote several hours to the taping and to clap on demand. If you would like to be an audience member at a live taping, write to the **LA Convention and Visitors Bureau**, 633 West 5th Street #6000, LA, CA 90071, and enclose a self-addressed, stamped envelope. (For more information, contact them at 213-624-7300 or go to www.lainc.com). Popular shows in particular are booked months in advance. Or you can go straight to the source: **Audiences Unlimited** is hired directly by the production companies to provide free tickets to people to attend tapings of their TV show or special, anything that requires a live audience. For listings, call 818-753-3470 or visit www.tvtickets.com. A similar service is available through **Audience Associates**, 323-653-4105, www.tvtix.com, which does a lot of game show tapings. Or, contact the network studio that carries your favorite live-taped show directly: **CBS**, 323-575-2345; **NBC**, 818-840-3537, www.nbc.com; and **Paramount Pictures**, 323-956-5575. Tickets are free, but more tickets than seats are always issued, so arrive early.

CONTEMPORARY MUSIC

CONCERT FACILITIES

Tickets can be obtained by standing in line at the venue itself or through Ticketmaster, 213-365-3500, www.ticketmaster.com.
- **Great Western Forum**, 3900 West Manchester Blvd., Inglewood, 310-419-3100
- **Greek Theater**, 2700 North Vermont Avenue, Los Feliz, 323-665-1927, www.greektheatrela.com
- **Hollywood Bowl**, 2301 North Highland Avenue, Hollywood, 323-850-2000, www.hollywoodbowl.org
- **John Anson Ford Amphitheatre**, 2580 East Cahuenga Blvd., 323-461-3673, www.fordamphitheatre.org
- **Kodak Theatre**, 6801 Hollywood Blvd., Suite 180, Hollywood, 323-308-6363, www.kodaktheatre.com
- **Los Angeles Sports Arena**, 3939 South Figueroa Street, 213-748-6136
- **Shrine Auditorium**, 665 West Jefferson Blvd., 213-748-5116, www.shrineauditorium.com
- **Staples Center**, 1111 South Figueroa Street, 213-742-7100, www.staplescenter.com
- **UCLA's Royce Hall**, 405 Hilgard Avenue, Westwood, 310-825-4401, www.uclalive.com
- **Universal Amphitheatre**, 100 Universal City Plaza, Universal City, 818-622-4440, www.hob.com
- **Walt Disney Concert Hall**, 111 South Grand Avenue, 323-850-2000, www.wdch.com
- **Wiltern Theatre**, 3790 Wilshire Blvd., 213-380-5005, www.thewiltern.com

COFFEEHOUSE PERFORMANCES

This relaxing, semi-Bohemian alternative to clubs and restaurants offers afi-cionados food, music, socializing and, of course, coffee and tea. Here are a few local coffeehouses that offer music and other performances on a reg-ular basis, as well an alternative to the omnipresent Starbucks.

- **Anastasia's Asylum**, 1028 Wilshire Blvd., Santa Monica, 310-394-7113
- **Cobalt Cafe**, 22047 Sherman Way, Woodland Hills, 818-348-3789
- **Cow's End**, 34 Washington Blvd., Venice, 310-574-1080
- **Highland Grounds**, 742 North Highland Avenue, Hollywood, 323-466-1507
- **Insomnia**, 7286 Beverly Blvd., Fairfax District, 213-931-4943
- **Kings Road Cafe**, 8361 Beverly Blvd., Fairfax District, 323-655-9044
- **Lulu's Beehive**, 13203 Ventura Blvd., Studio City, 818-986-2233
- **Novel Cafe**, 212 Pier Avenue, Santa Monica, 310-396-8566
- **Opus**, 38 East Colorado Blvd., Pasadena, 626-685-2800
- **Tsunami Coffeehouse**, 4019 Sunset Blvd., Silverlake, 213-661-7771
- **Un-urban Coffeehouse**, 3301 Pico Blvd., Santa Monica, 310-315-0056

NIGHTCLUBS

There are many, many, many nightclubs in LA. Cover charge varies by venue and day. Here is a sampling of the most well known; refer to other music genres in this chapter for more choices, or check out the *LA Weekly* for a complete guide:

- **House of Blues**, 8430 Sunset Blvd., West Hollywood, 323-848-5100, www.hob.com; the dance floor is close enough to the stage that your favorite blues singer might even climb down to boogie with you. Excellent sight lines and sound system for live bands despite it being a restaurant too.
- **The Joint**, 8771 West Pico Blvd., West LA, 310-275-2619; an eclectic venue for local bands.
- **Key Club**, 9039 Sunset Blvd., West Hollywood, 310-274-5800, www.keyclub.com; two-level showcase featuring a variety of acts. Three full bars feature a "tequila library."
- **Mayan Theatre**, 1038 South Hill Street, 213-746-4674; normally an LA nightclub, its cool, gothic building makes it irresistible as a concert venue.

- **The Troubadour**, 9081 Santa Monica Blvd., West Hollywood, 310-276-6168; considered the granddaddy since it's been in operation for more than 40 years.

ACOUSTIC PERFORMANCES

- **Genghis Cohen**, 740 North Fairfax Avenue, Fairfax District, 323-653-0640; half Chinese restaurant, half music den.
- **Luna Park**, 665 Robertson Blvd., West Hollywood, 310-652-0611; this restaurant/music hang-out plays host to a variety of acts, from folk to Brazilian pop.
- **McCabe's Guitar Shop**, 3101 Pico Blvd., Santa Monica, 310-828-4497; yes it's a guitar store, but there's a back room that features fine acoustic performances.

ALTERNATIVE, ROCK, HIP-HOP, AND POP

- **Al's Bar**, 305 South Newitt Street, downtown, 213-625-9703; a gritty, trendy downtown standard.
- **Alligator Lounge**, 3321 Pico Blvd., Santa Monica, 310-449-1844; this Westside club is a popular place with the alternative music scene.
- **14 Below**, 1348 14th Street, Santa Monica, 310-451-5040; live music and dancing every night, plus pool, darts, and lots of beer on tap.
- **Molly Malone's Irish Pub**, 575 South Fairfax Avenue, Fairfax District, 323-935-1577; for Irish, folk, rock, and R&B.
- **The Palace**, 1735 North Vine Street, Hollywood, 323-462-3000; a legendary club with a dance floor, balcony seating, and a patio.
- **Roxy Theatre**, 9009 Sunset Blvd., West Hollywood, 310-276-2222; this venue often serves as a showcase for the music industry's newest signs.
- **The Troubadour**, 9081 Santa Monica Blvd., West Hollywood, 310-276-6168; a tried and true venue for nightly live performances.
- **The Viper Room**, 8852 Sunset Blvd., West Hollywood, 310-358-1880
- **Whiskey-a-Go-Go**, 8901 Sunset Blvd., West Hollywood, 310-652-4202; for years a popular rock-and-roll club, the Whiskey now features mostly heavy metal.

COUNTRY

- **The Cowboy Palace Saloon**, 21635 Devonshire Street, Chatsworth, 818-341-0166; live country music and dancing seven nights a week.
- **Culver Saloon**, 11513 Washington Blvd., Culver City, 310-391-1519; a country nightclub featuring local acts.

JAZZ, R&B

- **Atlas Bar & Grill**, 3760 Wilshire Blvd., 213-380-8400; this jazz club/restaurant is located inside the landmark Wiltern Theater.
- **Babe & Ricky's Inn**, 4339 Leimert Park, 323-295-9112; LA's longest-running blues club, located in Leimert Park, which in the 1950s was the heart of the city's African-American music community.
- **The Baked Potato**, 3787 Cahuenga Blvd., North Hollywood, 818-980-1615; a small, well-known jazz spot that serves 38 kinds of baked potatoes. Cover charge. Also at 26 East Colorado Blvd., Pasadena, 626-564-1122.
- **B.B. King's Blues Club**, 1000 Universal Center Drive, Universal City, 818-622-5464; sister to the flagship club in Memphis, this large dinner club features a variety of live blues performances.
- **Catalina Bar & Grill**, 1640 North Cahuenga Blvd., 323-466-2210; an upscale jazz supper club, often with big-name acts on the bill.
- **Harvelle's**, 1432 Fourth Street, Santa Monica, 310-395-1676; funky, small blues spot that gets very crowded.
- **House of Blues**, 430 Sunset Blvd., West Hollywood, 323-848-5100; the restaurant's second floor overlooks the homey club below.
- **Jazz Bakery**, 3233 Helms Avenue, Culver City, 310-271-9039; a popular place to hear local and touring jazz acts.
- **St. Mark's**, 23 Winward Avenue, Venice, 310-452-2222; this two-story dinner and music venue is situated just up the street from the Venice Boardwalk.

LATIN, BRAZILIAN, AND SPANISH CLUBS

- **El Floridita**, 1253 Vine Street, Hollywood, 323-871-8612; Cuban music and food
- **Cha, Cha, Cha**, 17499 Ventura Blvd., Encino, 818-789-3600; Caribbean restaurant with a Latin beat
- **Grand Avenue**, 1024 South Grand Avenue, 213-747-0999

- **La Masia**, 9077 Santa Monica Blvd., West Hollywood, 310-273-7066, a supper club featuring the cuisine of northeastern Spain, plus live salsa and merengue music.
- **Zabumba**, 10717 Venice Blvd., West LA, 310-841-6525; for Brazilian food, music, and fun

FREE CONCERTS

In addition to all of the above, there are often free concerts throughout the city, especially during the summer months. The city of Santa Monica sponsors the **Twilight Dance Series** on Thursday nights from 7:30 p.m. to 9:30 p.m., located at the Santa Monica Pier. Featured musicians include jazz, rock, blues, salsa, gospel, and international artists. For more information, call 310-458-8900 or go to www.twilightdance.org. The Valley Cultural Center offers **Summer Concerts in the Park** in Warner Park at Woodland Hills. Past performers include Air Supply, the LAPD Concert Band, and the San Fernando Valley Symphony. Go to www.valley cultural.org or call 818-704-1358 for details.

For a free concert series experience within an urban setting, head downtown to the California Plaza (at Grand Avenue and 4th Street). In between two high-rise towers is the Watercourt Stage, which is ringed by a water fountain. This is where free noon and evening concerts are staged by **Grand Performances** in the summer. This city-sponsored event brings in a wide range of musical entertainment, from jazz to big band to ethnic/folk; consult their schedule for details at 213-687-2159 or go to www.grandperformances.org. Also, the **Pershing Square Summer Concert Series** runs one Sunday a month, from June to September. For more information, call 888-527-2757 or go to www.laparks.org. The **Los Angeles County Museum of Art** features a variety of free concerts, including Sundays Live, a chamber music series that performs 50 times a year from 6 p.m. to 7 p.m. in a museum auditorium (and also simultaneously broadcast live on 105.1 FM). For more information, call 323-857-6000 or visit www.sundayslive.org.

MUSEUMS

If it can be exhibited, it's on display somewhere in the LA area. Many museums offer free admission once a month; contact the museum for the specific day. If you're up for a full day of exhibit-hopping you might want to head for what is known as "Museum Row," along Wilshire Boulevard running east from Fairfax. In these few blocks you'll find the Los Angeles County Museum of Art, Craft and Folk Art Museum, Petersen Automotive

Museum, and the Page Museum at the La Brea Tar Pits. It could make for quite an interesting outing!

ART MUSEUMS

- **Craft and Folk Art Museum**, 5814 Wilshire Blvd., Fairfax District, 323-937-4230, www.cafam.org; international and American folk art is featured here in the heart of "Museum Row." Admission is $4, $2 for students and seniors, and free for children under 12.
- **Geffen Contemporary**, 152 North Central Avenue, 213-626-6222, www.moca-la.org; formerly known as the Temporary Contemporary, it began as a temporary space while MOCA was being built, but continues now as an extra exhibit space for MOCA events.
- **Huntington Library**, **Art Collections**, **and Gardens**, 1151 Oxford Road, Pasadena, 626-405-2141, www.huntington.org, features an extensive European art collection, a scholarly library, plus notable botanical gardens. Admission is $12.50 for adults, $10 for seniors, $8.50 for students, and $5 for children between 11 and 5. Free admission the first Thursday of every month.
- **J. Paul Getty Center**, 1200 Getty Center Drive, Brentwood, 310-440-7300, www.getty.edu; this $1 billion, 110-acre museum "campus" opened in 1997 and houses a vast and impressive collection of art and antiquities. European paintings and sculptures, drawings, decorative arts, and photographs are free to view, but parking is $7. The Getty Villa on the Malibu cliffs overlooking the Pacific Ocean, the original site of the Getty Museum, was closed in 1997 for extensive renovations. Reopened in the fall of 2005, its focus is ancient Grecian and Roman art.
- **Los Angeles Contemporary Exhibition (LACE)**, 6522 Hollywood Blvd., Hollywood, 323-957-1777, www.artleak.org, presents contemporary and experimental art in a variety of media.
- **Los Angeles County Museum of Art (LACMA)**, 5905 Wilshire Blvd., Fairfax District, 323-857-6000, www.lacma.org; houses everything from American and European art to photography to Southeast Asian art. It also has a fine film department featuring lectures and screenings. If a major traveling exhibition is coming to Los Angeles it will usually mount the show at LACMA. Admission is $9 for adults, $5 for students and seniors, free for those aged 17 and under.
- **Museum of African-American Art**, 4005 South Crenshaw Blvd., 3rd Fl., 323-294-7071; permanent and rotating exhibits by African-American artists, as well as seasonal events, performances, and lectures. Admission is free.

- **Museum of Contemporary Art (MOCA)**, 250 South Grand Avenue, 213-621-2766, www.moca-la.org; permanent collection features painting, sculpture, live performances, and environmental work, all in a landmark building designed by Arata Isozaki. Free admission Thursdays from 5 p.m. to 8 p.m. General admission is $8, $5 for seniors and students, free admission for children under 12.
- **Norton Simon Museum of Art**, 411 West Colorado Blvd., Pasadena, 626-449-6840, www.nortonsimon.org; recently renovated, houses a permanent collection of European art from the Renaissance to the mid-20th century. Admission is $6 for adults, $3 for seniors, free for those under 18.
- **Santa Monica Museum of Art**, Bergamot Station G1, 2525 Michigan Avenue, 310-586-6488, www.smmoa.org; this small museum features changing contemporary exhibitions. An admission donation is encouraged.
- **Skirball Museum**, 2701 North Sepulveda Blvd., Brentwood, 310-440-4500, www.skirball.org; features Jewish fine arts, archaeological artifacts, ceremonial and religious objects, photographs, and folk arts. Admission is $8 for adults, $6 for students and seniors, and free for children under 12. Admission is free on Christmas Day.
- **UCLA/Armand Hammer Museum of Art**, 10899 Wilshire Blvd., Westwood, 310-443-7000, www.hammer.ucla.edu; the permanent collection features more than five centuries worth of Western European art. Admission is $5 for adults, $3 students and seniors, those under 17 are free.
- **Watts Towers**, 1727 East 107th Street, Watts, 213-847-4646, www.culturela.org; though not a museum in the traditional sense, this monumental piece of folk art took artist Sam Rodia 33 years to complete. The towers are built of salvaged steel rods, dismantled pipes, bed frames and cement, and are covered with bottle fragments, ceramic tiles, china plates, and more than 70,000 seashells. The adjacent Watts Towers Art Center hosts visual and performing art exhibits, poetry readings, and other events.

HISTORICAL, CULTURAL, SCIENCE MUSEUMS

- **Autry Museum of Western Heritage**, 4700 Western Heritage Way, Griffith Park, 323-667-2000, www.autry-museum.org; founded by famed movie cowboy Gene Autry, this museum houses a permanent collection of art and artifacts depicting the history of the American West. Admission is $7.50 for adults, $5 for seniors and students, and $3 for children 2 to 12. Admission is free on the second Tuesday of every month.

- **California African-American Museum**, South Figueroa Street and State Drive, 213-744-7432, www.caam.ca.gov; focuses on African-American achievements in science, politics, religion, athletics, and the arts. Admission is free.
- **California Heritage Museum**, 2612 Main Street, Santa Monica, 310-392-8537, www.californiaheritagemuseum.org; admission is $2, free for children under 12.
- **California Science Center**, 700 State Drive, 323-SCI-ENCE, www.casciencectr.org (formerly the California Museum of Science and Industry); free admission to over 100 interactive exhibits within four themed worlds that demonstrate real-life examples of science at work— the largest of its kind on the West Coast.
- **The Erotic Museum**, 6741 Hollywood Blvd. Hollywood, 323-463-7684, www.theeroticmuseum.com; new in 2003, this museum specializes in human sexuality as interpreted through history and art. The first of its kind on the West Coast. Only 18 and over admitted, admission is $12.95 for adults, $9.95 for students and seniors.
- **Fowler Museum of Cultural History**, UCLA, Westwood, 310-825-4361; admission is $5 for adults, $3 for students and seniors, free for those under 17 (UCLA campus parking fees apply)
- **Griffith Park Observatory**, 2800 East Observatory Road, Griffith Park, 323-664-1181, www.griffithobs.org; closed for renovation and expansion in 2002 with plans to reopen in 2006. Renovations include an observatory that's doubled in size, new exhibit areas, theater, and cafe. Meanwhile, visitors can visit the temporary Griffith Observatory Satellite facility at 4800 Western Heritage Way. There's no charge to attend this modest display of astronomy exhibits, its mini-planetarium, and the monthly star viewing parties (the celestial kind) hosted by the Los Angeles Astronomical Society (www.laas.org).
- **Hollywood Guinness World Records Museum**, 6764 Hollywood Blvd., 323-463-6433; showcases record-breaking achievements in entertainment and sports, plus historic human endeavors; $10.95 for adults; $8.50 for seniors; $6.95 for children 6-12.
- **Hollywood Wax Museum**, 6767 Hollywood Blvd., Hollywood, 323-462-5991; admission is $10.95 for adults, $8.50 for seniors, $6 for children 6-12.
- **Japanese American National Museum**, 369 East First Street, downtown, 213-625-0414, www.janm.org; this cultural center illustrates the history of Japanese immigration to the United States. Admission is $6 for adults, $5 for seniors and students, children under 5 are free.
- **Los Angeles Natural History Museum**, 900 Exposition Blvd., 213-763-DINO, www.nhm.org; free admission the first Tuesday of each

month. Regular admission fees are $9 for adults, $6.50 for seniors and students, $2 for children 5-12.

- **Museum of Flying**, Santa Monica, 310-392-8822, www.museum offlying.com; hours of operation are limited and fall mostly on weekends, call or check the museum web site for specifics.
- **Museum of Jurassic Technology**, 9341 Venice Blvd., Culver City, 310-836-6131, www.mjt.org; features "exhibits of idiosyncratic and curious things throughout the world." A donation of $5 for adults, $3 for seniors, and $3 for those 12 to 21 is requested. Admission to the museum is free after 7:45 p.m. on Thursdays and 5:45 p.m. on Friday, Saturday, and Sunday.
- **Museum of Tolerance**, 9786 West Pico Blvd., Beverly Hills, 310-553-8043, www.museumoftolerance.com; features high-tech exhibits dedicated to the examination of racism and prejudice, with an exhibit devoted to reenacting the events leading up to the Holocaust. Some exhibits are not recommended for those under twelve. Admission is $10 for adults, $8 for seniors, $7 for students and children aged 3-11. Advance reservations and a photo ID are needed for admission.
- **Pacific Asia Museum**, 46 North Los Robles Avenues, Pasadena, 626-449-2742, www.pacificasiamuseum.org; the only museum in the southwest dedicated to Asian and Pacific Islands art and culture. Admission is $7 for adults, $5 for students and seniors, free for kids under 12.
- **Page Museum at the La Brea Tar Pits**, 5801 Wilshire Blvd., Fairfax District, 323-934-PAGE, www.tarpits.org; features fossils from La Brea Tar Pits, and other paleontology exhibits. Admission is $7 for adults, $4.50 for students and seniors, $2 for children 5-10. Admission is free the first Tuesday of every month.
- **Petersen Automotive Museum**, 6060 Wilshire Blvd., Fairfax District, 323-930-CARS, www.petersen.org; where else, besides Detroit, would you expect to find a museum devoted to the automobile? Admission is $10 for adults, $5 for seniors and students, $3 for children 5-12.
- **Southwest Museum of the American Indian**, 234 Museum Drive, 323-221-2164, www.southwestmuseum.org; Los Angeles' first museum, founded in 1907, it contains an important collection of Native American art and artifacts. Admission is $7.50 for adults, $5 for seniors or students, $3 for those 7-18.
- **Museum of Television and Radio**, 465 North Beverly Drive, Beverly Hills, 310-786-1000, www.mtr.org; ever wanted to hear Welles' infamous 1938 "War of the Worlds" broadcast or would you be tickled at viewing an old episode of "The Brady Bunch"? Then look no further. Make a reservation at the front desk to utilize its screening/listening consoles. There are also daily screenings and radio presentations usually

grouped around themes such as American Pop and Black History month. Free admission, but donations are accepted.

LITERARY LIFE

The *LA Times* **Festival of Books** is the largest book festival in the country. Hundreds of publishers, specialty booksellers, and authors come to the UCLA campus for one weekend each April to speak, sell books, give readings and demonstrations, and offer to autograph copies of recent best sellers. For details about this free festival, go to www.latimes.com or call 213-237-2366.

BOOKSTORES

Bookstores, such as Barnes & Noble and Borders, and specialty stores like Book Soup and Dutton's, host weekly readings and author signings, and organize book clubs to satisfy any bibliophile. Inquire with the stores or look at the Book Review section in the Sunday *LA Times* for listings.

GENERAL BOOKSTORES

- **Barnes & Noble** superstores, www.bn.com, offer vast selections of literary, reference, trade, and children's books, plus a large selection of magazines and newspapers from around the world. Hosts author readings and events, including an annual wine tasting, plus reading groups and workshops. Most locations have in-store cafes. Locations throughout the county; see the Yellow Pages or www.bn.com.
- **Borders Books & Music**; www.bordersstores.com; this national bookseller has many locations throughout LA as well. Offers a wide range of events from author readings to book groups to live music, all of which are free and open to the public. Check the Yellow Pages or www.borders.com for a location near you.
- **Bookstar** has three locations in Los Angeles (West Hollywood, Culver City, and Studio City). See your Yellow Pages for phone numbers.

SPECIAL INTEREST BOOKSTORES

If you're seeking a non-chain or specialty bookstore, try the following:
- **A-Z Technical Bookstore**, 1025 North Sycamore Avenue, 800-903-4567
- **Autobooks/Aerobooks**, 3524 West Magnolia, Burbank, 818-845-0707, www.autobooks-aerobooks.com; features aviation and automotive literature

- **Builders Book Inc.**, **Bookstore**, 8001 Canoga Avenue, Woodland Hills, 818-887-7828
- **Book'Em Mysteries**, 1118 Mission, South Pasadena, 626-799-9600, www.bookem.com
- **Book Soup**, 8818 Sunset Blvd., West Hollywood, 310 659-3110, www.booksoup.com; boasts an unusual collection of fiction and non-fiction titles not normally found in mainstream stores
- **Children's Book World**, 10580 3/4 West Pico Blvd., West LA, 310-559-BOOK, www.childrensbooksworld.com
- **Chevalier's Books**, 126 North Larchmont Blvd., 323-465-1334
- **Cook's Library**, 8373 West Third Street, 323-655-3141
- **Cook Books Janet Jarvits**, 1388 East Washington Blvd., Pasadena, 626-296-1638, www.cookbookjj.com
- **La Cité Des Livres French Books**, 2306 Westwood Blvd., 310-475-0658
- **A Different Light Bookstore**, 8853 Santa Monica Blvd., 310-854-6601, www.adlbooks.com; specializes in gay and lesbian literature
- **Dutton's Brentwood Books**, 11975 San Vicente Blvd. Brentwood, 310-476-6263, www.duttonsbrentwood.com
- **Dutton's Beverly Hills Books**, 447 North Canon Drive, Beverly Hills, 310-281-0997, www.duttonsbeverlyhills.com
- **The Legal Bookstore**, 316 West Third Street, 213-626-2139
- **Hennessey & Ingalls Art & Architecture Books**, 214 Wilshire Blvd., Santa Monica, 310-458-9074, www.hennesseyingalls.com
- **Medical Tech Book Center**, 8001 Canoga Avenue, Woodland Hills, 818-347-7438
- **The Mysterious Bookshop**, 8763 Beverly Blvd., 310-659-2959
- **Oriental Bookstore**, 1713 East Colorado Blvd., Pasadena, 626-577-2413
- **Russian Books**, 13757 Victory Blvd., Van Nuys, 818-781-7533
- **Samuel French's Theatre & Film Bookshops,** www.samuelfrench.com; 7623 Sunset Blvd., 323-876-0570; 11963 Ventura Blvd., Studio City, 818-762-0535
- **Shalom House Jewish Store**, 19740 Ventura Blvd., Woodland Hills, 818-704-7100
- **Storyopolis Children's Bookstore**, 116 North Robertson Blvd., 310-358-2500, www.storyopolis.com
- **Taschen,** 354 North Beverly Drive, Beverly Hills, 310 274 4300, www.taschen.com; the US flagship store of the German publisher of the same name peddles its eclectic art and culture titles in this super-glossy store.
- **Traveler's Bookcase**, 8375 West Third Street, 323-655-0575
- **Valley Book & Bible Stores**, 20936 Roscoe Blvd., Woodland Hills, 818-709-5610; 6502 Van Nuys Blvd., Van Nuys, 818-782-6101

USED BOOKS

The internet has made it possible for book collectors to conduct their own search for hard-to-find titles without ever leaving home. However, your local network of used and rare booksellers may have just what you need (and there is nothing quite like browsing through the old and rare titles of a used bookstore, often with a store cat snoozing nearby in a sunlit corner). Check your Yellow Pages under "Books-Used & Rare" for a complete listing of local stores. Here are just a few:

- **Bargain Books**, 14426 Friar, Van Nuys, 818-782-2782
- **Bodhi Tree Bookstore**, 8585 Melrose Avenue, West Hollywood, 310-659-1733, www.bodhitree.com
- **Books on the Boulevard**, 13551 Ventura Blvd., Sherman Oaks, 818-905-0988
- **Book Alley Fine & Old Books**, 611 East Colorado Blvd., Pasadena, 626-683-8083, www.bookalley.com
- **Book Castle's Movie World**, 212 North San Fernando Blvd., Burbank, 818-845-1563, www.bookcastlesmovieworld.com
- **Book City**, 6627 Hollywood Blvd., Hollywood, 323-466-2525, www.hollywoodbookcity.com; in addition to used books, it carries a good selection of screenplays from your favorite movies
- **Brand Bookshop**, 231 North Brand Blvd., Glendale, 818-507-5943
- **Dailey Rare Books & Fine Prints**, 8216 Melrose Avenue, 323-658-8515
- **Dutton's Books**, 5146 Laurel Canyon Blvd., North Hollywood, 818-769-3866; 3806 West Magnolia Blvd., Burbank, 818-840-8003; the most well-known secondhand bookstore in LA, famous for its friendly service, esoteric selection, and amazing ability to locate the rarest of books
- **Heritage Book Shop**, 8540 Melrose Avenue, West Hollywood, 310-659-3674

UNIVERSITY BOOKSTORES/LIBRARIES

College bookstores, such as the UCLA's and USC's, are another resource for general and specialized publications and are open to the public. As well, non-students can access libraries at many colleges and universities in the Los Angeles area. If you want to be able to check out books, but are not a student or alumnus, you may have to pay a fee. For more information, contact the following public schools:

- **California State University Los Angeles**, 323-343-3000, www.calstatela.edu

- **California State University Northridge**, 818-885-1200, www.csun.edu
- **Los Angeles City College**, 323-953-4000, www.lacc.cc.ca.us
- **Santa Monica College**, 310-450-5150, www.smc.edu
- **University of California Los Angeles**, 310-825-4321, www.ucla.edu
- **West Los Angeles College**, 310-287-4200, www.wlac.cc.ca.us

LIBRARIES

There are numerous **specialty libraries** in LA; some of those open to the public include:

- **Frances-Henry Library of Hebrew Union College**, 213-749-3424, www.huc.edu
- **LA County Law Library**, 310-288-1269, http://lalaw.lib.ca.us
- **Margaret Herrick Library** at the **Academy of Motion Pictures Arts & Sciences**, 310-247-3020, www.oscars.org/mhl
- **Norris Medical Library**, 323-442-1111, www.usc.edu/hsc/nml
- **University of Southern California**, 213-740-2311, www.usc.edu; houses several specialized subject libraries including architecture, education, philosophy, music, science, social work, and East Asian collections

PUBLIC LIBRARIES

City and county libraries offer a wealth of free to low-cost community services such as lectures, health and wellness programs, crafts workshops for adults or children, teen activities, computer and internet access and classes, movie rentals, book sales and clubs, storytelling, readings, and, of course, books. Los Angeles County and the City of Los Angeles operate separately; although a resident of the City of LA may use both systems; a library card application will need to be filled out for each card.

Call 213-228-7272 or visit the **City of LA Public Library's** web site, www.lapl.org, to investigate the locations of more than 60 branch libraries and to find out about upcoming community events.

The **LA County Public Library** system can be reached via www.colapublib.org, or call 562-940-8415 for assistance with locating a community branch near you. To view the entire catalog of library holdings of LA County Library, go to http://catalog.colapl.org.

Orange County's library system, which consists of 33 branches, can be contacted by phone by calling 714-566-3000 or go to www.ocpl.org; to search its database go to www.ocls.lib.fl.us.

Check the listings at the end of the **Neighborhood Profiles** for a branch library near you or visit one of these **main libraries**:

- **Los Angeles Central Library**, 630 West 5th Street, 213-228-7000, www.lapl.org/central; at the heart of this towering, multistoried library (and old, built in 1926) is a vast collection of books, magazines, audio/video tapes, and databases. Populated with unique architecture, murals, statues, fountains, and an eight-story atrium, the library offers public tours year round that run an hour. The Los Angeles Public Library is accessed by local residents, as well as libraries and other organizations from across the USA. In 2004, a public computer center with 55 stations was added.
- **Anaheim Central Library**, 500 West Broadway, Anaheim; 714-765-1880, www.anaheim.net
- **Huntington Beach Central Library**, 7111 Talbert Avenue, Huntington Beach; 714-842-4481, www.hbpl.org

CULTURE FOR KIDS

Children can keep busy year round in Los Angeles. Options range from visiting a working farm to participation in a youth chorus to viewing a children's theater production. In addition to the museums below, most of the "adult" museums listed in this chapter organize workshops and activities geared for kids. Contact the museums for more information.

MUSEUMS FOR KIDS

- **California Science Center**, 700 State Drive, 323-SCI-ENCE, www.ca sciencectr.org (see description above).
- **Kidspace Museum**, 480 North Arroyo Blvd., Pasadena, 626-449-9144, www.kidspacemuseum.org; participatory museum with exhibits scaled for kids 12 and under.
- **LA Children's Museum**, Administrative Offices, 205 South Broadway, Ste. 608, 213-687-8800, www.childrensmuseumla.org; the downtown museum closed in 2000 and is moving to the Hansen Dam Recreation Area, where a new facility is being built. When this 60,000 square foot building opens in 2007, it will include indoor and outdoor exhibit space, a café, playground, and a performing arts theater. Visit its web site for updates.
- **Museum of Flying**, Santa Monica, 310-392-8822, www.museum offlying.com; offers tours, model making classes, and an interactive children's area. Hours of operation are limited and fall mostly on weekends, call or check the museum web site for specifics.

- **Zimmer Children's Museum**, 6505 Wilshire Blvd., Ste. 100, 323-761-8989, www.zimmermuseum.org; a 10,000 square-foot museum located in The Goldsmith Jewish Federation Center. Open to the public.

PLAY/DISCOVERY FACILITIES

- **AdventurePlex**, Manhattan Beach, 310-546-7708, www.Adventure Plex.org; a health and fitness center designed especially for kids, with an outdoor climbing wall, gymnasium and fitness center, challenging mazes, tunnels, and slides.
- **Bright Child Children's Activity Center**, Santa Monica, 310-393-4844, www.brightchild.com; described as the granddaddy of indoor playgrounds for its innovative play space. An enormous main play structure features slides, a wind tunnel, and zip lines. Babysitting services and classes also offered.
- **Creative Leap**, Northridge, 818-366-3036; in addition to the expected play structures, there are yoga classes, a video game arcade, and a dinosaur room equipped with a fossilized climbing wall in a prehistoric setting.
- **Creative Kids**, West LA, 310-473-6090; offers classes in cooking, dancing, music, and art to keep kids 14 and under busy year round. Free trial classes offered. Also hosts birthday and slumber parties.
- **Gymboree Play and Music Center**, www.gymboree.com, 310-470-7780; Sherman Oaks, 818-905-6225; Northridge, 818-905-6225; Calabasas, 818-905-6225; padded, colorful playgrounds for youngsters, and music classes for kids 4 and younger. Sessions run 10 weeks.
- **Joey's Gym for Children**, Beverly Hills, 310-855-0146, is popular for birthday bookings; in addition to its fantastic play space, it will provide balloons, banners, streamers, tables, benches, and music for parties.
- **Kid Concepts, USA**, Torrance, 310-465-0075, www.kidconcepts usa.com; giant play structures, arts and crafts classes, toddler area, rock climbing, and a restaurant. Memberships available.

OUTDOOR

- **Cirque du Soleil**, 800-678-5440, www.cirquedusoleil.com; this funky Montreal circus-like-no-other pitches its colorful tents at the Staples Center parking lot when in town.
- **The Farm**, 8101 Tampa Avenue, Reseda, 818-341-6805; an animal farm with pony rides. Open weekends.
- **Green Meadows Children's Farm**, 323-224-8504, 4235 Monterey Road, Ernest Debs Park; take a guided tour of a farm filled with hundreds of farm animals. Open October through June. Admission is $9.

- **Griffith Park** offers pony and wagon rides, a miniature train and old-fashioned carousel, enough to take up a full day.
- **Kids Koncerts**, Theatricum Botanicum, 1419 North Topanga Canyon Blvd., Topanga, 310-455-3723, www.theatricum.com; summer series featuring popular, kid-friendly musical guests.
- **Long Beach Aquarium of the Pacific**, Shoreline Drive and Aquarium Way, Long Beach, 562-590-3100, www.aquariumofthe pacific.org; situated across from the Queen Mary, the aquarium shows off over 10,000 fish in 17 habitat tanks. Admission is $18.95 for adults, $10.95 for children 3-11, $14.95 for seniors.
- **Los Angeles Zoo**, Griffith Park, 323-644-4200, www.lazoo.org, is a modest sized zoo with a petting area that recently received a bond for expansion. Admission is $9 for adults, $6 for seniors, $4 for children 2-12.
- **Open House: Hollywood Bowl**, Hollywood Bowl Plaza, Highland Avenue, Hollywood, 323-850-2000, www.hollywoodbowl.org; a summer series of arts and crafts workshops for kids. Fees vary.
- **Pierce College Animal Farm**, 6201 Winnetka Avenue, Woodland Hills, 818-703-0826, www.lapc.cc.ca.us; a working farm that hosts special events during the year.
- **Ringling Bros Barnum & Bailey Circus**, www.ringling.com; the famous traveling circus makes the rounds from the LA Sports Arena to the Great Western Forum during select weekends in the summer. Visit its web site for specific dates.
- **San Diego Wild Animal Park**, 15500 San Pasqual Valley Road, Escondido, 760-747-8702, www.sandiegozoo.org, is a little like going on a safari, over 400 species roam together on 1,800 acres that visitors can see primarily by monorail.
- **San Diego Zoo**, 2920 Zoo Drive, San Diego, 619-234-3153, www.sandiegozoo.org; over 100 acres are devoted to the care and exhibition of animals for conservation, research, and education at this world class zoo.
- **Tierra Rejada Ranch**, 3370 Moorpark Road, Moorpark, 805-523-2957; animal farm with pony rides and pick-your-own vegetables. Open weekends.
- **Universal City Walk**, 1000 Universal Center Drive, 818-622-3801, www.citywalkhollywood.com; while this outdoor mall is popular with adults, it's the pulsing, interactive water fountain that kids can't resist. Free admission, but there is a fee for parking.
- **William S. Hart Park**, 24151 North San Fernando Road, Newhall, 661-259-0855, www.hartmuseum.org; in addition to a Western-themed museum, inside the park is a barnyard animal feeding area for kids.

THEATER FOR KIDS

The following theaters perform regularly to the delight of young audiences:

- **Bob Baker Marionette Theater**, 1345 West First Street, 213-250-9995, www.thepuppetstudio.com/BBTheater.html; the oldest of its kind in the USA, with an impressive collection of over 3,000 puppets.
- **Burbank Little Theater**, 1100 Clark Avenue, Burbank, 818-238-9998; performs children's stories and fairy tales such as "Treasure Island" and "Peter Pan"; the audience is encouraged to supply the sound effects.
- **Comedy Pups**, 4378, Lankershim Blvd., North Hollywood, 818-752-9566; stand-up comedians as young as six perform their funny antics for free at the Kindness of Strangers Coffeehouse.
- **LA Connection Comedy Theatre**, 13442 Ventura Blvd., Sherman Oaks, 818-784-1868, www.laconnectioncomedy.com; offers a "Comedy Improv for Kids" program, call for more information.
- **Occidental Children's Theater**, 1600 Campus Road, Eagle Rock, 323-259-2922, www.oxy.edu
- **Puppet & Magic Center**, 1255 Second Street, Santa Monica, 310-656-0483, www.puppetmagic.com; musical variety shows and home to a museum of more than 400 puppets, marionettes and ventriloquist figures.
- **Santa Monica Playhouse**, 1211 Fourth Street, 310-394-9779, www.santamonicaplayhouse.com; regular family-oriented performances by the Playhouse Actors' Repertory Theater Company and the Young Professionals' Company.

OTHER

- **American Youth Symphony**, 310-234-8355, www.aysymphony.org
- **Los Angeles Children's Chorus**, 626-793-4231, www.lachildrenschorus.org
- **Pasadena Junior Philharmonic**, 626-792-0463, www.laphil.org
- **San Fernando Valley Youth Chorus**, 818-888-6293 via the Angeles Chorale, www.sfvyc.org
- **Toyota Symphonies for Youth**, 213-850-2000, www.laphil.org

AMUSEMENT PARKS

The Los Angeles area is home to several amusement parks, including the granddaddy of them all, Disneyland. To avoid sticker-shock, you might want to call ahead to find out the various parks' admission and parking prices, which can be steep. The biggies include:

- **Disneyland** and **Disneyland's California Adventure**, 714-781-4565, www.disneyland.com

- **Knott's Berry Farm**, 714-220-5200, www.knottsberryfarm.com
- **Legoland**, 877-534-6526, www.lego.com
- **Raging Waters**, 909-802-2200, www.ragingwaters.com
- **Santa Monica Pier**, 310-260-8744, www.santamonicapier.org
- **Six Flags Magic Mountain**, 661-255-4111, www.sixflags.com
- **Universal Studios Tour**, 818-508-9600, www.universalstudios.com

COLLEGES AND UNIVERSITIES

Los Angeles has a number of first-rate institutions offering a wide range of higher education options. In addition to offering degree programs, local colleges and universities offer concerts, plays, lectures, and many other cultural opportunities to the public. Call the campus in which you are interested or visit its web site for more information.

Here are just a few local colleges and universities:

- **Art Center College of Design**, 1700 Lida Street, Pasadena, 626-396-2200, www.artcenter.edu; a four-year college known for its classes in both fine and applied arts.
- **Biola University**, 13800 Biola Avenue, La Mirada, CA 90639, 562-903-6000, www.biola.edu; Protestant university with a wide range of undergraduate and graduate programs, and host to cultural events.
- **California Institute of Technology**, 1201 East California Blvd., Pasadena, 626-395-6811, www.caltech.edu; a small, highly regarded school devoted to the study of science and mathematics, and the place where news cameras turn for information after local earthquakes.
- **California Institute of the Arts**, 24700 West McBean Parkway, Valencia, 661-255-1050, www.calarts.edu; referred to as Cal Arts, this avant-garde school focuses on visual, theatrical, and written arts. Now sponsored by Disney Studios.
- **California State University Long Beach** (**CSULB**), 1250 Bellflower Blvd., Long Beach, 562-985-4111, www.csulb.edu; offers degrees in business, education, engineering, health, and liberal arts. The CSULB Blue Pyramid is a popular venue for concerts and events.
- **Los Angeles City College**, 855 North Vermont Avenue, 323-953-4000, www.lacc.cc.ca.us; is a large, two-year community college with an ethnically mixed student body in an urban environment.
- **Loyola Marymount University**, 1 LMU Drive, 310-338-2700, www.lmu.edu; renowned Catholic University.
- **Mount Saint Mary's College**, 12001 Chalon Road, West LA, 310-954-4000, www.msmc.la.edu; located in the scenic hills above Brentwood with views of the city below, this Catholic school hosts art gallery shows and other cultural events.

- **Pasadena City College**, 1570 East Colorado Blvd., Pasadena, 626-585-7123, www.pasadena.edu; this two-year community college hosts cultural events, as well as special programs for part-time students.
- **Pepperdine University**, 24255 West Pacific Coast Highway, Malibu, 310-506-4000, www.pepperdine.edu; a marquee name and a magnificent ocean view.
- **Santa Monica College**, 1900 Pico Blvd., Santa Monica, 310-434-4000, www.smc.edu, is a well-respected, two-year community college with a high transfer rate to UCLA.
- **University of California, Irvine,** intersection of Campus and University drives, Irvine, 949-824-5011, www.uci.edu, currently enrolls more than 23,000 students, and is consistently ranked by *U.S. News and World Report* among the country's best public universities. A major research university, with undergraduate and graduate programs as well as a medical school, UCI sponsors numerous plays, concerts, and lectures that are open to the public.
- **University of California, Los Angeles**, 405 Hilgard Avenue, Westwood, 310-825-4321, www.ucla.edu, has the largest enrollment of all nine campuses in the UC system, with more than 35,000 students. Walking tours of the pretty, 419-acre campus are available. Don't miss the Franklin D. Murphy Sculpture Garden.
- **University of Southern California**, Exposition Blvd., between Vermont Avenue and Figueroa Street, 213-740-2311, www.usc.edu; this private school has a number of galleries and museums open to the public, as well as displays of scripts and movie memorabilia at the Cinema Special Collections Library. Its cinema, law, and dentistry schools are considered top-notch.

THE EXCELLENT YEAR-ROUND WEATHER IN LOS ANGELES MAKES IT a great place for those interested in watching or playing professional athletics. With professional teams that include an indoor football team, two baseball teams, two basketball teams, and an ice hockey team, and a powerhouse of college athletics, sports fans can keep very busy here. LA teams have bragging rights to the World Series, NBA Championships (three in a row), and the Rose Bowl, to name a few. The venues in which champs are made are equally top-notch. The slick and glossy Staples Center boasts a $1.5 million dollar sound system, two floors of luxury box suites, and excellent sight lines, making it the best and most popular sports venue in LA. An even newer arena, the Home Depot Center in Carson, opened in 2003. Sprawled over 85 acres, this complex of Olympian proportions features two world-class stadiums (one dedicated to soccer and tennis only) and track and cycling fields.

Fans keep tabs on their favorite teams through the extensive sports sections of the *LA Times* or *Daily News*. Radio stations KSPN 710AM and KMPC 1540AM are devoted to sports and more sports. All local television news broadcasts regularly set aside the last five to ten minutes of airtime for sports reporting. Fox Sports Net's Southern California Sports Report broadcasts every night from its studio in the Staples Center.

Possibilities for the fitness minded are vast, including a good selection of public tennis courts, soccer fields, city-run recreation centers, and loads of membership gyms. Also notable here is the world's largest public golf course system, the world's first disc golf course, and, for dedicated runners, Los Angeles hosts one of the largest marathons.

Clubs or leagues revolving around a particular sport are often the best place to start when seeking information about events, tournaments, and opportunities to join in. Sometimes the local sporting goods store will have a bulletin board that you can check for postings by sports leagues or even informal pick-up games. And for kids, parents of sporty tykes often refer to **Los Angeles Family,** www.lafamily.com, a free monthly magazine that lists child-friendly venues for baseball, swimming, summer camps, even yoga.

PROFESSIONAL AND SCHOOL SPORTS

Several ticket agencies handle professional games and venues in the Los Angeles area. Ticketmaster is the standard and official vendor, but if price is no object, other agencies may be worth checking into, after the box office and Ticketmaster are sold out. (Sometimes tickets are auctioned off at Ebay, www.ebay.com.) When purchasing from a ticket agency or online at the venue's box office, expect to pay a convenience charge.

- **Ticketmaster**, 213-480-3232 or 800-551-SEAT, www.ticketmaster.com
- **Barry's Tickets**, 818-990-8499, www.barrystickets.com
- **VIP Tickets**, 888-474-9490, www.viptickets.com

PROFESSIONAL SPORTS

BASEBALL

Baseball season runs from April through October.

- **The Angels** play at **Anaheim Stadium** (lovingly called "The Big A") in Orange County. Under Disney ownership, the Angels have had only sporadic success. Then they shocked the world with their game seven win in the 2002 World Series. Now general manager Bill Stoneman has his hands full as he attempts to repeat the Angels miracle. For ticket information, call 888-796-4256 or go to www.angelsbaseball.com.
- The **Los Angeles Dodgers** play at **Dodger Stadium** in Chavez Ravine. The Dodgers last won the World Series in 1988 under the leadership of famous manager, eater, and dieter, Tommy Lasorda. Just as Fernando Valenzuela's pitching success in the early 1980s drew a new crowd of fans to the park, pitching sensation Hideo Nomo from Japan produced what was locally known as "Nomomania" in the early 1990s. Today, they're struggling with their batting line-up, but a recent change in management and ownership has players and fans gunning for a trip to the World Series. Tickets for adults range from $6 to $37, giving Dodger games the moniker of "the cheapest ticket in town." For ticket information, call 323-224-1448 or go to www.dodgers.com.

- For minor league baseball, the nearest teams are the **Lancaster Jethawks**, 661-726-5400, www.jethawks.com, at The Hangar Ballpark; the **Lake Elsinore Storm**, 909-245-4487, www.stormbaseball.com, at The Diamond in Lake Elsinore, and the **Inland Empire 66'ers** (formerly the San Bernardino Stampede), 909-888-9922, www.ie66ers.com, at the Arrowhead Credit Union Park.

BASKETBALL

Basketball season picks up after baseball, and runs from October through April.
- Since 1999, the **Los Angeles Clippers** (season seats, 213-742-7555, www.nba.com/clippers) have called the **Staples Center** home. In this town, used to the Lakers glory days of Magic Johnson, Kareem Abdul Jabbar, and Shaquille O'Neal, the Clippers are often treated like poor second cousins. With the Clippers having gone 17 seasons out of 20 without a playoff game, in 2004 ticket prices were raised in hopes of funding stronger free agents. For ticket information, call Ticketmaster, 213-480-3232, www.ticketmaster.com, or the Staples Center, 877-5-ACT-NOW (premier seating), www.staplescenter.com.
- The **Los Angeles Lakers** (season seats, 800-4-NBA-TIXS, www.nba.com/lakers) have likewise nested in the Staples Center. Once the hottest ticket in town, the Lakers' future has become a little uncertain. After their failed bid to win a fourth NBA Championship in 2004 under head coach Phil Jackson, the team underwent a rapid and major exodus of players, including veteran players Shaquille O'Neal and Gary Payton. You can bet team management will be busy bringing around this younger team, still anchored by the outstanding Kobe Bryant—amidst very high expectations. For ticket information call Ticketmaster, 213-480-3232, www.ticketmaster.com, or the Staples Center, 877-5-ACT-NOW (for premier seating), www.staplescenter.com.
- The local WNBA team, the **Los Angeles Sparks** (tickets, 310-426-6033, www.wnba.com/sparks) also plays in the Staples Center, feasible because the women's season coincides with the men's off-season. Founded in 1997, the Sparks excited fans by becoming back-to-back WNBA champions in 2001 and 2002. Although they haven't gained a league championship since 2002, they do feature the amazing Lisa Leslie, who in 2004 received both the WNBA's Defensive Player of the Year and Most Valuable Player awards.

FOOTBALL

Purists have been pining for an NFL team franchise since the Los Angeles Rams played the last professional NFL game here in 1994. It wasn't until 2000 that the Arena Football League's **Los Angeles Avengers** kicked off their inaugural season. While not exactly what NFL fans were hoping for, many football fans were placated. Arena football is a fast-moving alternative to regulation football. It is played on an indoor field that is half the size of what NFL teams play on, resulting in a higher scoring game. The Avengers (for season tickets, call 888-AVENGERS or go to www.laavengers.com) play at the Staples Center from April to July. For ticket information, call Ticketmaster, 213-480-3232, www.ticketmaster.com; or the Staples Center, 888-5-ACT-NOW, www.staplescenter.com.

HOCKEY

- The **Los Angeles Kings** (season seats, 888-KINGS-LA, www.la kings.com) also play at the Staples Center. Ice hockey season begins in November and ends in March unless, as in 1993, the Kings make it to the Stanley Cup finals in June. "The Great One" Wayne Gretzky popularized hockey here in a city that only sees ice or snow on television. For ticket information, call Ticketmaster, 213-480-3232, www.ticketmaster.com, or the Staples Center, 877-5-ACT-NOW (premier seating), www.staplescenter.com.
- The **Long Beach Ice Dogs** play at the Long Beach Arena, 300 East Ocean Blvd., Long Beach, 562-436-3661, www.icedogshockey.com. Call the arena or Ticketmaster for tickets.

HORSE RACING

There are three racetracks in the Los Angeles area:
- **Hollywood Park**, Inglewood, 310-419-1574, www.hollywoodpark.com; races are run April through July, and November through December.
- **Los Angeles County Fairgrounds**, 909-623-3111, www.fairplex.com; races are held at the fair each September.
- **Santa Anita Park**, **Arcadia**, 626-574-RACE, http://origin.magnaent.com; races are run October through November, and then December through April.

SOCCER

Major League Soccer's (MLS) **LA Galaxy** is one of ten US Division One franchise start-up teams that date back to 1996. Over five seasons, head coach Sigi Schmid guided his team to three titles, winning the 2002 MLS Cup Championship, the 2001 US Open Cup Championship, and the 2000 CONCACAF Champions' Cup. Retired Galaxy player Paul Caligiuri was inducted into the Hall of Fame in 2004. More recently, a string of away game losses has cost the team some momentum, but their home games remain strong and playoff games are always anticipated for this perennial contender. The LA Galaxy play at the **Home Depot Center** in Carson (www.homedepotcenter). Call 877-3-GALAXY, www.lagalaxy.com for tickets. The season runs April through September.

TENNIS

The local major men's tennis event is the **Mercedes-Benz Cup**, which is played in July at the Los Angeles Tennis Center at UCLA. For professional women's tennis, don't miss the **WTA Tour Championships** (played in November), which moved from New York's Madison Square Garden to the Staples Center in 2002. Both events draw some of the world's top players. For more information on either of the tournaments, contact the local **United States Tennis Association** office at 310-208-3838, www. usta.com.

COLLEGE SPORTS

In Los Angeles, college games are plentiful and dependable. Many college sports enthusiasts find living here a heavenly experience, as the local schools consistently boast some of the nation's finest athletes and teams.

UCLA's basketball program is legendary, producing such stars as Kareem Abdul-Jabbar (then Lou Alcindor), Gail Goodrich, Jamaal (then Keith) Wilkes, Bill Walton, Marcus Johnson, Ann Meyers (sister of Dave), Reggie Miller, and Ed O'Bannon. The football program is no slouch either, with former players Troy Aikman and Ken Norton on the roster, and the home field being none other than the Rose Bowl. Likewise **USC** football can usually be described as nothing short of a powerhouse, energized in the past by the likes of Mike Garrett, Charles White, Marcus Allen, Ricky Bell, Ronnie Lott, Junior Seau, and yes, O.J. Simpson. Cheryl Miller, one of the greatest female basketball players ever, also was a Trojan. Other local college sports programs of note are baseball at **Cal State Fullerton**, **Pepperdine's** tennis and water polo, **Loyola Marymount** for basketball, **Long Beach State's** basketball, UCLA's volleyball, gymnastics, softball, and water polo, and USC's water polo.

For **athletic ticket information**, call the following numbers:

- **Cal State Fullerton**, 714-278-CSUF, www.fullerton.edu
- **Loyola Marymount**, 310-338-6095, www.lmu.edu
- **Long Beach State**, 310-985-4111, www.csulb.edu
- **Pepperdine**, 866-WAVE-TIX, www.pepperdine.edu
- **UCLA**, 310-825-2101, www.ucla.edu
- **USC**, 213-740-4672, www.usctrojans.com

PARTICIPANT SPORTS AND ACTIVITIES

PARKS AND RECREATION DEPARTMENTS

The **County of Los Angeles Department of Parks and Recreation**, 213-738-2961 or http://parks.co.la.ca.us, oversees an incredible 63,000 acres of parks, gardens, lakes, trails, natural areas, and the world's largest public golf course system. In addition, the City of LA runs many recreation programs and oversees the use of its city pools, green spaces, and urban forests. Contact the **City of LA Department of Recreation and Parks** at 888-LA-PARKS, www.laparks.org. Both organizations offer extensive information on park facilities, leagues, clubs, and lessons on their web sites. Additional city park departments include:

- **Azusa Recreation and Parks Department**, 626-812-5215, www.ci.azusa.ca.us
- **Beverly Hills Recreation and Parks Department**, 310-285-2537, www.beverlyhills.org
- **Burbank Parks and Recreation Department**, 818-238-5300, www.ci.burbank.ca.us
- **Calabasas Recreation and Parks Department**, 818-880-6461, www.cityofcalabasas.com
- **Carson Recreation and Parks Department**, 310-847-3570, www.ci.carson.ca.us
- **Cerritos Recreation and Parks Department**, 562-916-1254, www.ci.cerritos.ca.us
- **Culver City Recreation Department**, 310-202-5689, www.culver city.org
- **El Segundo Parks and Recreation Department**, 310-524-2300, www.elsegundo.org
- **Glendale Parks Recreation Department**, 818-548-2000, www.ci.glendale.ca.us

- **Long Beach Department of Parks, Recreation and Marine**, 562-570-3100, www.ci.long-beach.ca.us
- **Malibu Parks and Recreation Department**, 310-317-1364, www.ci.malibu.ca.us
- **Manhattan Beach Recreation Department**, 310-545-5621, ext. 325, www.ci.manhattan-beach.ca.us
- **Monterey Park Recreation and Parks Department**, 626-307-1388, www.ci.monterey-park.ca.us
- **Newport Beach**, 949-644-3151, http://recreation.city.newportbeach.ca.us
- **Orange County Resources and Development Management Department/Harbors, Beaches and Parks Division**, 866-OCPARKS, www.ocparks.com
- **Pasadena Parks and Recreation Department**, 626-797-1114, www.ci.pasadena.ca.us
- **Santa Clarita Parks and Recreation Department**, 661-250-3700, www.santa-clarita.com
- **Santa Monica Recreation Division**, 310-458-8300, www.ci.santa-monica.ca.us
- **Tustin Parks and Recreation Department**, 714-573-3326, www.tustinca.org
- **West Hollywood Recreation Department**, 323-848-6308, www.weho.org

BASKETBALL

Pick-up basketball games are available all over the city, with competition ranging from friendly to fierce. Particularly renowned is the busy pick-up basketball scene at Venice's Boardwalk. While it may seem like this is the spot with the best and flashiest players in town, there are good games to be found all over, from schoolyards to city parks. The Wooden Center's indoor courts at UCLA, 310-825-1135, are where the "big names" show up, and it's not uncommon for hot college players, former professionals, or even a current pro to drop by for a game of pick-up. Check out www.socalhoops.com for the latest leads. Here is a sampling of neighborhood parks and recreation centers with basketball courts:

- **Balboa Sports Center**, Burbank and Balboa boulevards, Encino, 818-756-9642
- **Roxbury Park**, South Roxbury Drive and Olympic Blvd., Beverly Hills, 310-550-4761
- **Reed Park**, Wilshire and Lincoln boulevards, Santa Monica, 310-458-2239

- **Victory-Vineland Recreation Center**, Victory Blvd. and Vineland Avenue, North Hollywood, 818-985-9516
- **Venice Beach Athletic Center**, Ocean Front Walk and Winward Avenue, Venice, 310-399-2775
- **West Hollywood Park**, North San Vicente and Santa Monica boulevards, West Hollywood, 323-848-6534
- **Westwood Recreation Complex**, South Sepulveda and Wilshire boulevards, Westwood, 310-473-3610

BASEBALL/SOFTBALL

There are numerous baseball and softball leagues throughout Los Angeles, many of which are organized through the workplace. There is, for instance, an advertising league and a law league. For more information, ask your colleagues, call your department of parks and recreation, or contact the **US Amateur Baseball Association**, 425-776-7130, www.usaba.com. If you've got money to burn and a dream to fulfill, sign up for the **Dodgers Adult Baseball Camp**, 800-334-7529, www.ladabc.com. The month-long camp provides pro-level baseball practice and coaching by the LA Dodgers staff and ex-players like Steve Garvey to anyone...with $4,000.

BICYCLING

Both tour bicycling and mountain biking are popular in Los Angeles. The most traveled bike path is the **coastal bike path** from **Pacific Palisades** in the north to **Torrance** in the south. On weekends, the path resembles a bicycling and skating freeway. If you don't own a bike, rentals are available at several shacks on the beach in Marina del Rey, Venice, and Santa Monica. Other popular trails include the **Ballona Creek Trail** and the **Pasadena bike trail**. Mountain bikers enjoy the challenging trails in the **Santa Monica Mountains**, including Sullivan Canyon along (and through) the creek bed, the **Malibu Canyon trails**, **Topanga State Park**, 310-455-2465, and **Sycamore Canyon**. For more information about area routes, call the **LA County Transportation Commission** at 213-236-9555. The site www.labikepaths.com is an excellent resource for bike enthusiasts, and includes an extensive list of trails and paths.

Local **bicycling groups** include:
- The **Los Angeles Wheelmen**, 310-556-7967, www.lawheelmen.org
- The **Los Angeles County Bicycle Coalition** (**LACBC**), 213-629-2142, www.labikecoalition.org; a membership-based advocacy organization that works to improve the bicycling environment and quality of

life in Los Angeles County. They also organize the annual Los Angeles River Ride in May.

For bicycling equipment and other information, check with the following **cycling retailers** and local **bike tour operator**:
- **Bikecology**: 9006 West Pico Blvd., Beverly Hills, 310-278-0915; 1515 Wilshire Blvd., Santa Monica, 310-902-1940
- **Helen's Cycles:** 1570 Rosecrans Avenue, Manhattan Beach, 310-643-9140; 2472 Lincoln Blvd., Marina del Rey, 310-306-7843; 2501 Broadway, Santa Monica, 310-829-1836; 1071 Gayley Avenue, Westwood, 310-208-8988; 142 East Huntington Drive, Arcadia, 626-447-3181; www.helenscycles.com
- **LA Bike Tours**, 6733 Hollywood Blvd., Hollywood, 323-466-5890, www.labiketours.com

BILLIARDS/POOL

Pool possibilities in Los Angeles run the gamut from lone tables in the middle of seedy bars to old-fashioned billiard halls to the trendy pool halls where pagers are handed out to those waiting for a pool table. Here are a few for you to sample:
- **Gotham Hall**, 1431 Third Street Promenade, Santa Monica, 310-394-8865
- **Hollywood Athletic Club**, 6525 Sunset Blvd., 323-962-6600; Universal City Walk, 818-505-9238
- **House of Billiards**, 1901 Wilshire Blvd., Santa Monica, 310-828-2120
- **Q's Billiard Club & Restaurant**, 11835 Wilshire Blvd., Brentwood, 310-477-7550; 99 East Colorado Blvd., Pasadena, 626-405-9777
- **Stick & Stein Eatery and Sports Parlor**, 707 Sepulveda Blvd., El Segundo, 310-414-9283
- **Yankee Doodles**, 1410 Third Street Promenade, Santa Monica, 310-394-4632; 21870 Victory Blvd., Woodland Hills, 818-883-3030

BOATING/SAILING/WINDSURFING

Marina del Rey is the spot for most boating and water sport activity in the Santa Monica Bay. Check Marina del Rey's Convention and Visitors Bureau web site, www.visitthemarina.com, for a complete list of boating/sailing clubs. For boating enthusiasts, contact the **Southern California Boat Club**, also in Marina del Rey at 310-822-0073. **Redondo Beach's** King Harbor, and **Long Beach's** downtown marina,

562-570-1815, are also busy with private sailboats, speedboats, jet-craft, and plain old yachts. In addition, many companies offer sailing lessons and rentals out of the marinas. Novices seeking basic sailing lessons should inquire with the City of Los Angeles, Recreation and Parks Department's **Aquatics Division**, 323-906-7953, www.laparks.org/dos/aquatic/ aquatic.htm. Some of the local colleges also offer sailing classes.

Not all water sports companies are located near a marina, so check your Yellow Pages under "Boat Renting & Leasing" for a complete list. Here are just a few:

- **Bluewater Sailing**, 13505 Bali Way, Marina del Rey, 310-823-5545
- **Pacific Sailing**, 14110 Marquesas Way, Marina del Rey, 310-823-4064
- **Rent-A-Sail**, 13719 Fiji Way, Marina del Rey, 310-822-1868
- **Offshore Water Sports**, 128 East Shoreline Village Drive, Long Beach, 562-436-1996

BOWLING

AMF operates a chain of bowling facilities in Southern California. Call 800-BOWL-AMF or go to www.amf.com to locate the one nearest you. Contact the **Los Angeles Bowling Association**, 818-784-3352, for more information about leagues. Area bowling lanes include:

- **Allstar Lanes**, 4459 Eagle Rock Blvd., 323-254-2579
- **Bahama Lanes**, 3545 East Foothill Blvd., Pasadena, 626-351-8858
- **Bay Shore Bowl**, 234 Pico Blvd., Santa Monica, 310-399-7731
- **Brunswick Bowlerland Lanes**, 7501 Van Nuys Blvd., Van Nuys, 818-989-1610
- **Canoga Park Bowl**, 20122 Vanowen Street, Woodland Hills, 818-340-5190
- **Jillian's Universal City Walk**, 1000 Universal Way, Universal City, 818-985-8234
- **Lucky Strike Lanes**, 6801 Hollywood Blvd., Hollywood, 323-467-7776
- **Mar Vista Bowl**, 12125 Venice Blvd., West LA, 310-391-5288
- **Pickwick Bowling Center**, 1001 Riverside Drive, Burbank, 818-846-0035
- **Pinz**, 12655 Ventura Blvd., Studio City, 818-769-7600
- **Woodlake Bowl**, 23130 Ventura Blvd., Woodland Hills, 818-225-7181

CHESS

The **Southern California Chess Federation (SCCF)** is the affiliate organization recognized by the US Chess Federation, www.uschess.org.

Inquire about membership, local tournaments, and club activities at 626-282-7412. The **Los Angeles Chess Club** is another chess resource: www.lachessclub.com.

It is not uncommon to find informal groups that meet for casual play. Chess tables are available daily from sunup to sundown at the **Santa Monica International Chess Park**, which is on the promenade just south of the Santa Monica Pier. Players gather for casual chess, blitz, and occasional summer tournaments.

Some "pick-up games" require a little sleuthing to locate. Many Starbucks serve as informal hosts to players on weekends. The unspoken rule is that players buy a cup or two of coffee while playing to compensate the establishment for the use of its tables. Here's a listing of just some local establishments that are known to welcome chess players. Call for specific dates and times and bring your own equipment.

- **Glendale**: Java City Café, 134 North Brand Avenue, 818-956-3925
- **Long Beach:** the chess room in Bixby Park, 130 Cherry Avenue, 562-570-1601; when this room closes, players gather for casual play at Golden Burger, 2301 East 4th Street, 562-434-2625.
- **Los Angeles**: The Exposition Park Public Library, 3665 South Vermont Avenue, 323-732-0169, is the Exposition Park Chess Club's turf. Go to www.chess.expoparkla.com to find out more. The Baldwin Hills Public Library at 2906 South La Brea Avenue (323-733-1196) hosts another group. Some players gather on Saturdays at Lulu's Alibi, 1640 Sawtelle Boulevard (310-479-6007). Tang's Donuts, 4341 West Sunset Boulevard (323-662-4085), hosts casual and speed chess players, mostly on weekends.
- **North Hollywood**: North Hollywood Public Library, 5211 Tujunga Avenue, 818-766-7185; mainly for students in grades K-12, but all ages are welcome. Sundays.
- **Santa Clarita**: the California Youth Chess League, 25864 Tournament Road, Suite G, 661-288-1705; open for casual play.
- **Santa Monica**: Joslyn Park, 633 Kensington Road, 310-827-2789; where the Santa Monica Bay Chess Club meets.
- **West Hills**: the West Valley Jewish Community Center at 22622 Vanowen Street (818-464-3300) hosts the West Valley Chess Club on Thursdays. It is one of the largest local clubs. All are welcome.

FISHING

If you are over 16 years of age, you must purchase a fishing license ($32.80 for freshwater, and an additional $2.65 for saltwater) good through December 31. Fishing licenses may be purchased from any bait and tackle shop; see your Yellow Pages under "Fishing Tackle Dealers" for locations. Sport fishing enthusiasts should inquire at such shops for information on fishing charters. The **California State Fish and Game Department**, located in Ontario, 909-484-0167, www.dfg.ca.gov, can provide more information on local fishing laws. They've also implemented a Fishing in the City program to teach urban dwellers the joy of fishing; call 562-342-7100 for more information and for details about annual fishing events.

Popular saltwater fishing spots are off the many piers in the Westside, particularly the Santa Monica Pier. For freshwater fishing, Castiac Lake is one of the most popular spots. It is just north of Santa Clarita at 32100 North Ridge Route Road in Castiac. Call 661-257-4050, for more information.

FRISBEE

An impromptu game of Frisbee can be had in any open field, especially the larger parks like Will Rogers State Park in the Pacific Palisades or Sepulveda Basin Recreation Area in Van Nuys. Contact area parks and recreation departments for contact information of Frisbee clubs or groups. Ultimate Frisbee is popular at many area colleges; the Los Angeles Organization of Ultimate Teams, www.laout.org, also provides information about pick-up games as well as team and league play. For disc golf, many head to Pasadena to the challenging Oak Grove Park Disc Golf Course, the world's first. Call 626-797-1114 for specifics.

GOLF

There are more than 100 **public golf courses** in the greater Los Angeles area. The City of Los Angeles operates seven 18-hole courses, and five 9-hole courses. For information, call 888-LA-PARKS or visit www.laparks. org/dos/golf/golf.htm. Los Angeles County operates 16 courses; for information, call 213-738-2961, or visit http://parks.co.la.ca.us/golfcourses.html.

Other popular spots include, but are not limited to:

- **Eaton Canyon Golf Course**, 1150 North Sierra Madre Villa Avenue, Pasadena, 626-794-6773; 30-year-old, 2,900-yard, 9-hole layout featuring two par fives
- **Griffith Park Golf Course**, 4730 Crystal Springs Drive, Los Angeles, 323-663-2555; two 18-hole courses, practice bunker, and lit driving range
- **Holmby Park Golf Course**, 601 Club View Drive, Westwood, 310-276-1604; 18-hole pony golf course, three-par
- **Malibu Golf Course**, 901 Encinal Canyon Road, Malibu, 818-889-6680; 18-hole course

- **Penmar Golf Course**, 1223 Rose Avenue, Venice, 310-396-6228; 9-hole course
- **Rancho Park Golf Course**, 10460 Pico Blvd., West LA, 310-838-7373; billed as one of the busiest golf courses in the country; features an 18-hole course plus a par three nine-hole pitch-n-putt
- **Roosevelt Golf Course**, 2650 North Vermont Avenue in LA, 213-665-2011; 9-hole course
- **Scholl Canyon Golf and Tennis Club**, 3800 East Glenoaks Blvd., Glendale, 818-243-4100
- **Sepulveda Basin Recreational Area**, Burbank and Balboa boulevards, Encino, 310-989-8060; there are two 18-hole golf courses at this 60-acre wildlife refuge

HIKING

The **Santa Monica** and **San Gabriel mountains** provide miles of varied hiking trails. The following are local state parks offering **hiking trails**:
- **Coldwater Canyon Park**, 310-858-7272, http://smmc.ca.gov; located along the southern slope of the Santa Monica Mountains, this park offers five-plus miles of hiking trails.
- **Elysian Park**, 213-847-0926, www.laparks.org; located in Echo Park; over 10 miles of hiking trails, winding through forested hills and lush valleys.
- **Franklin Canyon Park**, 310-858-7272, www.lamountains.com; part of the Santa Monica Mountains National Recreation Area, this 605-acre park is at the geographic center of Los Angeles, between the San Fernando Valley and Beverly Hills. Organized hikes are frequently held along the four-plus miles of hiking trails. Easy access from the Valley and Beverly Hills makes this a popular destination.
- **Griffith Park**, 323-913-4688, www.ci.la.ca.us/RAP/grifmet/griffith.htm; located above Hollywood, vast park with 35 miles of trails.
- **Malibu Creek State Park**, 818-880-0367, www.parks.ca.gov, with more than 15 miles of hiking trails weaving through this mostly undeveloped area, it offers a true retreat to unspoiled nature. The park's visitor center is only open on weekends.
- **Santa Monica Mountains National Recreation Area**, 805-370-2301, www.nps.gov/samo and 310-589-3200, http://smmc.ca.gov; the Santa Monica Mountains stretch almost 50 miles across Los Angeles. The range is host to the **Will Rogers State Historic Park**, 310-454-8212, www.parks.ca.gov (includes the 31-room former ranch home of actor, humorist, and columnist Will Rogers and the miles of trails behind his house). Most of the trails in the Santa Monica

Mountains are part of, or hook up to, the Backbone Trail (so named for its knobby resemblance to the human spine). Running 70 miles from Point Mugu State Park to Will Rogers State Historic Park, the Backbone Trail is situated along the crest of the Santa Monica Mountains.

- **Temescal Gateway Park**, 310-454-1395, http://smmc.ca.gov, is a 20-acre park in Pacific Palisades that includes a trail that travels north over 12 miles to the Backbone Trail.
- **Topanga State Park**, 310-455-2465, www.parks.ca.gov; 10,000-acre park that offers 32 miles of hiking.

Use of city, state, and federal trails is free, although there may be a parking fee. There are about 330 miles of country-side trails in Los Angeles (see www.parks.ca.gov, http://parks.co.la.ca.us, and www.laparks.org for more information), including **Frank G. Bonnell Regional Park Trail** in San Dimas; **Schabarum Trail**, from Whittier to Rowland Heights; **Colby Dalton Trail** in Glendora; **Altadena Crest Trail**, Altadena; **La Canada Open Space Trail**, La Canada Flintridge; **Los Angeles River Trail**, from Downey to Long Beach; **Devil's Punchbowl Nature Trail** in Antelope Valley; **Los Pinetos Trail**, Sylmar; **Coastal Slope Trail**, Malibu; and **Eaton Canyon Park Trail** in Pasadena. (For an informative guide to local hiking and biking trails, check the **Los Angeles Reading List** at the end of this book.)

HIKING/WALKING CLUBS AND PROGRAMS
Local hiking resources include:

- **William O. Douglas Outdoor Classroom**, Sooky Goldman Nature Center, Beverly Hills, 310-858-3834; organizes hiking and picnics
- **Nursery Nature Walks**, Santa Monica, 310-998-1151; offers walks throughout LA geared to parents and children
- **Placerita Canyon Nature Center**, Newhall, 661-259-7721, www.placerita.org; organizes Saturday hikes
- **Santa Monica Mountains Recreational Area**, Thousand Oaks, 805-370-2301, www.nps.gov/samo; numerous outdoor programs
- **Sierra Club**, Los Angeles headquarters, 213-387-4287, www.angeles. sierraclub.org; many join their organized evening hikes through Griffith Park and other locales
- **Trail Runners Club**, Pacific Palisades, 310-281-6083, www.trailrunners club.com
- **Will Rogers State Historical Park**, Pacific Palisades, 310-454-8212, www.parks.ca.gov; nature walks for adults and families on weekends

HORSEBACK RIDING

There are no city- or county-sponsored programs for horse riding and lessons. Several private stables that offer horseback riding rentals, lessons, and/or boarding include:

- **Altadena Stables**, Altadena, 626-797-2012
- **Griffith Park Horse Rentals**, Burbank, 818-840-8401
- **Circle K Horse Rentals**, Glendale, 818-848-8844/818-242-8443; trails in Griffith Park
- **Los Angeles Equestrian Center**, Burbank, 818-840-9063
- **Malibu Riding and Tennis Club**, Malibu, 310-457-9783
- **Mill Creek Equestrian Center**, Topanga, 310-455-1116
- **Sunset Ranch Hollywood Stables**, Hollywood, 323-469-5450; offers moonlight rides through Hollywood Hills and Griffith Park

ICE SKATING

If ice skating is your sport, try one of the following rinks for public skating or lessons:

- **Culver City Ice Arena**, 4545 Sepulveda Blvd., 310-398-5718, www.culvericearena.com
- **Ice'O Plex**, 8345 Hayvenhurst Place, North Hills, 818-893-1784, www.iceoplex.com
- **Iceland Ice Skating Rink**, 14318 Calvert Street, Van Nuys, 818-785-2171
- **Moonlight Rollerway**, 5110 San Fernando Road, Glendale, 818-241-3630, www.moonlightrollerway.com
- **Paramount Iceland Skating Rink**, 8041 Jackson Street, Paramount, 562-633-1171, www.paramounticeland.com
- **Pasadena Ice Skating Center**, 310 East Green Street, 626-578-0800, www.skatepasadena.com
- **Pickwick Ice Arena**, 1001 Riverside Drive, Burbank, 818-845-5300, www.pickwickcenter.com

IN-LINE/ROLLER SKATING

The parks and beaches of Los Angeles are bustling with in-line and roller skaters. Rentals can be found at several shacks along the coastal path of Marina del Rey, Venice, and Santa Monica. (Pedestrians beware, bicyclists and skaters turn the bike path into a fast-moving freeway on weekends.) For a unique experience, join the **Friday Night Skate**, 310-57-SKATE, www.fridaynightskate.org, a loosely knit group of bladers who get together the first and third Friday of every month. The effect is a roving 10-mile, traffic-stopping, three-hour long, noisy party on wheels in Santa Monica (and Hollywood once a month).

Pleasant year-round weather keeps the offering of **indoor skating rinks** to a minimum. The ones that remain are listed here:

- **World on Wheels**, 4645 1/2 Venice Blvd., 323-933-3333; hosts a roller disco party every fourth Saturday of the month
- **Moonlight Rollerway**, 5110 San Fernando Road, Glendale, 818-241-3630
- **Northridge Skateland**, 18140 Parthenia Street, Northridge, 818-885-7655
- **Robinson Park**, 1081 North Fair Oaks Avenue, Pasadena, 626-798-0926

PADDLE TENNIS

Those aren't kiddie-sized tennis courts you see dotting the beaches along the bike path, they're paddle tennis courts. Similar to tennis, paddle tennis is played on a smaller court with deadened tennis balls and with paddles rather than rackets. You can try your talent for this unique game at one of the following spots:

- **Santa Monica**, 310-294-6011; two paddle tennis courts located just off the beach in Ocean View Park
- **Culver City Paddle Tennis Park**, 310-202-5689; three courts at the corner of Culver Blvd. and Elenda Avenue, and two courts at Culver West Park, 4162 Wade Street
- **Venice Recreational Center**, 310-399-2775; eleven paddle tennis courts located on the beach
- **Marina Del Rey's Glen-Alla Park**, 310-305-9550; three paddle tennis courts at 4601 Alla Road

ROCK CLIMBING

Climbing enthusiasts head out of the city for the big rocks of **Stoney Point** in Chatsworth's Stoney Point Park, www.laparks.org. Being such a quick drive from LA, Stoney Point is particularly crowded on summer weekends. **Vasquez Rocks Natural Area Park** in Agua Dulce (www.parks.co.la.ca.us) and the **Joshua Tree National Park** (contact the Joshua Tree Rock Climbing School at 800-890-4745, www.climbing school.com) are also popular. The **California State University Northridge** (CSUN) Leisure Studies Department, 818-677-3202, offers mountain climbing training information. For alternatives, check with your local health club to see if they offer a rock-climbing wall or try one of the following indoor climbing centers:

- **Rockreation Sport Climbing Center**, 11866 La Grange Avenue, 310-207-7199
- **Rock Gym**, 600 Long Beach Blvd., Long Beach, 562-981-3200
- **Los Angeles Rock Gym**, 4926 West Rosecrans Avenue, Hawthorne, 310-973-3388

RUNNING

The miles-long beaches of the Pacific coast provide beautiful settings for runners. Another popular Westside running spot is the median park strip on **San Vicente Boulevard**, starting in Brentwood and continuing through Santa Monica to the cliffs above the ocean. In the Hollywood area, the path around the **Hollywood Reservoir** (also known as Lake Hollywood) is popular with runners.

Some Santa Monica runners like to include in their loop a strenuous staircase that runs from the end of 4th Street, north of San Vicente Boulevard, and leads into Santa Monica Canyon. In fact, many people bike or drive over to this spot, just to tread up and down these 200 steep steps, known as the **4th Street stairs**. Aside from a beautiful ocean vista and a good workout, the stairs also provide an active social scene, particularly on weekends when it gets downright crowded. But if you want to give the steps a try, watch your manners; climbers don't appreciate perfume or cologne wearing, which interferes with their huffing and puffing, and be sure not to mess with the stones and other markers at the top and bottom of the steps, which help exercisers keep track of how many flights they have completed.

Each March, the **Los Angeles Marathon** gathers more than 20,000 competitors. The course route, changed in 2004, runs through West Los Angeles. For more information, call 310-444-5544 or go to www.la marathon.com. For novice runners who have never accomplished a marathon or active runners who want to train with a group, the **LA Leggers**, 310-577-8000, www.laleggers.org, has a $50 one-year membership training/preparation program for the marathon.

Another popular running club (for gays, lesbians, and friends of) is the **Los Angeles Frontrunners**, 323-460-2554, www.lafrontrunners.com.

SCUBA DIVING

Many private scuba schools as well as local parks departments offer scuba instruction. While the diving in the **Santa Monica Bay** doesn't provide the greatest visibility, day trips to **Catalina Island** and the **Channel Islands** near Santa Barbara offer clear waters and exhilarating outings. For those particularly interested in diving with marine mammals like seals and sea lions, the California coast is the place.

LA County's Parks and Recreation Department **Underwater Unit**, 310-965-8258, www.lascuba.com, offers scuba certification and classes in scuba air snorkeling, basic and advanced scuba diving, and underwater instructor certification. Started in 1954, it was the first in the country to create a recreational scuba diving certification course.

Here are a few of the many private dive shops/schools in the area; check your telephone directory under "Diving Instruction" for others:

- **Blue Cheer Dive & Surf**, 1112 Wilshire Blvd., Santa Monica, 310-828-1217
- **Malibu Divers**, 21231 Pacific Coast Highway, Malibu, 310-456-2396
- **Reef Seekers**, 8612 Wilshire Blvd., Beverly Hills, 310-652-4990, www.reefseekers.com

SKATEBOARDING

Los Angeles is often host to the annual X Games, a professional competition for extreme sports of which skateboarding is one of the big draws. Many looking to perfect their ollie or bluntside grind head to the **Glendale-Verdugo Skateboard Park** at 1621 Canada Boulevard, Glendale, 818-548-6420, www.glendaleskatepark.com; the **Hollenbeck Skate Park** at 415 South St Louis Street, Boyle Heights, 323-261-0113; or the **Whittier Skateboard Park** at 7630 Washington Avenue, 562-464-3430. Inquire at these skate parks about monthly competitions. For more information about skateboarding in LA, go to www.socalskateparks.com.

SOCCER

Soccer is a popular sport in Los Angeles. **Balboa Park** in North Hollywood is a busy site for organized matches between multi-ethnic club teams. Check your phone directory under "Soccer Clubs" for more information. For youth soccer, check with your local parks and recreation program or contact the **American Youth Soccer Organization**, 800-USA-AYSO, www.soccer.org, for a soccer league in your area or check with Major League Soccer's LA Galaxy, which offers many programs for LA youth (see above under **Professional Sports**).

SURFING

As you probably know, beach culture and surfing go hand in hand in Southern California. All along the southern Pacific coastline there are beaches and coves where surfing reigns supreme. For information on where to surf, contact LA County's **Department of Beaches and Harbors** at 310-305-9503, http://beaches.co.la.ca.us; in Orange County, contact the **Department of Harbors, Beaches, and Parks** at 866-OCPARKS, www.ocparks.com. To learn how to surf, one option is trial by fire; head to Malibu for an afternoon to watch the veterans, then grab a board and give it a try. (Keep in mind that the locals can be territorial, and newcomers may not always be welcome.) If you have a buddy who already surfs, you might be better off letting him or her show you the ropes.

Before you head out, check the surf line web site for **surfing conditions**, live beach cams, and more: www.surfline.com.

SWIMMING—POOLS

Aside from that big outdoor pool called the Pacific Ocean, there are several places you can go to swim in Los Angeles. Contact the **LA Aquatics** office at 323-906-7953 or visit www.laparks.org for a complete listing of county pools and links to local clubs. Many **YMCAs** offer use of their pool for a fee, as do several city-run parks and recreation facilities, including those listed below. All are open year round.

- **Fremont Pool** (indoor), 7630 Towne Avenue, 213-847-3401
- **Griffith Park Pool**, 3401 Riverside Drive, 323-644-6878
- **North Hollywood Pool**, 530 Tujunga Avenue, North Hollywood, 818-755-7651
- **The Plunge** (indoor), 219 West Mariposa Avenue, El Segundo, 310-524-2738
- **Richard Alatorre Pool** (indoor), 4721 East Klamath Street, 323-276-3042
- **Eleanor G. Roberts Pool** (indoor), 4526 West Pico Blvd., 323-936-8483
- **Roosevelt Pool** (Olympic sized, outdoor), 456 South Matthews, 213-485-7391

- **Van Nuys-Sherman Oaks Pool**, 14201 Huston Street, Van Nuys, 818-783-6721
- **Venice Pool** (indoor), 2401 Walgrove Avenue, Venice, 310-575-8260
- **Westwood Recreation Complex**, 1350 Sepulveda Blvd., Westwood, 310-478-7019
- **Woodland Hills Pool**, 5858 Shoup Avenue, Woodland Hills, 818-756-9363

Local swim clubs include the **Southern Pacific Masters Association** (look for them online at www.spma.net), and the **Southern California Aquatic Swim Club**, 310-390-5700. For more about local swim clubs, check bulletin board postings at any of the pools listed above. (See the **Greenspace and Beaches** chapter for information about area beaches.)

TENNIS/RACQUET SPORTS

Public outdoor tennis and racquetball courts are scattered throughout the city and are open year round. Some courts require a small fee to make a court reservation (these pay-to-play courts are often in better condition than other public courts). The City of LA offers a list of free tennis parks (many of which also have racquetball courts) at www.laparks.org.

For more resources, including information about local clubs or upcoming events, contact the **Southern California Tennis Association**, 310-208-3838, www.scta.usta.com or the **Mid-Valley Racquetball Athletic Club**, 818-705-6500.

The following **tennis parks** charge by the hour (the fee is higher for nonresidents):
- **Echo Park**, 213-250-3578, Echo Park; six courts
- **La Cienega Park**, 310-550-4765, Beverly Hills; 16 courts
- **Lincoln Park**, 310-394-6011, Santa Monica; six courts
- **Plummer Park**, 213-876-1725, West Hollywood; six courts
- **Riverside Tennis Facility**, 323-661-5318, Griffith Park
- **Studio City Recreation Center**, 818-763-7651, Studio City; six courts
- **Van Nuys-Sherman Oaks Park**, 818-769-4415, Sherman Oaks; 10 courts
- **Westwood Recreation Complex**, 310-473-3610, Westwood; 12 courts

VOLLEYBALL

Several beaches offer beach volleyball courts, including **Zuma**, **Malibu Lagoon**, **Will Rogers**, **Santa Monica State**, **Venice**, and the granddaddy of them all, **Manhattan Beach**, which has more than 100 courts. Additionally, many parks have volleyball courts, including **Palisades Recreation Center**, 310-454-1412, **Barrington Recreation Center**, 310-476-3807 (summers), and **Westwood Recreation Complex**, 310-473-3610.

YOGA

Namaste! Hatha, Kundalini, Bikram...you name it and there is a center in Los Angeles that teaches it. Many accomplished gurus have made their home here, including Paramahansa Yogananda who founded a self-realization fellowship and lived and wrote near downtown Los Angeles for 30 years. Explore the various styles, levels, and teaching techniques to find one that best suits you. Always ask for a free demo clinic or class before joining. Most centers that offer classes also sponsor retreats. Here's a sampling of area yoga centers:

- **Bikram's Yoga College of India**, 1862 South La Cienega Blvd., 310-854-5800, www.bikramyoga.com
- **Center for Yoga**, 323-464-1276, www.centerforyoga.com; the city's oldest studio
- **City Yoga**, 1067 North Fairfax Avenue, 323-654-2125, www.city yoga.com
- **LA Sivananda Yoga Center**, 3560 Hughes Avenue #107, 310-837-3104, www.sivananda.org/la; founded by Swami Vishnu-Devananda, specializes in Sivananda yoga
- **Yoga Works**, 310-234-1200, www.yogaworks.com; four locations, two in Santa Monica, and one in Westwood, and one in Larchmont

HEALTH CLUBS

Los Angeles is the fabled land of "the beautiful people," and you may notice that physiques are trimmer and fitter here than elsewhere in the USA. The good weather makes it pleasant to exercise outdoors...and, alas, not so easy to hide under layers of clothing.

There are **YMCAs** located throughout the city (check the telephone directory for one near you), which traditionally offer good workout options at reasonable prices. On the other end of the spectrum, the most luxurious fitness complex in town is **The Sports Club LA**, 310-473-1447, www.the sportsclub.com, which offers everything from personal trainers and top-of-the-line equipment to a gourmet grill restaurant in its 100,000 square-foot complex.

Unfortunately, the health club industry is one with few fixed, publicly available prices, so words like "sale" and "discount" have little meaning. Take everything with a grain of salt. The person on the treadmill next to you may have paid half—or double—what you paid. Also, before you fork over money for a membership, ask for a free pass. Find out if this is the right place for you; skull-pounding music and grunting weight lifters may not be as healthful as you had imagined.

Major health clubs that fall somewhere in between, some local, some national, include the following (check the Yellow Pages for additional listings, including small neighborhood gyms and fitness centers):

- **Bally's Total Fitness**, 800-FITNESS, www.ballyfitness.com; numerous locations
- **Bodies in Motion**, www.bodiesinmotion.com; LA-based chain
- **Curves**, www.curvesinternational.com; numerous locations, specializes in 30-minute workouts for women only.
- **Gold's Gym**, 310-392-3005, www.goldsgym.com; the original Gold's Gym started in Venice, California in 1965. It was *the* place for serious, no-frills workouts.
- **LA Fitness Sports Clubs**, 800-LA-FITNESS, www.lafitness.com; numerous locations
- **LA Boot Camp**, 818-398-7002, www.labootcamp.com; a military-style training regimen
- **The Sports Connection**: Santa Monica, 310-829-6836; West Hollywood, 310-652-7440; West LA, 310-450-4464
- **Spectrum Club**, 310-829-4995, http://spectrumclubs.fitnessinsite.com; numerous locations
- **Total Woman Day Spa & Gym**, 818-552-2027, www.totalwomanspa.com; four in the Valley
- **Hollywood Gym**, 323-845-1420, www.hollywoodgym.com, 1551 North La Brea Avenue, Hollywood; open 24 hours
- **Venice Beach Athletic Center**, 1800 Ocean Front Walk, Venice, 310-399-2775, www.venicebeach.com/musclebeach/athleticcenter
- **World Gym**, 310-827-7705, www.worldgym.com; numerous locations, all World Gym fitness centers are a minimum of 9,500 square feet.

L OS ANGELES IS NOTORIOUS FOR ITS URBAN SPRAWL. WHAT IS LESS evident, until you live here, is that this area is rich with open spaces including parks, both urban and rural, and of course, beaches, lots and lots of beaches. The **County of Los Angeles Department of Parks and Recreation**, 213-738-2961 or http://parks.co.la.ca.us, is responsible for the county's 63,000 acres of parks, gardens, lakes, trails, natural areas, and the world's largest public golf course system. The **City of LA Department of Recreation and Parks**, 888-LA-PARKS, www.laparks.org, maintains the city parks and gardens. In Orange County, it's the **Harbors, Beaches, and Parks Division**, 866-OCPARKS, www.ocparks.com, that maintains its beaches and open spaces. (Information about California State parks and beaches can be found at www.cal-parks.ca.gov.)

CITY PARKS AND GARDENS

PARKS

Like mini-oases, urban parks dot the City of Los Angeles, offering amenities such as tennis courts, baseball diamonds, basketball courts, and plenty of grass on which to stretch out and relax. For a listing of the parks in your neighborhood, check the blue-bordered pages in the front of the Yellow Pages or call the recreation and parks department for your area (see **Sports and Recreation**). Two of the largest urban parks in Los Angeles are **Griffith Park** and **Cheviot Hills**.

Located in the Hollywood Hills, **Griffith Park**, 323-913-4688, www.laparks.org, is the largest municipal park in the United States, occupying 4,100 acres and featuring the Los Angeles Zoo, the Griffith Park Observatory and Planetarium (closed for renovation until 2006, but a temporary satellite facility has been set up just south of the Los Angeles Zoo), Travel Town Train Park, and the Autry Museum of Western Heritage. There are also pony rides, tennis courts, a soccer field, merry-go-round, picnic areas, and 50 miles of hiking and horseback riding trails.

Cheviot Hills Park, 310-837-5186, www.laparks.org, located in West LA near Cheviot Hills, offers 14 lit tennis courts, a pro shop, archery, swimming, basketball courts, soccer fields, baseball diamonds, a par course, a driving range, and what is reputed to be one of the busiest public golf courses in the country, Rancho Park (see **Sports and Recreation** for contact information).

If you're looking to be near some water but don't want to head for the beach, East Los Angeles's **Silverlake**, 323-644-3946, www.laparks.org, or **Echo Park**, 213-250-3578, www.laparks.org, in downtown LA, might do the trick. While Silverlake is actually a reservoir, so no water access is allowed, it offers basketball courts, a playing field, and a gymnasium for children, and is a pretty respite from the hustle and bustle of city life. At Echo Park you can rent canoes or paddle boats, use the tennis courts, baseball diamonds, and swim in its two pools, one indoor Olympic-sized, the other outdoor and shallow. Fishing is possible at Echo Park's stocked lake. Also downtown, the **Walt Disney Concert Hall** sports a small urban park around the third floor of its outer hull, wonderful for an impromptu break if you're in the area.

Nestled beneath the famed Hollywood sign is **Lake Hollywood**, 323-463-0830, www.hollywoodknolls.org, which is not really a lake at all but an emergency water reservoir managed by the LA Department of Water and Power. Nonetheless, it features open space, a jogging and pedestrian path around the lake, and a children's play area.

The largest recreational park in the Valley, just off the 405 Freeway, is the **Sepulveda Dam Recreational Area**, 818-756-8188, www.laparks.org. Spanning over 2,000 acres, it includes a lake where you can paddleboat or fish. There are three golf courses, an archery range, 10 soccer fields, and three cricket fields, and tennis, handball, and basketball courts abound. In addition, there are paved jogging and biking trails, and the Japanese Garden is open for tours (by reservation only, call 818-756-8166 or go to www.lajapanesegarden.org).

The **Van Nuys-Sherman Oaks Park**, 818-783-5121, www.laparks.org, is a grassy, tree-shrouded neighborhood recreation area, featuring six baseball fields, eight tennis courts, and walking trails. Additional intimate neighborhood parks perfect for a quiet picnic include the **Johnny Carson Park**, 818-238-5300, www.ci.burbank.ca.us, in Burbank, and **Verdugo Park**, 818-548-2000, www.ci.glendale.ca.us, in Glendale.

GARDENS

In the hills of Bel Air lies a peaceful excursion possibility at the two-acre **UCLA Hannah Carter Japanese Garden**, 310-825-4574, www.japanese garden.ucla.edu. Reservations are required (open only three days a week) and your 50-minute visit is self-guided. Ancient pagodas and bridges, koi fish, devil-casting stones, a teahouse, and a mix of indigenous Japanese trees and plants complement delightful views.

On the other side of the 405 Freeway in West LA is the **Getty Center** with a wooded walkway that leads to a spiral-shaped "floating" garden, designed to reflect the personality of each season. Guided tours of the garden are available, if you can get reservations: 310-440-7300, www.getty.edu.

The lush 207-acre **Huntington Library**, **Art Collections and Botanical Gardens**, 626-405-2141, www.huntington.org, in San Marino is a spectacular treat for garden lovers. Meander through the sculpture garden, view a towering cactus garden, and be transported to another land in the 9-acre Japanese garden. A glorious 12-acre Chinese garden, set to open in 2007, will be one of the largest classical Chinese gardens outside of China. The Huntington is also home to a giant Corpse Flower, one of the world's most unpleasant smelling and biggest flowers (if in bloom—which occurs about once every one to three years). Along with an afternoon tea room and mansion turned museum, which houses English and French art of the 18th and 19th centuries (the most famous of which is Gainsborough's *Blue Boy*), it is easy to spend a whole day at the Huntington.

Lest we forget, in this land of roses, out-of-town visitors and locals alike delight in the **Virginia Robinson Gardens**, 310-276-5367, http://parks. co.la.ca.us, in Beverly Hills as well as the **Exposition Park Rose Garden**, 213-763-0114, www.laparks.org, across the street from the University of Southern California—a true urban oasis that consists of a romantic seven and a half acres of roses.

STATE/COUNTY PARKS

Outside of LA proper, garden aficionados will want to visit the **Los Angeles County Arboretum & Botanic Garden** in Arcadia, 626-821-3222, www.arboretum.org, a 127-acre garden that features free-roaming peacocks, an extensive horticultural library, an orchid greenhouse, and several national and state historical landmarks from the 1880s: the Queen Anne Cottage, the Coach Barn, and the Santa Anita Railroad Depot.

Nestled in the Santa Monica Mountains near Pacific Palisades is **Will Rogers State Historic Park**, 310-454-8212, www.parks.ca.gov. The former ranch of actor, humorist, and columnist Will Rogers, the park features tours through the 31-room ranch home, a large grassy hill for picnics, and miles of trails behind the house. On weekend mornings you can sit alongside the polo field and enjoy the matches.

Other beautiful canyon parks are **Malibu Creek State Park**, 818-880-0367, www.parks.ca.gov, with more than 15 miles of hiking trails; **Temescal Gateway Park**, a 20-acre site that includes a trail that travels more than 12 miles north to the Backbone Trail; **Topanga State Park**, 310-455-2465, www.parks.ca.gov, with 10,000-acres and 32 miles of hiking trails; **Brookside Park**, 626-744-7195, www.ci.pasadena.ca.us, in Pasadena (home to the Rose Bowl, as well as a great gorge called the Arroyo Seco, and a golf course); and Newhall's 350-acre **Placerita Canyon Park and Nature Center**, 661-259-7721, www.placerita.org, with 10 miles of hiking trails, a nature center with live animal exhibits, and picnic and campsites. Visit any of these parks in the spring or early summer for a delightful traipse along trails in flower-strewn fields and valleys.

The **Kenneth Hahn Recreation Area**, 323-298-3660, www.parks. co.la.ca.us, in Los Angeles, is a 370-acre respite with hiking trails and a manmade lake, best known as the site of the 10th Olympiad (in 1932). The **Whittier Narrows Recreation Area**, 626-575-5526, www.parks.co. la.ca.us, offers lakes, trails, an equestrian center, and athletic complex sprawled over 1,000 acres. And in Rowland Heights is **Schabarum Regional Park**, 626-854-5560, www.parks.co.la.ca.us, with over 600 acres of open space and an equestrian center.

Campsites take a little digging to locate within Los Angeles County, but camp grounds can be found at **Malibu Creek State Park**, 818-880-0367, **Leo Carrillo State Park** (just north of Malibu), 818-880-0350, and **Saddleback Butte State Park** (near Lancaster), 661-942-0662 (campsites are first-come, first-served), and in the national parks described below. For more information on any of the above listed state parks, go to www.parks.ca.gov.

NATIONAL PARKS

The canyon parks offer a much different experience to what can be found in the immediate vicinity of LA. With only a short drive you'll leave the city behind, and a few minutes along a hiking trail can find you in a spot where cars can't be heard, houses can't be seen, and you're about as likely to meet a lizard or jackrabbit as a human being. The largest area of canyon parkland is the **Santa Monica Mountains National Recreation Area**. The Santa Monica Mountains stretch almost 50 miles across Los Angeles, and most of the trails here are part of, or hook up to, the Backbone Trail (see **Sports and Recreation**). For more information about parks throughout these mountains, call 310-589-3200 or go online to http://smmc.ca.gov.

Located on the northeastern edge of the San Fernando Valley is **Angeles National Forest**, one of seventeen national forests in California. Though accessible at many different points, the nearest point of entry for most Los Angeles residents is adjacent to Pasadena, in the San Gabriel Mountains. Here you'll find campgrounds, picnic sites, lakes, streams, and miles of hiking trails. For more information, call 626-574-1613 or go to www.fs.fed.us/r5/angeles.

Channel Islands National Park, 805-658-5730, www.nps.gov/chis/homepage.htm, is 70 miles north of Los Angeles, off the coast of neighboring Ventura County. It comprises five of the eight California Channel Islands and is accessible only by boat. One hundred forty-five species of plants and animals are unique to the islands and found nowhere else in the world. Camping, hiking, snorkeling, bird watching, and marine-mammal observation are some the activities possible here. Think of it as California's Galapagos Islands.

BEACHES

LOS ANGELES COUNTY BEACHES

Los Angeles is famous for its golden beaches, and they too provide an alluring place to get away from it all. There's nothing quite like standing at the edge of the continent, comforted by the knowledge that, although there may be millions of people and a bustling civilization behind you, there are no such distractions in front of you as far as the eye can see. Go to the **Los Angeles County Department of Beaches and Harbor** web site: http://beaches.co.la.ca.us or call them at 310-305-9546 for detailed information about local beaches, including surf reports, upcoming events, and permit applications. The **California Department of Parks and Recreation's** web site, www.parks.ca.gov, also has information about state beaches.

First, some safety advice: If you plan on swimming, swim in front of the nearest manned lifeguard tower. Take care to protect your eyes and skin; cover up with UV-safe glasses, hats, or clothing if necessary, and use sunscreen. Finally, being alone or even in a small group on the beach after dark is not safe; stick to beachcombing as a daytime activity.

At Malibu's northwestern-most end is **Leo Carrillo State Beach**, 818-880-0350, www.parks.ca.gov, named for the LA-born actor, preservationist, and conservationist. The 1,600-acre beach features nature trails, some of which lead to tide pools, and three campgrounds. The water is good for surfing and swimming, and you can explore Sequit Point, which has sea caves and a natural tunnel. Also in Malibu is the **Malibu Lagoon State Beach**, 818-880-0350, www.parks.ca.gov, located just west of the Malibu Pier. It consists of 22 acres of saltwater marsh, flower gardens, and sandy beach. Guided tours of the wetlands for grunion, the monarch butterfly, and the gray whale are scheduled seasonally; call 818-880-0363 for tour information. At the end of the Malibu Pier is **Surfrider Beach**, 310-305-9546, http://beaches.co.la.ca.us, famous for its good surfing conditions; it also has volleyball courts.

Further southeast is **Zuma Beach**, 310-305-9546, http://beaches.co.la.ca.us, which is known for its scenic views and rough surf. It also features volleyball, swimming, fishing, diving, and a children's playground. At nearby **Point Dume**, 310-305-9546, http://beaches.co.la.ca.us, you can explore tide pools and perhaps catch a glimpse of the migrating California gray whales, which travel through the area from November through May.

At the foot of Topanga Canyon are the small **Las Tunas Beach**, 310-305-9546, http://beaches.co.la.ca.us, and **Topanga State Beach**, 310-305-9546, http://beaches.co.la.ca.us. Although Topanga State Beach covers almost 22 acres, its most frequented site is a mile-long sandy stretch near Topanga Creek. Further south is **Will Rogers State Beach**, 310-305-9503, www.parks.ca.gov, a popular spot for board and body surfing and swimming. It too has volleyball courts and a playground.

Santa Monica State Beach, 310-458-8310, www.santa-monica.org, is one of the largest and most popular beaches in California, due to its proximity to the City of LA and its amusement amenities, which include the Santa Monica Pier, playgrounds, and basketball and volleyball courts. Though you will see many people swimming here, reports on the water quality at local beaches often rate this one poorly. For the most up-to-date water conditions, call the **Department of Beaches and Harbors**, 310-305-9503, http://beaches.co.la.ca.us or **Heal the Bay** (a volunteer advocacy group), 800-HEAL-BAY, www.healthebay.com. Clean-up efforts are under way, and actually the bay is safer now than in years past, though there are often swimming advisories near the major storm drains.

Just south of Santa Monica is **Venice Beach**, which features 238 acres of sand, but it's the adjacent boardwalk that has made it famous and brings more visitors. (See **Venice** in the **Neighborhoods** chapter.) Bicycles can be rented at several vendors along the beachfront, and there's a nice children's playground. For people watching, it can't be beat.

Marina del Rey's **Dockweiler Beach**, 310-305-9546, http://beaches.co.la.ca.us, is quieter, popular with families and young singles. Features here include three miles of shoreline, swimming, surfing, a picnic area, and a campground.

Busy **Manhattan Beach** boasts more than 100 volleyball courts. One of the main attractions here is The Strand, a concrete promenade for jogging, skating, and walking...and a whole lot of watching.

Long Beach, in Long Beach, is a long, long, long strip of waterfront. Here are just some of the local beaches that make up its 11 miles of ocean-front property: **Alamitos Beach, Bayshore Beach, Belmont Plaza Beach** (and **Belmont Pier**), **Belmont Shore Beach, Peninsula Beach, Colorado Lagoon, Junipero Beach**, and **Marine Park**. **Long Beach's Department of Parks, Recreation and Marine**, 562-570-1471, www.ci.long-beach.ca.us/park/facilities/beaches.html, oversees these beaches, as well as the largest municipally operated marina system in the nation.

A note: California was the first state in the nation to ban smoking in its restaurants and bars, and beginning in 2004, this health-minded prohibition extended to parts of the state's coastline. Beaches in the cities of Santa Monica and Malibu, and, in Los Angeles, the beaches of Venice, Cabrillo, Will Rogers, and Dockweiler, now have smoking bans in place.

ORANGE COUNTY BEACHES

The OC offers over 42 miles of coastline. Glamorized by the popular TV series of the same name, the glistening beaches of Orange County are a surfer's paradise and the stuff of dreams. The **Orange County Harbors, Beaches and Parks Division**, which oversees 37,000 acres of parkland and open space, including regional and wilderness parks, nature preserves and recreational trails, historic sites, as well as harbors and beaches, is the place to contact for information about its water-side facilities: 714-973-6865, www.ocparks.com.

On the north end of Orange County, **Seal Beach**, 562-431-1383, www.ci.seal-beach.ca.us, is at the opening of Alamitos Bay, providing access for boats and yachts entering the Pacific Ocean from Huntington Harbor. Fishing and strolling are just some of the activities to be enjoyed along the Seal Beach Pier. A little further south is **Sunset State Beach**, 831-763-7062, which offers bike paths and volleyball. **Crystal Cove State Park**, 714-661-7013, is just one of more than a handful of beaches to be found in the City of Laguna Beach. The park is made up of three and a half miles of shoreline and 2,000 acres of undeveloped woodland for hiking and horseback riding. **Dana Point Harbor**, 949-923-2280, is home to pleasure craft, restaurants and shops, tide pools, and the Orange County Marine Institute. Just a little further south is the county's most popular ocean-side campground, **Doheny State Beach**, 949-496-6172, www.dohenystate-beach.org, with picnic tables, volleyball courts, and a palm leaf–lined "Palapa" gazebo that's popular for weddings on the beach. **Sunset Beach**, 949-923-2220, spans 45 acres of sand, dotted by facilities that range from children's playgrounds to volleyball courts to lifeguard towers. **Newport's Municipal Beach**, 714-644-3044, is set among a backdrop of world-class shops, golfing greens, and yachts (in the very photogenic Newport Harbor). **Huntington State Beach**, 714-536-1454, a.k.a. "Surf City," is popular with bikers, skaters and, of course, surfers. Nearby is the 114-acre Huntington Beach Wetlands, which serves as a nesting sanctuary for threatened and endangered species. And sitting near the southern point of Orange County is **San Clemente State Beach**, 949-492-3156. The north end of this one-mile beach is popular with surfers. Trails lead from the bluffs down to the beach, where skin diving is popular, and hiking opportunities along the bluff trails abound.

THE LOS ANGELES AREA IS HOME TO A VARIETY OF FAITHS. IT IS HOST to substantial Roman Catholic and Protestant communities, the second largest Jewish population in the USA (behind the New York City metropolitan area) and is well represented by Muslims as well as Hindus and Buddhists among others.

Finding a suitable church, synagogue, mosque, or temple may be as simple as getting a suggestion from an acquaintance, or it may be as intensely personal and complex as choosing a spouse. The houses of worship described below are included for a variety of reasons, whether they are of historic or architectural note, renowned for their strong outreach programs, or host of popular music series. Certainly it is not a comprehensive list. A quick look at the Yellow Pages, listed by denomination, should provide you with all of the religious centers in your neighborhood; as well, **Faiths LA**, www.faithsla.org, describes the various meeting places/faiths within Los Angeles County. Nationally, you can contact the **National Council of Churches**, 212-870-2227, www.ncccusa.org, which publishes the *Yearbook of American & Canadian Churches*, a directory listing thousands of Christian churches. (Order one for $35 at 888-870-3325 or browse the directory links at www.electronicchurch.org.) Other national online directories of churches—generally limited to Christian denominations—include www.churchangel.com, http://netministries.org, http://churches.net, www.forministry.com, and www.adherents.com. Synagogues serving all branches of Judaism are listed at www.jewish.com.

BAHÁ'Í

Although Bahá'í houses of worship may differ from one another in architectural styles, they are often stunning, and are recognizable by their nine sides and central dome, which symbolize "the diversity of the human race and its essential oneness." For more information, go to www.bahai.org. The local Bahá'í community worships at the **Bahá'í Faith Los Angeles Center**, 5755 Rodeo Road, 323-933-8291 or go to www.labc.org.

BUDDHIST

Buddhism dates back over two millennia, and today over 350 million people across the globe consider themselves Buddhists. There are many different sub-traditions, including **Zen**, **Tibetan**, **Tantric (Vajrayana)**, and **Mahayana**.

Area temples include:

- **Wat Thai Temple** of Los Angeles, 8225 Coldwater Canyon Ave, North Hollywood, 818-785-9552, www.watthaiusa.org; the largest Thai Theravada Buddhist Temple in the United States. Many festivals are celebrated by the monks residing here, including "Taleung Sok Day" (Thai New Year's Day) in April. The temple complex is a major social hub for local Thais. Almost every weekend, Wat Thai's lower level turns into a busy, noisy Bangkok-style street scene where vendors sell Thai household wares, fabrics, and foods, including fiery spices and traditionally prepared foods.
- The **Zen Center** of Los Angeles, 923 South Normandie Avenue, 213-387-2351, www.zencenter.org

CHRISTIAN

Christian houses of worship, prayer retreat centers, and monasteries can be found throughout Southern California. While Roman Catholicism predominates, Christian churches of all persuasions are well represented.

One nondenominational church, while not exactly a house of worship in the traditional sense, has an interesting history and is where many love-struck couples have found themselves. The small (seats 150) **Little Brown Church**, 4418 Coldwater Canyon Avenue, Studio City, 818-761-1127, www.covonline.org, was built in the late 1930s. Open 24/7, this intimate and homey wood chapel with its white trim, pine interior, and hand-hewn pine pews, has hosted over 22,500 weddings. One of California's most famous couples to marry within the chapel was former President Ronald Reagan and his wife Nancy in 1952.

What follows are just some of the Christian faith groups in Los Angeles.

ORTHODOX (COPTIC, EASTERN, GREEK, ALBANIAN, MORAVIAN, RUSSIAN, ETC.)

In Los Angeles, the **St. Sophia Greek Orthodox Cathedral**, 1324 South Normandie Avenue, LA, 323-737-2424, www.stsophia.org, is a visual delight. Its stunning interior—gilded arches, lofty frescoes, ornate chandeliers, complete with a choir loft—seats 850. St. Sophia's Sunday school and youth programs are popular, as well as its camp and retreat center located in Crestline.

Contact information for Orthodox churches in the USA includes:

- **Greek Orthodox Church of America**, www.goarch.org/en/ archdiocese
- **Moravian**: Moravian Church in America, 800-732-0591, www.moravian. org
- **Orthodox Christian Foundation**, www.ocf.org
- **Orthodox Church in America**, www.oca.org

ROMAN CATHOLIC

Given the history of Southern California's early Spanish settlers and the continued Latino influence, it is no wonder that Roman Catholicism dominates the LA landscape. Roman Catholics should contact the **Roman Catholic Archdiocese of Los Angeles**, 213-637-7000, www.la-archdiocese.org, 3424 Wilshire Boulevard, Los Angeles, for a list of churches for each town as well as information about the Vatican, Catholic charities, marriage preparation, Catholic Social Services, and job opportunities. Another resource is the Catholic Information Center at www.catholic.net.

Roman Catholic churches of note include:

- The **Cathedral of Our Lady of Angels** at 555 West Temple Street (213-680-5200, www.olacathedral.org) in downtown Los Angeles; opened in 2002, the Cathedral of Our Lady of Angels is visually striking from the nearby 101 freeway. Designed by Spanish architect Rafael Moneo, its amber-colored contemporary lines feature virtually no right angles. Construction of this $189 million cathedral began in 1994, after the Northridge earthquake severely damaged the 120-year-old St. Vibiana's Cathedral and displaced the Archdiocese of Los Angeles. Tourists and locals alike can call to reserve a tour of the cathedral or casually drop by to enjoy the open plaza and even grab lunch from the café.
- The **Queens of the Angeles Old Plaza Church,** 535 North Main Street (in El Pueblo de Los Angeles Historic Park), 213-629-3101, www.la-archdiocese.org; originally called La Iglesia de Nuestra Senora de Los Angeles, it is the oldest church in the city. Considered the found-

ing site of the City of LA, it was here in 1781 that about 40 settlers established a farming community. Now consisting of 44 acres of city land (bounded by Alameda, Arcadia, Spring, and Macy streets), it is on these grounds where this lovely Spanish-style church sits, founded and built by the Franciscans in the early 1800s. Still an active church of the Roman Catholic Archdiocese of Los Angeles, it is within walking distance of the famed Mexican Marketplace on Olvera Street. If you pay a visit, be sure to stroll the northwest corner of Olvera Street; this is the oldest thoroughfare in Los Angeles.

- The **San Gabriel Mission**, 428 South Mission Drive, San Gabriel, 626-457-3048, www.sangabrielmission.org, is the oldest structure of its kind south of Monterey, California, founded on September 8, 1771, by Father Junipero Serra. The fourth mission in the 21-mission chain in California, it grew so prosperous that it earned another name, "Pride of the Missions." The early fathers planted orange trees and grapevines, crops of corn and beans, and raised cattle and sheep. The mission became known for its production of fine wines, soaps, and candles, which were used by the other missions and given to passing travelers. Catholic services are still performed at the mission's church, and outreach continues to be toward those in need, particularly recent immigrants. A museum as well as a gift shop is on site.

PROTESTANT CHURCHES

AMERICAN METHODIST EPISCOPAL (AME)

The **First AME Church** (FAME-Los Angeles), 2270 South Harvard Boulevard, South Los Angeles, 323-730-9180, www.famechurch.org, is the oldest African-American congregation in the City of Los Angeles. Former LA Mayor Tom Bradley and the Reverend Jesse Jackson are frequent guest speakers. FAME-Los Angeles was founded in 1872 by former slave Biddy Mason and housed the city's first black school. Several of the earliest African-American movie stars, including Hattie McDaniel and Ethel Waters, resided just north of the church. FAME-Los Angeles is an active church with a host of community outreach programs, including FAME Renaissance, a social and business development program that benefits impoverished communities in LA County. During his presidency, George H.W. Bush declared First AME Church the 177th Point of Light for its outreach in community services. Reverend Cecil L. "Chip" Murray, who was largely responsible for spearheading the church's community outreach, retired in 2004, after 27 years of service.

If you'd like to find an AME or Episcopal Zion church in your neighborhood, you can go to the directory link at the official AME site, www.amechurch.com.

ANGLICAN/EPISCOPAL

The Episcopal/Anglican Diocese of Los Angeles can be reached at 213-482-2040 (toll free 800-642-4427); online at www.ladiocese.org. For general information about the Episcopal Church of the USA, visit www.episcopalchurch.org; and for the Anglican Church, go to http://anglicansonline.org.

ASSEMBLY OF GOD

Assemblies of God are the largest Pentecostal denomination of the Protestant church in the USA. Their homepage, http://ag.org/top, is informative and provides a complete directory of its churches nationwide. **Assembly of God**, **Southern California District**, can be contacted at 949-252-8400, www.socalag.org, or www.ag.org.

BAPTIST

To find out more about the **American Baptist** community, contact the American Baptist Churches Mission Center, www.abc-usa.org, 800-ABC-3USA. To find out more about **Southern Baptists** in Los Angeles, go to www.sbc.net.

CHRISTIAN SCIENCE

Christian Science Churches and Organizations, 310-820-2014, www.cssocalifornia.com, is who to contact to find out more about this group.

CHURCH OF THE NAZARENE

Church of the Nazarene is the largest denomination in the Wesleyan–holiness tradition. For information about the Church of the Nazarene and a church locator service, go to the church's national web site, www.nazarene.org.

CONGREGATIONAL/UNITED CHURCH OF CHRIST

The Congregational Church is also known, since the 1950s, as the United Church of Christ (UCC). For more information on the local Congregational community, try the **Los Angeles Congregational Church of Christian Fellowship UCC**, 323-731-869, www.ucchristianfellow ship.org; nationally at 800-537-3394, www.ucc.org.

FRIENDS (QUAKER)

Members of the **Society of Friends** (a.k.a. Quakers) can trace their church's roots back to some of the first Europeans to settle in the Americas. Contact the **Southern California Religious Society of Friends** at 323-296-0733 (toll free 800-962-4766) or go online: http://scqm.org/index.htm or www.quaker.org.

JEHOVAH'S WITNESS

For information about Jehovah's Witness or to find a kingdom hall, you can call their local office at 323-660-1386 or visit www.watchtower.org or www.jw-media.org.

CHURCH OF JESUS CHRIST OF LATTER-DAY SAINTS (MORMON)

For more information on the Church of Jesus Christ of Latter-day Saints, contact the **Los Angeles California Stake**: 1057 West 30th Street, Los Angeles, 323-731-1350, www.lds.org.

LUTHERAN

Lutherans of the **Evangelical Lutheran Church in America** (**ELCA**), 800-638-3522, www.elca.org, and the **Missouri Synod** are both represented in LA. Contact one of the following for assistance with finding a church near you.
- **ELCA**: Southwest California Synod, 818-507-9591, www.socal synod.org

- **Missouri Synod**: Pacific Southwest District, 949-854-3232, www. psw.lcms.org, or 888-843-5267, www.lcms.org

MENNONITE

Until the 19th century, most Mennonites were concentrated in rural farming communities, speaking German, and leaving alone much of the secular world. Since the 1800s, there have been divisions in the church, yielding the Old Mennonite Church, General Conference Mennonite Church, Mennonite Brethren, and Old Order Amish. The regional office of the **Pacific Southwest Mennonite Conference** can be reached at 626-720-8100, www.pacificsouthwest.org.

METHODIST (UNITED)

The **United Methodist Church Los Angeles District** can be reached at 323-733-4100, www.cal-pac.org/districts/losangeles.htm or www.umc.org. Search their web sites for a church near you.

METROPOLITAN COMMUNITY CHURCH

The **MCC of Los Angeles**, 310-854-9110, www.mccla.org, welcomes all but specifically reaches out to the gay, lesbian, bisexual, and transgender Christian community. The founding church of the MCC movement, the MCC of Los Angeles has been blessing the unions of same-sex couples for more than 35 years.

PENTECOSTAL/CHARISMATIC

Some local Charismatic churches are organized through the offices of the **Southern California Renewal Communities**: 818-771-1361, www.scrc.org. Pentecostal contacts include the **Pentecostal Church of God in Christ**: First Jurisdiction of Southern California, 323-733-8300, www.cogic.org; and **Pentecostal, International**: World Agape Mission Church, 213-384-1882, www.iphc.org. For more information about the Pentecostal/Charismatic Churches of North America and to find a local church, visit www.pccna.org.

PRESBYTERIAN (USA)

A Protestant Church with its roots in 17th century England, it was the Scottish and Irish who brought Presbyterianism to the USA in the late 1600s. The largest Presbyterian branch in the USA is the **Presbyterian Church (USA)**; find them on the web at www.pcusa.org or call 800-872-3283. Of particular note in Los Angeles is the towering, neo-gothic structure that houses the **Hollywood First Presbyterian Church (FPCH)** at 1760 North Gower Street, Hollywood, 323-463-7161, www.fpch.org. The FPCH reaches out to the local community, which, being in Hollywood, has much to do with the entertainment industry. Beginning with the Actors Co-op in 1987, it now operates two theaters on its campus under a contract with Actors Equity Association. The Actors Co-op stages four plays each season and has received numerous Drama-Logue awards. Not to leave out writers, the church runs a month-long training program (Act One: Writing for Hollywood) for Christian scriptwriters.

REFORM CHURCH OF AMERICA (RCA)

The **Crystal Cathedral** in Orange County, 13280 Chapman Avenue Garden Grove, 714-971-4000, www.crystalcathedral.org, is a magnificent modern structure. More than 10,000 windows of silver glass are laced together by white steel trusses. Two 90-foot-tall doors open electronically behind the pulpit to allow the morning sunlight and breeze in during worship services, and the bell tower houses a 52-bell carillon. The Cathedral pipe organ is world renowned for its size and quality, and is among the five largest pipe organs in the world. This is a large church: Over 1,000 singers and instrumentalists can perform in the 185-foot long chancel area, and a giant indoor Sony "Jumbotron" television screen broadcasts the service. Programs include the internationally televised "Hour of Power," and its Christmas and Easter services are popular, large-scale productions that are frequently televised. Smaller "houses of power," which meet weekly in congregants' homes, are organized to meet the needs of its far-reaching congregation.

To locate a Reform Church of America near you, go to www.rca west.org and use its locator service.

SEVENTH DAY ADVENTIST

Contact the **Seventh Day Adventist: Southern California Conference**, 818-546-8400, http://scc.adventist.org (nationally at www.adventist.org), for a church near you.

UNITY CHURCHES

For information about local Unity Churches, go online to the **Association of Unity Churches** at www.unity.org.

UNITY FELLOWSHIP OF CHRIST CHURCH

The **Unity Fellowship of Christ Church**, 5148 West Jefferson Blvd., 323-938-8322, serves a predominantly gay and African-American community. Their motto is "God is Love and Love is for Everyone."

WESLEYAN

The local Wesleyan Church is part of the **Pacific Southwest District**: 619-660-0102, www.wesleyan.org. Contact them for a directory of area churches.

ETHICAL SOCIETIES

Not a conventional religious organization, ethical societies offer a meeting place and fellowship to members and visitors. Their "focus is on core ethical values that people have in common." Acknowledging that humans are both individualistic and social in nature, the society explores what it means to understand the inner workings of self and how to relate to each other in a respectful/ethical/moralistic way. For more information go to www.ethicalsociety.org or contact the **Ethical Culture Society of Los Angeles** at 818-784-9107 or online at www.ethicalsocietyla.org.

HINDU

Hinduism is as complex and multifaceted as the many gods it incorporates. Nearly 13% of the world's population is Hindu. Although most Hindus reside in India, there are roughly one million in the United States. In Los

Angeles, contact the **Hindu Temple Society of Southern California**, 1600 Las Virgenes Canyon Road, Calabasas, 818-880-5552, www.geo cities.com/malibutemple/main.htm. Designed by master architect Muthiah Sthapathi from India, this temple is one of the largest and most architecturally authentic Hindu temples in the western hemisphere. Built in the Malibu hills, the ornate temples, called shastras, comply with the strict architectural codes of the Silpa Shastra in the Chola style of temple architecture.

ISLAMIC

To tap into the local Islamic community try the **Islamic Center** at 434 South Vermont Avenue, between 4th and 5th streets in Los Angeles, 213-382-9200, www.islamctr.org; or go to www.islamicfinder.com.

JEWISH

Los Angeles has a sizable Jewish population, with the heaviest concentrations in the Fairfax District. The local media outlet is the *Jewish Journal of Greater Los Angeles*, which you can subscribe to online at www.jew-ishjournal.com or by calling 213-368-1661. If you are a student, professor, or otherwise affiliated with one of the many area colleges and universities, you can likely attend your school's Hillel or Chabad house.

Of note, the **Wilshire Boulevard Temple**, 3663 Wilshire Boulevard, 213-388-2401, www.wilshireboulevardtemple.org, is home to a prominent Jewish Progressive Reform congregation. Originating as Congregation B'nai Brith in 1862, it was the first synagogue in Los Angeles, with Rabbi Abraham Wolf Edelman as the first full-time rabbi in Southern California. Ten years later, they built their first temple. As membership grew, the congregation moved several times, eventually settling on Wilshire Boulevard in 1929. The Byzantine-inspired architecture was designed by A.M. Edelman, S. Tilden Norton, and David C. Allison; interior features include murals by Hugo Ballin. The Wilshire Temple is listed in the United States Register of Historic Places.

Contact information for branches of Judaism in Southern California include:

- **Conservative**: United Synagogue of Conservative Judaism, Pacific Southwest Region, 818-986-0907, http://uscj.org
- **Orthodox**: Orthodox Union, 310-229-9000, www.ou.org/west
- **Reconstructionist**: Jewish Reconstructionist Federation, www.jrf.org, Kehillat Israel, 310-459-2328, www.kehillatisrael.org
- **Reform**: Union of American Hebrew Congregations, http://uahc.org/conglist.html, 888-842-8242

SIKH

Although there are over 20 million Sikhs throughout the world, only 220,000 live in America. There is enough of a Sikh population in Los Angeles for several gurdwaras: In 1989 the **Sikh Sangat of Los Angeles** founded the gurdwara located at 7640 Lankershim Boulevard, North Hollywood, 818-765-9399; and the **Guru Ram Das Gurdwara** is at 1649 South Robertson Boulevard in Los Angeles, 310-201-0954. For more information, go to www.sikhs.org.

UNITARIAN UNIVERSALIST ASSOCIATION (UUA)

The Unitarian Universalist Association (UUA) dates back to 1961, when the Universalism and Unitarianism movements officially merged. The **First Unitarian Church of Los Angeles** can be reached at 213-389-2080, www.uula.org (nationally at www.uua.org).

G IVING BACK TO THE COMMUNITY IS A REWARDING EXPERIENCE. Whether you are skilled at building houses, caring for the elderly, tutoring underprivileged children, or canvassing neighborhoods (having bilingual skills in any of these areas can be particularly useful), you can find a volunteer project that suits your talents and beliefs. Helping out in your new community is also a great way to meet people and can make the transition to an unfamiliar place less stressful.

HOW YOU CAN HELP

THE HUNGRY AND THE HOMELESS

Scores of volunteers concern themselves with shelter for the city's homeless. Jobs include monitoring and organizing the shelters, providing legal help, ministering to psychiatric, medical, and social needs, raising money, manning phones, and caring for children in the shelters. Many people solicit, organize, cook, and serve food to the destitute at sites throughout the city. Still others deliver meals to the homeless and the homebound.

CHILDREN

If involvement with children is especially appealing you can tutor in and out of schools, be a big brother or sister, teach music and sports in shelters or at local community centers, run activities in the parks, entertain children in hospitals, and accompany kids on weekend outings. Schools, libraries, community associations, hospitals, and other facilities providing activities and guidance for children are all worth exploring.

HOSPITALS

The need for volunteers in both city-run and private hospitals is manifold: From interpreters to laboratory personnel to admitting and nursing aides, many volunteers are required. Assistants in crisis medical areas—emergency rooms, intensive care units, and the like—are wanted if you have the skills, as are volunteers to work with victims of sexual abuse. If you just want to be helpful, you might assist in food delivery or work in the gift shop. Most city hospitals are large and busy, and many are in need of help.

THE DISABLED AND THE ELDERLY

You can read to the blind, help teach the deaf, work to prevent birth defects, and help the retarded and developmentally disabled, among others. You can also make regular visits to the homebound elderly, bring hot meals to their homes, and teach everything from nutrition to arts and crafts in senior centers and nursing homes.

EXTREME CARE SITUATIONS

Helping with suicide prevention, Alzheimer's and AIDS patients, rape victims, and abused children is a special category demanding a high level of commitment—not to mention emotional reserves and in many cases, special skills.

THE CULTURE SCENE

Museums are always in need of volunteers to lead tours or lend a hand in any number of ways. Libraries, theater groups, and ballet companies have plenty of tasks that need to be done. Fundraising efforts also require many volunteers to stuff envelopes and/or make phone calls. The Public Broadcasting Service (PBS) is a good example. Its large volunteer staff raises money for its stations through extensive on-air fundraising campaigns that include collecting pledges.

THE COMMUNITY

Work in your neighborhood. You can help out at the local school, community garden, neighborhood block association, nursing home, or animal shelter.

VOLUNTEER REFERRAL SERVICES

The following organizations coordinate much of LA's volunteer activity, from feeding the hungry to counseling fire victims to mediation for the City Attorney's Office. Give them a call and they'll direct you to where help is most needed. **LA Works** is a clearinghouse for local short- and long-term volunteer opportunities; contact them at 323-224-6510 or go to www.laworks.com. **Volunteer Match**, www.volunteermatch.org, is a national service that matches volunteers with specific needs in your community; or check with the following:
- **Community Emergency Response Team** (**CERT-LA**), 818-756-9674, www.cert-la.com
- **Retired and Senior Volunteer Program** (**RSVP**), 818-908-5070, www.seniorcorps.org
- **Mayor's Volunteer Corps**, 213-978-0642, www.lacity.org
- **Volunteer Center Assistance League of Southern California**, 818-908-5066, www.vcla.net

OTHER CONNECTIONS
- **Check bulletin boards** at your office, church, neighborhood grocery store, laundries, and school.
- Walk into local **churches, temples, community organizations**, and/or **libraries**.

AREA CAUSES

The list below is just a small sampling of the many worthy organizations and causes that would appreciate your support. When calling, ask to speak to their volunteer coordinator.

AIDS

- **AIDS Project Los Angeles** (**APLA**), 323-993-1600, www.apla.org
- **LA Shanti Foundation**, 323-962-8197, 818-908-8849

- **LA Gay and Lesbian Center**, 323-993-7400
- **Minority AIDS Project**, 323-936-4949
- **Out of the Closet Thrift-Store**, 310-473-7787

ALCOHOL AND DRUG DEPENDENCY

- **Alcohol-Drug Council, West**, 310-451-5881
- **Alcoholics Anonymous**, 310-474-7339, www.lacoaa.org
- **Center for Chemical Dependency**, 310-855-3411
- **Focus on Recovery Helpline** (cocaine), 800-274-2042
- **Families Anonymous**, 800-736-9805
- **Narcotics Anonymous**, 310-390-0279, www.na.org
- **National Alcohol and Drug Abuse Hotline**, 800-252-6465

ANIMALS

- **Animal Regulations Department & Shelters, City of Los Angeles**, 888-452-7381, www.laanimalservices.com
- **Last Chance for Animals**, 310-271-6096
- **Pets are Wonderful Support (PAWS)**, 323-876-7297, www.paws la.org
- **ResQPet**, 818-346-1410
- **Society for the Prevention of Cruelty to Animals (SPCA)**, 323-730-5300, www.aspca.org

CHILDREN

- **Big Brothers of Greater Los Angeles**, 323-258-3333, www.big brothers.org
- **Big Sisters of Los Angeles**, 323-933-5749
- **Catholic Big Brothers and Big Sisters**, 800-453-KIDS
- **Children of the Night**, 310-276-9283
- **Jewish Big Brothers**, 323-761-8675, www.jbbla.org
- **Make-A-Wish Foundation**, 310-788-9474, www.wishla.org
- **School Volunteer Program of the Los Angeles Unified School District**, 800-933-8133, www.lausd.k12.ca.us
- **Starlight Foundation of California**, 310-286-0271, www.starlight can.org

CRIME PREVENTION

- **LAPD Volunteer Programs**, 213-485-8890, www.lapdonline.org
- **Neighborhood Watch Programs**, 323-526-5541, www.lapd online.org

CULTURE AND THE ARTS

Most museums, theaters, symphonies, chorus groups, and opera and dance companies routinely round up volunteers to help their programs run. Here are just a few to consider (Check the **Cultural Life** chapter for more):
- **Huntington Library, Art Collections, and Botanical Gardens**, 626-405-2100, www.huntington.org
- **Hollywood Bowl**, 323-850-2000, www.hollywoodbowl.com
- **Los Angeles County Museum of Art**, 323-857-6000, www.lacma.org
- **Los Angeles Philharmonic**, 323-850-2165, www.laphil.org

DISABLED ASSISTANCE

- **Association for Retarded Citizens**, 323-290-2000, www.the arc.org
- **Braille Institute**, 323-663-1111, www.brailleinstitute.org
- **Easter Seal Society of Los Angeles and Orange Counties**, 310-204-5533, www.essc.org
- **Greater Los Angeles Council on Deafness**, 323-478-8000, www.gladinc.org
- **Independent Living Center of Southern California**, 818-988-9525
- **Orton/Ryan Center for Dyslexics**, 323-748-9596
- **Los Angeles Caregiver Resource Center**, 800-540-4442
- **Westside Center for Independent Living**, 310-390-3611
- **Western Law Center for Disability Rights**, 213-736-1031

ENVIRONMENT

- **American Oceans Campaign**, 310-576-6162, www.americanoceans.org
- **Audubon Society**, 323-876-0202, www.audubon.org

- **California Conservation Corps**, 213-744-2254, www.ccc.ca.gov
- **Heal the Bay**, 800-HEAL-BAY, www.healthebay.org
- **Sierra Club**, 213-387-4287, http://angeles.sierraclub.org
- **TreePeople**, 818-623-4879

GAY AND LESBIAN

- **Gay and Lesbian Alliance Against Defamation**, 323-658-6775, www.glaad.org
- **Gay and Lesbian Counseling Center**, 323-936-7500
- **Gay and Lesbian Parents of Los Angeles**, 323-654-0307
- **Los Angeles Gay & Lesbian Center**, 323-993-7400
- **West Hollywood Cares**, 310-659-4840

HOMELESS

- **Chrysalis**, 213-895-7777, www.chrysalisworks.org
- **Los Angeles Mission**, 213-629-1227, www.losangelesmission.org
- **People Assisting the Homeless (PATH)**, 310-996-0034, www.epath. org
- **Saint Joseph Center**, 310-399-6878
- **Step Up on Second**, 310-394-6889
- **Union Station Foundation**, 818-449-4596, www.unionstation foundation.org
- **VOALA Hollywood Shelter**, 213-467-4006
- **West Hollywood Homeless Organization**, 213-850-4040

HEALTH AND HUMAN SERVICES

Refer to the **Useful Phone Numbers and Web Sites** chapter for contact information for local crisis centers, hospitals, and other health care organizations that are always in need of qualified volunteers for a host of jobs, from fundraising to manning call centers, to providing a listening ear and caring touch. Nationally, foundations that continually look for volunteers include the American Cancer Society, March of Dimes, United Way, and Visiting Nurse Service (you don't have to be a nurse). The list goes on.

Locally, contact one of the following:

- **American Red Cross of Greater Los Angeles**, 310-394-3733, www.acrossla.org

- **Bob Hope Hollywood USO at LAX**, 310-645-3716, www.bobhope uso.org
- **Catholic Charities**, 310-829-7944, www.catholiccharitiesla.org
- **Habitat for Humanity**, 818-765-2073, www.habitatla.org
- **The Salvation Army**, 818-361-6462, www.salvationarmy-socal.org

HUNGER

- **Meals and the Homebound**, 818-761-6224, www.mealcall.org
- **Project Angel Food**, 323-845-1800
- **SOVA Food Pantry**, 818-789-7633, http://jfsla.org/sova/
- **The Salvation Army**, 818-361-6462, www.salvationarmy-socal.org
- **Westside Food Bank**, 310-314-1150

INTERNATIONAL

- **EF Foundation for Foreign Study Cambridge**, 800-447-4273
- **Travelers Aid Society of Los Angeles**, 310-646-2270, www.tasla. org

LEGAL

- **American Civil Liberties Union of Southern California (ACLU)**, 213-977-9500
- **Bet Tzedek Legal Services**, 323-939-0506
- **Legal Aid Foundation of Los Angeles**, 800-399-452, www.lafla. org

LITERACY

- **Southern California Literacy Hotline**, 800-372-6641
- **Los Angeles Central Library**, 213-228-7000, www.lapl.org

MEN'S SERVICES

- **The Parent Support Group**, 310-659-5289
- **YMCA**, 310-553-0731, www.ymcala.org

POLITICS—ELECTORAL

- **League of Women Voters**, 213-368-1616 (LA, San Fernando Valley), 818-247-2407 (Glendale, Burbank); www.lwv.org
- **LA County Registrar of Voters**, 562-466-1323, http://regrec. co.la.ca.us
- **Orange County Registrar of Voters**, 714-567-7600, www.oc.ca. gov/election
- **Voter Registration and Poll workers**, 562-466-1373, Glendale, Burbank, http://regrec.co.la.ca.us/main.htm

POLITICS—SOCIAL

- **Amnesty International**, 310-815-0450, www.amnestyusa.org

SENIOR SERVICES

- **American Association of Retired Persons**, 310-496-2277
- **Jewish Family Services of Los Angeles**, 323-937-5930, www.jfs la.org
- **Retired Senior Volunteer Program**, 310-394-9871, 818-908-5070, www.seniorcorps.org
- **Los Angeles County Community and Senior Citizens Services**, 213-738-2600, http://lacounty.info
- **Senior Health and Peer Counseling**, 310-828-1243

WOMEN'S SERVICES

- **LA Commission on Assaults Against Women**, 323-462-1281
- **Planned Parenthood of Los Angeles**, 323-226-0800, www.pplos angeles.org
- **Progressive Health Services & Holistic Health for Women**, 323-650-1508
- **Safe Harbor Women's Clinic**, 213-622-4073
- **Santa Monica Hospital Rape Treatment Center**, 310-319-4000
- **Venice Women's Clinic**, 310-392-4147
- **Women's Commission for Los Angeles**, 213-974-1455
- **YWCA of Greater Los Angeles**, 213-365-2991, www.ywcagla.org

YOUTH SERVICES

- **Angel's Flight**, 800-833-2499
- **Children of the Night**, 818-908-4474, http://childrenofthenight.org
- **Exceptional Children's Foundation**, 323-290-2000
- **LA Works Youth Action Corps**, 323-936-1340
- **Los Angeles County Runaway Adolescent Project**, 323-466-5015
- **Los Angeles Youth Network**, 323-957-7757
- **McGruff House Program**, 801-486-8691, 877-367-6646, www.ut crimeprevention.org
- **MidValley Youth Center**, 818-904-0707

I N LOS ANGELES, WHERE THERE IS APPROXIMATELY ONE CAR FOR EVERY 1.8 persons, it is easy to understand why the city consistently ranks number one in the nation for traffic congestion. Los Angeles sprawls across 467 square miles and, while technically it is possible to get around by foot, bicycle, bus, and Metro light rail or subway, in most cases it is quicker and more convenient to drive. According to the Texas Transportation Institute, Los Angeles commuters spend an average of 90 hours a year sitting still in traffic—something to think about when choosing a place to live relative to where you work. To combat LA's reliance on the auto, the **South Coast Air Quality Management District (AQMD)** is doing its best to encourage use of public transportation, carpooling, bicycling, and walking, and many smog-conscious residents are trying to cut down on their driving, especially during peak commute hours. (There's even a hotline that you can call, 800-CUT-SMOG, to report a vehicle that you see emitting visible exhaust for more than 10 seconds.) In addition, the AQMD has mandated that companies with 100 or more employees must encourage smog-cutting transportation alternatives. In consideration of these mandates, some companies operate on flex time, which allows employees to work a compressed schedule of nine out of ten working days or to telecommute in certain situations, creating fewer cars on the road. To find out more about AQMD's initiatives, call 909-396-2000 or go to www.AQMD.gov. The **Los Angeles County Bicycle Coalition**, 213-629-2142, www.labikecoalition.org, has tips on commuting by bike. (If this interests you, consult with the LA County Bike Map Hotline, 213-244-6539, for route information.)

California law requires that everyone be buckled up, and children under age six or weighing less than 60 pounds must use a car safety seat.

GETTING AROUND

BY CAR

A quick glance at the map will tell you that Los Angeles is the land of free-ways. Any which way you look at it, morning (7:30 a.m. to 10:30 a.m.) and evening (3 p.m. to 6 p.m.) rush hours are a bear. If avoiding driving during these hours is not possible, be sure to check the electronic freeway condition signs along the road and heed any **"Sig-Alerts"** when driving (named after their inventor, the alert refers to any unplanned event that causes at least one lane of traffic to close for 30 minutes or more). You can also check www.sigalert.com as you're getting off work to plan your commute home. Two local radio stations, AM 1070 and AM 980, broadcast traffic reports every 10 minutes and "on the ones" (9:01, 9:11, etc.) respectively. **Caltrans**, the city crews responsible for maintaining Los Angeles and Orange counties' massive freeway network, posts real-time road incidents on the internet at www.dot.ca.gov/roadsandtraffic.htm. The **California Highway Patrol** (**CHP**) also posts real-time road alerts at http://cad.chp.ca.gov. For traffic condition maps, try www.sigalert.com; the **Los Angeles County Metropolitan Transportation Authority**–sponsored www.riits.net, with roadside traffic cams; and the **Travel Advisory News Network**'s site, http://traffic.tann.net/lartraffic, which also covers Orange County.

So, what is the best way to get around? In general, the freeways are a good choice if you need to go long distances. **Interstate 5** runs north-south, and is the fastest, though not the prettiest route, to other parts of Northern California. It is also the primary artery into Orange County. **US-101,** a more scenic route through the state, cuts through the San Fernando Valley and Hollywood. **Highway 1**, known as the **Pacific Coast Highway** (**PCH**) in the Los Angeles area, runs up and down the entire California coast. Most agree that, at some point, it's worth the extra hours on the road to take Highway 1 to or from northern California, as it covers some of the most beautiful terrain in the country.

Locally, **I-10** runs east-west, and is the most common way to get from West LA to downtown and points in between. The **I-405** runs north-south between the Valley and West LA, and down through the South Bay, and can have punishing traffic. Going north-south in south-central LA is the **I-110** freeway, which features an impressive elevated carpool lane. The rel-atively new **I-105** provides quick access from south-central LA to the west, ending at LAX. The **I-101** runs north-south in LA (called the **Hollywood Freeway**), but heads west in the Valley (and becomes the **Ventura Freeway**). **Highway 134** runs east-west and begins in Toluca Lake, then becomes the **I-210** in Pasadena.

Some of the stickiest interchanges in LA include the "four-level" in downtown, which is where on-ramps to the 110, 101, 10, and 5 freeways are clustered within a mile of each other. The interchange between the 405 and 101 is also tough, especially from the 405 to the 101. The addition of an extra lane in late 2003 did little to ease congestion. The 405 near LAX is another trouble spot, especially on Friday and Sunday evenings. Ditto for the junction where the 405 funnels into the 5 in Orange County. On the surface streets, the intersection of Wilshire and Westwood boulevards (in Westwood) is the busiest in the city. The junction of Wilshire and Santa Monica boulevards (in Beverly Hills) is also bad.

Most locals have their tried and true shortcuts around town (remember Steve Martin's cruise through alleys, parking lots, and front lawns in "LA Story"?), but they may be stingy about telling you what they are. After all, too much traffic on the shortcut defeats the purpose! It's worth experimenting yourself to see which byways move and which do not.

CARPOOLING

Most cars on local freeways hold one person—you guessed it, the driver. Local and statewide agencies are trying to change that. Carpooling lanes, located in the far left lane and marked by white diamonds and carpooling signs, are for the exclusive use of cars with two or more people (some diamond lanes require a minimum of three people). Check with your human resources office at work for carpooling incentives. Many employers offer gas coupons, parking spaces, and other freebies to those who make the trip with co-workers. For more information on commuter carpools and vanpools, call **Commuter Transportation Services** at 213-380-7433 or 800-286-7433.

For more information on transportation around Los Angeles, call the **Regional Transportation Information Network** at 800-2LA-RIDE. The **Smart Traveler Information Line** provides comprehensive information about every possible transportation option in LA, including ridesharing, 800-266-6883, www.smart-traveler.com.

PARK & RIDE LOCATIONS

Too many to list here (see your *Thomas Guide* index or http://mapsvr. scag.ca.gov/parkride for a full list). A few (located in Los Angeles unless otherwise noted) include:
- **Burbank Metrolink Park & Ride**, 201 North Front Street, Burbank
- **College of the Canyons Park & Ride**, 26355 North Rockwell Canyon Road, Santa Clarita

- **Glendale Metrolink Park & Ride**, 400 West Cerritos Avenue, Glendale
- **Hayvenhurst Park & Ride**, Hayvenhurst and Magnolia, Encino
- **Manchester Park & Ride**, Manchester Avenue and I-100
- **Parsons Company Park & Ride**, Pasadena Avenue and Union Street, Pasadena
- **Pasadena Park & Ride**, Sierra Madre Blvd. and Corson Street, Pasadena
- **Riverton Park & Ride**, Riverton Avenue and Ventura Blvd.
- **Sepulveda Pass Park & Ride**, 2350 Skirball Center Drive, Brentwood
- **South Pasadena Park & Ride**, 435 South Fairoaks Avenue, South Pasadena
- **Topanga Plaza Park & Ride**, 6600 Topanga Canyon Blvd., Canoga Park
- **Van Nuys Boulevard Park & Ride**, 7724 Van Nuys Blvd., Van Nuys
- **Veterans Administration Park & Ride**, Wilshire Blvd. and I-405
- **Washington & Fairfax Park & Ride**, Washington Blvd. and South Fairfax Avenue

CAR RENTALS

There are numerous car rental agencies near the airports, and throughout the city. Call the following phone numbers for information, reservations, and locations:

- **Alamo**, 800-327-9633, www.alamo.com
- **Avis**, 800-331-1212, www.avis.com
- **Budget**, 800-527-0700, www.budget.com
- **Dollar**, 800-800-4000, www.dollar.com
- **Enterprise**, 800-325-8007, www.enterprise.com
- **Hertz**, 800-654-3131, www.hertz.com
- **National**, 800-227-7368, www.nationalcar.com
- **Payless**, 800-729-5377, www.paylesscarrental.com
- **Rent-a-Wreck**, 800-535-1391, www.rentawreck.com
- **Thrifty**, 800-367-2277, www.thrifty.com

TAXIS AND SHUTTLES

Unlike New York or Chicago, Los Angeles is not a major taxi town. You will not, for instance, be able to step out of any building and flag down a cab. Nonetheless, there are taxis at airports, hotels, and tourist attractions. If you need a cab at a specific time, your best bet is to call and order one in advance. Group shuttles are almost always cheaper than cabs for one passenger, and may still be cheaper for groups. The listing here includes both taxis and shuttles:

- **Airport Shuttle**, 310-215-9950
- **Checker Cab**, 310-201-0307
- **Super Shuttle**, 800-258-3826, www.supershuttle.com
- **Prime Time Shuttle**, 800-733-8267, www.primetimeshuttle.com
- **United Taxi of San Fernando Valley**, 800-290-5600
- **United Independent Taxi**, 800-411-0303, www.unitedtaxi.com
- **World Shuttle Services**, 888-992-8600
- **Yellow Cab**, 877-733-3305, www.layellowcab.com

LIMOUSINES

Check the Yellow Pages under "Limousine" for a listing of the many companies that provide limo service—just don't expect to get a limo on the day of the Academy Awards.

BY PUBLIC TRANSPORTATION

METROPOLITAN TRANPORTATION AUTHORITY—METRO

LA County's **Metro** serves the greater Los Angeles area with more than 180 bus, rail, and light-rail routes. Base fare is $1.25; the unlimited local travel monthly pass is $52. For more on fares and passes, as well as routes and maps, visit www.mta.net or call 800-COMMUTE; TTY 800-252-9040, 6 a.m. to 8:30 p.m., Monday-Friday, and 8 a.m. to 6 p.m., Saturday and Sunday (outside of Los Angeles, call 213-922-6235, 8 a.m. to 4:15 p.m., Monday-Friday, or write to: Metro Customer Relations, 1 Gateway Plaza, Los Angeles, CA 90012-2952).

Metro's light rail and buses are ADA-compliant for passengers with hearing, mobility and visual impairments, and reduced fares are available to disabled passengers. If a disability prevents you from using regular bus or rail service, you may hire **Access Paratransit** for curb-to-curb service 24-hours-a-day. Contact Access Services' information specialists at 800-827-0829, TDD 800-827-1359, or online at www.asi la.org to obtain information for this and all accessible transportation options in Los Angeles County.

SUBWAY AND LIGHT TRANSIT

Los Angeles has an interesting history with public transportation. Until the 1940s, like most major American cities, LA had an extensive system of electric trolley cars run by the Pacific Electric Railway, known as "Red Cars." The old tracks can still be seen in Santa Monica and Beverly Hills. The system was famed for its efficiency and affordability. There's a long-held myth perpetuated by the movie "Who Framed Roger Rabbit" that car and tire manufacturers killed the railway in the interest of big business. But the less glamorous and more likely cause for the demise of the system included the growing popularity of automobiles, lack of public support, and unrecoverable losses in ridership from the Great Depression. Today you can relive a bit of history: The Port of Los Angeles has restored two Red Cars from the 1920s and operates them along a 1.5-mile route that retraces a portion of the original Red Car line in Long Beach. For schedule information: 310-732-3473, http://portoflosangeles.org.

LA's first subway was rolled out in the form of the **Metro's Red Line**. The project, delayed by shoddy workmanship and cost overruns, was unpopular with Angelenos ("A subway in earthquake country?" was the question commonly asked by those opposed to it). It was so unpopular, in fact, that in 1998 a proposition to outlaw the use of tax dollars to fund the Metro passed by a 68% majority. Today, however, ridership on the Metro subway continues to grow as commuters are taking advantage of this clean, predictable, and well-patrolled mode of transport. Currently, the Metro has four lines: the **Blue Line** (light rail) runs from downtown to Long Beach; the **Red Line** (subway) originates from Union Station in downtown and runs through Hollywood, finishing in North Hollywood; the **Green Line** (light rail) takes commuters through south-central communities, between Redondo Beach and Norwalk; and the **Gold Line** (light rail) connects Union Station to Pasadena, with plans to extend into East Los Angeles (see map at back of book). Fares at press time were $1.25 per boarding. An unlimited local travel monthly pass may be purchased for $52. Maps, timetables, tickets, and passes may be purchased in person at the Metro customer service center at Union Station, downtown, 800 North Alameda Street, or by calling 800-COMMUTE (out of state, call 213-922-6059 to purchase passes; 213-922-6235 for customer service). Online, go to www.mta.net for Metro and bus timetables and to download the "Metro Bus & Rail Rider's Guide."

The **Metrolink** is a long-distance commuter train connecting Los Angeles to surrounding counties, including Orange, Ventura, and San Diego. There is also a Ventura County Line that takes riders from Union

Station to Northridge, Van Nuys, Burbank, and Glendale. Fares are determined by distance traveled. Call 800-371-5465 or visit www.metrolink-trains.com for more information.

BUS

Due to the limited range of the Metro light rail lines, most residents who use public transportation rely on Metro buses to get around. For more information on using the bus in LA, call Metro's 800-COMMUTE line, an automated phone system that connects callers to over 40 transportation agencies serving Los Angeles and Orange counties. Also download Metro's "Metro Bus & Rail Rider's Guide" at www.mta.net. The *Transit Guide* ($6), published by the **Southern California Transit Advocates**, 3010 Wilshire Boulevard #362, Los Angeles, CA 90010, 213-388-2364, www.socata.net, lists over 50 fixed-route public transit agencies operating in Southern California, with tips on using the systems. Transit-rider.com (www.transitrider.com) is another comprehensive resource for getting around Los Angeles, Orange, and San Diego counties.

Seniors and the mobility impaired can utilize the Los Angeles Department of Transportation's **Cityride** (see LADOT contact information below), a service that provides substantial discounts on Metro passes, taxi rides, private lift van services, and dial-a-ride trips to those who qualify.

Additional bus service options in and around LA include:

- **LA Department of Transportation (LADOT)** operates **Commuter Express** and **DASH**. The Commuter Express links the San Fernando Valley with other parts of LA, including downtown, Burbank, Glendale, Pasadena, and LAX, with a limited number of stops. The DASH is a shuttle bus that runs short hops in the Valley and greater LA. Call 818/213/310-808-2273 or visit www.ladottransit.com for more information.
- The **Culver City Bus**, 310-559-8310 (recorded information), www.culvercity.org/depts_bus.html; provides local service in Culver City and to Los Angeles, LAX, Marina del Rey, UCLA, Venice, and the Westside. Adult base fare is $.75.
- **Foothill Transit**, 626-967-3147, www.foothilltransit.org; operates local and express buses within the Foothills area.
- Get around Glendale via the **Glendale Beeline**: 818-548-3960, www.glendale-online.com/transportation/beeline.
- **Orange County Transportation Authority (OCTA)**, 714-636-7433 or www.octa.net; serves Orange County. Plans are to begin work in 2006 on an OCTA light rail line, its first to be called the Center Line.

- **Santa Clarita Transit (SCT)**, 805-294-1287, www.santa-clarita. com/cityhall/field/transit; offers local bus service in the Santa Clarita Valley, as well as express buses to downtown LA, Westwood, and the Valley.
- **Torrance Transit**, 310-618-6266 or www.torrnet.com/city/dept/transit/ index.html; serves the South Bay area of LA County.
- **Santa Monica Municipal Bus Lines (Big Blue Bus)**, 310-451-5444, www.bigbluebus.com; services Santa Monica and the Westside, some routes extend to UCLA, LAX, and downtown.
- **Smart Traveler Information Line**, 800-266-6883, provides comprehensive information about every possible transportation option in LA, including ridesharing.
- The **West Hollywood CityLine** services the city of West Hollywood, fares are $.25 or free with a Metro pass. Call 323-848-6375 or go to www.weho.org for route and schedule information.

NATIONAL TRAIN AND BUS SERVICE

- **Amtrak**, 800-872-7245, www.amtrak.com; Los Angeles's Union Station is downtown at 8090 North Alameda Street. Amtrak offers a variety of departure times for San Diego commuters. Discount fares and promotions can be found on its web site.
- **Greyhound**, 800-231-2222, www.greyhound.com; the Los Angeles terminal is downtown at 1716 East 7th Street, 213-629-8402.

BY AIRLINE

AIRPORTS

Several airports serve this teeming metropolitan area. **Los Angeles International Airport** (LAX), 310-646-5252, www.lawa.org, is the largest and busiest airport on the West Coast. It is located just south of Playa del Rey.

Numerous public transportation service options to and from LAX are available. The Metro Rail Green Line stops at Aviation Station and provides free shuttle service to and from LAX. The Metro bus route #42 travels from LAX to downtown Los Angeles and to Union Station (train), which is about two miles from the Los Angeles Greyhound Bus Terminal. Board the bus at the LAX City Bus Center located in remote parking Lot C on 96th Street and Sepulveda Boulevard.

If you drive, LAX has almost 8,000 parking spaces in eight parking structures surrounding the passenger terminals, plus an additional two satellite lots (Parking Lot C at 96th Street and Sepulveda Boulevard and Parking Lot B at 111th Street and La Cienega). Check traffic flow to the airport on the web at http://trafficinfo.lacity.org/html/lax.html.

For lost or misdirected luggage from your flight, you should contact your airline. To retrieve items left behind at any of the passenger screening stations at LAX, contact the TSA Lost and Found in Terminal 6 at 310-665-7382. For assistance with items lost elsewhere at the airport, contact the LAX Airport Police Lost and Found at 310-417-0440.

Airlines serving LAX include (see further below for contact information):

- **Terminal 1**: America West, Southwest and US Airways
- **Terminal 2**: Northwest, Air Canada, Air New Zealand, Hawaiian, Virgin Atlantic, and others
- **Terminal 3**: Alaska, Frontier, Midwest Express, and others
- **Terminal 4**: American Airlines, Qantas
- **Terminal 5**: Delta Air Lines plus partner airlines, Air France, and American
- **Terminal 6**: Continental Airlines, United international and domestic flights, and AeroMexico
- **Terminal 7**: United Airlines
- **Terminal B** is The Tom Bradley International Terminal and serves most non-US airlines, including Air France, British Airways, Cathay Pacific, Japan, and Mexicana.

Additional **regional airports** include:

- **Bob Hope Airport** (formerly Burbank Airport), 2627 North Hollywood Way, 818-840-8840, www.burbankairport.com: Alaska, American, America West, SkyWest, Southwest, and United airlines offer domestic service.
- **Long Beach Airport** is located at 4100 East Donald Douglas Drive, 562-570-2600, www.lgb.org. Commercial airlines servicing this airport include Alaska, America West, Jet Blue, and American Airlines.
- **Ontario International Airport** is located about an hour southeast of Los Angeles at Airport Drive and Vineyard Avenue in Ontario. For general information, call 909-937-2700 or go to www.LAWA.org. Major airlines servicing LAX, as well as newcomer Jet Blue, also fly into Ontario.
- **Orange County's John Wayne Airport** is at 18741 Airport Way in Santa Ana, 949-252-5200, www.ocair.com. Airlines include America West, Northwest, Southwest, United, US Air, Alaska, American, Continental, Delta, Aloha, Frontier, and Midwest.

- **Santa Monica Airport**, 3223 Donald Douglas Loop South, 310-458-8591; no commercial flight service. For the exclusive use of private planes and helicopters.
- **Van Nuys Airport**, 16461 Sherman Way, 818-785-8838; for corporate and private planes and helicopters, no commercial flights.

CONTACT INFORMATION FOR THE MAJOR AIRLINES SERVING GREATER LOS ANGELES

- **AeroMexico**, 800-237-6639, www.aeromexico.com
- **Air Canada**, 888-247-2262, www.aircanada.ca
- **Alaska**, 800-252-7522, www.alaskaair.com
- **America West**, 800-235-9292, www.americawest.com
- **American**, 800-433-7300, www.aa.com
- **British Airways**, 800-247-9297, www.britishairways.com
- **Cathay Pacific**, 800-233-2742, www.cathaypacific.com
- **Delta**, 800-221-1212, www.delta.com
- **Continental**, 800-525-0280, www.continental.com
- **Japan Airlines**, 800-525-3663, www.japanair.com
- **Jet Blue**, 800-538-2583, www.jetblue.com
- **Mexicana**, 800-531-7921, www.mexicana.com
- **Northwest-KLM**, 800-225-2525, www.nwa.com
- **Qantas**, 800-227-4500, www.qantas.com.au
- **Southwest**, 800-I-FLY-SWA, www.southwest.com
- **US Airways**, 800-428-4322, www.usairways.com
- **United**, 800-241-6522, www.ual.com

FLIGHT DELAYS

Information about flight delays can be checked online on your airline's web site, or at www.fly.faa.gov. Similarly, the site www.flightarrivals.com offers real-time arrival, departure, and delay details for commercial flights.

CONSUMER COMPLAINTS—AIRLINES

To register a complaint against an airline, the Department of Transportation is the place to call or write: 202-366-2220, Aviation Consumer Protection Division, C-75 Room 4107, 400 7th Street SW, Washington, DC 20590.

LOS ANGELES AND THE GREATER METROPOLITAN AREA HAVE A GOOD selection of hotels and motels. Accommodations run the gamut from utilitarian to ultra luxurious. When reserving a room, be sure to ask about discounts or weekend packages. Many lodgings have unadvertised specials that they offer only if customers inquire, and some hotels offer senior citizen and/or automobile club discounts. Keep in mind that summer rates can be higher than the rest of the year, and that big conventions, or other area events, will cause hotels to fill up fast and rates to rise.

RESERVATION SERVICES

Once you've found the hotel, motel, inn, or other option that suits your fancy, you've got to decide how you want to reserve your room. Do you want to call and reserve directly or go through a reservation service? Here are a few reservation services and online travel agents that can assist you with finding a place to stay:

- **BizTravel**, www.biztravel.com
- **Central Reservation Services**, 800-548-3311, www.reservation-services.com
- **Cheap Tickets**, www.cheaptickets.com
- **Expedia**, 800-EXPEDIA, www.expedia.com
- **Express Reservations**, 800-356-1123, www.expressreservations.com
- **Hotel Locators**, 800-576-0003, www.hotellocators.com
- **Hotels.com**, 800-964-6835, www.hotels.com
- **LowestFare.com**, www.lowestfare.com
- **Orbitz**, www.orbitz.com
- **Quickbook**, 800-789-9887, www.quickbook.com
- **Room Exchange**, 800-846-7000
- **Tom Parsons' Best Fares**, www.bestfares.com

- **Travelocity**, www.travelocity.com
- **Travelweb**, www.travelweb.com
- **TurboTrip.com**, w3.turbotrip.com

A word of advice: When making reservations through any discount site it is always wise to ask about its cancellation policy and if the rate quoted includes the **hotel tax**, which in LA is a whopping 14%. Also, some services require a full payment when making the reservation.

The following list of hotels and motels is by no means complete. For more listings, check the telephone directory under "Hotels and Motels." If you are traveling and know the area in which you wish to book a room, you might call the local Chamber of Commerce or visit the city's web site for a list of what's available. The **LA Visitors Bureau**, 800-228-2452, www.lacvb.com, and **California Tourism** web site, http://gocalif.ca.gov, can also make some recommendations based on your budget.

LODGINGS

Unless otherwise noted, the following establishments are located in Los Angeles.

LUXURY LODGINGS

There is no shortage of luxury hotels in Los Angeles and the sky's the limit in terms of room rates ($5,000 a night for a suite at the Century Plaza Hotel, where visiting presidents and dignitaries stay). What follows are just a few in the $200- to $500-a-night range:

- **Beverly Hills Hotel**, 9641 Sunset Blvd., Beverly Hills, 310-276-2251, www.beverlyhillshotel.com
- **Chateau Marmont**, 8221 Sunset Blvd., Hollywood, 323-656-1010, www.chateaumarmont.com
- **Four Seasons Los Angeles**, 300 South Doheny Drive, 310-273-2222, www.fourseasons.com
- **Westin Century Plaza Hotel & Spa**, 2025 Avenue of the Stars, Century City, 310-277-2000, www.centuryplazala.com
- **Hotel Bel Air**, 701 Stone Canyon Road, Bel Air, 310-472-1211, www.hotelbelair.com
- **Loews Santa Monica Beach Hotel**, 1700 Ocean Avenue, Santa Monica, 310-458-6700, www.santamonicaloewshotel.com
- **L'Ermitage Beverly Hills**, 9291 Burton Way, Beverly Hills, 310-278-3344, www.lermitagehotel.com

- **The Peninsula**, 9882 Santa Monica Blvd., Beverly Hills, 310-551-2888, www.peninsula.com
- **Regent Beverly Wilshire**, 9500 Wilshire Blvd., Beverly Hills, 310-275-5200, www.regenthotels.com
- **Ritz Carlton Huntington**, 1401 South Oak Knoll Avenue, Pasadena, 626-568-3900, www.ritzcarlton.com
- **Ritz Carlton Marina del Rey**, 4375 Admiralty Way, Marina del Rey, 310-823-1700, www.ritzcarlton.com

MIDDLE RANGE LODGINGS

For hotels with multiple locations, call and inquire about their rates, as prices will vary according to location. The following hotels offer rooms that range between $100 and $300.

- **The Argyle**, 8353 Sunset Blvd., West Hollywood, 323-654-7100, www.argylehotel.com
- **Marriott Hotels/Inns**, 800-228-9290, www.marriot.com; Marriotts are located in Century City, Long Beach, LAX, Marina del Rey, Torrance, and Woodland Hills.
- **Hilton Hotels**, 16 in the LA area, call 800-445-8667, www.hilton.com
- **Hyatt Hotels**, 800-233-1234, www.hyatt.com; locations in LA, Century City, West Hollywood, and Long Beach.
- **Omni Hotel**, 251 South Olive Street, 213-617-3300, www.omni hotels.com
- **Radisson Huntley Hotel**, 1111 2nd Street, Santa Monica, 310-394-5454, 800-333-3333, www.radisson.com
- **Radisson Valley Center Hotel**, 15433 Ventura Blvd., Sherman Oaks, 818-981-5400, www.radisson.com
- **Shangri-La Hotel**, 1301 Ocean Avenue, Santa Monica, 800-345-7829, www.shangrila-hotel.com
- **The Standard**, www.standardhotel.com, two locations: West Hollywood, 8300 West Sunset Blvd., 323-650-9090; and downtown LA at 550 South Flower Street, 213-892-8080
- **Wyndham Checkers Hotel**, 535 South Grand Avenue, 213-624-0000, www.wyndham.com

BED & BREAKFAST INNS

The majority of B&Bs in Los Angeles are hosted, usually by the proprietors, and are reminiscent of a stay at a mini-hotel with a dash of an overnighter at grandma's house. Nearly all require a minimum stay of two nights. It is possible to book reservations through a B&B directly, though some only list with an agency. In comparison with the number of hotels in LA, the selection of B&Bs is limited. The following guides can assist you with locating a B&B that suits your needs and budget. Commissions, if any, are included in the price of the reservation.

- **California Association of Bed and Breakfast Inns**, 831-462-9191, www.cabbi.com
- **California B&B Travel Directory**, www.bbtravel.com; comprehensive listings
- **Bed and Breakfast Explorer**, www.bbexplorer.com
- **iBedandBreakfast**, www.ibedandbreakfast.com
- **LA Convention & Visitors Bureau**, 633, West Fifth Street, Suite 600, Los Angeles, CA 90071, 800-228-2452, www.lacvb.com; search its web site or call for referrals to local B&Bs.

EXTENDED-STAY HOTELS

Extended-stay hotels may be a good option for those simply needing more time in their search for permanent housing, although finding a summer sublet near a university will probably cost far less (see the **Finding a Place to Live** chapter for more information). Nightly, weekly, or monthly leases can be had, though a monthly lease may be the minimum at some extended stay chains. These fully furnished suites are large and offer more privacy than a standard hotel room. They also come with a fully equipped kitchen, data port, and on-premise laundry facilities. Some even offer gym and pool privileges.

- **Marriott Execustay Inc.**, 800-388-0004, http://execustay.com
- **Extended Stay America** and **Studio Plus Deluxe Studios**, 800-398-7829, www.extendedstay.com; various locations, including: 2200 Empire Avenue, Burbank, 818-567-0952; 18602 South Vermont Avenue, Gardena, 310-515-5139; 19200 Harbor Gateway, Torrance, 310-328-6000; 6531 South Sepulveda Blvd., near LAX, 310-468-9337; 4105 East Willow Street, Long Beach, 562-989-4601
- **Homestead Studio Suites Hotels**, 888-782-9473, www.extended stay.com: various locations, including 1377 West Glenoaks Blvd., Glendale, 818-956-6665; 1910 East Mariposa Avenue, near LAX, 310-607-4000; 930 South Fifth Avenue, Monrovia, 626-256-6999; 3995 Carson Street, Torrance, 310-543-0048
- **Oakwood Apartments**, 800-888-0808, www.oakwood.com; corporate apartments throughout Los Angeles

- **Residence Inn by Marriott**, 800-321-2211, www.marriot.com, various locations, including 321 East Huntington Drive, Arcadia, 626-446-6500; 1177 South Beverly Drive, Beverly Hills, 310-277-4427; 4111 East Willow Street, Long Beach, 562-595-0909; 1700 North Sepulveda Blvd., Manhattan Beach, 310-546-7627; 3701 Torrance Blvd., Torrance, 310-543-4566; 25320 The Old Road, Valencia, 661-290-2800

INEXPENSIVE LODGINGS

For hotels with multiple locations, call and inquire on their rates and reservations, prices will vary according to location. The following generally range between $40 and $150.

- **Best Western**, 800-528-1234, www.bestwestern.com; various locations in LA, including Santa Monica, Pasadena, and Westwood
- **The Beverly Laurel Motel**, 8018 Beverly Blvd., 800-962-3824
- **Beverly Terrace**, 496 North Doheny Drive, 310-274-8141; offers pleasant if small rooms in a great location
- **Comfort Inn**, 800-228-5150, www.comfortinn.com; there are 100+ locations throughout LA, including downtown, Burbank, Hollywood
- **Days Inn**, 800-329-7466, www.daysinn.com; various locations
- **Econo Lodge**, 800-553-2666, www.econolodge.com; a handful of Econo Lodges dot the LA area, including downtown, Hollywood, Glendale, and Inglewood. The accommodations are basic, but inexpensive.
- **Holiday Inn**, 800-465-4329, www.holidayinn.com; there are approximately 25 Holiday Inns in the Los Angeles area. Call for reservations and information.
- **Hotel Figueroa**, 939 South Figueroa Street, 800-421-9092, www.figueroahotel.com
- **Howard Johnson**, 800-654-2000, www.howardjohnson.com; there are five in the Los Angeles area.
- **The Magic Castle Hotel**, 323-851-0800, www.magiccastlehotel.com; 7025 Franklin Avenue, Hollywood; cheery two-story lodge type building located near Hollywood tourist attractions.
- **Motel 6**, 800-466-8356, www.motel6.com; various locations, including Hollywood
- **Orbit Hotel/Banana Bungalow Hollywood Hostel**, 7950 Melrose Avenue, Hollywood, 800-446-7835, www.orbithotel.com; dorm-style singles and some private rooms available with baths; no individual telephone lines

- **Ramada Inn**, 800-228-2828, www.ramada.com; multiple locations, including West Hollywood

HOSTELS

There are three **Hostelling International** locations in the Los Angeles area (go to www.hiayh.org for more information about this organization):

- **Fullerton**, 1700 North Harbor Blvd. (nearest to Disneyland), 714-738-3721
- **San Pedro**, 3601 South Gaffey Street, #613, 310-831-8109
- **Santa Monica**, 1434 2nd Street, 310-393-3413

YMCAs

Although there are multiple YMCAs (www.ymca.net) in Los Angeles, the Glendale location at 140 North Louise, 818-240-4130, is the only one that offers lodging. Dormitory rooms are for single men only and are $29 per night. Vacancies are rare and you must inquire in person.

HAVE CAR, WILL TRAVEL. MANY ANGELENOS USE THE WEEKEND AS an opportunity for a quick escape from the city. San Francisco, Las Vegas, San Diego, Santa Barbara, and Mexico are popular weekend destinations, as are Catalina and Palm Springs. But with LA as big as it is, just driving to a different community like Long Beach can be a quick getaway in itself. Don't forget to review the **Greenspace and Beaches** chapter of this book for other relaxing ways to fill up a weekend. Also, contact the **California Travel and Tourism Commission**, 800-862-2543, www.visitcalifornia.com, and request their fact-filled brochure on popular California getaway destinations. For more ideas on quick getaways and packages, go online to www.latimes.com/travel.

CATALINA ISLAND

Catalina Island is approximately 22 miles west of Long Beach, and is accessible only by a two-hour boat ride (or a helicopter ride) across the Pacific Ocean. Although getting to this resort town requires a little bit of planning, it is worth the effort. Once you land in Avalon, the island's port, scan the waters of the bay to receive greetings from the bright orange fish that are native to the waters here. Since the island is so small, 28 miles long and only eight miles wide, rented golf carts are the only means of transportation for visitors. Take your cart on a loop around the island for a self-guided tour. Over 80% of the land has been set aside for the preservation of native flora and fauna. Most hotels require a two-night minimum stay on the weekends, but you can also rough it at a campground. Contact the **Catalina Island Visitors Bureau**, 310-510-1520, www.visitcatalina.org, for trip-planning assistance.

PALM SPRINGS

Palm Springs is a popular (particularly with the gay crowd) golf and spa resort destination located in the upper Colorado Desert. National golf tournaments are frequently held here, making it a favorite destination for golf lovers. Upscale shopping is another prime activity. Don't miss the Palm Springs Tram, which whisks you from desert country to an Alpine forest within 15 minutes and provides a beautiful birds-eye view of the city. Contact the **Palm Springs Tourism Center**, 800-347-7746, www.palm-springs.org, for more information. You can request a Palm Springs Desert Resorts Vacation Planner by dialing 800-417-3529.

SAN FRANCISCO

San Francisco, charming and fresh, in spite of the crowds. Popular sight-seeing destinations include Fisherman's Wharf, the Golden Gate Bridge and Park, the Presidio, Alcatraz Island, Coit Tower, Chinatown, Union Square, and of course, the old-fashioned cable cars. A word to the wise, much of your sightseeing time can be spent seeking out street parking, especially on weekends. You're better off shelling out the bucks for garage parking. Contact **San Francisco's Visitor Bureau**, 415-391-2000, www.sfvisitor.org, for planning assistance. With frequent and inexpensive flights out of LAX and Bob Hope airports to San Francisco, San Jose, or Oakland, you may opt to skip the seven- to eight-hour drive north and fly instead.

LAGUNA BEACH

Laguna Beach, about an hour south of Los Angeles, is a picturesque resort town and artists' colony. Art collectors spend entire weekends just check-ing out the collection of exhibits at the town's popular summer Sawdust Festival (from July to August). The frequently sold-out Pageant of the Masters, a live-stage recreation of famous works of art by community actors set to live music, is a unique must-see as well. Many area hotels offer overnight packages that include tickets to the show; be sure to ask. **Laguna Beach Visitor Services**, 800-877-1115, www.lagunabeach info.com, can provide more information.

SAN DIEGO AND MEXICO

Two and a half hours south and you'll be in San Diego. Though now the second largest city in California, San Diego has still managed to maintain a laid-back beach town feel. In addition to being the largest naval air station on the West Coast, it is host to the world-renowned San Diego Zoo and Sea World Marine Park. The charming communities of La Jolla, Old Town, and Coronado Island are also popular with families. After a day of shopping and sightseeing, head over to downtown's Fifth Avenue, a popular street for nighttime dining, dancing, and people watching.

On the southern edge of San Diego are two international border crossings into Mexico. Young people jam the borders on long weekends (creating one-hour-plus waits) and head into Tijuana's main drag, Avenida de Revolution, for serious bar hopping and partying. The **San Diego Convention and Visitors Bureau**, 619-236-1212, www.sandiego.org, can provide additional information about San Diego as well as trips into Mexico.

SANTA BARBARA AND SURROUNDING TOWNS

Santa Barbara is another coastal community, located two hours north of Los Angeles. Highlights of this historically rich town include El Presidio State Historic Park, Mission Santa Barbara, the Zoological Dens, Sea Center, and downtown's State Street for its long thoroughfare of shops and restaurants. Antique collectors and flea market junkies should keep an eye out for **Summerland**, a tiny little town just five miles south of Santa Barbara. Many of the buildings along the town's main strip, Lillie Avenue, feature antique shops, cafes, and houses constructed in the late 1800s. The **Santa Barbara Visitor's Bureau**, 800-927-4688, www.santabarbaraca.com, can assist you with your vacation plans in both towns. Less than an hour north of Santa Barbara is **Solvang**, a city that gives a sense of visiting Denmark. A visit to this quaint, old-world village is a full-immersion experience of Danish restaurants, shops, and windmills. The **Solvang Visitors Bureau** will help with trip planning assistance: 800-468-6765, www.solvangusa.com.

Just off the coast of Santa Barbara are the **San Miguel** and **Santa Cruz Islands**, which offer scenic hiking, kayaking, caverns, and a petrified forest. Both islands are accessible only by chartered boat. Contact the **Channel Islands National Park**, 805-658-5730, www.nps.gov/chis/homepage.htm, for additional information.

LOMPOC

From May through September flower lovers head in droves to the flower beds of **Lompoc**, which is located about an hour's drive northwest of Santa Barbara. Many of the nation's flower seeds are harvested here, and the colorful flower fields are the primary attraction in this picturesque town. Its normal population of 37,000 multiplies by three during the

Lompoc Valley Flower Festival, held over a weekend in late June. Formal bus tours are arranged for the many tourists. Contact the **Lompoc Valley Chamber of Commerce**, 805-736-4567, www.lompoc.com, for more information.

BIG BEAR

An easy two-hour drive east of Los Angeles, Big Bear is a popular ski destination in the winter, and is one of the largest year-round recreational areas in the state. There are seven ski resorts here, offering a good selection of slopes with varying degrees of difficulty. Come summer, you can rent a boat, go horseback riding, hiking, camping, or picnicking. Quaint bed and breakfasts abound; perfect for romantic getaways. Contact the Chamber of Commerce, 909-866-4608, www.bigbearchamber.com, for more vacation ideas.

LAS VEGAS

And, on a completely different note, if you're in the mood for glamour and gambling, **Las Vegas**, Nevada is a mere four-hour drive away and the top destination for Angelenos on holidays. With popular themed mega-hotels in constant construction on the Strip, this city may have more hotel rooms clustered in one town than anywhere else in the world. The best room rates can be found on the weekdays, and many hotels require a two-night minimum on weekends. The buffets aren't as good a bargain as they once were, but food is still relatively cheap considering it's all you can eat. This glittering, restless city offers one of the most economical vacations around—unless you lose it all at the tables. Non-gaming options include the Bellagio's Art Museum, the MGM Theme Park, the spectacular Red Rock Canyon, and the Hoover Dam. Call the Las Vegas Convention and Visitors Authority, 702-892-7575, www.lvcva.com for more information.

STATE AND NATIONAL PARKS AND FORESTS

Nature lovers should consider the five-hour drive out to **Sequoia & Kings Canyon National Parks**. Among the park's lush old-growth pines, firs, and cedars are some of the world's oldest sequoia trees. In addition to camping in log cabins, there's hiking, fishing, climbing, and horseback riding in the spring and summer. During the winter, cross-country skiers delight in trekking through the snow-frosted sugar pine forest. Contact the **Sequoia-Kings Canyon Park Services Company**, 559-565-3341, www.nps.gov/seki/index.htm, or the **Sequoia Visitor's Council**,

877-847-2542, www.sequoia-regional-visitors-council.com, for camping reservations and trip planning information.

Much closer to home is the **Malibu Creek State Park**, 818-880-0367, www.parks.ca.gov. It consists of over 4,000 acres for hiking, fishing, and bird watching. Malibu Creek runs 25 miles through the park; a trail runs about 15 miles alongside the stream through oak and sycamore woodlands and chaparral-covered slopes. The park looks so convincingly remote that TV shows like Planet of the Apes and M*A*S*H were shot here.

There's also **Topanga State Park**, 310-455-2465, www.parks. ca.gov, a 10,000-acre park that's located entirely within the Los Angeles city limits and is considered the world's largest wild lands within a major city. Visitors should start at Trippet Ranch to head out on one of the many hiking trails (36 miles' worth) through oak trees and open grasslands.

The **Santa Monica Mountains National Recreation Area**, 310-589-3200, http://smmc.ca.gov or www.lamountains.com, encompasses a mind-boggling variety of parks and beaches. The Santa Monica Mountains stretch almost 50 miles across Los Angeles. Within this recreational area are over 20 parks, including the **Will Rogers State Historical Park** in Pacific Palisades, 310-454-8212, www.parks.ca.gov; **Griffith Park**, 323-913-4688, www.ci.la.ca.us/RAP/grifmet/gp/index.htm, which is one of the largest municipal parks in the United States; **Laurel Canyon Park**, 818-762-7246, www.lamountains.com, best known for its three-acre off-leash dog park in Studio City; and the popular **Coldwater Canyon Park**, 818-753-4600, headquarters to the urban forest advocacy group TreePeople in Beverly Hills.

For additional information on city parks, refer to the **Sports and Recreation** and **Greenspace and Beaches** chapters.

ORTUNATELY FOR RESIDENTS, NATURAL DISASTERS SUCH AS EARTH-quakes, forest fires, landslides, and floods happen infrequently. While some are inconvenienced by increased traffic due to flooding or a temporary loss of power due to a temblor, the vast majority of LA residents are unaffected. On the other hand, for those who are victim to such natural disasters, the results can be devastating. In any event, it is wise to have an established family emergency plan and to set up a stock of emergency supplies in case of a disaster.

The Southern California region offers a wealth of disaster preparedness programs, from natural disasters to terrorist attacks. To find out more about real-time earthquake activity, recent temblors, locations of fault lines, flooding zones, and fire activity, you can consult with the following **disaster preparedness** resources:

- **City of LA Fire Department**, www.lafd.org
- **City of LA Health and Human Services**, 800-339-6993, www.info line-la.org/disaster.html
- **Earthquake Hazards Program—Southern California**, http://pasadena.wr.usgs.gov
- **Emergency Preparedness Commission for the County and Cities of Los Angeles**, 323-980-2260, http://lacoa.org
- **LA County Fire Department**, www.lacofd.org
- **Southern California Earthquake Center**, 213-740-5843, www.scec.org

EARTHQUAKES

One of the biggest fears about living in California is earthquakes. While most natives aren't too frightened by the swaying or bumps of small temblors, no one relishes the thought of the proverbial "big one." The 6.8 Northridge earthquake that rocked LA in 1994 killed 57 people, with 1,500 more suffering serious injuries. It is believed that casualties would have been much greater had it struck in the middle of the day when the collapsed stores would have been filled with shoppers and the failed freeways crowded with cars. Twenty-two thousand people were forced to leave their homes (either permanently or while repairs were made) due to quake damage, and more than 3,000 buildings were declared unsafe for reentry. Yet, when you consider the millions of people who felt the quake that early morning, the number of people affected in more than a casual way was relatively small.

While only chance dictates who will be in the wrong place at the wrong time during a quake, there are precautions you can take to aid your survival in an earthquake. Here are some for you to consider.

IN YOUR HOME:
- Place your bed away from windows and bookshelves, and don't hang heavy objects above it.
- Heavy ceiling fans and lights should be supported with a cable that is bolted to the ceiling joist. The cable should have enough slack to allow it to sway.
- Be sure to store flashlights and batteries and a crowbar (in case your door gets jammed shut) in your bedroom.
- Store a disaster kit somewhere accessible. Local home improvement and specialty stores sell earthquake preparedness kits (see below).
- Heavy objects should always be placed on lower shelves.
- Use brackets to bolt bookshelves, file cabinets, and other heavy pieces of furniture to the walls. Be sure to connect brackets to wall studs.
- Brace chimneys (usually a professional will need to do this for you).
- Fasten down lamps and valuable objects, and use putty to hold breakables in place.
- Be sure your home is bolted to its foundation.
- Strap your water heater to the wall.
- Put latches on cabinet doors.
- Know where your water and gas valves are located, and how to shut them off.

IN YOUR CAR:
- Store the following: flashlight, batteries, portable battery-powered radio, first-aid kit, maps, food such as trail mix or non-melting energy bars, water, tools, and cash.

IN YOUR OFFICE:
- Store the following: a portable battery-powered radio, flashlight with spare batteries, and a first-aid kit. Most companies have emergency procedures in place to follow in the event of an emergency.

DISASTER KITS

Bottom line, if you live in LA, you should have a disaster kit ready. You may elect to purchase a prepared kit (see list of stores below) or do like most Angelenos, make your own. Any waterproof plastic container that's big enough to store all the items will do. The items on your list should be customized according to your specific needs, but generally, here is what the experts recommend:
- Portable radio and batteries
- Flashlights and batteries
- Candles and matches
- Medical and personal hygiene supplies
- Canned and/or dehydrated food
- Can opener
- Sleeping bags or blankets and sturdy shoes
- Three gallons of drinking water per person in your household
- Barbecue or camp stove
- Toiletries, including diapers for those with little ones
- Plastic sheeting and duct tape

Store your kit in a place that's easily accessible to the entire family. Don't forget to rotate your water and food every six months. And check that your batteries and first-aid supplies are still fresh.

Military supply surplus stores are a great resource for stocking a kit; turn to the Army and Navy Goods section of your Yellow Pages for a list of stores. Here are some mail order and walk-in stores that specialize in **disaster supplies**:
- **Grabbit Emergency Pack**, 310-471-8608, www.grabbit.com
- **Quake Kare Inc.**, 805-241-9898, www.quakekare.com
- **Recon-1**, 818-342-2666, www.recon-1.com
- **Safe-T-Proof Disaster Preparedness Co.**, 888-677-2338, www. Safe-T-Proof.com
- **SOS Survival Products**, 800-479-7998, www.sosproducts.com

FIRES, LANDSLIDES, AND FLOODS

While massive fires, landslides, and floods are seldom issues for people living in the most populated areas of Los Angeles, summer brush fires are a
normal occurrence in Southern California, especially in hilly canyon areas
where there is a good deal of vegetation. If you live in such an area (for
instance Malibu, Topanga Canyon, or other canyons), be sure to clear the
brush around your home before the summer dry season. Check with wild-
fire specialists on how to shield your home, especially in areas of high fire
danger. Expect to keep a clearing between your house and the surrounding forest, and having a metal roof is a good idea. The **Los Angeles City
and County Fire Departments**, www.lafd.org and www.lacofd.org
respectively, offer exhaustive tips for fire-proofing a home, as well as free
disaster preparedness handbooks.

Recently burned areas are especially vulnerable to landslides in the
rainy season, as the vegetation that normally holds the soil on the hillsides
has been burnt away. But fire sites are not the only places that landslides
occur. The sharp cliffs above the Pacific Coast Highway regularly slide during the rains, and slides are also common in all hilly neighborhoods.
Residents often use sandbags to shore up iffy areas, and tarps to cover pre-
carious hillsides. These same neighborhoods are particularly susceptible to
flooding. In particular, remote canyon roads may be inaccessible during
heavy rains, though not for longer than a few days.

WITH YEAR-ROUND GOOD WEATHER, IT'S NO WONDER THERE are so many things going on in Los Angeles. Scores of yearly events, including the popular Auto Show and the Home and Garden Expo, take place at the LA Convention Center alone. Museums and individual communities host their own events year round; keep an eye out for flyers and ads in the local publications for more happenings. The following is just a sample listing of annual festivities.

JANUARY

- **Auto Show**, 213-741-1151, www.lacclink.com; check out the latest models and concept cars at the LA Convention Center. Most of the new cars are open for viewing, touching, photographing, and dreaming.
- **Tournament of Roses Parade**, 626-449-7673, www.tournament ofroses.com; the January 1st parade travels along Orange Grove Boulevard in Pasadena. Folks typically camp out on the sidewalks the night before for the best views. You can also pay a nominal fee to see the floats up close after the parade—wear comfortable shoes, even though all the floats are parked nose to nose, you will walk the equivalent of two miles to view them all.
- **The Rose Bowl**, 626-449-7673, www.rosebowlstadium.com; this annual extravaganza hosts the champs of the Pac 10 as they duel with the champs of the Big 10.
- **Martin Luther King Jr. Awareness Day**, 323-290-4100, www. africanamericanla.com; a citywide celebration, featuring poetry, art, films, a gospel fest, and guest lecturers, culminating in the Kingdom Day Parade, 323-298-8777.

- **Marina del Rey Big Boat Show**, 310-645-5151, www.mdrboat show.com; boating and water sport enthusiasts head down to Burton Chace Park in Marina del Rey to check out the latest in aquatic equipment. Yes, it's now in January!

FEBRUARY

- **African-American History Month Celebrations**, 323-295-0521, www.africanamericanla.com; a citywide event featuring lectures, films, and performances.
- **Chinese New Year Celebrations**, 213-617-0396, www.chinatown la.com; 626-300-5933, www.lunarnewyearparade.com; punctuated by noisy firecrackers and lion dancing, a parade, street fair, and carnival are some of the celebrations to take place in Chinatown and San Gabriel Valley.
- **Mardi Gras Celebration**, 213-625-5045, www.cityofla.org/elp; on Fat Tuesday, head downtown to the El Pueblo de Los Angeles Historical Monument for a parade, costume contest, and general revelry.

MARCH

- **Annual Cherry Blossom Festival**, 888-527-2757, www.laparks.org; the City of LA and the West Los Angeles Japanese American Community Center team up to host this annual Japanese spring ritual of viewing blooming cherry trees at the Stoner Recreation Center in West LA.
- **Celebration of Cesar E. Chavez Day**, 213-624-3660; a parade, art exhibits, and speakers commemorate the Mexican-American farm laborer activist.
- **Environmental Education Fair**, 626-821-3222; a festival to increase environmental awareness held at the Arboretum of LA County.
- **LA Marathon**, 310-444-5544, www.lamarathon.com; nearly every community the marathon runs through throws a block party along the race route to cheer on the runners. A festival and fair are held downtown, which is the starting and finishing point of the race.

APRIL

- **Art Walk at the Brewery Art Colony**, www.breweryartwalk.com, is a biannual event at the world's largest art colony, in downtown LA. The public is invited to browse through local artists' loft studios and view their works. Held again in October.
- **Blessing of the Animals**, 213-625-5045, www.cityofla.org/elp; a Catholic priest will bless your feathered or furry friend at this centuries-

old ceremony at the El Pueblo de Los Angeles Historical Monument, downtown.

- **Brentwood, Pasadena Art Show**, 626-797-6803, www.delmano prod.com; art lovers flock to these annual shows in their respective neighborhoods to admire the works of local artisans.
- **Feria de los Ninos**, 888-527-2757, www.laparks.org; a Latin American festival featuring food, workshops, dances, and mariachi bands in Hollenbeck Park, Boyle Heights.
- **Fiesta Broadway**, 310-914-0015, www.fiestabroadwayla.net; this popular block party in downtown celebrates Latin American culture and bills itself as the largest Cinco de Mayo party in the world.
- **Los Angeles Times Festival of Books**, 213-237-6503, www.latimes.com; held the last weekend in April in Dickson Plaza on UCLA campus, this free festival attracts over 100,000 book lovers of all ages. Over 300 booths are set up by booksellers, publishers, and cultural organizations. Events include readings and signings by well-known and not-so-well-known authors and poets.
- **Thai New Year Festival**, 818-785-9552, www.watthaiusa.org; the Wat Thai Temple in North Hollywood is host to food booths, performances, ceremonies, and a beauty pageant. This popular festival is attended by Thais from all over California.

MAY

- **Affaire in the Gardens Fine Arts and Crafts Show**, 310-550-4796, www.beverlyhills.org; none of the typical costume jewelry or clothing is hawked during this fine weekend event held at the Beverly Gardens. Over 200 artists from around the country display fine art from sculpture to paintings for the discriminating art collector. The show takes place again in October.
- **Family Fun Fest**, 213-628-2725, www.jaccc.org; Little Tokyo's Japanese-American Cultural and Community Center hosts games, food and crafts booths, and other fun activities in honor of Children's Day.
- **Cinco de Mayo Celebration**, 213-625-5045, www.cityofla.org/elp; celebrate at the El Pueblo de Los Angeles Historical Monument in downtown.
- **Huntington Plant Sale**, 626-405-2141, www.huntington.org; every May, the Huntington Library, Art Collections, and Botanical Gardens has a parking lot sale of rare and unusual annuals and perennials, many propagated by seeds and cuttings from their botanical collections, a treat for beginning and experienced green-thumbers alike.
- **Museums of the Arroyo Festival**, 213-740-8687 www.museumsof thearroyo.com; five museums in Pasadena—The Gamble House,

Heritage Square Museum, The Lummis Home and Garden, Pasadena Museum of History, and Southwest Museum—offer free admission and shuttles between them for a day.

- **Los Angeles Fire Department Open House**, 213-485-5971, www.lafd.org; every year, on the Saturday before Mother's Day, city firehouses open their garages for visits by the public.
- **NoHo Theater & Arts Festival**, 818-763-5273, www.nohoarts district.com; North Hollywood's arts district, along Lankershim Boulevard in North Hollywood, celebrates with a weekend of music, food and crafts booths, and theatrical performances at area playhouses.
- **Santa Monica Festival**, 310-458-8350, http://arts.santa-monica.org; an impressive and eclectic selection of handmade arts and crafts booths, workshops, music, and food sponsored by the Santa Monica Cultural Affairs Division.
- **Renaissance Pleasure Faire**, www.renfair.com; starting in late May and running through June, this elaborate recreation of a medieval village takes place in the Glen Helen Regional Park in San Bernardino County. Many people attend in period costume to watch jousting matches, wander the crafts booths, and enjoy a stein of ale with fellow wenches, knights, and royalty.
- **UCLA Pow-wow**, 310-206-7513, www.studentgroups.ucla.edu/americanindian/powwowpage.htm; Native Americans and friends gather on the college campus to celebrate their heritage with song, dance, food, and displays.

JUNE

- **Annual Salute to Recreation Family Festival**, 888-527-2757, www.laparks.org; a weekend of carnival games, rides, and booths is capped off by an evening of fireworks.
- **Free Fishing Day**, 916-227-2245, www.dfg.ca.gov; no fishing license required to fish in California on two fishing days a year. Contact the Department of Fish and Game to find out the specific day in June (and September).
- **Gay and Lesbian Pride Parade and Celebration**, 323-860-0701, www.laglc.org; the West Hollywood portion of Santa Monica Boulevard is lined with bleachers for thousands of spectators of the gay and lesbian pride parade.
- **Irish Fair and Music Festival**, 818-501-3781, www.irishfair.org; the biggest Irish fair in the Western United States features bagpipes, Gaelic sports, and food.
- **Kids' Nature Festival**, 310-998-1151, www.childrensnatureinstitute. org; popular with young families, this annual event features face paint-

ing, storytelling, crafts, food, and animals. Held at Temescal Gateway Park in Pacific Palisades.

- **Playboy Jazz Festival**, 323-850-2000, www.hollywoodbowl.com; jazz aficionados flock to the Hollywood Bowl for performances by some of the top names in jazz.
- **Summer Solstice Folk Music, Dance, and Storytelling Festival**, 818-342-7664, www.ctmsfolkmusic.org; this is the country's largest folk festival, featuring workshops, concerts, and exhibits. Held at Soka University in the City of Calabasas.
- **San Fernando Valley Fair**, 818-557-1600, www.sfvalleyfair.org; held over a weekend at the Hansen Dam Sports Center, the rodeo is its main event, but the fair also features carnival rides, game booths, and gardening exhibits.

JULY

- **Fourth of July Celebrations**, 888-527-2757, www.laparks.org; citywide celebrations with fireworks displays from the Hollywood Bowl to Santa Monica. Contact the above number to locate the nearest fireworks show.
- **Hollywood Bowl Summer Festival**, 323-850-2000, www.hollywood bowl.com; the Hollywood Bowl begins its summer season each July (through mid-September), featuring varying orchestras and all genres of music from classical to pop. For many Angelenos, bringing a picnic dinner and heading to the bowl for an evening concert is an annual tradition.
- **Lotus Festival**, 888-527-2757, www.laparks.org; the largest lotus bed outside of China is located in Echo Park, which is a fitting host for a day filled with dragon-boat races, flower shows, and Pan-Asian food booths.
- **Malibu Arts Festival**, 310-456-9025, www.malibu.org/artfestival; over 100 artists display their wares at the city's civic center.
- **Shakespeare Festival**, 213-481-2273, www.shakespearefestival la.org; venues around the county pay homage to William Shakespeare by putting on professional productions of the bard's plays.

AUGUST

- **African Marketplace and Cultural Fair**, 323-734-1164, www. africanmarketplace.org; a festival filled with food and entertainment to celebrate African heritage.
- **Children's Festival of the Arts**, 323-871-ARTS, www.hollywood artscouncil.org; a wholesome event, held at Barnsdall Art Park in Los Feliz, filled with performances, food, and crafts for the entire family.

- **Los Angeles Greek Fest**, 323-737-2424, www.lagreekfest.com
- **Nisei Week**, 213-687-7193, www.niseiweek.org; Little Tokyo celebrates its culture with weeklong festivities including a parade, street fair, taiko drums and ondo street dancing.
- **Watts Towers Jazz and Arts Festivals**, 323-789-7304, www.watts festival.org; the Watts Towers Art Center plays host to a three-day event that includes a jazz festival, art exhibits, and fair booths.

SEPTEMBER

- **Los Angeles County Fair**, 909-623-3111, www.fairplex.com; this is billed as the world's largest county fair and is held on the Pomona Fairplex grounds.
- **Port of Los Angeles Lobster Festival**, 310-366-6472, www.lobster fest.com
- **Oktoberfest**, 310-327-4384, www.alpinevillage.net; bratwursts, a beer garden, and oompah bands—it must be the annual German celebration.

OCTOBER

- **Edwards Air Force Base Open House**, 661-277-3510, www. edwards.af.mil; annual open house and air show is an opportunity for the public to marvel at the best in aviation exhibits and flight demonstrations.
- **Los Angeles County Arts Open House**, 213-972-3099, www.la countyarts.org; in honor of the National Arts and Humanities month, the first Saturday of October features free admission to participating museums within LA County. This event is well attended, especially along Museum Row. Wilshire Boulevard, between Fairfax and Curson, is closed to cars, allowing the crowds to view outdoor performances.
- **Los Angeles Times Festival of Health and Fitness**, 800-350-3211, www.latimes.com; the campus of USC hosts a variety of exhibits to motivate healthy living.
- **Scandinavian Festival**, 323-661-4273, www.asfla.org; the American Scandinavian Foundation of Los Angeles organizes a Nordic costume parade, folk dancing, food, and entertainment.
- **West Hollywood's Halloween Carnival**, 323-848-6400, www.visit westhollywood.com; many might think of Halloween as a child's holiday, but in West Hollywood, adults claim it as their own. An estimated one million people, usually in elaborate costumes, jam Santa Monica Boulevard (west of La Cienega Boulevard) to strut their stuff.

NOVEMBER

- **AFI LA International Film Festival**, 323-856-7600, www.afi.com; screenings for one of the largest film festivals in the country, hosted by the American Film Institute, are held in theaters around Hollywood and Santa Monica.
- **Dia de los Muertos**, 213-625-5045, www.cityofla.org/elp; the Day of the Dead, a traditional Mexican festival to honor the departed, is observed at El Pueblo de Los Angeles Historical Monument, downtown.
- **Festival of Jewish Artisans**, 310-277-2772, www.templeisaiah.com; local and international artisans exhibit their wares. A concert and other activities are held for families.
- **Griffith Park Light Festival**, 888-527-2757, www.laparks.org; many families make a tradition of piling into the car for the free, mile-long display of holiday light scenes.
- **Harvest Festival**, 213-624-7300, www.lacclink.com; Angelenos head to the LA Convention Center to get a jump on holiday festivities and Christmas shopping among the hundreds of booths and vendors.
- **Hollywood Christmas Parade**, 323-469-8311, www.hollywood spectacular.com; the popular parade, held Thanksgiving weekend, is broadcast nationwide, but many Angelenos flock to Hollywood sidewalks with a thermos of hot chocolate to see it live.
- **Doo Dah Parade**, 626-449-3689, www.pasadenadoodahparade.com; fans of the irreverent or bizarre will want to check out this popular spoof of the Tournament of Roses Parade in downtown Pasadena.

DECEMBER

- **Burbank Mayor's Tree Lighting**, 818-238-5320, www.ci.burbank. ca.us; many residents of Burbank attend the mayor's tree lighting ceremony at city hall.
- **Los Angeles Harbor Holiday Afloat Parade**, 310-549-8111, www.sanpedro.com; go to the LA Maritime Museum or Ports O'Call to view decorated boats.
- **Kwanzaa Celebration**, 323-294-3229, www.lacvb.com; this Afro-centric holiday is celebrated with entertainment, crafts booths, and more in Leimert Park Village.
- **LA County Holiday Celebration**, 213-972-3099, www.lacounty arts.org; the Dorothy Chandler Pavilion is the site of annual holiday music and festivities.

- **Toluca Lake Open House**, 818-761-6594, www.tolucalakechamber. com; shops and restaurants along Riverside Drive in Toluca Lake stay open late the first Friday night of the month to offer free candy canes, cookies, and food samples. The neighborhood caroling truck also makes its rounds, adding to the charm of this holiday evening.
- **Santa Monica Open House**, 310-393-9825, http://santa-monica. org; similar to the Toluca Lake open house, but held on the first Saturday night of December, along Montana Avenue.

GENERAL NONFICTION

- ***Hollywood Dish! Recipes, Tips, & Tales of a Hollywood Caterer*** by Nick Grippo (Angel City Press); a unique combination of celebrity gossip and food from a local caterer to the stars.
- ***The Best of Only in LA***: ***A Chronicle of the Amazing, Amusing and Absurd*** by Steve Harvey (*LA Times*); a humorous collection of trivia and oddities that can only be found in Los Angeles.
- ***The California Cauldron***: ***Immigration and the Fortunes of Local Communities*** by William A.V. Clark (Guilford Press); in-depth study of immigration and how it's affecting California.
- ***How to Communicate with Your Spanish Speaking Help and Friends*** by Liora A. Cohen (Cohen Communications); English-Spanish guidebook for frequently used phrases in cooking, cleaning, childcare, and gardening.
- ***L.A. Unconventional*** by Cecilia Rasmussen (*LA Times*); collection of anecdotes about the offbeat characters found in LA.
- ***The Reluctant Metropolis***: ***The Politics of Urban Growth in Los Angeles*** by William Fulton (John Hopkins University Press); examination of the urban planning and politics that shaped LA into what it is today.

ARTS AND ARCHITECTURE

- ***Above Los Angeles, Revised Edition*** by Robert W. Cameron (Cameron & Co.); incredible aerial views of the city.
- ***An Architectural Guidebook to Los Angeles*** by David Gebhard, Robert Winter (Gibbs Smith Publishers); local architecture by notable architects.

- *Imagining Los Angeles*: *Photographs of a 20th Century City* published by the *Los Angeles Times*; beautiful photo-diary of the city's evolution over the last 100 years.

GUIDES

- *101 Hikes in Southern California*: *Exploring Mountains, Seashore and Desert* by Jerry Schad (Wilderness Press); a collection of the best hikes from Los Angeles to San Diego.
- *An Actor's Guide*: *Your First Year in Hollywood* by Michael Saint Nicholas (Allworth Press); advice and tips for newcomers who seek a career on the big screen.
- *Counter Intelligence*: *Where to Eat in the Real Los Angeles* by Jonathan Gold (LA Weekly Books); deliciously detailed guide to the savory options in town, written by the former restaurant reviewer of the *LA Weekly*.
- *Free L.A. The Ultimate Guide to the City of Angels* by Robert Stock, et al. (Corleyguide); fun stuff to do without opening your wallet.
- *Hollywood Creative Directory* by Hollywood Creative Directory Staff; published four times a year, this is the best listing of production companies and contact information that anyone looking to break into Hollywood needs.
- *Los Angeles A to Z*: *An Encyclopedia of the City and County* by Leonard Pitt, Dale Pitt (University of California Press); devoted to unique facts about the land, its people, and history.
- *On the Trail - Malibu to Santa Barbara* by Cathy Philipp (Cathy Philipp Publishing)
- *Rommelmann's Los Angeles Bar & Nightlife Guide* by Nancy Rommelmann (St. Martin's Press)
- *Thomas Guide Los Angeles County; Los Angeles County/Orange County;* and *Los Angeles County/Ventura County* by Rand McNally, Thomas Brothers; a necessary car accessory for getting around this city's sprawling roads.

FICTION

- *Another City: Writing from Los Angeles* by David L. Ulin (City Light Publishers); collected musings of local short story and essay writers.
- *The Assistants*: *A Novel* by Robin Lynn Williams (Regan Books); five different personalities struggle to stick their proverbial foot in tinsel town's doorway.
- *Hollywood Wives: The New Generation* by Jackie Collins (Simon & Schuster); juicy page-turning frolic amid power, sex, money, and fame.

- ***Kill the Messenger*** by Tami Hoag (Bantam); thriller set in Los Angeles.
- ***L.A. Confidential*** by James Ellroy (Mysterious Press); 1950's noir crime tale that was made into a movie in 1997.
- ***Less Than Zero*** by Bret Easton Ellis (Vintage); cautionary 1980s tale of rich young adults on a cocaine-laden, too fast trip to nowhere.
- ***Little Scarlet: An Easy Rawlins Mystery*** by Walter Mosley (Little Brown); shortly after the 1965 Watts Riots, a murder investigation threatens to fuel racial tensions further.
- ***The Pleasure of My Company*** by Steve Martin (Hyperion); the Saturday Night Live comedian and actor pens a delicious novella about a Santa Monica resident with Obsessive Compulsive Disorder.
- ***A Year in Van Nuys*** by Sandra Tsing Loh (Crown Publishing Group); struggling thirty-something writer toils in the Valley.

C ALL 911 FOR ALL POLICE, FIRE AND AMBULANCE EMERGENCIES. For 24-hour general information regarding county-wide public assistance, from shelters to food programs, call the **INFO Line of Los Angeles**: 800-339-6993, or go to www.la.infoline.org. The City of LA also has a **24-hour information line** for city services: 213-978-3231 (or 311—works only within city limits); online, go to www.lacity.org.

ALCOHOL AND DRUG DEPENDENCY

- **Alcoholics Anonymous**, 323-936-4363, www.lacoaa.org
- **Alcohol Abuse 24-hour Hotline**, 800-888-9383
- **Cocaine Abuse 24-hour Information and Treatment**, 800-274-2042
- **LA County Alcohol/Drug Helpline**, 800-564-6600
- **Narcotics Anonymous**, 818-773-9999, www.na.org
- **National Alcohol and Drug Abuse Hotline**, 800-252-6465
- **The Watershed**, an Alcohol and Drug Treatment Program 24-hour Hotline, 800-711-6402

ANIMALS

- **Animal Regulations Department & Shelters, City of Los Angeles**, 888-452-7381, www.cityofla.org
- **Dead Animal Pick-up**, 800-773-2489
- **Los Angeles County Animal Care & Control**, Downey Shelter, 562-940-6898, http://animalcontrol.co.la.ca.us

- **Los Angeles County Animal Care & Control**, Carson Shelter, 310-523-5966, http://animalcontrol.co.la.ca.us
- **Santa Monica Police Department Animal Control Division**, 310-458-8594
- **Society for the Prevention of Cruelty to Animals**, 323-730-5300, www.laspca.com

AUTOMOBILES

- **Automotive Repair Bureau, Department of Consumer Affairs**, 800-952-5210, www.dca.ca.gov
- **California Department of Motor Vehicles**, 800-777-0133, www.dmv.ca.gov

PARKING CITATIONS
- **Beverly Hills**, 800-752-1195, www.beverlyhills.org
- **Burbank**, 818-238-3120, www.ci.burbank.ca.us/police/parking_enforcement.htm
- **Glendale**, 818-548-3132, http://police.ci.glendale.ca.us
- **Irvine**, 949-724-7000 www.irvinepd.org
- **Los Angeles City**, 213-623-6533, 310-569-5561, 818-901-7027, www.lacity-parking.org
- **Los Angeles County Sheriff**, 323-526-5541, www.lasd.org
- **Newport Beach**, 949-644-3141, www.city.newport-beach.ca.us
- **Pasadena**, 626-744-6440, www.ci.pasadena.ca.us
- **Santa Monica**, 800-214-1526, http://santamonicapd.org/information/ticket.htm
- **Tustin**, 714-573-3200, www.tustinpd.org
- **West Hollywood**, 800-687-2458, www.weho.org

PARKING PERMITS
- **Beverly Hills**, 310-285-2551, www.beverlyhills.org
- **Burbank**, 818-238-3915, www.ci.burbank.ca.us
- **Glendale**, 818-548-3960, www.ci.glendale.ca.us
- **Irvine**, 949-724-6313, www.ci.irvine.ca.us
- **Los Angeles**, 323-913-4600, 310-843-5936, www.lacity-parking.org
- **Newport Beach**, 949-644-3121, www.city.newport-beach.ca.us
- **Pasadena**, 626-744-6440, www.ci.pasadena.ca.us
- **Santa Monica**, 310-458-8291, www.santa-monica.org
- **Tustin**, 714-573-3150, www.tustinca.org
- **West Hollywood**, 323-848-6392, www.weho.org

BIRTH AND DEATH CERTIFICATES

- **Los Angeles County Clerk**, 800-815-2666, http://regrec.co.la.ca.us/main.htm
- **Orange County Clerk**, 714-834-2500, www.oc.ca.gov/recorder

CONSUMER COMPLAINTS AND SERVICES

- **Better Business Bureau**, 818-386-5510, www.bbb.org
- **California Public Utilities Commission Consumer Affairs**, 800-649-7570, www.cpuc.ca.gov
- **City Ethics Commission Complaint Hotline**, 800-439-4666
- **Los Angeles Consumer Affairs Department**, 213-974-1452
- **State Bar of California Attorney Complaint Hotline**, 800-843-9053
- **State of California Consumer Affairs Department**, 800-952-5210, www.dca.ca.gov
- **US Consumer Product Safety Commission**, 800-638-2772, www.cpsc.gov

COUNTY OFFICES

LOS ANGELES COUNTY
- **Animal Care and Control**, 562-728-4882, http://animalcontrol.co.la.ca.us
- **Department of Beaches and Harbor**, 310-305-9546, http://beaches.co.la.ca.us
- **Department of Health Services**, 800-427-8700, www.dhs.co.la.ca.us/hospitals
- **Department of Parks and Recreation**, 213-738-2961, http://parks.co.la.ca.us
- **High Desert Health System**, 44900 North 60th Street West, Lancaster, 661-948-8581
- **Housing, Community Development Commission**, 323-890-7281, www.lacdc.org
- **INFO Line of Los Angeles**, 800-339-6993, www.la.infoline.org
- **LA County/USC Medical Center**, 1200 North State Street, Los Angeles, 323-226-2622
- **Library**, 562-940-8415, www.colapublic.org

- **Los Angeles County Government**, 213-974-1234, http://lacounty.info
- **Martin Luther King/Drew Medical Center**, 12021 South Wilmington Avenue, Los Angeles, 310-668-4321, www.ladhs.org/mlk
- **Office of Assessor**, 213-974-3211, 888-807-2111, http://assessor.co.la.ca.us
- **Office of Education (LACOE)**, 562-922-6111, www.lacoe.edu
- **Olive View Medical Center**, 1445 Olive View Drive, Sylmar, 818-364-1555
- **Parks and Recreation**, 213-738-2961, http://parks.co.la.ca.us
- **Police Department**, 323-526-5541, www.lapdonline.org
- **Public Defender**, 213-974-2811, http://pd.co.la.ca.us
- **Public Works, Department of Recycling and Household Hazardous Waste Program**, 888-253-2652, www.ladpw.org or www.888cleanla.com
- **Registrar-Recorder/County Clerk**, 562-462-2137, http://lavote.net
- **Sanitation District of Los Angeles County**, 323-685-5217, www.lacsd.org
- **Sheriff**, 323-267-3435, www.lasd.org
- **Transportation, Department of (LADOT)**, 818/213/310-808-2273, www.ladottransit.com
- **Treasurer-Tax Collector**, 213-974-2101, http://ttax.co.la.ca.us
- **UCLA Medical Center**, 100 West Carson Street, Torrance, 310-222-2345, www.humc.edu

ORANGE COUNTY
- **Animal Care Services**, 714-935-6943, www.ocpetinfo.com
- **Children's Hospital of Orange County**, 455 South Main Street, Orange, 714-997-3000, www.chochospital.org
- **Department of Education**, 714-966-4000, www.ocde.k12.ca.us
- **Harbors, Beaches, and Parks Division**, 866-OCPARKS, www.ocparks.com
- **Housing and Community Services Department**, 714-480-2900, www.oc.ca.gov/housing
- **Integrated Waste Management Department** (and Recycling), 714-834-4000, www.oclandfills.com
- **Library**, 714-556-3000, www.ocpl.org
- **Orange County Government**, 714-834-5400, www.oc.ca.gov
- **Orange County Health Care Agency**, 714-834-4722, ww.oc.ca.gov/hca/medical/ems/hospitals.htm
- **Police**, 714-744-7444, www.cityoforange.org/depts/police/contacts.asp
- **Registrar of Voters**, 714-567-7600, www.oc.ca.gov/election

- **Resources and Development Management Department/ Harbors, Beaches, and Parks Division**, 714-973-6865, www.oc parks.com
- **Sheriff**, 714-647-7000, www.ocsd.org
- **Transportation Authority (OCTA)**, 714-636-7433 or www.octa.net
- **Treasurer-Tax Collector**, 714-834-3411, http://tax.ocgov.com/treas/index.asp

RIVERSIDE COUNTY
- **Animal Control**, 909-358-7387, www.riversideshelter.com
- **Department of Public Health**, 909-358-5000, www.rivcoph.org
- **Housing Authority**, 951-351-0700, www.harivco.org
- **Library**, 909-685-8121, www.riverside.lib.ca.us
- **Office of Education**, 951-826-6530, www.rcoe.k12.ca.us
- **Parks and Open Space District**, 909-955-4310, www.riverside countyparks.org
- **Police Department**, 9009-787-7911, www.ci.riverside.ca.us/rpd
- **Recycling, Waste Management Department**, 951-486-3200, www.rivcowm.org
- **Registrar-Recorder/County Clerk**, 951-486-7000, http://riverside.asrclkrec.com/
- **Riverside Community Hospital**, 4445 Magnolia Avenue, Riverside, 951-788-3000, www.rchc.org
- **Riverside County Government**, 951-955-1000, www.co.riverside.ca.us
- **Riverside County Regional Medical Center**, 26520 Cactus, Moreno Valley, 951-486-4000, www.rcrmc.org
- **Sanitation, Local Solid Waste Management**, 951-955-8982, www.rivcoeh.org/lea.htm
- **Sheriff**, 951-955-2400, www.riversidesheriff.org
- **Transportation Department**, 951-955-6880, www.tlma.co.river side.ca.us/trans
- **Treasurer-Tax Collector**, 951-955-3900, www.treasurer-tax.co.river side.ca.us

SAN DIEGO COUNTY
- **Animal Services**, 619-236-4250, www.sddac.com
- **County Clerk**, 619-238-8158, www.sdcounty.ca.gov/arcc
- **Department of Beaches**, 619-221-8901, www.sdcounty.ca.gov/deh/lwq/beachbay
- **Department of Parks and Recreation**, 858-694-3049, www.sd county.ca.gov/parks

- **Health and Human Services Agency**, 619-230-0997 or 800-227-0997, www2.sdcounty.ca.gov/hhsa
- **Housing and Community Development**, 858-694-4801, www.sdcounty.ca.gov/sdhcd
- **Library**, 858 694-2414, www.sdcl.org
- **Metropolitan Transit System,** 619-238-0100, www.sdcommute.com
- **Office of Education**, 858-292-3500, www.sdcoe.k12.ca.us
- **Police Department**, 619-531-2000, www.sannet.gov/police
- **Recycling and Household Hazardous Waste**, 858-694-2212, www.sdcounty.ca.gov/dpw/management/recycling.htm
- **Registrar of Voters**, 858-565-5800, www.sdvote.com
- **San Diego County Government**, 858-694-3900, www.co.san-diego.ca.us
- **Sheriff**, 858-565-5200, www.sdsheriff.net
- **Trash, Environmental Services**, 858-694-7000, http://econtainer.sandiego.gov
- **Treasurer-Tax Collector,** 619-236-2424, www.sdtreastax.com

VENTURA COUNTY

- **Animal Care & Control**, 805-388-4341, www.ventura.org/animreg/main_shelter.html
- **Department of Harbor**, 805-382-3001, http://harbor.countyofventura.org
- **Department of Parks**, 805-654-3951, www.ventura.org/gsa/parks
- **Environmental and Energy Resources Department (Recycling)**, 805-289-3333, www.wasteless.org
- **Health Care Agency**, 805-677-5110, www.vchca.org
- **Housing Authority**, 805-480-9991, www.ahacv.org
- **Library**, 805-477-73331, www.vencolibrary.org
- **Police Department**, 805-339-4400, www.ci.ventura.ca.us/depts/pd/pdhome.shtm
- **Registrar-Recorder/County Clerk**, 805-654-2263, www.ventura.org/recorder/venclrk.htm
- **Sanitation Services Division**, 805-584-4829, http://publicworks.countyofventura.org
- **Sheriff**, 805-654-2311, www.vcsd.org
- **Superintendent of Schools**, 805-383-1900, www.vcss.k12.ca.us
- **Transportation Commission**, 805-642-1591, www.goventura.org
- **Treasurer-Tax Collector**, 805-654-3744, www.ventura.org/taxcollector
- **Ventura County Government**, 805-654-5000, www.countyofventura.org

- **Ventura County Medical Center**, 3291 Loma Vista Road, Ventura, 805-652-6000, www.vchca.org/mc

CRIME/CRISIS

- **Crime in Progress**, 911
- **Crime Prevention**, Santa Monica, 310-458-8473
- **Crime Victims Assistance**, 800-777-9229, www.boc.ca.gov
- **County Central Fraud Reporting Line**, 800-87-FRAUD
- **Criminal Fraud Reporting**, 800-78-CRIME, www.wetip.com

CHILD ABUSE AND FAMILY VIOLENCE

- **Abducted, Abused, and Exploited Children**, 800-248-8020
- **Childhelp USA**, 800-422-4453
- **Domestic Violence Hotline**, 800- 548-2722
- **Elder Abuse Hotline**, 800-992-1660
- **Sojourn Services for Battered Women**, 310-264-6644
- **Victims of Crime Resource Center**, 800-842-8467
- **YWCA Battered Women's Helpline**, 626-967-0658, www.ywca wings.org

CRISIS HOTLINES/RAPE AND SEXUAL ASSAULT

- **Boys Town National Hotline**, 800-448-3000
- **LA Rape and Battery Hotline**, 213-626-3393, 626-793-3385
- **Los Angeles County District Attorney Victim-Witness Assistance Program**, 800-380-3811
- **Los Angeles County Rape and Battering Hotline**, 310-392-8381, www.lacaaw.org
- **Rape Treatment Center, Santa Monica-UCLA Medical Center**, 310-319-4000, www.911rape.org
- **Sojourn Services for Battered Women**, 310-264-6644, www.opcc.net/sojourn
- **Suicide Prevention Center**, 877-727-4747
- **Suicide Prevention**, 310-391-1253
- **Youth Crisis Hotline**, 800-448-4663

DISCRIMINATION

- **California Fair Employment and Housing Department**, 800-884-1684, www.dfeh.ca.gov
- **Los Angeles County Commission on Disabilities**, 213-974-1053
- **Gay and Lesbian Alliance Against Defamation**, 323-933-2240, www.glaad.org
- **US Department of Fair Housing and Discrimination**, 800-233-3212
- **Women's Commission for Los Angeles County**, 213-974-1455

ELECTED OFFICIALS AND GOVERNMENT

- **California Governor's Office**, 916-445-2841, www.governor.ca.gov
- **City of Los Angeles Mayor's Office**, 213-978-0600, www.cityof la.org
- **Federal Citizen Information Center**, 800-688-9889
- **LA County Board of Supervisors**, 213-974-7207, http://la county.info

EMERGENCY

- **Police**, **Fire**, **Medical**, 911
- **American Red Cross Emergency Services**, 800-540-2000
- **City of LA Storm Water Hotline**, 800-974-9794
- **Earthquake Recovery-Debris Pick-up**, 800-773-2489, www.la city.org/SAN
- **LA County Office of Emergency Management**, 323-980-2260

ENTERTAINMENT

- **Audiences Unlimited**, 818-506-0067, www.tvtickets.com
- **City of Los Angeles Cultural Affairs Department**, 213-473-7700, www.culturela.org or www.lacountyarts.com
- **Ticketmaster** 213-480-3232, 213-365-3500 (fine arts line) www.ticket master.com
- **Tickets Los Angeles**, 323-655-8587
- **TV Tix**, 323-653-4105, www.tvtix.com

HEALTH AND MEDICAL CARE

- **AIDS Healthcare Foundation**, 213-741-9727, www.aidshealth.org
- **California Smokers Helpline**, 800-766-2888
- **Healthy Families Information Line**, 888-747-1222
- **Los Angeles County Health Services Department**, 800-427-8700, http://lacounty.info
- **Los Angeles County Mental Health Services**, 800-854-7771, http://lacounty.info
- **Los Angeles County Sexually Transmitted Disease Hotline**, 800-758-8080, http://phps.dhs.co.la.ca.us/std
- **Los Angeles Urban Search and Rescue–Fire Department**, 818-756-9677
- **Medi-Cal Information**, 877-597-4777
- **Minority AIDS Project**, 323-936-4949
- **National Health Information Center**, 800-336-4797, www.health.gov/nhic
- **Nursing Home Information and Referral**, 800-427-8700
- **Poison Control Center**, 800-876-4766, www.calpoison.org
- **South Coast Air Quality Management**, 800-CUT-SMOG, www.aqmd.gov

HOUSING

- **Assisted Housing Authority**, 323-260-2617
- **California Fair Employment and Housing Department**, 800-233-3212
- **Contractor's State License Board**, 800-321-2752, www.cslb.ca.gov
- **City of LA Housing Department**, 800-994-4444, www.cityofla.org
- **Culver City Housing Division**, 310-253-5780
- **Fair Housing Congress of Southern California**, 213-365-7184
- **Fair Housing Council of San Fernando Valley**, 818-373-1185
- **Fair Housing Council, Westside**, 310-477-9260
- **Fair Housing Hotline California**, 800-233-3212, www.dfeh.ca.gov
- **Fair Housing, Santa Clarita**, 818-373-1185
- **Fair Housing, Santa Monica**, 310-458-8336
- **Homeowners and Renters Assistance, Franchise Tax Board**, 800-852-5711, www.ftb.ca.gov
- **HUD Fair Housing Information**, 800-767-7468

- **US Department of Fair Housing and Discrimination**, 800-669-9777

LEGAL REFERRAL

- **American Civil Liberties Union of Southern California**, 213-977-9500, www.aclu-sc.org
- **Asian Pacific American Legal Center of Southern California**, 213-977-7500, www.apalc.org
- **Bet Tzedek Legal Services**, 323-939-0506, www.bettzedek.org
- **Legal Aid Foundation of Los Angeles**, 213-640-3883
- **Los Angeles County Bar Association Referrals**, 213-243-1525
- **Los Angeles Gay and Lesbian Center Legal Services Department**, 323-993-7670
- **Police Misconduct Attorney Referral Service**, 213-387-3325
- **Public Defender Information Line**, 213-974-2811, http://pd.co.la.ca.us
- **San Fernando Valley Neighborhood Legal Services**, 800-433-6251

LIBRARIES

See also **Libraries** in **Cultural Life**, and end-listings in the **Neighborhood Profiles**.
- **Los Angeles Central Library**, 213-228-7000, www.lapl.org
- **Orange County Public Library**, 714-566-3000, www.ocpl.org

MARRIAGE LICENSES

- **LA County Marriage License and Ceremony Information**, 562-462-2137, http://lavote.net/recorder/birth_death.htm
- **Orange County Marriage License Information**, 714-834-2500, www.oc.ca.gov/recorder

MUNICIPALITIES

- **Beverly Hills**, 310-285-1000, www.ci.beverly-hills.ca.us
- **Burbank**, 818-238-5850, www.ci.burbank.ca.us
- **City of Bellflower**, 562-804-1424, www.bellflower.org

- **City of Downey**, 562-904-7246, www.downeyca.org
- **City of La Mirada**, 562-943-0131, www.cityoflamirada.org
- **City of Norwalk**, 562-929-5700, www.ci.norwalk.ca.us
- **Culver City**, 310-253-6000, www.ci.culver-city.ca.us
- **Glendale**, 818-548-2090, www.ci.glendale.ca.us
- **Lakewood City Information Line**, 562-925-4357, www.lakewood-city.org
- **Long Beach**, 562-570-6101, www.ci.long-beach.ca.us
- **Los Angeles**, 213-978-3231, www.cityofla.org
- **Malibu**, 310-456-2489, www.ci.malibu.ca.us
- **Pasadena**, 626-744-4000, www.ci.pasadena.ca.us
- **Santa Clarita**, 661-259-2489, www.santa-clarita.com
- **Santa Monica**, 310-458-8411, www.ci.santa-monica.ca.us
- **South Pasadena**, 626-403-7200, www.ci.south-pasadena.ca.us
- **West Hollywood**, 323-848-6400, www.ci.west-hollywood.ca.us
- **Irvine**, 949-724-6000, www.ci.irvine.ca.us
- **Tustin**, 714-573-3000, www.tustinca.org
- **Newport Beach**, 949-644-3309, www.city.newport-beach.ca.us

PARKS AND RECREATION DEPARTMENTS

Please refer to **Sports and Recreation** chapter for a full listing of area parks and recreation departments.

POLICE

- **Central Bureau Operations**, 213-485-3101
- **LA County Sheriff**, 323-526-5541, www.www.la-sheriff.org
- **Los Angeles Police Department Divisions**, www.lapdonline.org
- **South Bureau Operations**, 213-626-4251
- **Valley Bureau Operations**, 818-756-8303
- **West Bureau Operations**, 213-473-0277
- **Orange County Sheriff**, 714-647-7000, www.ocsd.org

POST OFFICE

For a list of Post Offices with extended hours, see **Mail Receiving and Delivery** in the **Helpful Services** chapter.
- **US Postal Service**, 800-275-8777, www.usps.com

SANITATION AND GARBAGE

- **LA County Sanitation District**, 323-685-5217, http://lacounty.info
- **LA County Recycling and Hazardous Waste**, 888-CLEANLA, http://ladpw.org/epd
- **Orange County Sanitation District**, 714-962-2411, www.ocsd.com
- **Orange County Integrated Waste Management** (recycling), 714-834-4000, www.oclandfills.com

SCHOOLS

See **School Districts** in the **Childcare and Education** chapter for listings of LA County and Orange County schools.
- **LA County Office of Education**, 562-922-6111, www.lacoe.edu
- **LA School District Boundaries**, 213-241-4500, http://lausd.k12.ca.us
- **LA Unified Parent Resource Network Hotline**, 800-933-8133, www.lausd.k12.ca.us
- **LA Unified School District**, 213-241-1000, www.lausd.k12.ca.us
- **Orange County Department of Education**, 714-966-4000, www.ocde.k12.ca.us

SENIORS

- **Alternative Living for the Aging**, 323-650-7988
- **City of LA Department on Aging, Senior Services Referral**, 213-368-4030, www.cityofla.org/doa
- **Elder Abuse Hotline**, 800-992-1660
- **Elder Care Locator**, 800-677-1116
- **Jewish Family Service of Los Angeles**, 323-761-8800, www.jfsla.org
- **Long-Term Care Ombudsman, California**, 916-323-6681, www.aging.com
- **LA County Area Agency on Aging**, 800-510-2020
- **LA County Community and Senior Citizens Services**, 213-738-2600, http://dcss.co.la.ca.us
- **National Council on the Aging**, 626-791-5010, www.ncoa.org
- **Social Security and Medicare Eligibility Information**, 800-772-1213, www.ssa.gov

SHIPPING

- **DHL**, 800-247-2676, www.dhl.com
- **FedEx**, 800-463-3339, www.fedex.com
- **UPS**, 800-742-5877, www.ups.com
- **US Postal Service**, 800-275-8777, www.usps.com

SPORTS

- **Angels**, 888-796-4256, www.angelsbaseball.com
- **Cal State Fullerton**, 714-278-CSUF, www.fullerton.edu
- **Long Beach State**, 310-985-4111, www.csulb.edu
- **Los Angeles Avengers**, 888-AVENGERS, www.laavengers.com
- **Los Angeles Clippers**, 213-742-7555, www.nba.com/clippers
- **Los Angeles Dodgers**, 323-224-1448, www.dodgers.com
- **Los Angeles Kings**, 877-522-8669, www.lakings.com
- **Los Angeles Lakers**, 800-4-NBA-TIXS, www.nba.com/lakers
- **Los Angeles Sparks**, 877-44-SPARKS, www.wnba.com/sparks
- **Loyola Marymount**, 310-338-6095, www.lmu.edu
- **Pepperdine**, 866-WAVE-TIX, www.pepperdine.edu
- **UCLA Bruins**, 310-825-2101, www.uclalive.com
- **UCLA**, 310-825-2101, www.ucla.edu
- **USC Trojans**, 213-740-4072, www.usctrojans.com

STATE GOVERNMENT

- **California Legislative Information**, www.leginfo.ca.gov
- **California State Senate**, 916-445-1353, www.sen.ca.gov
- **California State Assembly**, 916-319-2042, www.assembly.ca.gov
- **Governor's Office**, 916-445-2841 or 213-897-0322, www.governor.ca.gov/
- **Senate Office of Research**, 916-445-1727, www.sen.ca.gov/sor/
- **State of California**, 916-657-9900, www.ca.gov
- **US House of Representatives**, 202-224-3121, www.house.gov

STREET MAINTENANCE

- **Caltrans Highway Information Network**, 800-427-7623
- **City of LA Streetlight Repair**, 800-303-5267

- **LA County Road Maintenance**, 323-776-7552
- **Pot holes, sidewalk repair**, 800-675-4357, http://ladpw.org/general/dpwrequest
- **Traffic signals, sign repair, LA County**, 800-675-4357

TAXES

- **Internal Revenue Service**, 800-829-4477, www.irs.gov
- **LA County Treasurer-Property Tax**, 213-974-2111, http://lacounty.info
- **State Franchise Tax Board**, 800-852-5711, www.ftb.ca.gov

TELEPHONE

- **AT&T**, 800-222-0300, www.att.com
- **GTC Telecom**, 800-486-4030, www.gtctelecom.net
- **IDT**, 800-889-9126, www.idt.net
- **MCI**, 800-444-3333, www.mci.com
- **Sprint**, 800-877-4646, www.sprint.com
- **Verizon**, 800-870-9999, www.verizon.com
- **Working Assets**, 800-362-7127, www.workingforchange.com

TIME

- From any area code, dial 853-1212

TOURISM AND TRAVEL

- **California State Parks and Recreation**, 800-777-0369, www.cal-parks.ca.gov
- **California Travel and Tourism Commission**, 310-854-7616, www.visitcalifornia.com, http://visitcwc.com/losangeles
- **INFO Line of Los Angeles**, 800-339-6993
- **Los Angeles Convention and Visitors Bureau**, 213-624-7300, www.seemyla.org

TRANSPORTATION

- **Cal Trans Highway Conditions**, 800-427-7623, www.dot.ca.gov

- **City of LA Department of Transportation** (**LADOT**), 818/213/ 323/310-808-2273, www.ladottransit.com
- **Commuter Transportation Services** (carpools), 800-266-6883
- **LA County Metropolitan Transportation Authority** (**Metro**), 800-COMMUTE, 213-922-6235, www.mta.net
- **Smart Traveler Information**, www.smart-traveler.info

AIRPORTS
- **Bob Hope Airport** (formerly Burbank Airport), 818-840-8840, www.burbankairport.com
- **Long Beach Airport**, 562-570-2600, www.lgb.org
- **Los Angeles International Airport** (**LAX**), 310-646-5252, www. lawa.org
- **Ontario International Airport**, www.lawa.org/ont
- **Orange County's John Wayne Airport**, 949-252-5200, www.ocair. com

NATIONAL TRAIN AND BUS SERVICE
- **Amtrak**, 800-872-7245, www.amtrak.com
- **Greyhound**, 800-229-9424, www.greyhound.com

UTILITY EMERGENCIES

- **Castaic Lake Water Agency**, 259-2737, www.clwa.org
- **City of LA City Storm Water Hotline**, 800-974-9794
- **LA County Water District**, 310-456-6621, www.ladpw.org
- **LA County Waterworks and Sewer**, 626-458-4357, www.la dpw.org
- **Los Angeles Department of Water and Power**, 800-342-5397, www.ladwp.com; Electric Trouble, 800-821-5279; Water Trouble, 800-499-4611
- **Southern California Gas Company**, 800-427-2200, www.socal gas.com
- **Southern California Water Company**, 310-838-2143
- **Underground Service Alert**, 800-227-2600

VOTING

- **California Voter Registration Hotline**, 800-345-8683
- **LA County Clerk's** directory is at www.lausd.k12.ca.us/district_directory

JOAN WAI is a Southern California native and has resided in the Los Angeles area since 1987. Her favorite Los Angeles pastimes include browsing ethnic supermarkets and farmers' markets, getting into free sneak previews of feature films, and people watching at The Grove. When not sitting in traffic, she works as a freelance writer and screenwriter. Her articles have appeared in print and on the web. Joan is also the author of *100+ Wedding Games: Fun & Laughs for Bachelorette Parties, Showers, & Receptions*.

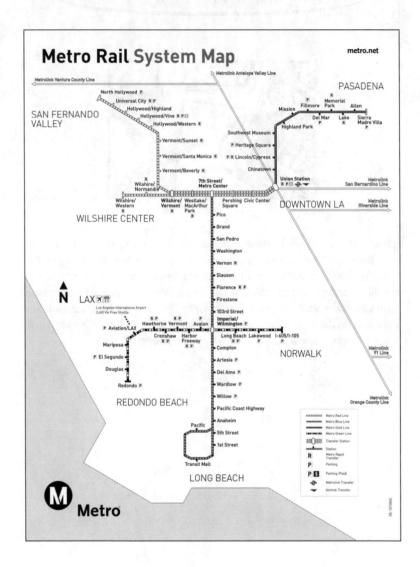

Metro Rail System Map

metro.net

THE ORIGINAL, ALWAYS UPDATED, ABSOLUTELY INVALUABLE GUIDES FOR PEOPLE MOVING TO A CITY!

Find out about neighborhoods, apartment and house hunting, money matters, deposits/leases, getting settled, helpful services, shopping for the home, places of worship, cultural life, sports/recreation, volunteering, green space, schools and education, transportation, temporary lodgings and useful telephone numbers!

	# COPIES	TOTAL
Newcomer's Handbook* for Atlanta	_____ x $21.95	$_____
Newcomer's Handbook* for Boston	_____ x $23.95	$_____
Newcomer's Handbook* for Chicago	_____ x $21.95	$_____
Newcomer's Handbook* for London	_____ x $20.95	$_____
Newcomer's Handbook* for Los Angeles	_____ x $23.95	$_____
Newcomer's Handbook* for Minneapolis-St. Paul	_____ x $20.95	$_____
Newcomer's Handbook* for New York City	_____ x $22.95	$_____
Newcomer's Handbook* for San Francisco	_____ x $23.95	$_____
Newcomer's Handbook* for Seattle	_____ x $21.95	$_____
Newcomer's Handbook* for the USA	_____ x $23.95	$_____
Newcomer's Handbook* for Washington D.C.	_____ x $23.95	$_____
The Moving Book: A Kids' Survival Guide	_____ x $20.95	$_____
The Pet-Moving Handbook	_____ x $ 9.95	$_____
	SUBTOTAL	$_____
POSTAGE & HANDLING (*$7.00 first book, $1.00 each add'l.*)		$_____
	TOTAL	$_____

SHIP TO:

Name _____

Title _____

Company _____

Address _____

City _____ State _____ Zip _____

Phone Number (   ) _____

E-mail _____

Send this order form and a check or money order payable to:
First Books
6750 SW Franklin, Suite A, Portland, OR 97223-2542

Allow 1-2 weeks for delivery

www.firstbooks.com

We would appreciate your comments regarding this third edition of the *Newcomer's Handbook* for Moving to and Living in Los Angeles. If you've found any mistakes or omissions or if you would just like to express your opinion about the guide, please let us know. We will consider any suggestions for possible inclusion in our next edition, and if we use your comments, we'll send you a *free* copy of our next edition. Please send this response form to:

Reader Response Department
First Books
6750 SW Franklin, Suite A
Portland, OR 97223-2542
USA

Comments:

_____

_____

_____

_____

_____

_____

Name: _____

Address _____

_____

_____

Telephone (   ) _____

E-mail _____

6750 SW Franklin, Suite A
Portland, OR 97223-2542
USA
503-968-6777
www.firstbooks.com